THE
SOCIALIST REGISTER 1983

THE
SOCIALIST REGISTER
1983

EDITED BY

RALPH MILIBAND

and

JOHN SAVILLE

THE MERLIN PRESS

LONDON

First published in 1983
by The Merlin Press Ltd.
3 Manchester Road
London E14

©The Merlin Press Ltd 1983

British Library Cataloguing in Publication Data
Socialist register.—1983
1. Socialism—Periodicals
335'.005   HX3

ISBN 0-85036-309-8
ISBN 0-85036-310-1 Pbk

Printed in Great Britain by
Whitstable Litho, Whitstable, Kent.

Typesetting by Heather Hems
The Malt House, Chilmark, Wilts.

TABLE OF CONTENTS

PREFACE

This is the twentieth issue of the *Socialist Register* and this volume follows the pattern of its predecessors in tackling issues of major significance for socialist theory and practice. The first two essays, one by Dorothy Smith and the other by Varda Burstyn, present different approaches to the 'theorisation' of feminism from a socialist and Marxist perspective. The issues raised here have been forced on to the socialist agenda by the feminist movement and are of the greatest importance for all socialists; and we hope that we shall be able to pursue the discussion begun here in further volumes of the *Register*.

The following five essays are concerned in different ways with the condition of the left after the General Election of June 1983. David Coates and Ralph Miliband discuss the situation of the Labour Party in the light of the election results and what implications it has for socialist advance in Britain. Richard Taylor's essay recalls the experience of the peace movement in the sixties and discusses the crucial question of the relationship of the peace movement to socialist struggle. John Saville takes the occasion of a new biography of C.R. Attlee to reflect on some neglected influences on the Attlee Government's conduct of affairs after World War Two, and Paul Foot suggests what the diary of the former Ambassador of the Shah of Iran to the Court of St James shows about the attitudes of the British Establishment to dictatorships of the right.

The following three articles are concerned with critical international questions: Roy Medvedev writes from Moscow about what may be expected from the change of leadership in the Soviet Union; and Paul Joseph discusses recent developments in American nuclear strategy and links them with the purposes of American foreign policy. James Petras and Morris Morley for their part provide a timely analysis of the roots of American intervention in Central America.

The last three articles deal with the crucial question of the role of the working class in socialist struggles. Ellen Meiksins Wood analyses the ways in which seemingly abstract questions of socialist theory have a crucial bearing on socialist strategy; and Richard Hyman provides a critical appraisal of André Gorz's recent and influential work *Farewell to the Working Class?* Finally, Monty Johnstone offers a scholarly analysis of

Marx's view of *putschism* and majority rule.

Dorothy Smith teaches in the Department of the Sociology of Education at the Toronto Institute for Studies in Education; and Varda Burstyn is doing research and writing in Toronto on feminist themes. David Coates is in the Department of Politics at the University of Leeds and Richard Taylor is the Warden of the Adult Education Centre, also at Leeds. Paul Foot writes for *The Daily Mirror* and *Private Eye*. Roy Medvedev is doing research and writing on Soviet history in Moscow. Paul Joseph teaches in the Department of Sociology at Tufts University, Mass. James Petras is Professor of Sociology at the State University of New York at Binghamton and Morris Morley lectures in Political Science at the American University, Washington, D.C. Ellen Wood is Professor of Political Science at Glendon College, York University, Toronto, and Richard Hyman is in the School of Industrial and Business Studies at the University of Warwick. Monty Johnstone is doing research and writing on socialist democracy and related themes in London.

We are grateful to our contributors for their help and to Brian Pearce for his translation of Roy Medvedev's article. We also gladly record once again our appreciation of the help and encouragement we have had from Martin Eve, Philippa Jones and David Musson, of Merlin Press, and we take this opportunity to congratulate them on having produced such an excellent volume in 1982, when pressure of other work made it impossible for us to edit that year's *Register*.

August 1983   R.M.
                                                                 J.S.

WOMEN, CLASS AND FAMILY

Dorothy E. Smith

1. *Introduction*

This paper explores the relations between patriarchy and class in the context of the capitalist mode of production. The relations between these terms, patriarchy and class or patriarchy and capitalism have been, in the women's movement, embedded in an often rancorous debate. For Marxist-feminists in particular, the dilemmas of how to locate ourselves in what were often represented by both sides as contradictory and opposing struggles, were serious and painful. On the one side, radical feminists posed men as the 'main enemy'.[1] For them, therefore, any struggle must oppose patriarchy directly as a form of domination imposed by men on women. For them, Marxist-feminists, who link the struggle against patriarchy with a struggle with men against the ruling class, work with the oppressor and are thereby complicit in the reproduction of patriarchal relations. They have gone over to the other side. On the other side, Marxist-feminists, viewed as traitors by radical feminists, encountered a parallel accusation from the Left. Basing arguments on the theoretical work of Engels, women's oppression was identified with the historical emergence of private property and hence of class relations. The struggle for a classless society subsumed the struggle for women's emancipation. To struggle separately for immediate gains for women, or worse, to struggle within Marxist organisations against male chauvinism, served only to divide and weaken organisations committed to class struggle. The problems for Marxist-feminists have been how to represent feminism within class struggle, how to understand the relations between patriarchy and capitalism, how to confront and oppose male chauvinism in the working class and in the often petty bourgeois character of Left organisations, how to relate revolutionary organisation and struggle to the autonomous women's movement and how to bring understandings learned there into the struggle for socialism.

This is a highly oversimplified rendering of the deep political rift underlying theoretical discussions of the relation between patriarchy and capitalism. It produced a tendency to view patriarchy and capitalism as mutually exclusive and opposing terms. More recently, however, formulations have been developed providing a theoretical ground enabling Marxist-feminists to bring feminist positions into Marxism. Perhaps the most influential have

1

been those which seek to create a bridge between the two terms and sides by understanding patriarchy and capitalism as distinct but interacting systems. Hartmann, for example, has written of the unhappy marriage of Marxism and feminism, reflecting on the tendency to collapse feminism into Marxism and proposing as an alternative to understand patriarchy and capitalism as assembled historically. Patriarchy in her view pre-dates capitalism and has been incorporated into capitalism as the latter developed. Some aspects of patriarchy have served capitalism and others have been in contradiction with it. Neither system is reducible to the other; each is shaped by and shapes the other.[2] Similarly Eisenstein has argued that patriarchy is a universal principle and that its local historical forms are expressions of this. There is feudal patriarchy, capitalist patriarchy and socialist patriarchy. Patriarchy takes on its distinctive character in the context of a particular mode of production and in the case of capitalism, patriarchy provides the hierarchical ordering of political control of the political economy and capitalism its economic system.[3]

The tack I have taken is somewhat different. I cannot see a mode of production as excluding the organisation of gender relations.[4] In pre-capitalist societies, gender is basic to the 'economic' division of labour and how labour resources are controlled. In other than capitalist forms, we take for granted that gender relations are included. In peasant societies for example, the full cycle of production and subsistence is organised by the household and family and presupposes gender relations. Indeed, we must look to capitalism as a mode of production to find how the notion of the separation of gender relations from economic relations could arise. It is only in capitalism that we find an economic process constituted independently of the daily and generational production of the lives of particular individuals and *in which therefore we can think economy apart from gender.* In treating patriarchy and capitalism as distinct systems, we are reading back into history and into other kinds of societies a state of affairs peculiar to our own.

We have come slowly to the discovery that gender permeates all aspects of social, political and economic organisation; that what has been seen as not gendered is in fact largely an exclusively male arena of action and that from that viewpoint, gender relations are only present when women are. But from the standpoint of women, we are coming to recognise the pervasive effect or presence of gender.[5] To posit a distinct sex/gender system[6] is to inhibit analysis and understanding of the gender-saturated character of social relations by sectioning off those involving women. I have taken the view that we must begin by including women from the outset in our attempt to make out the historical processes in which we are implicated and which launch us towards the future we try to grasp and make. In so doing the concepts we are familiar with and which have been built upon an assumption of a universe which has excluded gender by excluding women must be pulled, stretched and if necessary remade. For we are addressing the reality of a world which is put together as it is in the actual activities of actual individuals and in that world women are really present. They are as much in class, part of class and class struggle as men. Gender relations are, I shall try to show, an integral constituent of the social organisation of class.[7]

To begin from the standpoint of women means finding a method of thinking which does not insist that we put aside aspects of our experience of what we know by virtue of the living we do in an ordinary everyday way in an ordinary everyday world. We are confident of the discoveries we have made as women in reflecting on and consulting our experience. In the making of the women's movement, we opened our consciousness to the experience of other women and found our own oppression reflected in theirs. In the process of consciousness-raising, we sought to objectify and make real an oppression we shared. As women outside the dominant classes, which was the first site of the women's movement, became active the voice of women's experience was for them how they discovered their common oppression with others and how we and they learned of forms of women's oppression which we did not all share and which had different class sites.

The concept of patriarchy names relations, events, suffering, power-lessness, repression, which happen in many forms in our experience. Yes, violence is done to women. There are the ordinary daily ways in which women find they don't count. There are the ordinary ways in which women's labour and sexuality is used and appropriated. The experience named 'patriarchy' is a real experience. We experience it inwardly as a product of how women and how men have been socialised in the relations of dominance and subordination. We are trapped again and again into relations and situations we do not and have not chosen, but cannot escape because, among other reasons, patriarchy as an ideological practice has sought to deprive us of moral sanction and the inward surety to speak up for ourselves. What we see is a society which directly oppresses women, which has written books, tracts, constructed laws, made regulations, created organisations, work relations etc., systematically subordinating women to men and systematically placing us in relations which render us politically and economically powerless. Of course it is not a conspiracy. But as we learn more, it becomes clear that it has been *done,* actively. The social, political and economic forms of women's oppression have been and are the actual work, actual activities, actual doings of actual indivi-duals. Of course women are part of these institutions, participating in the ways in which they have been rendered powerless—at least until recently.

Looked at in this way, the problem of patriarchy versus class takes on a different cast. The interpersonal relations of direct dominance, between women and men, are implicated in a larger organisation of the society.

Even if we see the patriarchal principle at work in each new setting, in government, business, professions, labour unions, yet that personal relation of dominance and inequality is articulated to the larger social, political and economic organisation of the society. It cannot be separated from it. The direct and personal character of men's domination over women takes on its actual character within determinate social relations specific to capitalism and to its development over the past 150 or so years. The relation between the actual forms of men's dominance over women, and women's general inequality in the society, are specific to this kind of society, to this historical epoch. These are the forms in which we experience oppression. They are the only forms of oppression we know. Whether there is something beyond or beneath which is general is not our first question. Our first question is to understand the relation between what we find at the level of experience and the larger social, economic and political process, viewing the latter as historical processes. For of course, this place, this time, these material conditions, these social relations, are where we do our work. This is what we must understand.

The first and fundamental step is to begin where women are in the society, with the everyday worlds of our experience, and to be prepared to reconceptualise the accepted concepts, frameworks and theories. These are built upon and presuppose how the world appears from positions and from within discourses from which women have for centuries been excluded. Much thinking and research on the family in the past has failed even to recognise that what women were doing in the home was work. The concept of role as it was developed and used provided a means of analysing family relations as interpersonal processes in which the work process was invisible. The absence of women's work in the home has become for many of us a major presence in the work of many writers. Here then we will attempt to place women and their work in the centre of the picture—not to rewrite a new and female chauvinist version of the family but to redress a gross imbalance and in part also because we cannot move towards the full picture until this imbalance has been rectified.

This means raising questions about our conceptual practices and conceptual organisation. The ordinary ways of our thinking and research begin in the intellectual world, with questions arising out of debates among social scientists, intellectuals, administrators, etc. We begin ordinarily *outside* experience and *in* the discourse (the interaction between thinkers and researchers exchanging knowledge and thinking in the form of texts). This approach gives us trouble when we want the ordinary experience of women in the everyday world at the heart and centre of our inquiry.

Let us look at what happens with the concept of 'The Family'. When we start in the intellectual world, that concept 'The Family' defines our concerns. We are oriented first by the work done in studying 'The Family' and thinking about 'The Family'. Beginning with the concept leads us into a special set of procedures. These leave out the actualities of people's work, lives and experience and the varying actual settings and the actual social relations in which people live and work. 'The Family' becomes the topic and object of investigation. Actual families are examined with respect to how they may be seen to have common features and properties which can be assembled as aspects of 'The Family'. Questions then arise concerning what families across time, culture and class have in common with one another—their size for example, their constitution in terms of membership—is the nuclear form of the family a universal form? and so forth.[8]

This approach focuses upon conceptual problems and upon the problems of finding in the real world features corresponding to the conceptual structure. The actuality is examined in terms of 'family structure' or the like. Structures are read into the world as its features. This is not how we will proceed here. For there is another way. It is to make the actual practices visible so that we can locate our inquiry in an everyday world.

In Engels' *The Origin of the Family, Private Property and the State*[9], he uses a method of analysis which shows how we can get out of the difficulty we are left in once we have deserted 'The Family' concept and want to find out how to begin where people are and where the work is actually done.

This method takes an actual work process and locates it in a determinate social relation. Then we can see how the articulation of an individual's work to the social relations of a given mode of production determine how she is related and the ways in which she becomes subordinate. There is on the one hand a work process, an actual activity, and on the other social relations (also activities) which articulate the society. With the shift from communal to private property—

> The administration of the household lost its public character. It was no longer the concern of society. It became a *private service;* the wife became the first domestic servant, pushed out of participation in social production.[10]

Engels oversimplified, but the method he used is important. He did not see the division of labour simply as a distribution of work in work roles. Rather he saw the work process as articulated to social relations which defined its relation to others and hence defined how the doer of that work was related in society.

If we follow Engels' method we will see that we cannot treat the material basis and work organisation of home and family as constituting an independent entity, independently determined. Rather they are articulated to and organised by social relations which *are* the social relations of a mode of production. The very separation, the very privatisation of women's work in the home and how it is mediated by private property (according to Engels) is a feature of the social relations of a definite mode of production. This approach does not draw a boundary on the mode of production at the door of the home. Rather home and family are seen as integral parts of and moments in a mode of production. Our method is one which raises as empirical questions in every instance both concerning the work which is done, and the relations which organise and articulate that work to the social economic and political processes beyond and outside the home. Thus we don't cut across class and other differentiations or rural/urban differences in a society to discover the lineaments of 'The Family' and then return to the abstracted family to discover how it 'varies' in differing class, historical and other contexts. We begin with a method which locates the family and women's work in the home in the actual social relations in which they are embedded. The inner life and work of the family, and the personal relations of power between husband and wife are understood as a product of how family relations are organised by and in the economic and political relations of capitalism. The relation between internal and external, between the personal dimensions of relations, i.e. those wherein particular individuals confront, cooperate, engage sexually, are related as parents and children, work together as individuals, and those relations which are organised as economic and political relations, is the key to women's experience of the personal as political as a relation of oppression. In back of the personal relations of women and men in the familial context is an economic and political process which provides the conditions, exigencies, opportunities, powers and weaknesses in terms of which the interactional process goes on. Choice, decision, moral commitment, love, hate, alienation, are there in a context and in conditions in relation to which family members have no choice, where their particular commitments to each other may make a difference in terms of the fate of individuals and of the family as a relational working unit, but do not change the conditions, means, grounds, of what they may or can do. No matter how it is done, where men are wage earners and women cannot earn enough outside the home to provide for their children independently of a man and his wage, dependency permeates every aspect of the interpersonal process in the home—regardless of how loving, how caring, how much or little respect each has for the other, how they have been able to work together, how much the man has learned to grant autonomy to his wife, or she has learned to assert herself *vis-à-vis* him. The economic and political process is there as a continual presence giving shape, limits and conditions to what goes forward, and, as in every other aspect of a capitalist mode of production, supplying change, and necessitating adaptation in ways which render the examples of lifetime experience of previous generations irrelevant as models for each new generation.

Our strategy then seeks for the determination and shaping of the inter-personal forms of domination and oppression of women in how the economic and political relations in which the family is embedded constitute inequality, creating relations of dominance and dependency within the family. Of course other things are going on. But I want to push as far as possible an analysis which investigates how capitalism works in relation to women's situation in the family so that we can grasp the specific forms and processes of women's oppression—so that we can see what it is, how it is there, and perhaps be clearer about how to work for change.

In the analysis which follows, class and family, or class and patriarchy, will not be viewed as opposing and incompatible terms—placing us in an either/or situation at every point. Rather our strategy will be one relating the specific form of the family to the class organisation of a changing capitalist society. The basic conception of class we will work with is Marxist. This differentiates classes on the basis of a differing relation to the means of production. A dominant class appropriates and controls the means of production. It is supported by a class which labours to produce the subsistence of the ruling class as well as for itself. In capital-ism this relation takes the form of the mutual constitution of capital and wage labour, surplus value is the form in which surplus labour appears and is appropriated by the dominant class. This dichotomous class structure does not become visible in a simple way for reasons which will in part be a topic of parts of this paper. For we shall see that rather than an analysis of family relations leading us away from an examination of class, it brings into focus class and the divergence between the underlying relation of capital and labour and the surface features blurring the sharpness of the underlying opposition. By beginning with class as a dynamic relation central to capitalism, by recognising families as organised by and organising social relations—among them class relations—by avoiding the concept of 'The Family' and thereby avoiding making class relations invisible by using the concept to make differences between classes unobservable, we can begin to see the social organisation of class in a new way. We discover the family or forms of family work and living, as integral to the active process of constructing and reconstructing class relations, particularly as the dominant class responds to changes in the forms of property relations and changes in the organisation of the capitalist enterprise and capitalist social relations.

It is important to preserve a sense of capitalism as an essentially dynamic process continually transforming the 'ground' on which we stand so that we are always continually experiencing changing historical process. It is one of the problems of the strategy of the intellectual world that our categories and concepts fix an actuality into seemingly unchanging forms and then we do our work in trying to find out how to represent society in that way. This we must avoid. We must try to find out how to see our society as continually moving and to avoid introducing an artificial fixity into what we make of it. The society as we find it at any one moment is the product of an historical process. It is a process which is not 'complete' at any one time. The various 'impulses' generated by the essentially dynamic process of capitalism do not come to rest in their own completion or in the working out to the point of equilibrium of systematic inter-actions. The process of change is itself unceasing and at any moment we catch only an atemporal slice of a moving process. Hence to understand the properties, movement, 'structure' of the present, we must be able to disentwine the strands of development which determine the character and relations of the present in Western capitalism.

In our discussion we will rest at one major theoretical indecision by avoiding a clear distinction between 'bourgeoisie' and 'middle class'. The uses of terminology here will be descriptive rather than analytic. The current state of the debate on class and stratification is quite inconclusive and does not yield a satisfactory terminology, let alone theoretical account. I have become inclined to treat the capitalist elite, the middle class and the so-called petty bourgeoisie as a single class in relation to contemporary forms of property and the contemporary modes of maintaining domina-tion of the means of production and the processes of expropriating surplus labour. It is an internally differentiated class articulated to the regional basis of the capitalist economy, actively organised and reorganised as a class by ideological processes, by the organisation of networks of personal relations, by the maintenance of privileged access to state and state services including education, governmental regulation and so forth. This section of society appears as dominant and corresponds to the ruling class as Marx and Engels used that term in *The German Ideology*.[11] It refers there not to a political group, but to that class which controls and dominates the means of production. The ruling of the dominant class or classes in contemporary capitalist society is mediated by a ruling apparatus of bureaucracy, legislature, management, intellectual discourse, professional organisation, etc. The payoff for the dominant classes is various forms of expropriation of surplus value where surplus value can no longer be seen as arising in a relation of individual capitalist to individual worker but must increasingly be understood as the organisation of relations between dominant classes and a working class as major segments of society and hence as having systemic properties. The class which rules, the dominant class or classes is, as I have said, internally differentiated. We can distin-guish different sectors including the locally based petty bourgeoisie con-tributing his or her own labour to the enterprise, a large middle class salaried and occupying positions in managerial, bureaucratic or professional organisations, and an elite who come nearest to being describable as 'owners' particularly closely linked to finance capital and top levels of government. The working class can also be seen to be internally differentiated into different sectors though its internal structure is as much organised by forces external to it than by initiatives arising from within. The major class organisations of the working class are trade unions and these in fact have served as part of the organisation of a dual labour market separating a core or central work world from a marginal or peripheral sector. The internal structure of the working class must be seen largely as responses to conditions and pressures originating in the economic process and as a defence against exploitation.

It must be clear by this point that questions concerning the designation of class and relations in contemporary capitalism cannot, in my view, be answered definitionally. Nor wholly at the level of theory. They can indeed be resolved at the theoretical level only by empirical inquiry examining the social relations mediating control and domination of the means of production and expropriating surplus labour, as they actually are today. Indeed this present essay can be seen as part of such an inquiry concerning itself with how the organisation of relations between women and men can be understood as integral to the forms of domination securing the means of production and expropriation to dominant classes and subordinating a working class in a relation of exploitation to them.

2. Individual, Family and Property Relations

At the beginning of the *Grundrisse,* the work which lays the foundations for the developed formulations of *Capital,* Marx analyses the social construction of individuality. He presents the individual as a social creation, a form which arises in social relations characteristic of capitalism.[12] Of course individuals exist under all modes of production, but it is only with capitalism that the individual emerges as a determinate social actor, entering into social economic relations *as* an individual. This conception was important in Marx's thinking about the stage represented by capitalism in the historical processes of transforming society towards human emancipation in classless society. The individual appears as a free agent with the breakdown of feudal relations tying serf to household and to land, lords and serf, and ordering relations of exploitation and appropriation as relations of obligation between persons embedded in personalised relations of fealty and force. Capitalist relations externalise the relations of inter-dependency in general forms—the relations of exchange between money and commodities and the distinctive form of these taken as capital appears. The individual, whether as capitalist or as wage labourer, is detached from personal forms of interdependency and is constituted as a free agent in market relations. Thus capitalism as it destroys feudal relations and creates the autonomous individual also creates the conditions for the democratic processes of civil society.

The promise of democracy was, however, withheld from the mass of humankind. Democracy proved partial. The egalitarian claims and advances on the basis of which the alliances of the English, American and French revolutions had been created were in the event necessarily restricted. Underlying the egalitarian principles and egalitarian forms of government were class differences radically modifying the social and political effects. The individual had indeed arrived upon the historical scene, but he was of two kinds—an individual owning the means of production and seeking to put it to use by buying labour-power to apply to it and an individual lacking the means to produce for himself or for the market, owning only his own labour power which he must sell in order to live. The truly egalitarian society promised by democratic forms of government can emerge only when this basis of inequality among individuals is eliminated. Until then, democracy remains a means to the exercise of state power by the dominant classes.

Taking the standpoint of women discloses a further barrier to equality. The universe of individuals thus constituted as such is a universe of men and not of women. Marxist thinkers have done much work recently to analyse the specific relation of women's domestic labour to the labour-power sold as a commodity by the worker.[13] This work hones in on what is missing from Marx's model. The constitution of the individual worker as an individual appearing on the market with his labour-power to sell presupposes a work organisation 'behind the scenes' which is not articulated directly to the market process, but appears as a personal service to the individual worker. That individual depends upon domestic labour as the essential basis of his capacity to sell his labour-power to the capitalist, hence to appear as an individual in the marketplace. Marx and Engels believed that the development of capitalism would progressively break down these vestigial forms of personal dependence, that all members of a family would enter directly into the industrial process as individuals, and that the final transformation of family relations would be through the socialisation of private domestic labour.[14] This has not happened, at least not in the way in which Marx and Engels anticipated. Rather, our times until recently have seen a consolidation of the privatised relation in which the individual worker is 'produced' through his wife's domestic labour. This relation is integral to the appearance of the worker as individual on the market. Hence the social form of the individual as worker is, like the wage, an appearance which conceals an actual relation between the domestic labour done largely by women in the home and the individual wage-earner in the productive process.

The analysis of the significance of domestic labour has however addressed only one side of the appearance of the individual. It addresses the construction of individuals only of the working class. On the other is the individual owner of the means of production. In Marx's work private property as constitutive of the individual capitalist as economic agent remains unexamined and unexplicated as a social relation. The individual as one participating in the appropriation and control of the means of production must also be reproduced daily as an individual through the domestic labour in the home. Further than that, when the means of production were identified with an individual or individuals, the property relations of entrepreneurial forms of capitalism also depended on relations within the family. In the first stages of capitalism the continuities of property and the consolidation and continuity of capital transgenerationally depended upon an organisation of family relations which subsumed the wife as a civil person under the person of her husband and gave to the father significant control over the relations formed in marriage by his sons and daughters. Marriages among the bourgeoisie brought into being relations among properties appropriated by individuals. The actor on the economic and political scene, the civil person, legally constituted as such, was the husband and father whose rights to appropriate his wife's property and earnings, as well as those of his minor children, mobilised property, resources, and labour of the family in the interests of the capitalist enterprise on whose successes and failures the family depended. The family became a corporate economic unit identified with an individual man. At various levels of the economy different aspects of this control and appropriation came into prominence. For the smaller entrepreneur, the petty bourgeois, owning and working in his own shop as well as employing others, women's domestic labour (of wife, daughters and servants) was integral to the subsistence organisation of the enterprise. At levels where the specialisation of merchant, financial and similar roles created actual forms corresponding to the theoretical category of agents of capital, the bourgeois appropriated the domestic labour of the women of his household; and controlled the women of his family's capacity to create social linkages. He was legally accorded exclusive access to his wife's sexuality since that provided the essential corporeal connection between men of one generation and men of the next through which the continuity of property could be established. He also disposed of similar rights in his daughters' sexuality as a means of forming connections between his capital and property and that of others. As Hall and others have pointed out, marriages between kin of appropriate degrees was a significant mechanism for the consolidation of capital transgenerationally in the absence of specialised capital-holding institutions, trusts, joint stock companies, corporations, etc.[15]

These relations are more than relations in which men exploit women.[16] If we examine the legal relations closely and their changes, we would see how they are geared to constituting formally the forms required by the relations of capital, of the market, and of the developing property-owning forms. They are the social constitution of the capacities of an individual, whether an individual person or later a corporate form, to act as an economic agent, to incur debts, to make loans, to hold mortgages, to hold property in land in ways which articulate it to a real estate market, etc. These are the kinds of linkages and requirements which are constitutive of the form of the bourgeois family, given its character as an economic unit and they determine how domestic labour and resources are appropriated. Hence as these institutions change, and of course they have changed greatly, the relations determining the form of the bourgeois and middle-class family, the internal structure of appropriation and the relation of domestic labour to these, have also been modified. In particular as property (in the sense of ownership of the means of production) shifts to the corporate form of ownership and the chief actor on the economic scene ceases to be the individual person and becomes the corporate person (so that even a one-man enterprise would be constituted as a company), a radical separation between the company or corporation and the bourgeois or middle-class family emerges. These are changes in the middle-class family. They are great changes in the roles and activities of women, and the contexts in which women's domestic labour in the home is done.

In the earlier stages of capitalism, the social relations which were key as contexts for women's domestic labour in the middle class were those of the property institutions and other institutions organising and constituting economic agency, and indeed agency in political and professional spheres in general. The development of the corporate form of ownership of the means of production implies new forms of social relations. Corporate ownership is accompanied by the extension of bureaucratic forms of government, and the rise of a scientific and technological establishment located in a variety of organisational forms. An integration of the functions of 'ruling' in the society emerges. The organisation of relations and activities in all spheres becomes increasingly differentiated as specialised practices, in government, management and the professions, in ideological processes and in education. These came over time to form a loosely integrated apparatus in which forms of action are characteristically in words or mathematical symbols. This apparatus I shall call the 'ruling' apparatus, where in the economic context of Marxist thought 'ruling' identifies the processes and functions which reserve and control the means of production in the interests of a class. The ruling apparatus of contemporary capitalism comes into view as such in a special way from the standpoint of women of the dominant classes, since they have been excluded from all but subordinate and generally menial positions within it.

3. *The rise of the corporation, the externalisation of property and the changing role of the family in the reproduction of the ruling class*
The development of the corporate forms of ownership and economic agency increasingly separate the spheres of economic relations of the family and household unit. The social construction of the individual man as agent or actor arises at the juncture of the two spheres. The forms of

property and the social relations of the economy organise domestic labour in relation to the individual man in determinate ways. Under capitalism these relations are in a continual process of change producing an ever-increasing concentration of capital. Quantitative changes have been accompanied by major modifications in the forms of property ownership, in the organisation of the market and of finance and commercial processes, as well as of management and technology. These modifications have also radically modified the organisation of the middle-class family.

The externalisation of the relations of inter-dependency which were earlier primarily market relations began to develop as an externalisation of property relations and an objectification of managerial and organisational processes. The continuity of accumulation of capital so precariously provided for by individual forms of property were externalised as corporations, trusts, cartels, joint stock companies, etc. Markets organised earlier as a series of independent transactions are progressively integrated as a single sequence of ordered transactions from original seller to final destination. This required coordination at a different level than could be met by economic units tied in to the household and family. Economic organisation became increasingly separated from the local organisation of the household. Men moved to and fro between the two 'levels' of organisation, participating in each. With the rise of corporate forms, they became the agents of capital by virtue of their positions in an organisation, whatever their capacity. Director, manager, so-called owner—the relations, powers and activities of each are features of large-scale organisation. Their relations, roles, performances, are mediated by the corporation as a property-holding form. The new forms of property are a differentiated structure externalising property relations as a system of specialised roles.

Over time the corporate form becomes the legal constitution for all sizes of business, although for small business it is elective. Organisationally it completes the separation of family and household from economy—or rather from the economy as differentiated and specialised processes. Economic relations became increasingly differentiated and specialised at an extra-local, national and international level. Earlier, forms of externalised economic relations depended upon networks of kinsfolk in varying degrees. Among the middle class, the family was a broader conception than the household representing an organisation of common interests vested in more than one privately owned enterprise or professional occupation. The separation of family and business world was blurred. Economic organisation was supported and organised by kin and familial relations. The primarily domestic work of women was not isolated from the relational politics of business—quite apart from other ways in which women's skills could be involved in business enterprise. The advancement and security of the family involved the active participation of women in more than one way. Allegiances, decisions about character, the backdoor informational processes known as gossip—these were all part of the ordinary world in which business was done and were integral to it. But the corporate form supplants these processes with its own. Those employed must owe allegiance to the organisation and not to family. Specific competences and qualifications become of greater importance than family ties. Alliances established within the business structures and networks themselves become more central than alliances in the local area or within a kin network. As the economic process is sealed off, women in the household are isolated from it. The middle-class domestic world becomes truly privatised. The locus of advancement for the individual ceases to be identified with his family connection and with the advancement of the kin constellation. It becomes identified with his individualised relation to the corporate enterprise. It is this which later becomes institutionalised as a career. The domestic labour of the middle class household is increasingly organised as a personal service to the individual man. Its relation to the business enterprise in which he is actor arises in how the household work and organisation is subordinated to its requirements as they become his.

The relation through which men appropriated women's labour is changed. It is no longer part of the organisation of an economic enterprise in which women are included. Now an individual man appropriates as his the work done by his wife or other women of his family. The individual man becomes the enterprise so far as the family is concerned. The earliest and most typical form of this is that of the individual professional. It becomes general as the *career* rather than individual ownership structures the entry and activity of the individual as economic agent. As the corporate form of organising agency and ownership become primary, the individual's agency and relation to the means of production are organisationally mediated. The relation of appropriation becomes highly personalised. It becomes a general form characterising the relations of middle-class women and men in work situations in the home and outside.

This is visible in many forms. It is there, for example, in what we do not know about women in the past. It is present for example in our ignorance until recently of the fact that the figure of the British astronomer William Herschel concealed that of a second astronomer, his sister, Caroline, who shared his work, perhaps shared his discoveries, made discoveries of her own, kept house for him and acted as his secretary.[17] When a group of eminent sociologists wrote accounts of how one of their major pieces of work was done, some described a very substantial contribution by their wives. No one raised questions then about the fact that the husband appropriated that work as his and that the wives' work contributed to the advancement of their husbands' careers and reputations and not to theirs.[18] The middle-class relation of appropriation by men of women's work is incorporated into professional, bureaucratic and managerial organisation. It appears as a differentiation of women's and men's roles providing for the structuring of a career for men in positions which are technically specialised and superordinate, and a truncated structure of advancement for women in positions which are skilled but ancillary and subordinate to those of men, and, of course, low paid. Women were and are secretaries, graduate nurses, dental hygienists, and elementary classroom teachers. Men were and are managers, doctors, dentists and principals and vice-principals of elementary schools. Prentice's study of 'the feminisation' of teaching in nineteenth-century Canada indicates that as the school system expanded, the structuring of women's and men's roles was consciously designed to permit men in the teaching profession a career and salaries at a professional level. This was possible only by allocating a substantial part of the work to women teachers whose rates of pay were depressed and whose advancement was limited.[19] Until recently these forms of employment for middle-class women were institutionalised as a transitional status between childhood and marriage. Possible competition and social contradiction between women's occupational status and subordination to the husband after marriage were avoided by terminating employment on marriage or by ensuring that married women did not occupy professional positions of any authority.[20]

In these developments we find the social and material bases of the form of family which we have taken as typical and which we are only now becoming aware of as a distinct historical and cultural form in moving away from it. This is the household and family organisation which is a distinct economic unit, primarily a 'consuming' unit—i.e. one in which women's domestic labour producing the subsistence of its individual members depends upon a money income. Household and family are increasingly tied to the individual man's career and less to an interlinking of family relations and enterprises. Household and family are enucleated. The interests of the wife are held to be intimately bound up with her husband's career. In various ways she is expected to support him morally and socially as well as through the ways in which her domestic labour ensures both his ordinary physical well being and his proper presentation of self. His career should pay off for her increments of prestige in the relevant social circles and in home furnishings, a larger home—in general in the material forms in which his advancement in the organisation may be expressed in relations between neighbours, friends and colleagues. As corporations increase in size and the managerial structure is increasingly objectified, a sharp contradiction arises between individual autonomy and subordination to authority. For men there is a peculiarly difficult combination of the need to exercise initiative, to give leadership, and to take risks as ingredients of a successful career and the requirements of conformity to organisational exigencies, norms and criteria of achievement in a hierarchical structure. Hence tension management comes to be seen as an important responsibility of middle-class wives.

As the professional, government and corporate apparatus becomes consolidated as a ruling apparatus, forms of action in words and symbols become a fully differentiated form. Language is constituted as a discrete mode of action. This requires a division of labour which will organise and provide for the necessary material aspects of communication. Processes of action which are merely communicative depend on specific divisions of labour as well as a technology. Hence the elaboration of clerical work. But women's domestic labour also comes to be organised specifically to service this conceptually organised world of action.

> It is a condition of a man's being able to enter and become absorbed in the conceptual mode that he does not have to focus his activities and interest upon his bodily existence. If he is to participate fully in the abstract mode of action, then he must be liberated also from having to attend to his needs, etc. in the concrete and particular. The organization of work and expectations in managerial and professional circles both constitutes and depends upon the alienation of men from their bodily and local existence. The structure of work and the structure of career take for granted that these matters are provided for in such a way that they will not interfere with his action and participation in that world. Providing for his liberation from the Aristotelian categories (of time and space) . . . is a woman who keeps house for him, bears and cares for his children, washes his clothes, looks after him when he is sick and generally provides for the logistics of his bodily existence.[21]

The home then becomes an essential unit in organising the abstracted modes of ruling in the context—the necessary and ineluctable context—of the local and particular.

These changes introduce a new subordination of the home to the educational system. The technological, accounting and communicative practices of the emerging ruling apparatus require appropriate skills as a condition of entry and of action in its modes. Language skills, indeed perhaps just those styles of speech identified originally by Bernstein as an elaborated code,[22] are essential to participation in this form of action and being. The work of mothering in relation to the work of the school becomes an essential mediating process in the production and reproduction of class relations among the bourgeoisie and the working class.[23]

The educational system and access to the educational system mediated and controlled by family, home and, above all, by the work of women as mothers, comes to provide the major transgenerational linkage of class. Children are no longer prospectively actors in the moving history of family relations entwined with property and economic enterprise. Sons are no longer propsectively those who will carry on family businesses and hence provide for the continuity of capital built in the work of one generation forward towards the next. Daughters are no longer those who will consolidate alliances or relations linking social, economic and political relations into a network of kin. Children progressively become the object of parental work, particularly the work of mothers, aimed at creating a definite kind of person, with distinct communicative skills in speech and writing and with capacities to take advantage of an educational process through which boys will have access to career-structured occupations and girls will have access to men with career-structured occupations.

At a certain point there appears to be a reversal in the relation between the domestic unit and the economic organisation. At the outset of the development of capitalist property relations, the family/household unit supported and was subordinated to the economic enterprise. With the increasingly sharp separation of household and family from a role in the social construction of property relations and the declining significance of the broader social network based on kin and family, the original relation becomes reversed. Economic activity more and more takes the form of paid employment and the career is a means of private accumulation. For the managerial or professional employee of corporation or the state, the salary is a means of building personal and family assets—a home investment, life insurance, a better pension, leisure 'capital'—a summer cottage, a boat, etc. The emergence of the sphere of 'personal life' which Zaretsky attributes to the appearance of industrial capitalism as such seems rather to be a later development.[24] It seems to be correlated with this shift from economic agency directly identified with the individual capitalist as property-owner, to the form of agency mediated by the corporate form of property holding. 'Personal life' becomes the object of investment. Salaries, their increments and careers build private assets rather than the advancement of an enterprise with which the small capitalist is identified as an individual. Such accumulation of private wealth has been organised in relation to the marital unit. New forms of matrimonial property legislation are sought to accommodate these newer patterns. These changes indicate that capital no longer depends upon the family to constitute those forms of property relations enabling the individual man to act as an individual property-owner yet providing for the perpetuation of capital beyond the lifetime of the individual. They indicate that the property holding form constitutive of capital is fully separated from dependency upon the economic persona of the individual subsuming the family organisation which earlier provided for its continuity.[25]

4. *The extra-local social organisation of the dominant classes*

We have proceeded with the analysis of the bourgeois and middle-class family as an aspect of the organisation of a dominant class. We have also taken for granted that the organisation of a class, of the dominant class at least, is an actual activity or activities, that it involves work, that it is continually produced and reproduced with respect to how the means of production are controlled. We have been viewing the middle-class family as an active part of the internal organisation of the class and, most recently, in relation to the social organisation of preferential access to the educational system. We have focused also upon changes taking place in capitalism which arise from its essential dynamic. The latter feeds effects to the 'surface' creating problems, new alignments and divisions requiring an active work to reorganise the intra-class relations of the ruling class. The family and the work of women in the family have been central in the work of organising and re-organising the internal structure of the dominant classes, as a class. A major change in the basis of the dominant classes has been the progressive reorganisation of property relations and the emergence of a differentiated basis of class, giving rise to sections structured as differentiated forms of agency in relation to the division of property functions represented by the corporate form. These changes continue with a movement towards an increasingly hierarchical organisation more and more tightly articulated to the structures of financal capital.[26]

In this section we will draw attention to the relation of this ruling apparatus and the general social relations of capitalism to relations among particular people necessarily always located in particular places, viewing the world from their actual bodily location and in very ordinary ways, eating, fucking, suffering, giving birth, loving, hating, working, living and dying. The organisation of these relations—the ways in which the living of particular individuals is organised in relation to the abstracted generalised relations of exchange and ruling is a major work of the family and in particular of the middle-class family under capitalism.

A major shift took place in the basis of dominant class organisation with the emergence of a class based on the extra-local organisation of commodity exchange relations and the organisation of financial and mercantile activities at an international and national level. This shift is the basis of a developing centralisation of the ruling class in Europe as well as the formation gradually of international linkages. Marshall has pointed out that the class structure of Britain, as he observed it in the 1940s and 1950s was distinctly differentiated with respect to local and national structures. The dominant classes (a term he did not use) were organised nationally, whereas the working class was still locally and regionally organised.[27] The significance of dialects and 'accents' in England was the expressive aspect of this structure. In North America, the organisation of the ruling class in the late nineteenth century had more regional structures, sometimes cross-cutting national boundaries, as for example the west coast elite of the ruling class based on lumber, railroads and coal linked California, Oregon, Washington, and British Columbia. Though the north-eastern establishment of the US exercised a centralising pull, the geographical dispersion of its bases prevented the increasingly extra-local and abstracted forms of property, finance, marketing and management from developing the strongly centralised organisation of the ruling class characteristic of Britain. In Canada the indigenous development of class is given a distinctive character in the late nineteenth century by the inter-section of the leading section of the Canadian ruling class with that of Britain. But whether centralised or regional, the generalised and abstracted relations of commodity exchange progressively detached the dominant classes from particular localities and regions and from the organisation of class relations on a local basis. Hence intra-class relations had to be re-formed on the national or non-local level. These relations had also to be organised in and as part of an actual everyday world, a world inhabited by particular individuals, embodied, who necessarily exist in local and parti-cular places. The social organisation of the ruling *trans-local* class must be accomplished at the *local* and *particular* level in the everyday world. The everyday world and its order had to be redesigned so as to realise in *local* settings the properties, settings and order of a non-local, abstracted general order. Class as an everyday social phenomenon came to consist of highly developed codes of dress, manners, etiquette, furnishings, organising practices of exclusion and inclusion and the ordering and control of the settings in which intra-personal encounters occurred. Everything that we have laughed at about women in reading novels, fashion magazines and the like becomes less silly and more intelligible when we see that this is what is and was going on. The attention to fashion, the eagerness to learn and imitate what is being worn this season in New York, in London, in Paris, these were part of the formation of a non-locally organised class as a lived everyday world. These are part of the social organisation of the ruling class *as a class*. Davidoff has stressed this change in the local organisation of class relations in her study of the *Best Circles* in nineteenth-century London. She describes how rules of access to privatised settings and to social circles provided a new basis of class organisation. Kin relations could be treated selectively, those that were advantageous could be exploited while others were dropped. Barriers against newcomers could be more effectively maintained.[28]

So there is a change in the internal organisation of the ruling class away from localised and localising networks of kin and towards a distinctly created order of relations and settings, a definitely stylised, expressive and staged everyday world, identifying, marking, and re-forming intra-class relations, and securing and *organising closure* of the interpersonal relations of the ruling class. The elaboration of a code, or a system of codes in furnishing and dress styles, in etiquette, conversation, etc., provided for mutual recognition among members of the class and the routine accomplishment of social 'circles' as a hierarchy within the ruling class. Entry to the best, or even the next best, circles depended upon already being a member in the sense of knowing how to recognise and to reproduce the expressive codes which announced membership and having therefore capacity to participate in the circles defined by their codes. Subordinate sections of the ruling class oriented towards the styles, manners and etiquette as a means of establishing in their local setting their claim to membership in it. Through these means too they sharply differentiated themselves from others in their local community whose local economic and social roles might be little different from theirs.

In this type of class organisation, being an outsider is a distinct way in which class is experienced. Being present and yet knowing oneself to be an outsider and knowing oneself to be known as an outsider, who does not know how to speak, does not know how to dress, does not know how to address the appropriate topics appropriately, does not recognise the differentiating signals of dress, does not know which fork to use, or what a finger bowl is for, or how to speak or not to speak to servants; who does not know what to wear at what times of day, and in what settings—these were features of the social organisation of the ruling class at this extra-local level. In this way an extra-local everyday world is formed building in rules of exclusion and inclusion as codes and knowledge of codes.

At the stage of entrepreneurial capitalism, the small town was still an important locus of extra-local class formation. Though members of the bourgeoisie and middle class looked towards a centre such as Boston or New York or London in terms of fashion and culture, the actual locus of organisation was decentralised. The structure of entrepreneurial capitalism relates locally organised enterprises via market and monetary processes which are extra-local. But market functions themselves were enterprises located in towns and cities and tied into a locally organised class structure. At this stage of capitalism we find the work of producing class and class relations and intra- and extra-class relations within the local community. We can identify this localised organisation of class in novels such as those of Mrs Gaskell and Anthony Trollope in England, or of Sara Jeanette Duncan in Canada. Typical is the interplay between local neighbourhood, kin and political relations. At this stage (which of course did not develop nor disappear at the same time everywhere) there is a direct transfer from the relations generated by the economic organisation of the community to its political and civil relations. The local social organisation of the ruling class is largely the work of the women and implicates the family and familial relations. The boundaries are drawn by admission into the family setting, a family setting which is specifically designed and organised so as to intersect with and create the class linkages and allegiances coded in furniture, styles of meals and serving meals, conversational topics, and so on. The domestic labour of the middle-class woman and her servants were directed of course towards the comfort and health of her family members, but also and very importantly towards maintaining the material aspects of the codes articulating the family setting and social process to the extra-local organisation of class.

The basis of the family and domestic organisation of classes as an extra-local structure within the local setting changes with the change from entrepreneurial forms of capitalism to the corporate form. A study of the history of Glossop shows a sequence from the emergence in the late eighteenth and early nineteenth century of a multitude of small manufacturers owning small shops who at the outset worked along with their wage-labourers, through the consolidation of larger units on which a *local* bourgeoisie was established, to the shift away from that to an externally structured strata of salaried managers linked to the rise of what Birch calls combinations.[29] These are changes which shift the locus of economic organisation as a practice of management and of relations among the differing functions of the economic process out of the local community.

This progressive transposition of economic functions from individual enterprises locally organised to corporate form organised at the national or international level is the same movement which creates the salaried middle class. C. Wright Mills has described this change statistically for the United States in the changing ratios of salaried professionals and managers to independent businessmen and professionals.[30] It is a change also in the basis of class organisation, hence the work of the middle-class family in constituting the internal relations of class is modified accordingly.

Mills represents this as a decline of the old middle class and indeed it is.[31] But it should be emphasised also that it is a social re-organisation of the internal relations of the bourgeoisie and middle class in response to changes in economic organisation. New forms of local relationship emerge. The relations of the abstracted economic forms are no longer an active and integral process of neighbourhood and community relations. Now they must be expressed and organised as an everyday world in the local setting. The house, household, furnishings become a key then to forms of relations between neighbours in which house properties lie alongside one another so to speak, unrelated by the various working relations which linked members of a community in the earlier period. In this setting their relations are mediated by the visible signs which constitute for each other their mutual class status and hence bring into being the actual social organisation of class and its internal structures *as status*.

The suburb becomes an alternative mode of constituting the extra-local relations of the dominant classes. Suburban enclaves establish distinctive types of housing, types of schooling, and exclude 'undesirables' by informal real estate practices and zoning regulations restricting the financial basis of the area. This type of suburban development constitutes a total environment controlled with respect to the bases of participation. The control is built into the material environment and the use-value it embodies. Restricting entry provides for residents a controlled social environment which ensures that others are at least minimally appropriate as class associates and that as far as children are concerned the contacts they make, the associations they form and what they learn informally, will be within the desired class level. These forms of class residential organisation correspond to the abstracted form of organisation arising with the corporate form of capitalism in a way that is analogous to how science fiction writers have imagined that an alien form of life might reproduce its specialised and controlled climatic form and air supply in a variety of specific local settings.

The process then is one of constructing the social relational basis of a class that is no longer organised on a local basis in relation to land and local organisation of general market processes, but on a basis of modes of identifying persons in terms of performance in social occasions, knowing how to behave, how to dress, how to appear, and therefore upon behaviours which can be learned even though access to opportunities of learning may be restricted. Identification of class membership is no longer particularistic but is based upon and constitutes persons as kinds of currency whose value is determined by qualifications, by styles, by dress, and by knowing how and what to say, how to participate. The inculcation of this rather specialised culture requires intensive training, much of which is done in the early years of life prior to the child's going to school. The articulation of such trained and specialised behaviours to types of formally organised settings such as schools is part of the social construction of class transgenerationally, the social construction aspect of the distinctive mode in which the dominant classes are organised in contemporary corporate capitalism. It establishes both a relatively closed system of entitlement to settings and occasions provided by the various forms of corporate enterprise, including those of university and school, and an interchangeability of persons corresponding to the generalisation and interchangeability of settings and occasions established by the generalisation of corporate forms of organisation.

5. *A contradiction within the dominant classes and its management*
The emergence and progressive integration of the new form of ruling apparatus, distinctively a communicative practice, is also an ideologically informed and organised practice. It is socially organised to be differentiated and separable from particular individuals, and particular places. We can find in Weber's analysis of the bureaucratic type of authority, the essential prescription for the formation of a managerial or administrative structure serving the objectives of an enterprise quite separate from and independent of the objectives of those who 'perform' it, its employees make its objectives theirs and thereby bring it into being. The bases of access to positions in the ruling apparatus change. As these no longer clearly differentiate on sex lines, but call for technical knowledge, qualifications and so forth, the barriers to women's entry are weakened. In response the barriers are artificially and actively reinforced and ideological forms aimed specifically at the organisation of middle-class women's

relation to the ruling apparatus are developed.

The earlier form of economic agency constitutes the biological differences of sex as components of individual private property among the bourgeoisie. As property functions are transferred to the corporation and as the state and professional apparatus grows concurrently, skills acquired through education become increasingly important. So does the formation of the person socialised to roles structured now by the planful and rationally ordered logic of corporate action rather than the individual skills and working relations of actual individuals as actors in a given enterprise. The general capacity to participate in an elaborated world of literate action becomes essential. With these developments, the original basis of married women's exclusion as a component of property relations is no longer a barrier. The 'natural' basis of differentiation between the sexes was fundamental to the economic and political organisation of pre-capitalist social formations. With the rise of capitalism the basis of differential power and participation in civil society begins to dissipate. The barriers become weak. Major women novelists of the nineteenth century stood on the margins of power sensing in themselves unused capacities for participation. Their intellectual powers, their energetic intelligence, and exceptional language capacities gave them a natural access to an arena in which they could not act. The social barriers placed on them by their sex emerges in the work of Charlotte Bronte, George Eliot, and others, as a powerful contradiction generating the movement of their novels and the tragic dilemmas of their heroines. The period which first sees a theory of the education of women specifically recommending training for subordination, domesticity and personal servitude to men, notably of course the teachings of Rousseau, also sees the counter-statement in the work of Mary Wollstonecraft. The rise of capitalism rather than instantly precipitating women into the private sphere seems rather to initiate a struggle on one side to reinforce and re-organise the barriers to women's participation and on the other to break through barriers already weakened by the advance of capitalism on the other.

This struggle has focused particularly on women's education. The conception of a specialised education for women preparing them for domesticity points to a new need to plan and organise women's relation to the home. Importantly also, it provides that the very ideological channels through which women's potential access to a wider arena opens, should be those through which they would learn the practice of their confinement. Ideological organisation has been central in organising the role and social relations of bourgeois and middle-class women. It has been of special significance for women whose material situations have been such that they could make the everyday realisation of ideological forms an objective. They could adopt styles of being, manners, etiquette, dress, moral relations, in accordance with ideological developments. Intra-class relations were increasingly ideologically organised. Ideological forms began to shift the basis of culture from the inherited forms of previous generations, passed from mother to daughter, to an orientation towards the authority of print and hence of ideology generated within the ruling apparatus itself by specialists of various kinds—by authorities in women's feelings; by experts in women's physiology, biology and sexual capacities; by writers of fiction who created the mirrors in which women sought to discover their reflection; by the makers of moral tales who prescribed the forms of heroism and sacrifice proper to women; by the physicians who packaged ideology and treatment for the nebulous but real suffering arising from the regime of ideological living. Over the shifting requirements of changing social relations of capitalism, ideologies continue to design and redesign the modes of women's subordination and service to the ruling apparatus.

The importance of the domestic labour of dominant class women and of their subordination to the economic and political roles played by men and to the work of organising intra-class relations, has been secured using ideological as well as other means of class control. As education became the key link in the access to economic agency women's access to education had to be regulated. Steps were taken to exclude women from professional, bureaucratic and political positions as these were found to be vulnerable. Active forms of ideological and state repression responding to incursions by middle-class women were developed. For example, the rise of women novelists in the nineteenth century elicited, as Showalter has shown,[32] a critical enterprise amounting almost to censorship on the part of male publishers and literary leaders. Typically 'female' styles and topics were institutionalised in the novel through the influence of men whose critical treatment laid down the topics women writers could properly address, how they could address them, and the range of feeling and moral issues which could properly be taken up by the woman writer.

Over time an educational system was put in place which systematically differentiated boys from girls. Girls were streamed into programmes ensuring their disqualification from the kinds of advanced training giving access to the professions. The hidden curriculum trained them to be responsive and open to the ideological initiatives and technical practices increasingly originating in experts located in academic settings—instructors on home management, child rearing, interpersonal relations in the family, and the like. Women's post-secondary training came to focus largely within the arts and social sciences, or in subordinate forms of professional training such as nursing, pharmacy and teaching. School and post-secondary education emphasises women's language abilities, their knowledge of social science, art and literature, and trained them to respond and to make use of the work of experts. Women are prepared for their ancillary clerical roles in management. They are provided with the language skills needed to give the 'cultural background' on which their future children's success in school will depend. They are also trained to respond to the work of psychological and sociological experts, to psychiatry, and to medicine as authorities and to make practical use of their understanding of the new ideologies produced by such specialists. Women of the dominant classes learned to treat the academic and professional sources of guidance with deference and to look to the expert for guidance in child rearing and in the management of interpersonal relations in the home. They learned in university the essential conceptual organisation articulating their daily work lives in the home to categories and concepts of the scientific establishment. They learnt indeed to think in terms of role and interpersonal relations, to analyse their situation and work in these terms, hence not to see what they were doing as work, to understand it as 'love', as 'role structures' and 'interpersonal processes'. They learned to look for problems and issues as these were analysed and constituted by experts. These skills are pieces of an ideological organisation linking the private domestic sphere to the professional bureaucratic and managerial controls of the ruling apparatus. The ideological organisation coordinated and coordinates the family and women's role in relation to the changing and various needs of the ruling apparatus. Education not only ensured that women would not end with the types of skills giving them an undeniable claim to entry as active participants to the ruling apparatus, but also laid down specific ideological controls through which the changing relations of a rapidly shifting capitalist development could be reformulated and reorganised as they were fed through to the family and to women's work in the family. Women learned in post-war North America, a 'feminine mystique' extolling the devotion of women to children, husband and suburban home.[33] Middle-class women were learning and participating in a work role ancillary and subordinated to the educational system. The ideological organisation provided the organisational linkage which seemed like no linkage at all. The 'causal' rhetoric of psychology and sociology was a one-way street. What mothers did affected how children did in school. What went on in the home was the 'wild' factor uncontrolled by the hierarchical structure of the educational process. Ideological organisation originating in a scientific establishment and mediated by the mass media came to coordinate the private and state sectors of responsibility for children, as indeed in other spheres.

These relations among ideological organisations, a family form subordinating women in a subcontractual relation[34] to a ruling apparatus of government, management and professions mediated as personal services to husband and children, and an educational system preparing them for these family functions and for the essentially subordinate clerical and professional roles middle-class women came to play, are the matrix of the experience of patriarchy among middle-class women. The authority of men over women is the authority of a class and expresses class 'interest'. The inner complicity of women in their own oppression is a feature of class organisation. The concept of 'patriarchy' explicates as a social relation between women and men the conjunction of institutions locking middle-class women into roles ancillary but essential to the ruling apparatus and specifically silencing them by giving them no access to the ideological, professional and political means in which their experience might be communicated to other women.

6. *The working-class family: the emergence of women's dependency on men*

Dependency of married women, and particularly women with children on men and men's salaries or wages is a feature of both middle-class and working-class family relations in contemporary capitalism. This is not simply a matter of universal family form characteristic of a species rather than a culture or mode of production. Women's dependency must be seen as arising in a definite social form and, we have suggested, organised rather differently in differing class settings and relations. One view identifies the emergence of this type of family organisation with the rise of capitalism. As the productive process is increasingly taken over by the industrial organisation of production, the family becomes a consuming rather than a producing unit, and women's domestic labour ceases to play a socially productive role and becomes in the working class a personal service to the wage earner. Her domestic labour reproduces the labour power of the individual worker.

But as we acquire more historical knowledge of women we find that the sharpness of this supposed historical moment becomes blurred. The emergence of the dependent family form is slow and seemingly contingent upon elaborations and developments of the original separation of domestic economy from the industrial process. As we explore the dynamic process at work we can recognise a contradiction in the rise of capitalism so far as women and their relation to the family are concerned. It seems that the same industrial capitalism leading apparently to a restriction and narrowing of the scope of women's work in the home and to her and her children's dependency on a man's wage, is also a process which potentially advances women's independence by making it in principle at least possible for women to earn enough to support themselves, perhaps even to support their children. Productive labour formerly tied to sex differences by different physical and biological situations and also by the intimate ties of skills which were earlier a true specialisation of persons from childhood or youth on. As production is increasingly mediated by machine technologies and increasingly organised as a form of enterprise specifically separated from particular individuals and their local relations, it is also increasingly indifferent to social differentiation, such as gender or race.[35] At every new

level in the development of productive capacity in capitalism, this contradiction is apparent. Capitalism continually represents the possibility of
women's independence and at the same time engenders conditions and
responses which have constituted a fully dependent form of family unit.
It seems then that the dependency of both middle-class and working-class
women on the individual man's salary or wage must be examined in
relation to the organisation of the labour market and employment
possibilities for women outside the home.

Over time working-class and middle-class patterns of family organisation have become more alike with respect to the wife's dependency on
her husband's wage or salary. But the history of that relation is very
different. The earlier civil status of a man simply obliterated his wife's
as she was subsumed in the family economic unit identified with him.
She had no place in civil society, no capacity for economic action, at
least so long as she was married. What she produced, what she earned,
if she did earn, was his. Later her domestic labour becomes subordinated
to the enterprise of his career, and employment outside the home is
organised to ensure that the jurisdiction of male authority and appropriation of women's labour both inside and outside the home do not
interfere with one another. Dependency is part of a perpetuated pattern
of excluding women and married women in particular from functioning
as independent economic agents.

This history of the present family form among the working class is very
different. It does not begin with women's exclusion from economic
activity and it does not involve the formation of a property-holding unit
identified with the man. The legal forms were the same and those gave men
the right to women's earnings, but the actual practice and organisation of
work relations and economic contributions did not conform to the
bourgeois or middle-class pattern. The exclusive dependency of women on
men's wages is only gradually established and is differently structured. For
working-class women, dependency is directly on the man's wage-earning
capacity and role and a man's status and authority in the family is directly
linked to his capacity to earn.

The dependence of the mother-children unit on the male wage earner
emerges rather slowly. Scott and Tilly have identified a distinct form of
working-class and petty bourgeois family economy in which each member
earns and contributes to a common fund out of which the family needs
are met. They argue that although a relatively small proportion of married
women were employed in industry until relatively late in the nineteenth
century, the pattern of women not contributing actively to the household
economy comes very late. A wife who did not earn or otherwise contribute directly to the family means of subsistence and who had to depend
upon her husband's wage was most definitely undesirable. Married women
worked outside the home, and brought money or goods into the home in

all kinds of ways.[36] They took in lodgers. Some had gardens and produced for their families and sold the small surplus; or they baked and sold the product. Women were small traders, peddlars, and scavengers. They went into domestic service, took in laundry, were seamstresses, labourers on farms, took in homework and worked in factories.

Children too were essential contributors to the family economy. They might be employed in factory work but there were also a variety of opportunities for casual labour such as running messages. In addition there were many tasks around the house which children could perform while parents were at work outside. They did housekeeping, looked after younger children, fetched water, gardened and did other odd jobs.

With the institutionalisation of universal education, children cease or have already ceased to be regular wage earners contributing to the family wage from early in life. They cease progressively to contribute to the everyday work activities of household work and childcare. The withdrawal of child labour from the household as well as from the labour force required the presence of mothers in the home. Indeed the home comes to be organised around the scheduling of school and work so that the mother is tied down to the household in a way which was in fact new. Both husbands and children might come home for a mid-day meal. The school imposed standards of cleanliness which themselves represented a serious work commitment on the part of women who had to pump and heat water for washing. In the school context the child appears as the public 'product' of a mother's work. Her standards of housekeeping and childcare began to be subject to the public appraisal of the school system through the appearance and conduct of her child in the school. The working-class home as a work setting began to be organised by a relation to the school as well as the place of work. The school itself set standards for women's work as mothers and in various ways enforced them.

7. *The patriarchal organisation of the working-class family*

The dynamic processes of capital accumulation involve an increasingly extensive use of machines making labour more productive. From these processes, two consequences flow for working-class women. The first is a tendency of machines to displace labour, generating over time a surplus labour population. This functions as a reserve army of labour in relation to the opening up of new areas of capital investment. The expansion of markets and of opportunities for investment regards the actual appearance of a surplus as such, but the steadily increasing rate of unemployment over time identifies a tendency which cannot be wholly suppressed and is quickened by the monopolistic process of corporate capitalism. The emergence of a permanent surplus labour population is relatively independent of unemployment created in the crises which periodically throw capitalist economies into recession. The presence of this 'reserve army of labour' tends to sharpen the competition of workers for jobs and hence to lower the price of labour-power (the wage). A second consequence is that technological advances have also made differences in physical strength and in skills developed over a lifetime of practice of decreasing significance in the productive process. Parallel to the developments of capitalism which among the ruling class make participation in the exercise of power indifferent to sex, is a development of the productive process rendering it too increasingly indifferent to the sex of the worker. Hence as the surplus labour population increases and competition sharpens, women come into competition with men for jobs. The traditionally lower wages of historically disadvantaged groups such as women and blacks gave them an advantage in competing for jobs which employers had no hesitation in deploying to their own advantage.

Through the nineteenth and early twentieth centuries, this problem was a recurrent theme in male working-class views concerning women in the labour force and in the policies of trade and labour unions. The issue for men was not only that of jobs. It was also the implications for the family and for men's traditional status in the family. Various nineteenth century writers, including Marx himself, saw women's participation in industry as destructive of their 'natural' female virtues and modes of being. These 'virtues' were intimately tied to notions of passivity and subordination and a restriction of women's spheres of action to a narrow conception of the domestic. Both working class and middle class were marked by the prohibition for women (and for children) of self-knowledge of their sexuality and control of their own bodies. The physical fragility of women, their supposedly natural weakness, is also related to the ways in which women's physical existence was subordinated to that of the husband and children.[37]

When women were employed outside the home and could earn a wage sufficient for independence, their departure from the ideals of feminity became a subject of reprobation. Of the early nineteenth century, Malmgreen writes:

> There was a psychological as well as an economic basis for the male worker's uneasiness, for the chance to earn a separate wage outside the home might free wives and daughters to some extent from the control of their husbands and parents. The piteous image of the sunken-cheeked factory slave must be balanced against that of the boisterous and cheeky 'factory lass'. Lord Ashley, speaking on behalf of the regulation of child and female labour in factories, warned the House of Commons of the 'ferocity' of the female operatives, of their adoption of male habits—drinking, smoking, forming clubs, and using 'disgusting' language. This, he claimed, was 'a perversion of nature', likely to produce 'disorder, insubordination, and conflict in families'.[38]

The voice here is that of the ruling class, but on this issue the working-class man and the ruling class were united. Malmgreen notes that in the early nineteenth century this view appears particularly prevalent among leading artisans in the working-class movements of Britain in that period.[39]

This stratification of the labour force within those trades and industries organised by craft unions survives in the differing job classification, which, for example, separates bartenders and chefs from waitresses and cooks. These divisions have their base in the internal division of labour resulting from differentiating tasks requiring specialised capacities from those which 'anyone' could do.[40] The internal differentiation becomes the basis of a stratified labour force separating a central workforce. This comes about in part as the outcome of union struggles, particularly in the early part of the twentieth century.[41] The central labour force is 'insulated', to use Friedman's terms[42] from the 'reserve army of labour'. It has access to the internal labour market of the corporation and hence to possibilities of mobility within the workplace. Pensions and other benefits have been won and seniority in transfers, layoffs and rehiring has been established; working conditions are regulated to some degree. By contrast, the peripheral labour force is defined by categories of dead-end jobs in the corporation and in localised small industries and service businesses with fluctuating labour needs.[43] It is not insulated from the reserve army of labour—indeed it is in part constitutive of that reserve. Workers tend to be bottled up in the peripheral labour force by lack of differentiating skills or experience. Rates of turnover, unemployment and underemployment are endemically high. Wages are low, benefits lacking or inadequate, working conditions poorly regulated.

Advances for workers according to Friedman have been won through struggle.[44] The struggle for a family wage and to reduce the competition of capitalist with man and family for women's labour is the obverse of the struggle to secure stability, good wages, benefits, to control working conditions, on the part of what becomes the 'central' section of the labour force. The central section is characterised by union organisation whereas the peripheral labour force has been relatively less organised. Struggles which have made gains for the central section of the labour force have also been part of the organisation of a racially and sexually segregated labour force. Under Gompers' leadership, the trade-union movement in North America became for women a systematic organisation of weakness relative to men and a systematic organisation of preferential access to skills and benefits for white men. There was little interest in unionising women other than as a means of control. There was fear that bringing numbers of women into a union would result in 'petticoat government'. Women's locals were sometimes given only half the voting power of men on the grounds that they could only contribute half the dues.[45] The Canadian Trades and Labour Congress in the early twentieth century had as an avowed goal that of eliminating women, particularly married women, from the work-force. In Britain, though women had a longer history of trade-union organisation and there was an entrenched though small number of women in leadership positions, there was a similar lack of interest in actively organising women workers or in representing their distinctive interests.[46]

Struggles to restrict women's participation and particularly married women's participation in the labour force went on under various guises. Union efforts alone could not have been effective in reconstituting the family in a way that fixed women's dependence on men's wages. At that period, however, the state begins to enact legislation in various ways constitutive of a family in which dependency of women and children, or conditions become legally enforceable and are progressively incorporated into the administrative policies of welfare agencies, education, health care, etc. There is an implicit alliance forming during this period between the state and the unions representing predominantly male working-class interests in the subordination of women to the home and their elimination from an all but marginal role in the labour force.

The emergence of national and international markets and financial organisations, of an organisation of productive process implanted into local areas rather than arising indigenously, conforming to standardised technical plans and standardised machines, tools and other equipment, and of a universalising and managerial and technical process, called for a new kind of labour force. Similar exigencies arose also in relation to the military requirements of imperialist expansion and the devastating wars resulting from the conflict of rival empires. This new labour force had to be capable of entering the industrial process anywhere in the society. The need was not only for technically skilled workers, but more generally for a *universalised* labour force, stripped of regional and ethnic cultures, fully literate, English-speaking, familiar with factory discipline and the discipline of the machine and, in relation to the military enterprise in particular, physically healthy. In the production of this labour force, mothering as a form of domestic labour was seen as increasingly important. The mother's ancillary role *vis-à-vis* the school and the school as means of setting standards for children's health, cleanliness and character has been mentioned before. The liberation of women for work in the home became an objective of the ruling class of this period.[47] Here then we find steps taken to reduce the competition of industry and home for women's labour. Legislation restricting the length of women's working day, night shift work, the physical exertion which could be required of women, was passed.

In these changes we see under a different aspect some of the same developments we have described earlier, in relation to the changing basis of the social organisation of the dominant class. It is the period during which in the United States the corporations began to predominate. Various legislative steps and administrative developments re-organised, at least the legal and administrative basis of the family and united the interests of the AFL type of union with those of the section of the ruling class represented by the state. Laws which earlier entitled husband and father to appropriate both his wife's and his children's earnings disappeared. New legislation was passed requiring men to support their wives and children, whether they lived together or not,[48] and administrative processes were developed to enforce the law. Laws such as these became the bases of welfare policies both during the depression years and later. They are built into the welfare practices of today, so that a man sharing the house of a woman welfare recipient may be assumed to be supporting her and her children, hence permitting the suspension of welfare payments to her.[49] Furthermore, the state entry into the socialisation of children through the public education system provided an important source of control. Davin has described the early twentieth century policies for educating working-class girls. They are in line with ruling-class interest in a healthy working class and stress the girl's future role as mother.[50] As secondary education developed streaming patterns similar to those characterising the experience of middle-class women prevented working-class women from acquiring the basic manual and technical skills on which access to skilled and even semi-skilled work in industry came increasingly to depend. Vocational training became almost exclusively a preparation for clerical employment.

The depression years established a clear conjunction between the interests of organised labour and of the state (and of some sections of the ruling class) in as far as possible eliminating married women from the labour force. The state adopted various measures designed to ensure that one wage would provide for two adults and their children (some of the legislation mentioned above was passed during the depression years). The emergence of Unemployment Insurance and Pension Plans created an administrative organisation building in the wife's dependency on her husband. In the United States, job creation programmes omitted to create jobs for women.[51] The man as wage earner and the woman as dependent became the legally enforceable and administratively constituted relation. In this way the increasing costs of reproducing the new kind of labour force including the costs of women's specialisation in domestic labour would be borne by the working man and his wage. As Inman points out:

> The law makes it mandatory on the husband to 'support' the woman in this workshop (the home), and their children. And while the 'support' the husband gives his wife must come out of production, and the owners of the means of production are not unaware of her existence, and while they also know that children must be raised if the supply of labour and soldiers is to remain adequate to their needs, yet the working man who is the support of his family is not secure in this amount.[52]

It would be, however, a serious mistake to see these reactions as merely the expression of a patriarchal impulse. Women's domestic labour was of vital and survival value to the family unit. Subsistence was still dependent upon the work of women in a way which it is no longer. The adequacy of shelter, the preparation and cooking of food, including making break, the making and maintenance of clothing, the management of the wage, are crucial. The availability of a woman's unpaid labour was highly consequential to the household standard of living. The physical maintenance of the male breadwinner was an essential feature. When food was short, women and children would go without to ensure that the 'master' got enough, or at least the best of what there was. As the family was increasingly integrated into the monetary economy, the role of women was more and more that of managing and organising the expenditures of the wages. Women became experts in managing and experts also in going without themselves.[53] It seems likely that at a certain point the requirements of domestic labour began to come into direct competition with work outside the home. A family could manage better if the mother did not go out to work, but was able to devote herself full-time to domestic labour and the production of subsistence. The concentration of the wage earning function in the man also liberated women's domestic labour to maintaining and increasing the family's standard of living. More time spent in the processing of food, more time to give to mending and making clothes, more time to give to cleanliness and maintaining of warmth and shelter resulted in material improvements in the family's standard of living. Where men could not earn enough, women with young children were confronted with the dilemma of whether to go out and earn what little they could so that the children could eat, running the risks that lack of adequate care for the children created, or whether to stay home and give the children adequate care when they could not get enough to eat.[54] The improvement over time in men's wages reduced, though it has not eliminated, this dilemma. It is implicit in the situation of working classes because it is always present in the wage relation. As real wages decline, the spread of families in which the wife goes out to work increases. The family is always dependent upon the state of the economy and of the particular industry in which the man works, and upon which his role and livelihood and his family depend.

Characteristic also of the working-class family, in which the man is the breadwinner, and the women and children are dependent, is a marked subordination of women to men's needs. Control over funds is a distinct male prerogative. A husband's resistance to his wife's going out to work goes beyond the practicalities of the family's economic well-being.[55] Working-class women learn a discipline which subordinates their lives to the needs and wishes of men. The man's wage is his. It is not in truth a 'family' wage. Varying customs have developed around the disposal of this. Sometimes there appears to be a survival of the older tradition whereby the wife takes the whole wage and manages its various uses, including a man's pocket money. But it is also open to men not to tell their wives what they earn and to give them housekeeping money or require them to ask for money for each purchase. It is clearly his money and there is an implicit contract between a husband and wife whereby he provides for her and her children on whatever conditions he thinks best and she provides for him the personal and household services that he demands. The household is organised in relation to his needs and wishes; meal times are when he wants his meals; he eats with the children or alone as he chooses; sex is when he wants it; the children are to be kept quiet when he does not want to hear them. The wife knows at the back of her mind that he can, if he wishes, take his wage-earning capacity and make a similar 'contract' with another woman. As wages have increased, the breadwinner's spending money has enlarged to include leisure activities which are his, rather then hers—a larger car, a motorcycle, a boat and even the camper often proves more for him than for her, since for her it is simply a transfer from convenient to less convenient conditions of the same domestic labour as she performs at home.

Unemployment of the man has a shattering effect on this type of family. Men's identity as men is built into their role as breadwinner, as spender in relation to other men, as patriarch within the family. The extent to which their masculinity is dependent upon capitalism appears powerfully in the context of unemployment when the claims and entitlements built into the 'contract' are undermined. No matter how hard wives may attempt to replicate the forms of the proper relation, over time the situation itself falsifies their efforts and it is apparent to both.

This situation is often represented as one which is somehow the product of women's arbitrary ill-will. But as we begin to understand the basis of the patriarchal structure of the working-class family in its relation to capital and the founding of masculine identity on the wage and the wage relation imported into the home, we can see that it is not a matter of choice for the unemployed workers' families. Rather the underlying basis of relations has changed. The man is not what he was, his relations are not what they were, because the material determinations outside his control and the control of members of his family are not what they were. Hence his moral claims, his right to authority, based on these material relations, are undermined. He was not what he thought he was. His masculine identity, his authority over his wife and children, his status with other men, was always based on relations outside the family and not within his grasp. His masculinity was not really his after all.[56]

For working-class women, this relation has a political dimension. The discipline of acceptance of situations over which they have no control and the discipline of acceptance of the authority of a man who also has in fact no control over the conditions of his wage-earning capacity, is not compatible with the bold and aggressive styles of political or economic action necessarily characteristic of working-class organisation. Women's sphere of work and responsibility is defined as subordinate to that in which men act and it is indeed dependent and subordinate. The children s well-being, the production of the home, these require from women a discipline of self-abnegation and service as exacting as that of a religious order and just as taxing emotionally. Masculinity and male status is in part expressed in men's successful separation from the subordination of the sphere of women's activity as well as the visibility of his success in 'controlling' his wife (what may go on behind the scenes is another matter). The fact that the wage relation creates an uncertain title to male status and authority by virtue of how its conditions are lodged in the market process and exigencies of capital, make the visible forms of relations all the more important. Men subordinate themselves in the workplace to the authority of the foreman, supervisor and manager. A condition of their authority in the home is this daily acceptance of the authority of others. They assume also the physical risks and hazards of their work. (Indeed as Willis shows these became the basis of a distinctively masculine identity on the shop floor.)[57] They live with the ways in which capital uses them up physically and discards them mentally and psychologically. They undertake a lifetime discipline also, particularly if they elect to marry and support a wife and children. That responsibility is also a burden and it can be a trap for working-class men as much as for working-class women. Through that relation a man is locked into his job and into the authority relations it entails. His wife's subordination, her specific personal and visible subservience, her economic dependence, is evidence of his achievement. Her 'nagging', her independent initiatives in political or economic contexts, her public challenges to his authority—these announce his failure as a man. In the political context, we find a subculture prohibiting women's participation in political activity other than in strictly ancillary roles essentially within the domestic sphere. When for example women organised militant action in support of the men striking in the Flint, Michigan strike in 1937, they had to go against norms restraining women from overt forms of political action.

Union organisation is based upon and enhances the separation and powers created by the wage relation. Obviously and simply the union is an organisation of wage-earners. The individualised appropriation of the wage by he or she who earns it is institutionalised in a collective organisation of workers attempting to control the wage and the conditions under which it is earned. Wives and families dependent upon the wage have no title to represent their interests. I am not suggesting that these interests are always ignored. I am pointing rather to how collective policy and decision-making of wage earners institutionalises an individual worker's exclusive right to a wage. The separation of the sphere of economic action from the domestic is completed. The interchange between the two is a matter for the individual wage earner. The consequences of union decisions and policies are consequences for wives and families, but they have no voice other than through the individual wage earner. In strike situations women may organise to support within the sphere of domestic activity; or they may be accessible to manipulation by management propaganda and have even occasionally developed organised oppositional strikes. Both are aspects of a single underlying relation and both conform to the appropriate boundaries and relations of women's political activity *vis-à-vis* men's.

Earlier we cited Malmgreen's description of an instance of ruling-class fear of the 'ferocity' of female operatives. Lord Ashley clearly identified the subordination of women to men in the home with their political suppression. The ideology of the weak and passive women, needing protection and support and subordinated 'naturally' to the authority of men in the home, as it was adopted by working-class men and working-class political and economic organisations, served to secure the political control of one section of the working class by another. In the first part of the nineteenth century in England, working-class women had been active in radical politics.[58] Their subordination to men in the family was perfected progressively over the latter half of the nineteenth century and the first quarter of the twentieth. It is integral to the attempt of the ruling class to establish a corporate society. The range of organised working-class action is narrowed progressively to economic organisation restricted to the workplace. A whole range of concerns and interests arising outside the workplace in relation to health, housing, pollution, education, remain unexpressed or expressed only indirectly. Localised neighbourhood and community concerns have yet to develop an organised and continuing political voice. Inadvertantly working-class men combine to suppress and silence those whose work directly engages them with such problems and concerns. Indirectly and through the mechanism described above they come to serve the interests of a ruling class in the political and economic subordination of half the working class.

8. *Patriarchy and Class*
At the outset we confronted the terms 'patriarchy' and 'class' as key terms in contrasting and opposed accounts of women's inequality in contemporary capitalist society. Resolution of the opposition has been sought in an empirical questioning of family organisation as a basis for women's subordination to men. As we have examined the development of a form of the family in which women depend upon men and the ideological and political institutions enforcing it, we can begin to see patriarchy (in the sense of men's political and personal domination over women) in relation to class as part of the institutions through which a ruling class maintains

its domination. At different stages in the transformation of property relations from the individual to the corporate form, bourgeois and middle-class women have been subordinated to the changing requirement of class organisation and of the transgenerational maintenance of class. For working-class women we have seen the emergence of a dependent form of family subordinating women to men, locked in by legal and administrative measures instituted by the state and a stratified labour market fostered by trade unions, capitalists and the state. These are the institutional forms which have secured the uses of women's domestic labour in the service of a ruling apparatus, ensuring and organising the domination of a class over the means of production. They are political institutions in the sense in which the women's movement has come to understand that term, where it refers to the exercise of power as such whether it is a feature of special-ised political institutions such as political parties, government and the like, or of less formal interpersonal processes.

Throughout the foregoing analysis we have been aware of capitalism as continually generating changes in material conditions and of these changes as they are fed through to the 'surface' necessitating innovations, adapta-tions, re-organisation. Forms of political and ideological organisation relatively successful in stabilising the position of the dominant classes at one point may at the next confront situations in which they are no longer effective or appropriate. This today is surely the situation with respect to women. The institutions of patriarchy organise and control in a material context other than that they can handle effectively. The ground has shifted under our feet.

We have pointed to a major contradiction arising for both middle-class and working-class women as capitalism advances. It is the contradiction between a developing and essential indifference of capital to the sex of those who do its work, and the gender organisation of the domestic economy as an integral part of the reproduction of class. With the rise of corporate capitalism the balance begins to shift away from the domestic. Women's exclusion becomes then a political institution built into the organisation of education, into the uses of power characteristic of the self-governing process of professions and professional organisations, and of union organisation, and into other institutional processes. Earlier the contradiction emerges as a latent and sometimes actual competition between the domestic and the political economies for women's labour—a competition resolved for some time by restricting women's success to the labour force after marriage and in general to a limited range of occupations with an earning capacity below that enabling them to maintain a family unit without a husband. The political aspects of women's subordination are the institutions of patriarchy. But they could not have been effective without a corresponding material base.

Earlier women's domestic labour was essential to subsistence. It had no substitutes. It has also been essential to advances in the family standard of living which would have been originally unobtainable without the inter-position of women's work in the home. Women of both the middle class and working classes at different income levels could by their personal skills, their hard work and commitment, take the wage and salary, pur-chase materials and tools and combine these with labour and skill—their knowledge of cooking, cleaning, managing, laundering, shopping, etc.—to produce a subsistence level or better, essential for family health, comfort and under minimal income conditions, for survival. In the households of the dominant classes the production of the 'coded' settings expressing class status also depended upon women's skills and labour, although until the first decade or so of the twentieth century much of that labour would have been that of hired domestic servants.

Over time the labour women contributed to the domestic production of subsistence was displaced by labour and skill embodied in the product of industry. Progressively capital has inserted a labour process embodied in the commodity into the home and has reorganised the work process there as it has reorganised so much in every part. At some point what women can contribute in the form of labour no longer balances off what she can earn and hence add to the purchasing power of the family. The wife can no longer significantly reduce costs to the wage earner by contri-buting more of her labour to the household process. This moment is not single nor simple since it is also related to income levels and the standard of living at which the family aims. Nonetheless the basic process is one which increases the significance of a monetary contribution and depresses the significance of skilled domestic labour. Additional money comes to be the primary if not the only means of improving the family's standard of living or of avoiding economic hardship. The exigencies of care of small children comes to be the chief claim reserving women from labour force participation.

Along with the transfer of labour and skill in the production of sub-sistence from housewife to product, the market process provides increasing-ly for the daily needs of individuals. Many functions earlier belonging to the home have been socialised in various ways—cleaning clothes, cooking and feeding, care of the sick, of the old and handicapped, amusement, social life, etc., have become commercial or state services. Even though recently state support in some areas has been reduced or withdrawn, the massive transfer from the domestic to the social realm still generally holds. In practice this means, among other things, the existence of alternatives where formerly there were none. This is consequential in particular for men for whom the home no longer represents the sole and exclusive source of food, shelter and comfort. For men the assumption of the 'burden' of a family no longer so clearly provides a standard of well-being and comfort which would otherwise be unobtainable.

For women of the dominant classes the importance of their local work in the maintenance of class relations has declined. The rise of suburbia first transferred some elements of the formation of the extra-local forms of class to the selective processes of the real estate market and the organisation of stylistic and price enclaves as neighbourhoods of similar kinds of people. The further detachment from the local of the ruling apparatus accords for men increasing importance to linkages based on their business or professional associates. There is at first a characteristic split between the zones of social activity of men and women. Men's is increasingly articulated to their work and women's increasingly in relation to their work and responsibilities in the suburban territory of childcare and the eight-to-six working week of women at home. This split becomes visible in social settings in the conversational separation of men from women. The evolution of the ruling apparatus as an elaborately interlaced network of the state, managerial, financial and professional division of the work of ruling is more and more divorced from specific local places and individuals rooted as such in neighbourhood and community. This evolution diminishes the significance of family and family-formed transgenerational linkages for the dominant classes.

The slow but consistent upward creep of the labour force participation of married women, and indeed of women in general, points to the diminishing power of the domestic economy to compete with paid employment for women. The demand for certain types of women's labour increased greatly as corporate capitalism called for clerical, sales and service workers at low cost, a demand which has more and more been met by women. The 'compact' restricting the employment of married women and hence the direct competition of paid employment with the domestic economy controlled by the husband has been weakened and is in decline. The assertion of individual authority by a man in restraining his wife from taking on paid employment outside the home is weakened by the disappearance of complementary restrictions in the work setting. With inflation and increasing levels of unemployment more and more married women enter the labour force. Money earnings are essential to the family and if the man's wage or salary does not bring in enough then women's responsibilities to her home and family are increasingly calling for her to seek employment outside the home.

Nonetheless, the earlier political and ideological accommodations institutionalised in the labour market and the educational system come to function so as to depress arbitrarily women's capacity to earn a living, to survive, to provide for children. Patriarchal institutions continue to reduce women's capacity to compete on the labour market. The organisation and perpetuation of a stratified labour force has vested powers and privileges in men which give them an advantage in the context of the sharpening competition for employment as well as for positions of power and opportunity in the ruling apparatus. In particular the educational system as a whole including both schools and post-secondary institutions of all kinds, is effectively sealed off from initiatives seeking to modify the processes by which it has systematically served to disquality women at every level of the occupational structure from access to more highly skilled, more advanced and better paid employment. Government attempts to modify women's access to skilled trades had been restrained by business and organised labour and by its own unwillingness to adopt policies which would exacerbate problems of unemployment. Depression has its gender organisation. It appears in the government statistics as the high proportion of women on welfare; in the uses by high school girls of pregnancy as a means of independence through child care payments; in the increased numbers of single parents; in the increases in prostitution; in the increased availability of working-class women for jobs such as office cleaning, textile manufacture, waitressing, where rates of pay are kept down by the vast reserve army waiting in the wings, and the like. It appears also in the increases in violence of parents against children and of husbands against wives, as children and wives with children become a trap.

In these historical movements which transform the internal gender relations of class we can see both the bases among women for a common struggle against patriarchy and the bases for class divisions. In the analysis developed in this paper patriarchy comes into view as located in the same set of institutional processes which organise class hegemony. The ruling apparatus of managerial practices, state, textual discourse, professional organisation and so on is gender organised and still dominated by men. It confronts women of the dominant classes primarily in its gender aspect: its class dimension does not appear. For working-class women, on the other hand, its patriarchal practices are not easily distinguishable from its class rule. Nonetheless there are common bases for struggle against a common enemy. And while the local patriarchal forms of the working class are oppressive to women and have been reinforced and sustained by the patriarchy of the ruling apparatus, they do not take on the same political significance as the coincidence of the local and personal with institutional domination which is the experience of women of the dominant classes. The issues for women of the dominant classes revolve around the possibilities of transforming the internal gender relations of class without transforming class itself. Clearly those for working-class women confront a more fundamental contradiction, particularly as the ambiguous local patriarchal forms of the family are eroded by changes in the bases of the family economy. The women's movement provides for the possibilities both of alliance and of opposition. More important, however, than the almost certainly illusory dream of unity among women, is the creation of a wholly new arena of discourse within which such issues as these are debated and in which class relations among women are given expression and definition.

NOTES

1. c.f. Christine Delphy's early paper, 'The main enemy: a materialist analysis of women's oppression', Women's Research and Resources Centre, *Explorations in Feminism*, No. 3, 1979.
2. Heidi Hartmann, 'The unhappy marriage of Marxism and feminism: toward a more progressive union' in Lydia Sargent, ed., *Women and Revolution: A Discussion of the Unhappy Marriage of Marxism and Feminism* (South End Press, 1981). An earlier version of this influential paper was published in 1975, pp. 2-41.
3. Zillah Eisenstein, 'Developing a theory of capitalist patriarchy and socialist feminism' in Zillah Eisenstein, ed., *Capitalist Patriarchy and the Case for Socialist Feminism* (New York, Monthly Review Press, 1979), pp. 5-40.
4. Veronica Beechey's admirable appraisal of the range of feminist thinking on patriarchy concludes with a call to develop a materialist method of analysis integrating 'production and reproduction as part of a single process' and revealing 'that gender differentiations are inseparable from the form of organization of the class structure'. Veronica Beechy, 'On Patriarchy', *Feminist Review*, No. 3, 1979, pp. 66-82.
5. c.f. Sandra Harding, 'Why has the sex/gender system become visible only now?' in Sandra Harding and Merill B. Hintikka, *Discovering Reality: Feminist Perspectives on Epistemology, Metaphysics, Methodology and Philosophy of Science* (Dordrecht, Holland, D. Reidel Publishing, 1983), pp. 311-24.
6. Gayle Rubin originated this concept with her paper, 'The traffic in women: notes on the "political economy" of sex' in Rayna Rapp Reiter, ed., *Toward an Anthropology of Women* (New York, Monthly Review Press, 1975), pp. 157-210.
7. V. Beechey, op. cit.
8. See Rayna Rapp's critique of the acceptance of 'the family' as a natural unit and her recommendation that we view it rather 'as a social (not a natural) constructtion, the. . . boundaries (of which) are always decomposing and recomposing in continuous interaction with larger domains'. Rayna Rapp on 'household and family' in Rayna Rapp, Ellen Ross and Renate Bridenthal, 'Examining family history', *Feminist Studies*, Vol. 5, No. 1, Spring 1979, pp. 174-200, and her more recent 'Family and class in contemporary America: Notes toward an understanding of ideology' in Barrie Thorne and Marilyn Yalom, eds., *Rethinking the Family: Some Feminist Questions* (New York, Longmans, 1982).
9. Frederick Engels, *The Origin of the Family, Private Property and the State* (Moscow, Progress Publishers, 1968).
10. Ibid., p. 73.
11. Karl Marx and Frederick Engels, *The German Ideology* (Moscow, Progress Publishers, 1976).
12. Karl Marx, *Grundrisse: Foundations of a Critique of Political Economy*, trans. Martin Nicolaus, (Harmondsworth, Middx., Penguin Books, 1973).
13. Examples of an extensive debate include: Margaret Benston, 'The political economy of women's liberation', *Monthly Review*, September 21, 1969, pp. 13-27; Peggy Morton, 'Women's work is never done', in *Women Unite* (Toronto, the Women's Press, 1972), pp. 45-69; John Harrison, 'The political economy of housework', *Bulletin of the Conference of Socialist Economists*, Winter 1973, pp. 35-52; Wally Seccombe, 'The housewife and her labour under capitalism',

New Left Review 83, January–February 1974, pp. 3–24; Jean Gardiner, 'Women's domestic labour', *New Left Review*, January–February 1975, pp. 47–59. This is only a partial list. The most recent contribution to the discussion is a collection of papers edited by Bonnie Fox, *Hidden in the Household: Women's Domestic Labour under Capitalism* (Toronto, the Women's Press, 1980).

14. Engels, op. cit., p. 77.
15. Peter Dobkin Hall, 'Marital selection and business in Massachusetts merchant families, 1700-1900' in M. Gordon, ed., *The American Family in Social-Historical Perspective* (New York, St. Martin's Press, 1978).
16. Christine Delphy's analysis of marriage as establishing a relation of appropriation between man and woman appears to be based on the middle-class family. Delphy, 'Continuities and discontinuities in marriage and divorce' in Diana Leonard Barker and Sheila Allen, eds., *Sexual Divisions and Society: Process and Change* (London, Tavistock Publications, 1976), pp. 76–89.
17. H.J. Mozaus, *Women in Science* (Cambridge, Mass., The M.I.T. Press, 1974), pp. 182–90.
18. Philip E. Hammond, *Sociologists at Work: Essays on the Craft of Social Research* (New York, Basic Books, 1964).
19. Alison Prentice, 'The feminization of teaching' in S. Trofimenkoff and A. Prentice, eds., *The Neglected Majority* (Toronto, McClelland and Stewart, 1977), pp. 49–65.
20. Kathleen Archibald describes this development in her study of gender in the Canadian Public Service, *Sex and the Public Service: A Report to the Public Service Commission of Canada*, Information Canada, 1973, pp. 14-17.
21. Dorothy E. Smith, 'Women's perspective as a radical critique of sociology', *Sociological Inquiry*, Vol. 4, No. 1, 1974.
22. Basil Bernstein, *Class, Codes and Control: Theoretical Studies Towards a Sociology of Language* (St. Albans, Paladin, 1973).
23. Dorothy E. Smith, 'Women's work as mothers: A new look at the relation between family, class and school achievement', paper presented at the meetings of the Western Association of Sociology and Anthropology, Brandon, Manitoba, February 1983.
24. Eli Zaretsky, *Capitalism, Family and Personal Life* (London, Pluto, 1976).
25. Sachs and Wilson suggest that the nineteenth century changes in matrimonial property enabling wives to hold separate property are associated with the emergence of property-owning institutions independent of the family such as joint stock companies. Albie Sachs and Joan Hoff Wilson, *Sexism and the Law: A Study of Male Beliefs and Judicial Bias in Britain and the United States* (New York, Oxford University Press, 1978).
26. David Mole, 'An approach to finance capitalism', unpublished paper, University of Toronto, 1979.
27. T.H. Marshall, *Citizenship and Social Class* (Cambridge, UK., Cambridge University Press, 1950).
28. This analysis depends heavily on Leonore Davidoff's *The Best Circles: Society, Etiquette and the Season* (London, Croom Helm, 1973).
29. Anthony H. Birch, *Small Town Politics: A Study of Political Life in Glossop* (New York, Oxford University Press, 1959).
30. C. Wright Mills, *White Collar: The American Middle Classes* (New York, Oxford University Press, 1956).
31. Idem., p. 58.
32. Elaine Showalter, *A Literature of Their Own: British Women Novelists from Bronte to Lessing* (Princeton, NJ, Princeton University Press, 1977).
33. Betty Friedan, *The Feminism Mystique* (New York, Norton, 1963).
34. Dorothy E. Smith, 'Women, the family and corporate capitalism' in Marylee

Stephenson, eds., *Women in Canada* (Toronto, New Press, 1973), pp. 1-35.

35. Patricia Connelly, *Last Hired, First Fired: Women and the Canadian Work Force* (Toronto, the Women's Press, 1978).

36. Louise A. Tilly and Joan W. Scott, *Women, Work and Family* (New York, Holt Rinehart and Winston, 1978).

37. Oren suggests that women were regularly undernourished because they went without food so that husbands and children should have more. Laura Oren, 'The welfare of women in laboring families: England 1860-1950', *Feminist Studies* I, 1973, pp. 107-125.

38. Gail Malmgreen, *Neither Bread Nor Roses: Utopian Feminists and the English Working Class, 1800-1850*, in 'Studies in Labour History' pamphlet, John L. Noyce, publisher, Brighton, UK, 1978, p. 23.

39. Idem.

40. Harry Braverman, *Labor and Monopoly Capital: The Degradation of Work in the Twentieth Century* (New York, Monthly Review Press, 1974).

41. Andrew L. Friedman, *Industry and Labour: Class Struggle at Work and Monopoly Capitalism* (London, Macmillan, 1977).

42. Idem, p. 105.

43. See, for example, R.C. Edwards, 'The social relations in the firm and labor market structure' in R.C. Edwards, M. Reich and D.M. Gordon, eds., *Labor Market Segmentation* (Lexington, Mass., D.C. Heath Company, 1978); and Donald H. Clairmont, Martha McDonald and Fred C. Wien, 'A segmentation approach to poverty and low-wage work in the Maritimes', Paper No. 6, Marginal Work World Program, Institute of Public Affairs, Dalhousie University, 1978.

44. Friedman, op. cit.

45. Joan Sangster, 'The 1907 Bell Telephone strike: Organizing women workers', *Labour: Journal of Canadian Labour Studies*, Vol. 3, 1978, pp. 109-130; and Philip Foner, *The Policies and Practices of the American Federation of Labor 1900-1909*, Vol. 3 of *History of the Labor Movement in the Unites States* (New York, International Publishers, 1964).

46. See Sarah Boston, *Women Workers and the Trade Union Movement* (London, Davis-Poynter, 1980) and Sheila Leuwenhale, *Women and Trade Unions: An Outline History of Women in the Trade Union Movement* (London, Ernest Benn Ltd., 1977).

47. See Anna Davin, 'Imperialism and motherhood' in *History Workshop: A Journal of Socialist Historians*, Issue 5, Spring 1978, pp. 9-65.

48. See National Council of Women in Canada, *Legal Status of Women in Canada* (Ottawa, Canada Department of Labour, 1924).

49. Elizabeth Wilson, *Women and the Welfare State* (London, Tavistock Publications, 1978).

50. Anna Davin, op. cit.

51. See Jane Humphries, 'Women: scapegoats and safety valves in the Great Depression', *Review of Radical Political Economics*, Vol. 8, No. 1, Spring 1976, pp. 98-117.

52. Mary Inman, 'In women's defense', Committee to Organize the Advancement of Women, Los Angeles, 1940, excerpted by Gerda Lerner in *The Female Experience: An American Documentary* (Indianapolis, Bobbs-Merrill, 1977).

53. For descriptions of how working-class women 'managed', see Mrs. Pember Reeves, *Round About a Pound a Week* (London, G. Bell and Sons, 1913), and Richard Hoggart, *The Uses of Literacy* (London, Chatto and Windus, 1958).

54. Clementina Black's investigations of the situation of married women in the labour force exhibits this dilemma clearly. Clementina Black, *Married Women's Work* (London, G. Bell and Sons, 1915).

55. Lillian Rubin, *Worlds of Pain: Life in the Working Class Family* (New York,

Basic Books, 1976).
56. Inman, op. cit.
57. Paul Willis, 'Shop floor culture, masculinity and the wage form' in John Clarke, Charlas Critcher and Richard Johnson, eds., *Working Class Culture: Studies in History and Theory* (London, Hutchinson, 1979), pp. 185-98.
58. Dorothy Thompson, 'Women and nineteenth century radical politics: a lost dimension' in Juliet Mitchell and Ann Oakley, eds., *The Rights and Wrongs of Women* (Harmondsworth, Middx., Penguin Books, 1976), pp. 112-38.

MASCULINE DOMINANCE AND THE STATE

Varda Burstyn

The speech from which this article has been developed was given at a session of the Winnipeg Marx Centenary Conference[1] entitled 'Women and the Economic and Political Crisis'. That a crisis exists in the world economic and political order there can be no doubt. There can also be little doubt that there is a crisis in the organised Marxist movement— defined in general terms as composed of the far Left groups, the Communist and parts of the Social Democratic Parties, and important parts of the socialist networks which exist in mass movements and institutions. The causes of Marxism's crisis are both historical and contemporary. Historically speaking, Marxism is only now beginning any large-scale recovery from its Stalinist deep-freeze as far as its own capacity to generate the kinds of answers demanded by the questions posed by the class struggle today is concerned. In the meantime, its liberatory potential has been tarnished in the eyes of millions of people, and insofar as it continues its association with the bureaucratic regimes of the transitional societies, that potential will continue to be dulled. There are a number of contemporary problems which also present major obstacles to Marxism's overall capacity to provide revolutionary solutions. The one I want to single out in this discussion is the crisis between the genders that has hit and rocked the Marxist movement, from the smallest local study group to the largest workers' party, during the preceding decade and continuing into the eighties. These two crises are distinct problems, but they overlap in important ways historically, and need to be addressed together in the period to come. One of the most crucial areas of both anti-Stalinist and feminist concerns is the enormous set of issues regarding the nature and role of the state. In this article I want to tackle the general problem feminists have described when they talk about Marxist categories obscuring relations of masculine dominance by a specific discussion of the state, and the ways in which it acts as an organiser and enforcer of male supremacy. Socialist feminists have been developing a body of scholarship and theory over the last ten to fifteen years that has until now barely been engaged by most Marxist men. It is in the spirit of the positive gains that can flow from such an engagement that this article is offered.

INTRODUCTION

In the long-standing debate between Marxism as a whole (if one may still speak of Marxism in such unified terms) and the political science of the liberal democratic tradition, Marxism has from the beginning insisted that whatever the state may be, it is not a neutral arbiter, which mediates disinterestedly between different social groups, changing its laws and institutions according to a historically shifting consensus of the 'whole society'. Marxism has claimed that the state is both a reflection of actual social relations and the central set of institutions which maintain and perpetuate the privileges of the ruling classes—with their different fractions, sectors and parties—in all complex, hierarchical societies. For Marxists the state is a class state by definition, even though it may grant concessions to the dominated classes through a number of its institutions or functions. Such concessions are usually understood to be either necessary in some form to the growth and stability of the mode of production, or means by which the state can appease the oppressed, thereby reinforcing its hegemony through an appearance of justice and flexibility, or both. Thus for Marxists, the state in capitalist society is a capitalist state. It acts to administer, enforce and mystify the interests and needs of the capitalist system and the capitalist class as a whole. Its class character is expressed both in its policies and in its forms of power, as these are inserted into the economic, sexual, cultural and political life of the whole society.

Clearly, the term 'state', like the term 'mode of production' or 'class' for that matter, is a generalisation and abstraction. It sums up and schematises a system of relations, structures, institutions and forces which, in industrialised society, are vast, complex, differentiated, and as an inevitable result, contradictory at times as well. For example, one part of the state, in its capacity as legitimator of the overall system of privilege, may agree to fund a Marxist conference by way of showing its openness and neutrality. Another part of the state, say a part of the coercive apparatus, may then tap the telephones of its organisers. Or, to choose an example with somewhat more importance, one part of the state may attempt on a local level to set up childcare facilities, rape crisis centres, community enterprises, and local decision-making bodies which involve non-elected representatives, while another level of the state, inevitably a 'higher', more centralised level, will cut off the funds for these projects, or declare them illegal, or otherwise swamp, contain or dismantle them. Because of the hierarchy of power in the state, moving from less at the local to more at the central levels, less in the department of legitimiation to more in the departments of economic facilitation and coercion, Marxists have stood their ground regarding the major functions of class domination played by the state in capitalist society. They have argued that for all its complexity, differentiation and even contradiction, the state works to facilitate the appropriation and centralisation of wealth (which in capital-ist society primarily takes the form of surplus value produced by the working class); to protect this appropriation through the means of coer-cion, both domestically and internationally; and to legitimate these two functions in the interests of social stability, which in turn creates optimal conditions for surplus extraction. Not surprisingly, then, for Marxists the state is an exceptionally important site of power in capitalist society. As the major set of executive and coercive instruments supporting the owning classes, though by no means the only site of the ruling apparatus,[2] it has been targeted by Marxists as the most important strategic focus alongside of the collectivisation of the means of production in the larger socialist project, and rightly so.

The state is also crucial for Marxists because it is indispensable, in a transformed way, to the employment of resources and the organisation of large-scale public effort in the construction of a new society. Without public coordination of economic and social reorganisation at all levels—local, regional, national and international—new societies cannot be built. The state is not only an issue for Marxists because of its importance to the class enemy, but also because of the role that it must play in our own project of human liberation.[3] Although Marx's vision projected the 'withering away' of the state as a necessary condition to the end of social domination, in the transitional societies,[4] history has played an ironic and painful trick: we have seen the opposite development. In the absence of a free market and, in most cases, even the limited forms of bourgeois democracy, the state has become an even more ubiquitous and powerful source of economic, social and political regulation than in the capitalist countries. As a result, not only does the bureaucratic elite have privileges of power and material wealth which place them in the same league as their capitalist counterparts, but their very existence makes a mockery of any notions of workers' democracy based on these models. Indeed, the most powerful weapon capitalist ideology can wield against socialism today is the example of the political monoliths in the transitional societies. These developments present an enormous strategic headache to Marxism as well, both in terms of formulating the correct attitudes to these societies, and in terms of developing an understanding of state building and transformation which will fulfil Marx's promise that communist democracy will qualitatively surpass the kind produced by capitalism.

Within the revolutionary socialist movement there have always been large minority currents—utopian socialists, anarchists and many kinds of Trotskyists—who have stressed that the construction of socialism requires the creation of forms of public authority which can challenge and break those of capitalist society and the bureaucratic transitional regimes. Occupying first place among these forms and principles are vehicles such as workers' and popular councils (soviets), and socialist pluralism in terms of political parties and socialist governments.[5] These kinds of vehicles have been thrown up and the democratic impulse expressed in the course of political struggle over and over again, and their use has enabled the people to find forms of unity which have mobilised the creative and strengthening possibilities of *difference* within the ranks of progressive movements. Their existence challenges political monolithism as a theory and as a coerced practice. Crises in various Communist Parties and Marxist-Leninist groups over Poland, Afghanistan and other issues of nuclear disarmament and other questions of struggle indicate that more and more Marxists are beginning to open up to the issues and criticisms raised by these currents.

However, an outstanding problem remains. For the very categories that Marxism has developed—notions of the working class, the economy and the state for example—while illuminating one crucial set of economic class relations have also obscured, much as the use of the word 'Man' to describe humanity has obscured the specific reality of women, another set of class relations—gender-class. In what follows I want to explain my use of this term and to discuss the ways in which its major features are expressed at the level of the state. I will do this by looking briefly at some aspects of pre-capitalist sexual divisions of labour, and then take a more detailed look at the state in capitalist times, drawing on material from Britain, Canada and the US to illustrate the main points. Following that, I will explore in schematic terms some related aspects of state formation in industrialised transitional societies. I will conclude by drawing out some practical implications of this analysis and suggesting areas for further discussion.

Problems of terminology

In order to analyse and to act on the totality of a social system which is itself comprised of many interrelating sub-systems, we need conceptual tools and language which can enable us to see, describe and question aspects of our reality which have been rendered invisible by the dominant ideology. Indeed, the very notion of the dominant ideology, along with such concepts as the labour theory of value, the exploitative relation embedded in the wage, and alienation, for example, are concepts which had first to be articulated in language by Marx before much larger numbers of people could see many of the ways in which they were being stripped of the fruits of their labour by those whose sole relation to them was one of exploitation, and to understand the necessity of expropriating the capitalist class as a rock-bottom precondition to the ending of that relation. Within Marxist discourse today one need only say 'class' or for that matter 'state' to convey in shorthand form a complex, sophisticated set of meanings about *appropriation, inequality, conflict* and *domination.*

I hope that it is within this commitment to demystification and revolutionary clarification that we can grapple with the problems of concepts and terminology in our search for ways to express and communicate the political implications of hierarchical divisions between the sexes. The problem with present terminology is this: if terms like state and class denote inequality, conflict and organised domination with respect to the relations of economic stratification, terms like sex or gender carry no such denotative or even connotative meanings in relation to men-as-a-group and women-as-a-group. Sex brings to mind either the biological and physiological characteristics of organs and hormones which distinguish male and female, or the acts through which humans propagate their species and/or seek pleasure from zones of the body. There is nothing logically or necessarily hierarchical and political in this term, nor is there anything desirable in attaching such meanings to it. The word gender, on its own, is little better. Although it has been used in the discourse of the social sciences to distinguish social and learned behaviour from the biological substrata to which such behaviour is culturally assigned, it carries with it connotations of sex 'role' and 'appropriate division of attributes' which also do not contain any necessary sense of domination. Within liberal and Marxist discourses it may carry a sense of inequality in the interpersonal interaction of women and men, or in the impersonal machinations of capitalism's need for cheap labour. But so far no terminology yet contains and communicates the extent of the relation of appropriation and domination between the two genders. Given the existence of some foraging societies with separate but equal gender spheres, I am not persuaded that we should draft the term gender into position as the sole bearer of these meanings. Will there be no gender, in a non-sexist society? The jury is still out on this one.

The term 'patriarchy' is also problematic, because of the way in which Marxists and Marxist-feminists have attacked its general use, insisting that it means a specific form of masculine power and privilege and not a 'transhistorical' arrangement. The specific form is seen most particularly as the patrician organisation of kin and slaves with the oldest owning male, the patriarch, at the head of the entire productive and reproductive unit; most generally the term can be used to characterise the rule of the ruling-class father in other agrarian—notably feudal—modes of production. My own feeling about this attack is that in some instances it has been carried out with positive intentions and results, refining our understanding of the ways in which masculine privilege and power have changed through different modes of production and, as a result, underlining the capacity of gender relations to change in more positive terms in the future.[6] At other times, the attack has served a less positive role and has in part cloaked an attempt to discredit the analysis of those features of masculine power and privilege which have remained continuous over time in many post-foraging and all known agrarian and industrial societies—in other words, to attack the validity of a notion of a system of gender hierarchy which has crossed modes of production. This is the sense in which the term partiarchy is used in much feminist discourse, and as such, I have no major objection to it. But the important thing is not to lose ourselves in false debates, and the objections to the use of the term have had sufficient impact that, at least in theoretical work which bridges the discourses, it is probably useful to use another one to signify a system of gender hierarchy which is no more and no less 'transhistorical' than class society itself, conceptually speaking, and which is quite clearly older than class society in chronological or developmental terms (as I shall soon explain). That is to say that it has appeared in a number of different guises at different times, but retains certain essential features which enable us to identify it as such throughout.

The term I prefer at this time for this cross-mode-of-production system is *masculine dominance*. The term certainly lacks elegance but it allows us to name both the relation (dominance) and the agent (the gender men). For the two opposing groups, I suggest the best we can do at this time is to call them *gender-classes*, because only the use of the term class can adequately add the dimension of appropriation and domination in such a way as to include automatically and by definition a full sense of the politics of masculine dominance. The adoption of this term requires that we specify 'economic-class' to characterise what Marxists have until recently called simply 'class'. I am aware of the very real problem in the relation between these concepts and realise that they opt to emphasise two distinct forms of social hierarchy rather than reach for one term which will collapse these two systems into one. But at this stage I think it is important to retain a vocabulary which allows us to express the distinct effectivity—to borrow Annette Kuhn's phrase—of these systems, in order to understand how the two do work together to create whole systems of domination. This choice does not preclude the possibility that an adequate term for the whole system of domination may be developed, when we better understand its structures and dynamics, and it certainly does not mean that work being done by socialist-feminist historians today using an emerging method which looks at the ways in which gender arrangements organise and reproduce classes and to a certain extent, vice versa, is not on the right track.[7] I think this work is very important and points us in the right direction methodologically. Nevertheless, because of what I perceive to be a relative autonomy in the forms of economic-class and gender-class, I think we need to retain the theoretical distinctions which these two terms afford us, while continuing to strive for a more totalistic appreciation of their interaction.

Regarding the politics of masculine dominance and gender-class as they are expressed in the state, the first step is to explain how and why women do constitute a class in terms which Marxists can employ. If one accepts the notion that the politics of class society are expressions of its economic contradictions, then the first crucial issue from the Marxist point of view is that of the economics of gender. The literature on this question is by now very extensive.[8] It covers historical periods ranging from foraging to advanced industrial societies, and everything else 'in between'. As all of the best Marxist historiography has been reminding us recently, the changes in people's ways of life under different modes of production, during different periods within modes and production, and in different regional or national social formations should be emphasised rather than minimised if we are to develop a refined understanding of the way in which people create and recreate their life, and their resistance to its most oppressive features. Nevertheless, such reminders have not served to invalidate abstract concepts and social realities such as 'the labouring classes' or 'the ruling classes', and we must be able to generalise at the same level of abstraction when looking at genderic relations.[9] The criterion which defines the relation of subordinate to ruling classes in orthodox Marxist terms is the relation of appropriation of surplus labour. The labouring classes produce more than is strictly necessary for their subsistence according to a historically determined standard of living; the ruling classes appropriate that surplus and use it to aggrandise their own wealth and power. Does such a generalisation apply to relations between men and women across modes of production in such a way as to justify the use of the term gender-class? As I will now explain, I think it does.

Pre-capitalist roots
In the briefest possible of historical terms, anthropological and historical research suggests that in many foraging societies, especially prior to their contact with post-foraging populations, a sexual division of labour obtained between men and women which was not (and among the Mbuti, for example, still is not) characterised by the same forms of women's oppression that we find in many horticultural and post-horticultural societies. Engels, in *The Origin of the Family, Private Property and the State*,[10] working brilliantly with far less data than we have today, suggested that this discrepancy was explained by the way in which women's labour lost status as herds of domesticated animals, owned by men, created a surplus 'in which women enjoyed' but which they did not produce. In other words, Engels believed that it was women's lack of contribution to the sources of surplus which was in the final analysis responsible for their oppression. Since for Engels the creation and ownership of that surplus was identical with the process through which the differentiation of economic classes took place (in Engels's term, 'social' classes), women's oppression was a direct by-product of (economic) class stratification, and could only be resolved when such stratification had disappeared. For him and most Marxists following him, the most important steps to over-

coming women's oppression, in addition to general socialist activity, would consequently be subsumed under women's 'integration' into 'production', and the 'socialisation' of women's work. The actual sexual division of labour was not to blame in any way for women's oppression, and was thus not, for Engels or Marx, a target of specific concern as a site of political power or lack of it. From pastoral societies on, so to speak, it was entirely determined by the economic-class division of labour, of which its oppressive features were by-products. For Engels the sexual division of labour was 'natural' and 'primitive', that is to say unproblematic, as compared to economic-class divisions of labour, which were 'great social divisions of labour', distinctions between the haves and have-nots, the exploiters and exploited, the dominators and the oppressed.[11]

Today, Engels's sanguine view of the fate of the sexual division of labour has been challenged and, to my mind, decisively defeated. Although many, myself included, agree that there have been societies with a sexual division of labour in which women are not oppressed, the consensus around the role of the sexual division of labour in economically stratifying societies has broken down, and different interpretations have been advanced to explain its vicissitudes. The one which I support, and about which I have written elsewhere,[12] is fundamentally different from that of Engels. I see the sexual division of labour very much as a 'great social' division of labour, likely the first such division of labour, and one which pre-, sub- and co-structures the division of labour of economic-classes.

In my opinion, the most useful starting place for tracing the sexual division of labour from its status of 'rough and ready equality' to an oppressive division between gender-classes lies in horticultural societies. Although one can see certain latent forms of masculine dominance in a number of foraging societies relatively unaffected by post-foraging populations[13] (e.g. exclusion of women by men from the most sacred and decisive rituals of the band, greater prestige to men and to hunting than to women and to gathering, even when women produce the *greater* proportion of food and other means of subsistence), it seems to me that only with the development of certain kinds of horticultural societies are the relations of gender-class fully fleshed out. The development of horticulture—small-scale cultivation—is credited by the majority of anthropologists to women, who are thought to have begun cultivation as an extension of their involvement with plants as the major consistent source of food. Women are indeed the central productive workers in horticultural societies, and thus the major producers of most of the surplus accumulated. Under conditions of advanced horticulture, that surplus is very considerable, and it allows for a very advanced form of cultural and political life. But how that surplus is utilised and appropriated is not the same in all horticultural societies.[14] From the point of view of this discussion, the decisive difference regards whether that utilisation works through communitarian distribution of the surplus by those who produce it (as in Engels's favourite group, the admirable Iroquois, where women controlled the production and distribution of most of the means of subsistence) or whether it is appropriated and distributed through increasingly private means. If it is appropriated in this latter fashion, it will usually display the key element of gender-class: women's productive and reproductive labour will be amassed and distributed within family units of usually three generations in which men have the power to appropriate, control and therefore benefit from that labour internally to the family. The surplus thus accumulated will establish degrees of man-to-man ranking, and as a result, the position of men and women in the larger group will be determined by the relative status of their family in a constellation of families, as well as by their gender. Wives are the most important source of labour for surplus accumulation in such arrangements, and warfare for the capture of women is common once these conditions generalise. It is out of this latter arrangement that fully developed (economic) class society emerges. The former path has come to a series of dead ends in bloody confrontations which are scattered through history: societies exemplary of it have been overcome by the insurmountable might of populations in which the unequal sexual division of labour and commitment to surplus accumulation provided the fighting edge needed to overcome the generally more pacific and egalitarian groups.

There are several key features of this sexual division of labour which should be established here. First of all, the nature of women's labour must be clarified if we are to understand the nature of its appropriation, because it has always been different than men's. Women's labour has always had a twofold character and has consequently been embodied (congealed) in two different kinds of entities. The first aspect of women's labour is what has been called productive. Like men's productive labour it is congealed in *things* which make life livable: food, clothing, shelter and the like. Men's control over women's labour in cultivation, with domesticated animals, in craft production, has all been part of generic appropriation in pre-capitalist societies, including in the transition from feudalism to capitalism. The second aspect of women's labour is what has been called 'reproductive' and it is embodied in *people*. From the economic point of view the use-value of people is realised in their labour power; from the cultural point of view, of course, in many other things. In any case, first and most importantly these people are children. Men's control of children formalised in family authority patterns and masculine inheritance systems in pre-industrial (overlapping into industrial) societies is an essential form of masculine appropriation and control of women's labour. This is not to deny the important role which men played in the post-childhood preparation of their male children for their gender and economic-class determined means of livelihood in such societies, but it is to stress the fact that early childhood care and the ongoing labour for family members in terms of daily sustenance were different and more time-consuming for women than for men in most post-foraging societies, and in all agricultural and industrial societies. The other people in which women's labour is embodied are men-as-a-group, who both as children and as adults benefit from the private service of women who take care of their bodily needs through the performance of domestic labour organised through the normative, legal and physically enforced relations of subservience. Finally, women's labour is embodied in the lives of the old and the sick, economically non-productive members of society who are enabled to survive because of women's care. Women's labour is thus different from and more extensive than men's, and men-as-a-group, in and across different classes, have appropriated that labour to themselves, even if the extent of the labour has differed for women of different economic-classes. Men are the leisured gender-class across economic-class lines, and across modes of production, as we shall see a little farther on.[15]

Second, the central mechanism for masculine control and appropriation of women's labour has been in the first place control over women's sexuality. As the Iroquoian example demonstrates, it is difficult to control women's labour when women control their own affective, sexual and economic unions, and their own children. To bring these essential things under masculine control, men had to find ways to regulate women's (hetero-)sexual activities and procreative issue. Engels understood the origins of what he called 'monogamy for women only' in this imperative, but he did not understand the connection between that and compulsory heterosexuality as the major psycho-sexual organising principle of gender-class society, with its attendant subordination of women's right to erotic pleasure as well as masculine control of children and property.[16] Given the connection between sexuality and feeling, the element of control over the actual body of the labouring class in generic terms is thus much greater than that element between members of ruling and labouring classes in economic terms, with the exception of some kinds of slavery. Thus while gender-class is a social construction because there is nothing biologically given about the division of labour between the sexes which it expresses, one of its central and most contested terrains is in fact the physical body of woman herself. What is at stake is how she will use that body in the service of her male kin, both in terms of her productive and reproductive labour, and will not use that body in the service of her own or her daughter's independent interests, need and desires. This terrain is divided and cordoned off according to rank and privilege between men, both *de facto* and *de jure*. *De facto* control is exercised through rape and coercion (what happens in the conjugal bed, what armies always bring in their wake, what happens to unaffiliated or disowned women); *de jure* control through taboos, laws and eventually ecclesiastical and secular courts. Although in their capacity as dependent wives and mothers, women have passed on the norms of sexual chattelhood to their children, they have also as sexual and social beings resisted this status and rebelled in a myriad of different ways, from the women's 'crime' of adultery, to the more conscious choice of outlaw status by women who were once labelled witches[17] because they rejected the validity of men's claims on women through their lives and their medicinal work, to the mass epidemics of 'frigidity' which so preoccupied the late Victorians, the early psychoanalysts and sexologists. Generic relations have been characterised by strife and conflict between the genders with outbreaks of resistance on the part of women, individually and collectively, directly and indirectly, throughout history.

This point brings us to the third feature of the sexual division of labour—and that is of course what *men* do within it that is so different from, exclusive of, and 'better than' what women do. Statistics presented at the 1975 United Nations Conference on women in Copenhagen set the stage for this aspect. They remind us that women form fifty-two per cent of the world's population, perform two-thirds of the world's labour, receive one-tenth of the world's wages, and own less than one-hundreth of its property.[18] Crossing modes of production, and so in a sense historical periods, these statistics throw into high relief important continuities in women's condition. What is as important to compute, however, is what is missing from the statistics: women form less than five per cent of the world's top governmental cadres and, if one calculates informally from a number of different sources,[19] something like the same proportion, or perhaps even less, in terms of their presence in the upper echelons of the church hierarchies and the positions of authority within the military. Men are present in the sexual division of labour where women are absent, and those places are not the loci of productive labour, either in terms of petty commodity production, or full-blown capitalist production, or industrial production in the transitional societies. These places are at the top of the economic, religious, political and military systems of power in human society, and women's exclusion from these stratified and stratospheric realms is just as fundamental, historically-rooted and defining a characteristic as their relegation to primary responsibility for childhood caretaking and bodily sustenance of men and non-productive adults.

Men's freedom from the necessity to care for their own bodies and those of children, the sick and the elderly, through men's appropriation of women's productive labour and men's access to women's bodies and control of their issue—that is, men's appropriation of women's reproductive labour—indicates that we are talking about class relations between men and women. But a fully-fledged class relationship has a politics of domination, not simply a set of economic relations, and it is this politics of domination that can be illustrated by going back to the formation of the exclusive men's groups and networks in aboriginal societies and seeing how they evolved, through the stratification and complexification of society, into the institutions and networks of what Marxists have until now called simply class power, but which such an examination will reveal to be not only economic- but also gender-class power,[20] culminating in the virtually exclusive masculine monopoly of the major positions of power in the world today. Masculine dominance has been a central organising principle of economic class society, not by virtue of some historical accident which, as in Engels's view, gave to men the source of social surplus, but through men's conscious and systematic relegation of women into an increasingly domestic space and set of functions called in our time 'the private'; and exclusion from the social space and set of functions in which men have taken charge of the life of increasingly larger numbers of people, called in our time 'the public'.[21]

In our own time, industrial society has greatly increased the numbers, kinds and relations of the ruling structures. Women are conspicuous by their miniscule or non-existent presence in the church hierarchies, the boardrooms of multinational corporations, the upper echelons of government bureaucracy, and professional associations and schools, the military, especially combat forces, and also, alas, from the top trade-union leaderships in many countries. The state itself is condensed, to use Zillah Eisenstein's term, out of these structures—the networks and systems of power. I want to move on now to look at how the politics of masculine domination have been and are expressed in industrial states. I regret that space does not allow for a lengthier treatment of pre-capitalist societies, and I am aware that I have tied together enormous spans of time and changes in modes of production, speaking in terms of economic-class. But the characteristics of the sexual division of labour which I have described are important in their fundamental outlines to this day, and the mode of masculine appropriation of women's labour from the family system of advanced horticulture to that of late feudal—early capitalist times does possess a central element of continuity, which is its organisation through the power, privilege and authority of the ruling-class father, replicated in miniature within the households of the labouring classes. While from the standpoint of economic-class there are several distinct modes of production involved, from the standpoint of gender-class I think it correct to term all these arrangements together as patriarchy, a particular form and organisation of masculine dominance. That form began very slowly to change with the emergence of capitalism and the full-scale development of industry, but masculine dominance itself has not disappeared. On the contrary, it has continued to reassert itself both by attempting to reassert the control of the father during the nineteenth and early twentieth centuries, and by producing new forms since then. I want to close this section by saying that I hope I have made my preference for the term 'gender-class' over 'gender' clear at this point, and indicated its essential features. However, I am not attached to the term as such, and if another capable of better communicating the relations of appropriation, conflict and domination between men-as-a-group and women-as-a-group can be proposed, I would certainly welcome it.

MASCULINE DOMINANCE AND CAPITALISM IN THE STATE

In comparison with all previous modes of production, capitalism develops with dizzying speed, rushing in only a few hundred years through several distinct stages of development, and accelerating all the while. Each stage has had its own heavy impact on kinship and gender relations, the relative stability of which acted as a profound element of stability and continuity in and between different epochs in pre-capitalist times. For the proletarian-isation of the peasantry and the primitive accumulation of capital, a period of a hundred and fifty or two hundred years; from early industrial-isation to mature capitalism/imperialism, barely a century; from imperial-ism to the beginnings of anti-imperialist struggle with a socialist dynamic, less than half a century; from mature capitalism to late capitalism, again less than fifty years, and if one sees several distinct sub-periods within this larger one, the pace really quickens. Because capitalism is such a dynamic force of surplus extraction, it wreaks havoc with the ways in which people can arrange their lives in order to reproduce themselves on a daily and generational basis.[22] Each new stage creates pressures and demands for particular kinds of labour, different in important respects from the labour of the preceding period, and often required in locations different from earlier places of work and residence. In pre-capitalist societies, men and women within household systems essentially raise their children to replace them in the economic and generic divisions of labour. Not so for the generations who have lived at the starting or ending edges of the major stages of capitalist development. All the more reason why it is important to understand the role of the state during these times, to see whether it has been consistently generic as well as distinctly capitalist. While the amount of material is not lavish, enough has been generated to demon-strate adequately that as each stage of capitalism has developed and been negotiated, the state has taken on the crucial role of mediation and regula-tion to advance capitalism's needs for a given form of labour power and surplus extraction in such a way as to retain masculine privilege and control—masculine dominance—in society as a whole. I will restrict myself to a few examples chosen to indicate major aspects of this behaviour through several developmental stages.

Women's oppression is expressed both in ongoing, living patterns expressing deeply seated norms and genderic behaviour—in etiquette, feeling and ritual—and in formalised laws, encoded and enforced by institutions of social domination. In the transitional period between feudalism and capitalism formalised laws affecting women were encoded and enforced by both the church and the state. The church was in charge for the most part of reproductive aspects of gender-class relations: its rules pertained to the issues of marriage, divorce and sexual practice (adultery, sodomy and the like) and, as part and parcel of this function, the church was involved in maintaining explicit genderic authority. The regulation of property relations, on the other hand, usually devolved onto secular laws and courts. In the societies out of which capitalism developed, women were frequently denied the right to hold property in their own name, and to exercise the civic duties and rights that followed with such ownership for men. Women were, as a rule, legally infantilised, and able to exercise power in society only through whatever paths were open to them in terms of their masculine affiliations.[23] In families of the land-owning classes and, for a considerable time in the transitional period, in the families of the urban middle-classes, that power could be considerable within the limited but important sphere of the manorial and/or domestic economy, insofar as women acted as managers of these enterprises in the upper classes and as manager-workers within the domestic economies of the bourgeoisie. In farm and peasant households, the necessity of women's labour is thought by many to have created within the domestic and perhaps village sphere certain norms of respect because of its indispensability. But women were proscribed from a host of religious, sexual and political rights which were reserved for men only.

As far as the state development is concerned, as capitalism consolidates in the nineteenth century genderic regulations lag well behind changes in actual life conditions. They do not seem to become visible until well into the nineteenth century in Britain, and if we can take the British case as a general model for key trends (allowing for variations according to uneven and combined developments in other national formations), we can discern at least the main lines of changing modalities of masculine dominance. According to Rachel Harrison and Frank Mort,[24] there were two sets of changes in women's legal status as measured through changes in legislation, one having to do primarily with issues of women's rights to property and money, the other with women's right to divorce and greater sexual autonomy. The first set of issues received a lot of attention from the state during the latter half of the nineteenth century, under the impact of agitation on the part of middle-class women. That attention can be seen to consist in a set of extremely interesting state accommodations, each one attempting to juggle the demands of capitalist property relations (which require a much greater mobility of capital in comparison with landed property which requires stability and continuity of property) and the evident need to maintain masculine control of those property relations with the need to make some concessions to the demands of bourgeois women who wanted to have full control of property in their own right. The concessions that were made in the nineteenth century in Britain had a clear masculinist character: they were made very slowly and only in degrees that allowed for inheritance from father to daughter while simultaneously favouring the appropriation of the daughter's property and capital by her husband. Women's right to hold and dispose of their own property was won very late (it is still being contested in many ways in the courts of capitalist countries to this day) and in the nineteenth century the legal victories were often no more than formalities since fathers and husbands continued to make their own arrangements, superceding the formal and rather shaky rights of the daughter/wife. Harrison and Mort argue most convincingly that these grudging changes are undertaken by the state only because they fit in with changes in inheritance and control of property necessary for the growth of capitalism. What is not addressed in their article is why the state, now a fully-fledged capitalist state, should not have wrought rather larger and more generous changes if, in Michéle Barrett's terms, gender oppression is not a 'logically pregiven element of the [capitalist] class structure'.[25]

The notion of a distinct generic commitment as such on the part of the state would account for the conundrum. Such a commitment is even more strikingly revealed by state actions on the marriage and sexuality fronts. Again, drawing on the British example, changes in sexual and marriage law were not at all substantive or progressive during most of the nineteenth century. They consisted primarily in the transference of previously ecclesiastical jurisdiction virtually whole hog into secular jurisdiction in mid-century. In this way the capitalist state took on a set of generic laws which can quite correctly be characterised as patriarchal, with respect to norms of marriage, procreation, and to ('deviant') sexualities. Major change on these issues has only begun in the latter half of the twentieth century, and even these are precarious. Again, while there is much to be said about these changes—or lack of them—what is essential from our point of view is that where capitalism did not require change in terms of the exigencies of its immediate economic development, the state retained and attempted to retrench masculinist and patriarchal privilege, in specific opposition by mid-century in the US and Britain to a developed and articulated feminist campaign for changes in this sphere.

Nevertheless, accommodation and refusal to change in property and sexual law respectively neither stopped important changes in the actual life conditions of the genders, nor contained women's opposition to their subservient status and oppression. By the last quarter of the nineteenth century in Britain, the United States and Canada, the state was confronted with a series of contradictions that were exploding as a result of the

effects of almost a century of industrialisation and urban proletarianisation. Although the numbers and concentration of women workers in
large-scale factories differ according to regions as well as countries, and the
pattern of women's employment in such industries is still a matter of
some contention, there seems to be general agreement that the intense
exploitation of women and children as well as working-class men had
by that time undermined the capacity of the working class to reproduce
itself adequately on both a daily and a generational basis.[26] Such a situation was acceptable neither to the working class as a whole nor to significant sectors of the capitalist class. *Chez les bourgeois,* in stark contrast to
the sweated conditions of working-class women, the ladies of the affluent
classes had reached the nadir of infantilisation, pressured by their
husbands and families to do nothing more than 'adorn' the domestic
retreat from the hostile public world of capitalist business and politics,
and turn a blind eye to the conditions of their working-class sisters—
labourers, domestics and prostitutes—all working for their husbands and
fathers.[27] Such a situation was quite acceptable to bourgeois men, but
not to many of the women, and it spawned the middle-class revolt which
was eventually to give birth to the term feminism.

From the last quarter of the nineteenth century to the first quarter of
the twentieth, the masculinist nature of the state was clearly visible in two
extended operations of generic mediation. The first, primarily at the level
of the economy, was the role the state played in enabling the institution
of what has come to be called *the family wage system* as an ideological
standard for the whole working class, and a reality for only its most
privileged layers.[28] As others have written at much greater depth, this
system validated and attempted to generalise as normative within the
working class a situation in which the husband/father of a nuclear family,
emulating his upper-class counterpart, earned a wage large enough to
maintain children and a wife who did not labour outside the home. While
we know that many working-class women eventually welcomed this
system, as many today still hearken back to it because of the terrible
conditions under which women worked and work, we also know that
many women resisted this system up to and including fighting pitched
battles with men outside of factories and other workplaces to maintain
their right to work for a wage, and an unequal one at that. The family
wage system was not simply a clever economic-class manoeuvre to maximise worker productivity, although its normalisation did better correspond to capitalist needs for a more stable and healthy workforce, a
continuing source of cheap (female) labour and larger, healthier standing
and conscriptive armies.[29] It was rather an arrangement elaborated,
constructed and enforced by a cross-class masculine coalition—an operation of gender-class as well as economic-class—in which the state played a
pivotal and decisive role. The state enacted a series of laws which excluded

women from most trades and professions (or supported such exclusions), which institutionalised unequal pay for work of comparable worth and effectively ghettoised working women of which a majority remained in a very limited number of low paying job ghettos. The state further structured social policy in such a way as to economically and socially coerce women into marriage, through welfare-state policies structured on the assumption of masculine labour and authority within the family, and social punishment for the transgression of sexual norms deriving from this arrangement. That the family wage system in fact hindered the development of revolutionary consciousness and struggle by economically atomising working-class people into isolated family units responsible for reproduction, and ideologically accentuating and reinforcing the working-class man's identification with the men of the bourgeois class, did not seem to trouble many of the 'class conscious' (read economic-class conscious) workers who fought for that system. From the working class in gender chaos documented by Engels in the nineteenth century to the 'breadwinner power' of the workingman in the first half of the twentieth, capitalism, with the essential mediation of the state, landed on masculinist feet.

In the necessary attention we devote to matters of economics during this period, we must not, however, forget what the state was doing in the most direct of political terms from approximately 1850 to 1920 in the United States, and from 1880 to 1920 in Britain: it was resisting the demand for women's suffrage with all its might.[30] The breadth and militancy of the more than fifty-year battle for women's suffrage is well known, and need not be repeated here. What does need elucidation is the reason behind the generally masculine, specifically state resistance to these campaigns, if indeed women's oppression is not required logically by capitalism. Over and over again the position that women's right to vote would undermine women's appropriate role and work in society was articulated, indicating that even where economic-class considerations were very remote, masculinism retained its imperatives, its rules and its laws. The sexual division of labour under masculine dominance requires women's exclusion from political power, and the right to vote is the most basic and elementary component of that right in liberal-democratic societies. It is also, in and of itself, a very, very limited form of political power, as the bourgeoisie and men in general learned when the mass workers parties and large chunks of the women's suffrage movement capitulated to the imperialist war drive in 1914. It was no accident that women's suffrage was granted in the period directly after the one in which the limitations of electoral power within a capitalist society with an enfranchised workingmen's population were becoming so terribly clear.

From the point of view of generic relations, the history train really moved into high gear following the Second World War. The family wage system, while it applied consistently only to the privileged layers of the working class (and at that, differently than among the petty bourgeoisie and capitalist class) was nevertheless stabilised ideologically and material-ly prior to and following the First World War. Many women who had been mobilised for non-traditional occupations during that war were summarily returned to marriage and the family,[31] and the norms of the family wage—if hardly its consistent reality—were reinforced between wars. During the Second World War, the mobilisation of women into heavy industry and other non-traditional occupations was even more substantial than in the previous war—a mobilisation engineered, of course, by the state—and women's consequent demobilisation in the name of men's rights to well-paid jobs rankled much more deeply as a result.[32] The demobilisation and its aftermath had the usual twofold character: it excluded women from well-paid, traditionally masculine proletarian jobs and it relegated them to low-paid, increasingly 'feminine' and extremely limited job ghettos. But these measures, engineered by the state in the name of preserving mascu-line dignity (read privilege) have not succeeded in re-establishing the previous 'breadwinner power'[33] form of masculine dominance, for with the economic developments of the fifties, sixties, seventies and eighties, the full *contradictions* between capitalism and masculinism have really begun to explode.

The explosion has a number of different fuses, each of which has been lit by developments in the last forty years. First, as has been endlessly documented, the post-war capitalist economy with its expansion of service sectors and clerical work to facilitate the workings of finance capital has created the need for many new workers, and has drawn women out of the home to fill these jobs. Thus women have taken their place in new sectors alongside of their traditional place in labour-intensive, low-paid jobs—for example, in the garment and cleaning industries. As has also been endlessly documented, whatever carrot was constituted by these opportunities was more than compensated for by the stick of in-flation which reduced the power of the family wage and increasingly compelled working-class and even petty-bourgeois families to rely on two wages to maintain, and today to chase after, a previous standard of living obtainable on the basis of the earnings of the single male breadwinner. Because of the pharmaceutical companies' search for profits, because of capitalism's need for a smaller labour force, and because of women's increasing unwillingness to drown in domestic labour, contraception became used on a mass scale, so that the life of the adult woman was no longer taken up exclusively with child-bearing, lactating and all the rest of it. These three developments alone were enough to blow the old generic arrangements sky-high, but of course there is more. Not only have women had to take on work outside the home which is by and large more menial and boring, less remunerative (by 40 per cent) and socially prestigious than, but equally as exhausting as, men's, but they have not been relieved of any domestic labour in a qualitative way by men. In fact, through the sixties and seventies, we can see an aggravation of women's condition in her double day of labour within marriage on the one hand, and in the increasing tendency of family units to dissolve, leaving women without even the nominal aid of a husband and father, and more often than not (something like two-thirds of men default on their support payments in Canada and the US)[34] without even financial aid for the children. These trends have been accompanied by a masculinist ideological onslaught which has two rather different prongs, each one lethal, but in different ways: on the one hand, the movements of orthodox patriarchal retrenchment call for a return to the father-headed family and the 'non-working' mother, the banning of abortion rights, pre-marital sex and homosexuality, and the absolute right of parents (read fathers) over children. On the other hand, movements representing new modalities of masculine dominance argue implicitly and explicitly for the loosening of sexuality from all relations of social solidarity and mutual aid, for the objectification and commodification of women's sexuality, for the end of a special status for childhood in psycho-sexual terms, and for support to abortion, birth control and homosexual rights, as essential means by which men can be divested of their responsibility for others within the context of an obsolete and confining family system.[35]

These movements which represent new modalities of male supremacy have greater affinity with certain aspects of late capitalism: above all the sex industries *per se*[36] (which, according to some estimates, outgross—so to speak—all other 'entertainment' industries combined) and the advertising and the (non-directly sexual) film, television and video industries. But while these represent new capitalist sectors, and seem to confront and clash with the forces of orthodox patriarchal ideology, they should not be understood as in any clear sense representing capitalism's *resolution* of the gender problem and therefore vanguard paths which will surely be followed by majority fractions of the capitalist class as a whole, and supported consistently by the state. This is because while the new masculinism seeks to subordinate women through erotic and ideological control, and a further delegitimation of the family, in important ways it aids the material disintegration of what Eisenstein refers to as the 'neat distinction' between 'Man' and 'Woman' *in the paid workforce, and* by direct reverberation, *in the home.* That neat distinction, while not very profitable to the newer industries, is still exceptionally profitable to other, older and more established sectors of the capitalist class (insurance, banks, all finance capital whose labour force is massively female) and to the state as employer of service workers; and tremendously important to capitalism as a whole economic and political system which depends on material and ideological divisions in the working class as a precondition of maximum surplus extraction. Further, that distinction as it embodies women's service to men is evidently very valuable to men-as-a-group, who show little inclination to give up their privileges, either in the workforce or in the realm of reproductive labour—what is usually called the home.[37]

In negotiating a way through these treacherous waters, the state has taken on a qualitatively new relationship with respect to the regulation of women's productive and reproductive labour: it has become for large numbers of women, especially mothers, drawn now from the petty bourgeoisie and the proletariat as well as the chronically poor, the great collective father-figure, a new representative of men-as-a-group, but now a new kind of group, totally divorced, as it were, from these women in terms of kinship and mutual aid, a bureaucratic, impersonal pyramid of a group of men, who have taken the place of all those absent fathers.[38] Women's labour and sexuality are the two most important things to control for any society of masculine dominance. Policies delineating everything from unemployment insurance benefits to daycare subsidies to the modalities of socialised medicine to the (lack of) abortion facilities to prosecution and persecution of lesbian mothers are all up-to-date expressions of a generic state, in the process of developing new forms of masculinism corresponding to the really acute crisis and change in gender arrangements. These new collective modalities of control are also modalities of *appropriation*, to return to our first criterion of relations of domination between men and women. As women's previous functions in domestic labour become severed from individual men on a stable, long-term basis (from father to husband to the arms of death was the way the usual pattern read, with maybe a little fooling around in between), their so-called 'caring' role is replicated in the paid workforce. Far from being the road to liberation, as Engels's admonition to women ('Get a job') suggested, women's large-scale wage labour has resulted in what Nicole Laurin-Frenette has called a 'publicisation' of the previously privatised labour of women such that even women who live most of their lives as single are appropriated through the work they do in the paid labour force, or through their mothering work regulated through state welfare agencies, or through the nurturing kinds of functions they perform even in non-traditional jobs, or, and most likely, through all three forms of collective appropriation at some time or another.[39]

More work needs to be done on these new forms, and on other emerging manifestations of masculine dominance which are products of industrialisation and late capitalism, but it is important here to point out that the contradictions feminists have described between capitalism and the sexual division of labour intrinsic to masculine dominance are real contradictions, as real as the affinities the systems have with one another.[40] These contradictions allow of no easy solution, not only structurally but also politically, since they have been creating an absolutely massive movement of resistance—the women's movement—whose successive waves have spanned a period of almost one hundred and fifty years, and whose demands and forms of organisation have been given greater impetus by the widening gap between generic and economic-class relations in the capitalist system, and which is now threatening to further the politicisation of the working class itself. If the state is the most important site of mediation of contradictions for gender and economic classes, we should find that its role in the regulation of women in the interests of continued masculine dominance increases rather than decreases. I think that the evidence for this is more than ample, despite what appear to be numerous concessions around divorce criteria, reproductive rights, equal pay and human rights legislation. Those concessions, like unemployment insurance or socialised medicine under different circumstances, were forced by struggle and/or threat of struggle from a state in great need of maintaining an appearance of some neutrality in the tense, politicised years of the late sixties and early seventies, but which is increasingly retrenching in the bleaker years of the late seventies and early eighties. Moreover, as in relation to the working class as a whole, so in relation to women, what the state hath given, the state taketh away. Reproductive rights legislation, representing the territory of women's bodies and men's right to control them, is under constant attack by important fractions of the ruling class with their petty-bourgeois and working-class troops rallied behind, and is even being carried out by social democratic governments.[41] Ditto for equal pay legislation, which, when magnanimously legislated by one arm of the state, is subsequently subverted by the courts, labour relations boards, and police who protect the strike-breaking companies which have received a whole new lease on life as an enormous number of first-contract battles by women workers just beg to be crushed. In any case, for Marxists, concessions have never indicated a change in the class nature of the state—only the need for a refined understanding of the ways in which class states make concessions and reforms without disrupting, indeed at times positively reinforcing, dominant class rule.[42] The same analysis needs to be made with respect to gender-class as it does with respect to economic-class, since capitalist states, like all other states, have functioned, in the final analysis, to preserve and in new ways extend masculine control, rather than to end it.

MASCULINE DOMINANCE IN TRANSITIONAL STATES

Although debates rage over any number of pertinent questions regarding the forms and functions of the state in capitalist societies, one question has not troubled Marxism as such: Marxists agree that the state is a capitalist one. This broad unanimity of characterisation breaks down dramatically as soon as Marxist discourse shifts to the political economy and the nature of state formation in those societies which I prefer to call transitional, but which others call everything from 'actually existing socialist' to 'state capitalist'. Where there is great diversity of characterisation of the (economic) class aspect of these states, there is great silence with respect to their gender-class nature. Debates between major positions articulated by theoreticians like Ernest Mandel, Hillel Ticktin, Charles Bettleheim, Bogdan Krawchenko and many others who dissent from official Communist apologetics contain no consideration, let alone a sustained theoretical treatment, of the ways in which gender divisions operate in societies ostensibly attempting to evolve from domination to equality. These considerations are in fact extremely extensive and affect both separately and in their interaction all the essential spheres of life: the economy and the problems associated with the conditions of production, distribution and consumption; sexual relations and the growth of the new person (still called the new 'man' in most instances) out of conditions of psycho-sexual health; cultural life and the creation of vital, open and critical expressive and analytic work; and culminating out of all of these, political life and the creation of truly self-regulating and egalitarian forms of public coordination of all aspects of social existence.

In recent years an impressive body of much empirical and some theoretical work has been generated by feminists studying the condition of women in almost all of the transitional societies—from the USSR (which includes a number of diverse social formations within it) to the distinct societies of Eastern Europe, to China, Cuba, and now Nicaragua and the states of southeast Africa.[43] The weight of the descriptive material is staggering in its stark and unavoidable conclusions concerning women's oppression in the transitional societies. These provide a truly fundamental challenge to the capacity of Marxist theory as it is presently elaborated to account for the situation of women in these countries.

By way of an introductory summary, this situation for women in the USSR and Eastern Europe and China may be described as astoundingly similar, both across national boundaries within these societies and to that of women in the West. Although married women's participation rate in the paid workforce is higher than in the capitalist countries, the patterns of women's employment are rather painfully similar: women are ghettoised into jobs where their work tends to reflect their roles as sustainer and drudge, in much the same way as noted above. While women have penetrated the ranks of previously male-exclusive professions in perhaps greater numbers, their concentration at the lower- and, in thinning numbers, mid-level of some of these professions, and their absence from the elite, speaks of an identical process of structural and ideological discrimination. Moreover, the social devaluation of currently female-dominated professions like medicine in the USSR indicates that the importance placed upon a given occupation has more to do with generic prejudice than with the intrinsic merit of the job. (Just compare the status and remuneration of doctors in the West with that of those in the East.) Most importantly, women's central condition is that of the double day of labour—the condition which we can with justification describe as the dominant form of masculinist appropriation of women's labour in industrial societies. It should hardly be necessary to add that, given the greater scarcity of consumer goods—from food and clothing to household appliances—women's second workday in the transitional societies is more arduous, not less, than that of their counterparts in advanced capitalist countries.[44] In terms of women's presence in places of authority, that is in the ranks of the bureaucratic elite which spans top posts in all spheres and which is coterminous with both state structures and party membership, women form less than five per cent of ruling cadres, sometimes as little as zero per cent.[45] Although their percentage in elected positions at regional or national levels is somewhat larger than that of women in capitalist legislatures, familiarity with the political systems in question reveals that these positions are symbolic, without real power, and chosen for their ideological value in enabling the elite to claim women's representation as a 'gain' of 'socialist' society.

From the point of view of orthodox Marxism, what is bizarre about these patterns is their similarity. If indeed differences in the development of the productive forces in the first place, and differences of national cultural life in the second place, really are the decisive factors in determining the position of women, how is it possible that the economic, social, sexual and political patterns characteristic of women's condition should be so strikingly, so depressingly similar, not only to women's condition in capitalist countries, but across a range of societies which include highly industrialised, 'advanced' political economies such as those of Hungary, Czechoslovakia and Poland and also quite agrarian, 'backward' political economies such as Uzbekistan, Mongolia and the like? If bureaucratic rule has no distinctly masculinist or generic commitment, if it is precipitated independently out of the development of the productive forces in which there is no central and specific set of dynamics flowing from and reconstructing masculine dominance, if despite everything it should be possible to put politics in command to work towards the equalisation of the sexes—how is it that these remarkably similar patterns of masculine dominance appear so uniformly across these societies? Marxist explanations which grant no autonomous and major effectivity to masculine dominance cannot, even with the most sophisticated of bureaucratic-deformation elaborations, account for these patterns. Feminists' contention that Marxist positions on women in fact obscure the relations of masculine dominance rather than reveal them has been borne out by the experiences of these societies both with respect to the role of the state and with respect to the emergence of important forms of opposition.

All discussions of the role of the state with respect to any given problem must begin with a grasp of its ubiquitous and, when confronted with any sort of opposition, sinister and repressive presence in all spheres of life—from the factory creche to the factory manager, in the schools, offices, hospitals—in a word, everywhere. The state is everywhere, and as the chief organiser of life in these societies, must be held accountable for the policies and forms which it adopts. The patterns of women's condition I have already summarised speak directly to its policies in a number of crucial respects, and I refer the reader to the extensive material detailing these conditions country by country, stratum by stratum, nationality by nationality. Here I want to discuss briefly how the orthodox Marxist theory of women's oppression, in its capacity as the official ideology, has served to obscure and perpetuate masculine dominance and gender-class with respect to women's labour and sexuality, and then to look at the relation of this to the issue of anti-bureaucratic struggle.

Marxist ideology has formulated the goal which would embody the answer to the 'Woman Question' as one of *equality between men and women*. This in turn has been seen to depend on Engels's prescriptions to 'integrate women into production' and to provide some socialised services to relieve women of domestic burdens so that they may partake of that integration. Between 80 and 90 per cent of able-bodied women do work outside the home in the industrialised, transitional societies, and indeed that percentage has been achieved through a much larger network of childcare centres, and in the case of China through collective eating centres and laundries which have enabled women to find eight hours a day, six days a week, without the immediate responsibility of children, to work outside the home. But in fact the limitations of this 'socialisation' are products of a purposeful choice, not only of struggling and beleaguered economies, because the companion piece to 'equality of men and women' in the ideological set is *'the family as the building block of socialism'*. These two major planks are fraught with problems. First, the notion of equality for women rather than the notion of women's liberation denies a transformative dynamic to women's struggle. (This is of course a problem socialist and radical feminists have pointed out with respect to bourgeois feminism in capitalist countries as well.)[46] It implicitly but firmly sets the life-ways and goals of masculine existence as the standards to which women should aspire and against which official estimates of their 'progress' will be made. It poses the problem as one of the women's 'catching up to men', rather than as a problem for women and men to solve together by changing the conditions and relations of their shared lives—from their intimate to their large-scale social interaction. The commitment to the 'family'—in that case the mostly two but sometimes three generational non-extended biological kinship structure—as the central means through which responsibility and labour for daily and generational reproduction takes place seals off this necessary transformative dynamic, because it assumes women's unpaid labour in performing domestic tasks of a physical and managerial nature, and men's relative leisure and freedom to pursue extra-domestic goals and activities. If the results of a study conducted in the Soviet Union some years ago are in any sense typical, and informal reportage indicates they are, the tendency to this masculinist sexual divison of labour is accentuated, rather than the other way around, as one goes up the social scale.[47] In her investigation of Soviet data Gail Warshafsky Lapidus found that of the groups of men likely to 'help' their wives with the housework (no group assumed that housework was anything other than the woman's main responsibility), non-politically active industrial workers scored highest and upwardly mobile or already established party members lowest. Here is very disturbing evidence of a mechanism which reproduces the generic division of labour in reality regardless of official notions of equality and sharing, and insofar as the standards of the privileged strata become standards for the whole society, reinforces masculinism ideologically as well. 'Equality' coupled with the commitment to the 'family as the building block of socialism' have served to reinforce, legitimise and reproduce the generic sexual division of labour, not to change it, while at the same time mystifying its reality and its potential solutions.

If we look at this issue in relation to sexuality and procreation, at first glance it may seem the hypothesis won't hold. After all, millions upon millions of abortions are performed in the transitional societies, and in China women's mothering labour will soon be reduced to a minimum if the one-child-per-couple campaign really gets off the ground. But the real issue is not abortion as against the lack of it, or children as against sterility, but of who controls fertility and erotic relations and how the standards for that control are established. Because there are a number of very different needs as perceived by the ruling elites of the transitional states, policies concerning things like abortion and sterilisation, economic incentives and penalties around children, and questions of erotic relations differ from country to country. Several key features are continuous, however, and prove the principle of masculine control. First, demography has a very high place as a branch of social science and social control, and demographic policy is discussed and decided upon at the level of the politbureaus (less than two per cent women). Second, and ideologically justified by the demands of the first, women are not considered to have the right to control their own bodies and reproductive capacities, rather the state is considered supreme in this matter. So long as this is the case, of course, there can never be an equality even of access to non-domestic activity because women will, as a group, have to cope with the major obstacles which child-bearing and rearing constitute to full public participation when reproductive labour is their sole responsibility. Third, the availability and quality of contraception (preventive measures which give women far greater real control than the horrendous, but government-controlled, recourse to high numbers of abortions) is appallingly bad. In the Soviet Union, for example, diaphragms, cervical caps and birth control pills are virtually unavailable (except for women affiliated to the elite) forcing resort to condoms whose reliability is a pan-national joke.[48] In the capitalist world the struggle against abortion rights represents an attempt to preserve the relations of masculinism on a face-to-face level, between men and women, because of the reluctance to allow the state the kind of control it exercises in the transitional societies. In the latter countries, however, the mass, grotesque reliance on abortion represents masculine dominance just as much as Western variants, but in a different— a collective—form. Fourth, and related to this, the repressive nature of the availability of information and education about sex itself, and the masculinist heterosexist bias of that information, is extraordinary by Western standards, especially so in China but not only there. (Recent personal communication described some Chinese family planning information as completely lacking the word for penis, because this is considered taboo for public discourse in certain regions!) And finally, erotic freedom in choice of sexual orientation is viewed primarily as a social crime and sign of bourgeois decadence. The harsh and repressive maintenance of compulsory heterosexuality is a very powerful component of generic power. These ideologies and policies throw all the responsibility for change onto women, absolve men of any need to change in either private or public life, and completely subvert the possibility for real change, as they further entrench masculine privilege.

The oppression of women in economic, sexual, social and political spheres acts as a massive block to the transition to socialism, and constitutes an immense pillar of bureaucratic dominance in a number of crucial ways. Women's atomised labour in nuclear and less-than-nuclear (mother-children only) units blocks the ways in which the contradiction between the socialised production of the social surplus and its private appropriation can be overcome, the most important economic contradiction in transitional societies according to Ernest Mandel.[49] Women's labour in the home and in the female ghetto jobs of the paid workforce blocks the transformation of the content of and relationship between production, distribution and consumption. As long as reproductive labour is performed privately by individual women and collectively by groups of women in under-remunerated and overcentralised social services in which men refuse to work, domestic labour cannot be socialised in a way that equilibrates the balance between heavy industrial and military production on the one hand and consumer goods and services on the other, for structural and social reasons. Structurally, the funds for quality services and consumer goods will remain tied up, and women's unpaid and low-paid labour will continue to maintain the society at a low standard of living. Socially, people will remain isolated from each other, a horizontal process of social bonding, community organising and political planning prevented by the single-family-to-central-state relationship. New values which truly do put the needs of human life—that is, in another vocabulary, the needs of reproduction—first will not develop because of the generic divisions which both derive from and maintain this form of isolation.[50]

The consequences of all this are political in every respect. From the point of view of the creation of a socialist mass psychology (or consciousness, if one prefers the term), the bifurcation of human qualities into gender-appropriate behaviour, characteristics, activities and spheres creates the classical authoritarian personality[51] incapable of the full range of human activities, unable to be truly self-regulating and therefore always inclined to look to some to lead and decide from above, and to others to serve and submit from below. Overlaid on or intertwined with or even regardless of this mass psychology, the present gender arrangements lead parents, and especially mothers, to reject the whole notion of socialised domestic labour and childcare because it seems a mechanism for their super-exploitation economically, and their impoverishment emotionally, socially and politically (for example, this is expressed in the second of Solidarity's 'women's demands': extension of maternity leave—note, not parental leave, but maternity leave—to *three years*). These psychological and practical conditions create the living basis for a cross-class gender coalition which divides the working classes along gender lines in ways most profitable to the elite. In the Soviet Union, the incidence of women's physical and emotional demoralisation, men's alcohol-induced domestic brutality, and all-round sexual misery for both sexes is of tragic proportions. Imploding discontent and alienation prevents the full development of resistance, which is especially important in a society where the elite benefits very little from the kind of ideological hegemony of capitalist states. The kind of alienation between the sexes so many have reported in the USSR seems worse than in other transitional societies—and this makes sense insofar as gender relations are part of the overall reality of atomisation and repression. But the general points are valid for all transitional societies—and in China, where we do not have the same kind of atomisation, we still hear of female infanticide, and very sexist practices and customs among party members and intellectuals who, like their Soviet male counterparts, benefit from the personal services of their wives.

Masculine dominance has reasserted itself and remains a fundamental organising principle, constitutive element and political commitment of the bureaucratic regimes of the transitional states, but never named as such even by Western Marxists. Even more problematically, it has largely been ignored by the oppositional currents, inside and outside of these societies,[52] despite the fact that the privileges it actually delivers to the men of the working class are miniscule when compared to the liabilities. The quality of life which masculine dominance degrades in economic, sexual, social, cultural and political spheres—in short, everywhere—affects men as well as women. The majority of men stand to gain everything from renouncing its norms, customs and relatively speaking miserable rewards. Perhaps this explains why the elite continues to reinforce masculine dominance so consistently.

PERSONNEL

When we discuss the state as a manifestation of social relations, as a relation of production, as the major organiser of class hegemony, as the site of conflict mediation, we are using conceptual terms which enable us to express real attributes and functions. But these terms, though absolutely necessary, also tend to depersonalise the state, to hide the fact that it is created by, made up of, and maintained by real people who are not simply cogs in an inexorably rolling wheel but active, conscious human beings—more active and more conscious, it is probably safe to say, the closer one approaches the central seats of power. Until now I have been arguing the generic nature of the state on the basis of its policies and interventions into society, not on the basis of its personnel. But the two are related, and while the former considerations need to be established, perhaps in the first place, they are completely bound up with the latter. In terms of state personnel examined from the point of view of masculine dominance, it is important to understand who makes up state structures, how they got to where they are, and how they manage to stay there. One of the most useful publications to date with respect of the purely political cadres of industrial states is *The Politics of the Second Electorate,* an anthology which covers women's electoral fortunes (participation and representation) in all the advanced capitalist countries, Eastern Europe and the Soviet Union. The articles contained in it provide invaluable empirical and descriptive material, but for the most part decline to undertake theoretical elaborations. Perhaps rightly so, for fuller generalisations need to look at the relation and interaction between the elected, the bureaucratic, the legal and coercive repressive systems and follow this with a further examination of how all of these interact with the other ruling structures—among them the professional associations, the schools, and, in various places, the top bureaucracies of the unions and even (as in the transitional societies) state women's organisations themselves. Nevertheless, since I am of the opinion that the central state systems do represent a massive condensation of real power and do act quite instrumentally—to use a deliberately controversial term[53]—in constant, recurring ways to enforce class domination, I think it valid and necessary to understand something about their personnel as well as about their policies and forms of governing.

For the purposes of this article, I am going to take as given that the people at the top of these systems are not as a rule children of the working class, nor do they for the most part represent the interests of the working classes in their decisions and activities. What I want to talk about here is that the people at the top of these systems also tend not to come from the female sex,[54] and have the same record with respect to women's interests that they have *vis-à-vis* those of workers.

First, with respect to the question of elected representatives in the capitalist countries: women are most highly represented in local and municipal governments where elections are not dominated by political parties. When local politics are organised along party lines women's presence drops, and continues to diminish with each 'higher' level of centralisation, until they are hardly to be found in the rarefied atmosphere of government benches and cabinet meetings at all. Up to the present it has been acceptable to suggest that women's absence from these levels was due to their 'socialisation', the burden of domestic responsibilities and the sexism of the electorate. But with the publication of recent material, scholars have been forced to conclude what any politically active woman has known all along: the primary responsibility for women's absence lies with none of these factors, although they play a sometimes important secondary role. It is found, first, foremost and most importantly, in men's conscious exclusion of women from positions of authority and responsibility.[55]

In liberal democracies, governmental teams are made up of elected representatives of a number of political parties, and it is within these parties that the most important systematised exclusion primarily takes place. It happens through several related mechanisms. First there is the most blatant form of the sexual division of labour, still institutionalised in all the major capitalist parties and in most of the worker's parties to this day: the separate organisation of women into women's 'committees' or 'sections' or 'auxiliaries'. These organisations are charged with and actually do perform the majority of daily party maintenance work, such as meeting organisation, local fundraising, secretarial functions, envelope stuffing and electoral canvassing. Unfortunately, the performance of these duties appears for the most part not to qualify persons for positions of party responsibility. Research (and experience) shows that these positions go to the people who control the funds and make political policy and alliances; people who are almost always men freed from much of the organisational nitty-gritty by the women's support work.[56] (Note that appropriation structures political party relations as well.) Thus in the mixed gatherings of party life where political policy, strategy and selection of candidates is formally decided, the men predominate and dominate. Candidate selection itself is a process which has various modalities in various parties, but is usually decided upon with the criterion of party service uppermost—the criterion reflecting priority to those with experience in the masculine side of affairs.

There have always been women who have refused the sexual division of political labour, and sought to be politically active in the fullest sense of the term. But the sexual segregation of the mass parties has worked against them, and against their ability to represent women. In cutting them off from the majority of women in the parties, it has deprived them of a feminine base of support and forced them to seek the approval of the male party membership and leadership. This has so effectively undercut their capacity to speak out aggressively on behalf of women and against masculine dominance that we can find almost no strong feminists among the women who have reached the apex of party power in industrialised societies (Margaret Thatcher being the quintessential example of those who have).[57] For women who do evade the sexual division of labour and/or are strong feminists, major parties have a back-up, highly effective form of discrimination which usually works where others have failed: these women are simply denied winnable constituencies. It thus requires a major mobilisation of women and sympathetic men in the constituency associations (where these even have supreme power of selection) to obtain such candidacies, and these in turn require a great deal of time and money, two things that women, who in general are less affluent and more over-worked than men, have in scant supply. Sexual segregation and masculine control of candidacies then set a series of catches in motion which guarantee that few women and fewer feminists will make it to the top. Non-political party positions mean no good candidacies; no good candidacies means irregular legislative experience at best; this in turn means no cabinet participation, which means no real power, in and out-side the party. Finally, for those women who manage to get elected and to get appointed to cabinet posts, there is the final catch. They are assign-ed primarily to portfolios which are concerned with matters relating to 'women and the family'—health, education, community services, culture (leisure, arts and sports)—and restricted from the high-powered depart-ments such as transport, finance, foreign affairs and the military.

These extremely blatant and powerful mechanisms of masculine control by no means exhaust the list of ways in which men order and keep unto themselves political associations which are in name representative of both sexes. The routines of party life, the skills which are valued, the extra-ordinary double standard of behaviour for men and women, and the priorities and values of programmatic elaboration have all been analysed and shown to embody masculine dominance in a series of ways ranging from the most overt to the most subtle. I think that these are as important as, for example, the issue of selection of candidates.[58] Indeed, as far as the crisis of the far Left is concerned, these other forms of masculine power are more important than the issue of candidatures *per se*. But I have become increasingly convinced that internal party power, while in and of itself protected jealously by men as a group (sometimes unconsciously, especially on the Left), is profoundly connected to the notion of power that will eventually be held in society as a whole, and that it is the deeply rooted generic exclusion of women from governing, authoritative positions as well as the protection of position, petty privilege and brittle egos, that is working against women within party structures, and in the name of which the internal divisions are perpetuated and reinforced. Men have been raised to experience their masculinity—inseparable in any meaningful way from their identity—as defined by their political control over women. Women's appearance as full-scale political beings is the most threatening phenomenon of all *vis-à-vis* the generic division of labour. If women adopt the forms, values and standards of masculine dominance (as the majority of top-level women politicians do today), they are much more easily assimilable, although even then they are as scarce as hen's teeth. When they challenge those forms and standards, they are either summarily excluded, as in the parties of the conservative Right (the Tories in Britain and Canada, the Republicans in the US, and the more conservative wings of Canadian Liberals and American Democrats), or exploited and contained, as in the parties of the Centre (the British Social Democratic Party, the American Democratic Party, the Canadian Liberal Party). In the reformist mass workers parties the relationship between masculinism and feminism is more complex: feminism tends to be both exploited and contained for purposes of party recruitment and electioneering, respectively, but the ideology of commitment to the underdog opens up a political space for women and men who want a more serious approach to the issues of masculine dominance, and thus enables a far more real process of protracted political struggle to take place than in any of the bourgeois parties. In the groups of the far Left, the problems are in some ways worse: a more rigid ideology than that of the opportunistically pragmatic mass parties means, ironically, a greater resistance to the theoretical and programmatic elaborations from a feminist point of view; and the same is true with respect to organisational innovations. Moreover, and most crucially, the marginalisation of the far Left in this historical period denies its women and sympathetic men members a mass base amongst sectors who not only want to see progressive change in the relation between the sexes but see those changes as desirable for and in the far Left groups.

The other system I want to address here is the government bureaucracy, the non-elected army of workers and managers who run the administrative machinery of state. The by-now-familiar pyramid pattern is in evidence here as well, with women making up the vast majority of clerks and secretaries who type, process, file and retrieve the mountain of forms and letters on which the upper echelons rest. At the top we are once again in a men's club. As in the political parties, the *de facto* sexual segregation of the work force at the bottom of the pyramid is the single most important factor in determining who will move up it, and we need spend no more time elaborating on that. But since the goals of bureaucratic upward mobility can be achieved only through formal promotion, not election, and since promotion is a process in which those from below are selected by those from above, with little room for the kind of alliance-making that goes on in political parties (you deliver x, I'll deliver y, etc.) the mechanisms operating for female exclusion are a little different in form, if not in substance. The woman who now heads a small federal department in the Canadian government called Status of Women Canada, and who is *de facto* occupying a deputy minister's position (she is the only woman at this level in Ottawa, and her title is, despite the job, director, not deputy minister) says,[59] as does a growing body of research, that the differences in men's and women's job performance works against women in the following way: women tend to spend *more* time on the substance of their work. . . and less on the different kinds of activities which will move them up the bureaucratic ladder. For when it comes to actual personnel selection, the men at the top tend to choose those with whom they are most 'compatible' and with whom they can work most 'comfortably', those whose 'performance' and 'style' they've come to 'know and like'. The jargon may be different in London or Washington, but the effect is the same. Women who do not organise their worklives the way men do—from the connection-making to the odd hours for important meetings (like dinner-time, Saturday mornings and Sunday nights), who do not identify with the goals and methods of the male-dominated bureaucracy—will by definition not be seen as 'compatible' with the men, and the very few women, who do. Of course, as with party politics, women who seek upper-level appointments not only accept these conditions of work and the havoc they play with personal life, they must also cope with the resistance which the very construct 'masculinity' puts up to their presence in the male realms. This is expressed by a rather more rigorous, if sometimes circuitous, weeding-out process of feminist civil servants than of those women who accept the masculinist modalities.[60] Sexual harassment plays an important, if little understood, role in keeping strong women down as well, and the double standard of evaluation and behaviour also comes sharply into play, with women being judged not only more harshly but on the basis of sex appropriate behaviour which in itself creates an insurmountable obstacle: women who are aggressive, verbal and decisive are judged negatively and rejected for breaking gender rules, yet upper echelon positions demand aggressive, decisive and literate qualities in their members. And on it goes. The sexual division of labour which relegates women to sustaining roles at home and in the paid workforce, and assigns to men responsibility for large-scale social decision-making on the basis of their freedom from such labour, is reproduced within the government bureaucracy as well.

The implications of masculine power within these two systems of the core state apparatus are important to understand from a strategic point of view, and I will briefly return to this in the concluding section. Here I want to add a few more general points about the reproduction of masculine power within state apparatuses more generally. First of all, it would be useful to have detailed and exact understandings of the way in which masculine dominance reproduces itself in the other central apparatuses, and the differences between apparatuses in local, regional and national formations. It would also be very helpful to understand the impact that a growing number of women are having on these apparatuses— from the political parties to, say, the legal system where, in parts of the US and Canada for example, graduating classes in law school are now composed of almost one-third women. What will be crucial to a mapping of that impact is a clear sense of the distinction and relation between feminism, capitalism and socialism. For, as we have seen with the so-to-speak renegade sons of the working class, it is not only or so much one's background but also one's present and future orientation that determines one's position in the overall scheme of things. If we have whole female generational cohorts adopting the modalities of masculine, as well as capitalist, politics, aspiring collectively to the Thatcher role-model, this will not constitute a qualitative step forward. I think such a uniform development *extremely* unlikely, but what is probable is that some important segment of the seventies cohort will adopt the positions and functions of masculinism and capitalism, just as important cadres thrown up by working-class organisations adopt social-democratic, and worse, liberal and conservative policies and positions. One's sex will be no more a guarantee of progressive politics than one's class origins.

It is also important for Marxists and feminists to familiarise themselves with the information regarding the reproduction of masculinist power in the apparatus of transitional states. Many of these are of course identical, in terms of face-to-face interaction, sexual divisions of labour, sexual harassment and coercion, double standards of political and sexual behaviour and the like. But it is important for strategic reasons to understand the peculiarities of these systems as well, including the traditions and modalities of the respective national Communist Parties, and special power bases of the male bureaucracy in heavy industry,[61] the centralised seats of political power, the overt repression of explicit feminist forces,[62] and the relation between symbolic functions and positions of real authority and power. Such an understanding would lay the basis for targeting the necessary changes, practically speaking. Theoretically speaking, it helps to bring into even sharper focus the autonomous effectivity of masculine dominance as an organising principle of state formations.

Last, but not least, is the serious and essential question of the coercive and repressive apparatus of industrial states, capitalist and transitional: the military, para-military and intelligence operations which constitute such enormous positions of the state as a whole, and whose power is both massive and ubiquitous. Marxists have always seen standing armies as instruments of naked ruling-class power within capitalist state formations, and have accorded them important study and weight in the political life of transitional societies.[63] But nowhere to my knowledge has there been any speculation or sustained consideration of the consequences of the masculinist composition and traditions of armies in this most masculinist of all systems of power. In capitalist countries, armies organise men into a men's society in which the rules and conditions which affect one's well-being are entirely severed from those with reflect, even if in partial and stunted terms, the needs of women and children—in other words, the productive and reproductive needs of the species. This principle works in less extreme, but nevertheless clearly discernable terms in police forces and intelligence services as well, and thus characterises the whole of the repressive apparatus. In transitional societies, with pre- and post-insurrectionary periods, there is potential for the army to play more progressive roles insofar as it plays a major role in mobilising the population for the process of social reorganisation and reconstruction. But as the insurrectionary period recedes, the army loses its nature as a force of liberation, a chain of rank and command independent of the control of the troops becomes institutionalised, and the armies of the transitional societies come to look and act more and more like those of the capitalist states. Invariably this process brings with it a new retrenchment of masculine dominance in every sense of the term.

The lack of Marxist discussion concerning the relation between masculine dominance and militarism, in fact the resistance to this discussion among many men Marxists, is in my opinion one of the most serious problems in Marxism's inability to come to terms with and grow from the feminist contribution. Feminists argue that there is in masculinism an orientation to conflict resolution trapped within the modalities of brute force; a system of ranked command which abstracts and absolves its members from responsibility for life, a lack of connection with the conditions of life (human and biospheric) so profound as to mystify the material limits of it; a sense of the need for the endless exploitation and domination of nature rooted in the masculinist orientation to life itself.[64] I am aware that as I write these words I have left behind the vocabulary of Marxist discourse, but like many other feminists, I am profoundly convinced that it is Marxists who must learn to understand the meaning of these perceptions and the theoretical and empirical material which has generated them. For if it is true that some of the feminist analysis has obscured issues of economic class and imperialism in more general discussion, it is equally true that the Marxist analysis has obscured issues of gender-class with even more disastrous results.

SUMMARY AND CONCLUSION

Having argued very hard for a conceptualisation of the relations between the genders that involves systematic appropriation, inequality, conflict and domination, it is now necessary to add one mandatory point: I have no wish to obscure economic-class differences between women by insisting on the category of gender-class. Obviously not all women are equally oppressed, and women affiliated to ruling-class men are as a rule less oppressed than working-class women. Class privilege has always softened and continues to ameliorate the conditions of life for ruling-class women and even to buy them off from feeling and expressing solidarity with their working-class sisters, whose labour they also appropriate, directly and indirectly. But I do not think that this dynamic is qualitatively different from the way in which gender-class has organised cross-economic-class masculine privilege, and bought off labouring men who have opted to retain their gender-class privilege rather than unite in struggle with their working-class sisters against the oppressors of the ruling economic-class. In other words, class divisions of both kinds cut across one another, but this makes them no less real, just more complicated. The situation is complicated further still by the fact that gender-class relations are lived in different ways than the relations between economic-classes because women and men have, for the most part, depended on one another for mutual, if unequal, aid, and have shared for the most part a mutual, if unequally free, sexuality. Generic relations of stable mutual aid are breaking down very fast in capitalist society, but not to any great sense of joy or liberation as 'free' men and women with children confront the expanse of masculinist capitalist chaos on their own. Likewise, the old sexual arrangements are in process of profound turmoil and change, with the women's and gay movements representing the socially positive poles of possibility, and the commodification of sexuality representing the negative. Gender-class relations need to be understood in terms of the ways in which every human being feels and experiences them, as well as in terms of the way that impersonal states manipulate them, if we are to find humane and liberatory means of transcending them. They cannot be 'smashed'—they must gradually be dismantled and wither away. Gender relations are passed on generationally and interiorised within the personality at a profound level, but with all the inevitable contradictions that must exist as a result of, among other factors, the lack of fit between what we learn as children and what we must live as adults. The intrapsychic and social experience of such contradictions is a pool of potential transformative consciousness and desire, but also of painful and terrified reaction which when mobilised acts as a massive brake on social change. Again, strategically, we must address ourselves to the political problems posed by the crisis of gender relations and the existence of masculine dominance.

Thus a revolutionary strategy which aims at real transformation must have feminist as well as classically socialist principles. Socialist-feminist or feminist-socialist, it needs to help those seeking progressive change to learn to draw the feminist line much as up till now it has helped people to draw the economic-class line. Because of the non-economically centralised nature of masculine dominance and because of men's and women's mutual sexuality, we cannot speak of the need to 'expropriate' the dominant gender-class. But if the power men possess in political life (based on their appropriation of women's labour and women's exclusion from politics) is not both shared and transformed, socialism will be blocked just as surely as if no capitalist expropriation had occurred. Thus we must speak of *displacing,* over time and through processes of qualitative change, at least half of the masculine cadres who now rule society on a planetary basis, and of changing the whole relation of the genders to political power and reproductive labour. The path to socialism can only travel through the transformation of gender as well as economic relations if social relations really are to lose their character as matrices of domination. The practical implications of this position are as extensive as are the programmatic, strategic, tactical and organisational aspects of common work and struggle, and are expressed at all these levels simultaneously. To tackle these we need to work at change on each distinct but linked level in which unequal gender relations express themselves: the intrapsychic, in which each individual man and woman must take responsibility for overcoming the legacies of sexism; the interpersonal—in couples and families and close friendship groups; in social and political associations in which we work or which we alternatively construct to express and organise our public life as a species. We must, as many feminists argued during the British debate on the Alternative Economic Strategy, change the values that guide our efforts in these associations, and place the values which stem from the reproductive aspects of our lives at centre stage. The existence of human life depends on its actual, day-to-day, bodily reproduction, and on the existence of a biosphere of which it is a part and without which it cannot survive. Because of the genderic division of labour the principles which guide the masculinist state are those based on an abstraction from and a denigration of those aspects of existence, a smash-and-grab attitude to the world, a rape of nature, an endless plunder and greed for domination.

Until now, Marxism has not seen this problem, for two important reasons. First, Marxism itself is a product of what Mary O'Brien has called male-stream thought, a stream which has taken the sexual division of labour for granted as natural and unproblematic. Its categories have assumed and therefore mystified that division of labour, and Marxism's organisations have reproduced it, adopting forms of functioning and power which have been labelled proletarian and revolutionary, when in reality they have masked significant forms of masculine privilege, values and priorities. Second, and not unrelated, Marxist men (the majority gender in the Marxist movement) have benefitted from women's re-productive and nurturant labour just as much as any other men, and they have been tremendously reluctant to give it up. The reasons for this reluctance are similar to those of men outside the movement. Practically, it is much harder to go to meetings, organise campaigns, run for parlia-ment or write complicated, demanding theory if one has to wash socks, cook meals, clean house, nurse sick relatives, do homework with the kids and spend a lot of time figuring out how to mediate between the conflict-ing emotional and material needs of family members and/or close friends—all of which women do, and all of which are absolutely indispensable labours to human existence. Additionally, connectedly and no less compellingly, Marxist men are socialised like other men and share with them deeply felt values of masculine identification, the negative aspects of which require (unless worked through consciously) certain forms of ritualised as well as practical subordination from women. (It is not only time-consuming but also 'unmanly' to do many aspects of reproductive labour; it is definitely a blow to one's masculinity to be rejected in favour of a woman for a political position, or for that matter as a sexual partner.) The problem is that all these masculine investments serve the camp of the class enemy, and make it impossible to build the kinds of alliance between socialist men and women that we need.

But, and this is why so many feminists are engaged in this debate with Marxist men, Marxism is also the most radical of the world views to come out of the male-dominated epoch of human history, and many of us still think that it carries within it the possibility for the correction of its internal omissions and distortions, and the practical transcendence of its internal weaknesses. The commitment to a human society free from domination and the implacable opposition to ideological mystification put Marxism as a theory and a movement in a qualitatively different position *vis-à-vis* feminism than any other male-stream social theories. This is not simply a rhetorical point: there is evidence for it in the superior performance of workers parties, even of the most reformist nature, on issues affecting women when compared to those of the bourgeoisie, and in the fact that some of the most important strategic discussions about the actual making of a non-sexist society take place through and around women and men who are Marxists, or Marxist-feminists. But these positive achievements are too small and partial in comparison with what is demand-ed by the reality of masculine domination and more must be done.

The challenge for Marxism is to help bring the so-called feminine values into the public sphere, and to help guide political life on that basis. Marxism must break from its Stalinist and masculinist heritage by learning to work with modalities of self-activity and self-organisation that take into account the gender division of labour in the working class and other oppressed social strata. There must be a conscious commitment on the part of Marxist men to take all appropriate means at all times to dismantle that division of labour, whether in mass campaigns and parties or in local politics, study groups and smaller political organisations. Through affirmative action in all political and social associations, we must all attempt to implement the inverse law of masculine domination: a greater presence for feminist women the more centralised the level. Men need to meet in workshops within all manner of political and social associations to discuss together the questions and problems they encounter in dealing with sexism and masculinism so that they can begin to hold *each other* accountable. This will set the precondition to their being able to set goals with women in what must be, at many crucial levels, a mutual battle to overcome masculine domination. And insofar as Marxist theory *per se* has a useful role to play in the longer and larger process of social transformation, Marxist men must begin to engage as seriously with feminist political theory as feminists have done with Marxist political theory. If we really do want to constitute forms of public coordination and cooperation which maximise the creative potential in both individuals and collectivities, Marxist men really must engage with feminism at all levels, to see what can be learned and changed, so that we can go forward together towards human liberation.

NOTES

1. Marx Centenary Conference, Department of Economics, University of Manitoba, March 12–15, 1983. For their special concentrated contributions of intellectual stimulation and practical help, I want warmly to thank Suzanne Findlay, Jackie Larkin and Pamela Walker. In addition, since this paper comes out of a long process of thought, discussion and practical work, I want also to thank Deirdre Gallagher, Roberta Hamilton, Meg Luxton, Heather-Jon Maroney, Wally Seccombe, and at a somewhat greater distance from my day-to-day life, Zillah Eisenstein and Nicole-Laurin Frenette, for the important contributions they have made over time to its production. Of course, I take sole responsibility for the contents of this paper.
2. The state is not the sole repository of the ruling apparatus. See Dorothy Smith, 'Women's Inequality in the Family', in Alan Moscovitch, ed., *Essays on the Political Economy and Social Welfare* (Toronto, University of Toronto Press, 1981); Zillah Eisenstein, *The Radical Future of Liberal Feminism* (New York, Longman, 1981).
3. See Ralph Miliband, *Marxism and Politics* (Oxford, Oxford University Press, 1977).
4. There is no one term which is satisfactory to describe all the societies in which

some sort of collectivisation of the means of production has occurred. But I do not agree with the term state capitalism, and certainly not with 'actually existing socialism'—transitional societies seems preferable to me.

5. See for example *Socialist Democracy*, Statement of the United Secretariat of the Fourth International (1979), available from: 2 rue Richard-Lenoir, 93108 Montreuil, France.

6. Sheila Rowbotham, 'The trouble with "patriarchy" ', and Sally Alexander and Barbara Taylor, 'In defense of "patriarchy" ', in Raphael Samuel, ed., *People's History and Socialist Theory* (London, Routledge and Kegan Paul, 1981); Joseph Interrante and Carol Lasser, 'Victims of the Very Songs They Sing: A Critique of Recent Work in Patriarchal Culture and the Social Construction of Gender', *Radical History Review* No. 20, Spring/Summer 1979; Barbara Ehrenreich and Deidre English, *For Her Own Good* (Garden City, Anchor, 1979), Introduction; Michèle Barrett, *Women's Oppression Today* (London, Verso, 1980); Lydia Sargent. *Women and Revolution* (London, South End Press, 1981).

7. Catherine Hall, 'Gender Division and Class Formation in the Birmingham Middle Class, 1780–1850', in Raphael Samuel, ed., op. cit.; Joseph Interrante and Carol Lasser, op. cit.; Dorothy Thompson, 'Women and Nineteenth Century Radical Politics', in Juliet Mitchell and Ann Oakley, eds., *The Rights and Wrongs of Women* (London, Penguin, 1976); Nicole Laurin-Frenette, 'The Women's Movement and the State', *Our Generation* Vol. 15, No. 2, Summer 1982; Meridith Jax, *The Rising of the Women* (New York, Monthly Review Press, 1980); see also Peggy Reeves Sanday, *Female Power and Male Domination* (London, Cambridge University Press, 1981) for an interesting approach to much earlier periods.

8. Michelle Zimbalist Rosaldo and Louise Lamphere, eds., *Women, Culture and Society* (Stanford, Stanford University Press, 1974); Rayna R. Reiter, *Toward An Anthropology of Women* (New York, Monthly Review Press, 1978); Margaret Benston, 'The Political Economy of Women's Liberation', *Monthly Review*, Vol. xxi, No. 4, September 1969; Rae Lesser Blumber, *Stratification: Socioeconomic and Sexual Inequality* (Milwaukee, W.C. Brown, 1978); Hugh Armstrong and Pat Armstrong, *The Double Ghetto* (Toronto, McClelland and Stewart, 1978); Annette Kuhn and Ann Marie Wolpe, *Feminism and Materialism* (London, Routledge and Kegan Paul, 1978); Meg Luxton, *More Than A Labour of Love* (Toronto, The Women's Press, 1980); Bonnie Fox, ed., *Hidden in the Household* (Toronto, The Women's Press, 1980); Mary O'Brien, *The Politics of Reproduction* (London, Routledge and Kegan Paul, 1981). Also see notes 7., 11. and 15. for additional material; and see note 43. for material dealing with women's labour in the transitional societies.

9. The term 'generic' was coined by Mary O'Brien, op. cit. It is used here and throughout to indicate the relations characteristic of gender-class. As expanded on below, and adapted from Ehrenreich and English, op. cit., the term 'patriarchy' will be used to refer to pre-industrial forms of masculine dominance and 'masculinism' to new ones characteristic of advanced industrial societies.

10. Frederick Engels, op. cit.

11. See Varda Burstyn, 'Economy, Sexuality and Politics: Engels and the Sexual Division of Labour', *Socialist Studies*, University of Manitoba, July 1983 (forthcoming) for a detailed analysis of Engels's text and an elaboration of the summarised interpretation given here.

12. Ibid.

13. Colin Turnbull, *Forest People* (Touchstone Books, 1968); Richard Lee, *The !Kung San* (Cambridge, Cambridge University Press, 1979); Patricia Draper, '!Kung Women, Contrast in Sexual Egalitarianism in Foraging and Sedentary

Contexts', Rayna Reiter, op. cit.; Peggy Reeves Sanday, op. cit.; Rae Lesser Blumberg, op. cit.; Stanley Diamond, *In Search of the Primitive* (New Brunswick, New Jersey, Transaction Books, 1974); Evelyn Reed, *Women's Evolution* (New York, Pathfinder Press, 1975); Elizabeth Fisher, *Women's Creation* (Garden City, Anchor Press Doubleday, 1975).

14. Rae Lesser Blumberg, op. cit., ch. 4 and 5.

15. See Nicole Laurin-Frenette, op. cit.; Christine Delphy, *The Main Enemy: A Materialist Analysis of Women's Oppression* (London, Women's Research and Resource Centre, 1977); Christine Delphy, 'Continuities and Discontinuities in Marriage and Divorce', in L. Barkett and S. Allen, eds., *Sexual Divisions and Society* (London, Tavistock) for an analysis of appropriation in late capitalist society; see also Dorothy Smith, op. cit., and Mary O'Brien, op. cit.

16. Varda Burstyn, op. cit.; Gayle Rubin, 'The Traffic in Women: Notes on the Political Economy of Sex', in Rayna R. Reiter, op. cit.; Gad Horowitz, *Repression* (Toronto, University of Toronto Press, 1977); Nancy Choderov, *The Reproduction of Mothering* (Berkeley, University of California Press, 1978); Dorothy Dinerstein, *The Mermaid and the Minotaur* (New York, Harper Colphon Books, 1976); see also Adrienne Rich, 'Compulsory Heterosexuality and Lesbian Existence', *Signs: A Journal of Woman in Culture and Society*, Summer 1980. Clearly this is not to say that homosexual practices have been treated identically in all genderic societies.

17. Gordon Rattray Taylor, *Sex in History* (New York, Harper and Row, 1970); Barbara Ehrenreich and Deirdre English, *Witches, Mid-Wives and Healers* (Boston, Feminist Press, 1972).

18. Cited in Greta Nemiroff, 'The Empowerment of Women', *Alternatives* (Oberlin College, Oberlin, Ohio, Spring 1982)

19. Margaret Stacey and Marion Price, *Women, Power and Politics* (London, Tavistock Publishers, 1981), ch. 3.

20. Exceptional women of the ruling economic-classes have at times played important roles in mature state formations. But in virtually all these cases we are either talking about women administering a masculine-dominated state in the interests of the men to whom they are affiliated by kin, class or ideology in most cases (up to and including M. Thatcher) or, as in the case of women like Theodora of Byzantium, of even rarer cases of women trying to use the state to ease women's lot—an attempt that has met with the same fate as the social democratic effort to use the capitalist state to better proletarian fortunes. Even in these cases, up to the twentieth century, these women's access to the machinery of state was determined by their masculine affiliation and not by their own rights.

21. For definitions of public and private in this context see Mary O'Brien, op. cit.; Stacey and Price, op. cit.; Eisenstein, op. cit.

22. Meg Luxton, op. cit.; Wally Seccombe, *Reproduction of Labour Power in Three Modes of Production* (working title; NLB, forthcoming).

23. Roberta Hamilton, *The Liberation of Women* (London, George, Allen and Unwin, 1978).

24. Rachel Harrison and Frank Mort, 'Patriarchal Aspects of Nineteenth Century State Formation: Property Relations, Marriage and Divorce, and Sexuality', in Philip Corrigan, ed., *Capitalism, State Formation and Marxist Theory* (London, Quartet Books, 1980).

25. Michèle Barrett, op. cit., p. 138.

26. Frederick Engels, op. cit.; Meg Luxton, 'Women, Work and Family', in Heather-Jon Maroney and Meg Luxton, eds., *The Political Economy of Women* (working title; Toronto, University of Toronto Press, forthcoming, 1984); Fraser Harrison,

op. cit.; Sheila Rowbotham, *Hidden from History* (London, Pluto Press, 1973); Sheila Rowbotham, *Woman, Resistance and Revolution* (London, Penguin, 1972); Sally Alexander, 'Women's Work in Nineteenth Century London, A Study of the Years 1820–1850', in Mitchell and Oakley, op. cit.

27. Fraser Harrison, op. cit.; Lori Rotenberg, 'The Wayward Worker: Toronto's Prostitutes at the Turn of the Century', in *Women at Work*, op. cit.

28. Michèle Barrett and Mary McIntosh, 'The "Family Wage": Some Problems for Socialist Feminists', *Capital and Class*, No. 11, 1980; Meg Luxton, op. cit.; see also Jane Hamphries, 'Class Struggle and the Persistence of the Working Class Family', *Cambridge Journal of Economics*, Vol. 1, No. 3, 1977 for another analysis of the family wage.

29. See for example Anna Davin, 'Imperialism and Motherhood', *History Workshop Journal* 5, Spring 1978.

30. A wide range of material is available on this question. See for example Andrew Rosen, *Rise Up, Women!* (London, Routledge and Kegan Paul, 1975); Eleanor Flexner, *Century of Struggle* (New York, Atheneum, 1971); Catherine Cleverdon, *The Woman Suffrage Movement in Canada* (Toronto, University of Toronto Press, 1950).

31. Denise Riley, 'The Free Mothers: Pronatalism and Working Mothers in Industry at the End of the Last War in Britain', *History Workshop Journal* 11, Spring 1981; Ceta Ramkhalawansingh, 'Women During the Great War', in *Women at Work*, op. cit.; Carol Hymonwitz and Michelle Wisson, *A History of Women in America* (New York, Bantam, 1978).

32. Betty Friedan, *The Feminine Mystique* (New York, Dell Books, 1963); Hymonwitz and Weisson, op. cit. For interesting discussions about the way in which this demobilisation was experienced (and aided) in one important area of cultural life in the US, see Molly Haskell, *From Reverence to Rape: The Treatment of Women in the Movies* (New York, Penguin Books, 1975), chapters 4 and 6; Marjorie Rosen, *Popcorn Venus: Women, Movies and the American Dream* (New York, Avon Books, 1974), chapters 3–6; Joan Mellen, *Big Bad Wolves: Masculinity in the American Film* (New York, Pantheon Books, 1977). A number of feminists have argued that this present wave of the women's movement has developed at least in part because its organising cadre are the daughters of their mothers' emotional and ideological revolt, which was absorbed along with and in contradiction to the renewed patriarchal and masculinist ideology of the fifties. I share this analysis of *ideological* roots.

33. This term is borrowed from Wally Seccombe, op. cit. For discussion of its collapse see Varda Burstyn, *Feminism in the Political Arena*, Part I (CBC Transcripts, Box 500, Station A, Toronto, Canada M5W 1E6); Zillah Eisenstein, op. cit.

34. Barbara Ehrenreich, *The Hearts of Men* (New York, Doubleday, 1983); Barbara Ehrenreich writes in *Ms.* (June 1983, Vol. xi, No. 12):

> Women's earnings average out to a little more than $10,000 a year each—nowhere near enough to support a single in a swinging lifestyle, much less a single mother and her children. For most women the obvious survival strategy has been to establish a claim on some man's more generous wage, i.e. to marry him. For men, on the other hand, as *Playboy*'s writers clearly saw, the reverse is true: not counting love, home-cooked meals, or other benefits of the married state, it makes more sense for a man to keep his paycheque for himself, rather than to share it with an underpaid or unemployed woman and her no doubt unemployed children. A recent study by Stanford University sociologist Lenore J. Weitzman suggests the magni-

tude of men and women's divergent interests—upon divorce, a woman's standard of living falls, on average, by 73% for the first year, while the standard of living for her ex-husband rises by 42%. For men, the alternative to marriage might be loneliness and TV dinners; for women, it is, all too often, poverty (pp. 14–15).

35. Varda Burstyn, 'Art and Censorship', *Parallelogram*, forthcoming Summer 1983; Varda Burstyn, 'Freedom, Sex and Power, 6', *Fuse*, Vol. 6, No. 5, January/February 1983; Varda Burstyn, 'Eroticism and Pornography', *Fuse*, Vol. 6, No. 2, April/May 1982; Varda Burstyn, 'Masculinity, Violence and Profit: A Look at the Mass Entertainment Media', *Canadian Women's Studies*, forthcoming Fall, 1983; Barbara Ehrenreich, *The Hearts of Men* (New York, Doubleday, 1983); see also Elizabeth Janeway, 'Incest, A New Look at the Oldest Taboo', and Judith Lewis Herman, 'Incest: Prevention is the Only Cure', *Ms.*, Vol. x, No. 5, November 1981; see also letters and editorials on incest in *Playboy* and *Penthouse*, 1980–83; on childhood sexuality see Gad Horowitz, op. cit. Dorothy Dinnerstein, op. cit.; see also Elizabeth Janeway, 'Who is Sylvia? On the Loss of Sexual Paradigms', and Irene Diamond, 'Pornography and Repression: A Reconsideration', in Catherine R. Stimpson and Ethel Spector Person, *Women, Sex and Sexuality* (Chicago, University of Chicago Press, 1980).

36. By the sex industry *per se,* I mean prostitution, massage parlours, gay and heterosexual gathering places (i.e. steam baths), live sex shows, peep shows, telephone fantasy services, pornography of the film, video, magazine and literary varieties, and sexual aids from lingerie to whips and chains. The commodification of sexuality is not restricted to these phenomena, but forms a part of many other (not directly sexual) enterprises.

37. This statement is made with the full knowledge that under the impetus of feminist union leaders and strong women's organising in important sectors of the trade-union movement, we have begun to see important instances of men workers striking and otherwise supporting the demands of women in their unions, and even, very occasionally, in other unions. The issues have ranged from equal pay to maternity leave to abortion to sexual harassment, and this support is perhaps the most heartening single feature of the beginnings of visible change within the male membership of mass movements and organisations. But these struggles are still few and far between. For each instance of support, we have far too many of indifference or resistance. For each time a complaint about sexual harassment is taken up by a union, we have hundreds, thousands of instances of harassment and assault on the streets, at work, in the home. Side by side with growing support for feminist demands we have the growth of the sex industries. For every initiative to win abortion rights, we have counter-initiatives to deny them again. And for every successful interpersonal struggle between a woman and a man to share the responsibility for domestic and emotional labour, we have—how can we even measure the number?—endless defeats: separations or a return to the sexist *status quo* being the most common variants. We would benefit very much from post-seventies studies showing the extent of masculine participation in domestic labour—perhaps a breakthrough invisible to my own eyes has occurred during this most important of all decades. But I doubt it. The victories in the paid workforce and in the home are certainly to be welcomed. But they are too scant to mask the saddening reality of continuing masculine dominance.

38. Nicole Laurin-Frenette, op. cit.; Elizabeth Wilson, *Women and the Welfare State* (London, Tavistock Publishers, 1977); Mary McIntosh, 'The State and the Oppression of Women', in Kuhn and Wolpe, op. cit.

39. Laurin-Frenette, op. cit.
40. Eisenstein, op. cit.
41. In June 1983, the New Democratic Party government of Manitoba presided over the violent police entry into an abortion clinic organised and supported by the Women's Movement, where doctors, nurses, and clients were all arrested. The Attorney General's Office is planning to press charges.
42. From 1970 to 1982 Suzanne Findlay worked in developing what was called 'the Woman's Programme' in the Department of the Secretary of State in Ottawa; she headed that programme and also served as Vice-President of the Advisory Council on the Status of Women—a body designed to advise cabinet on issues and policies of concern to women. In two unpublished papers she has taken an in-depth look at those experiences in terms both of existing political theory and its ability to account for the experience of feminism within the state and the lessons the women's movement and the Left need to draw from those and similar experiences. Suzanne Findlay, 'Lobbying Our Way to Revolution', 1982, and 'Struggles Within the State: The Feminist Challenge to Hegemony', 1983. That challenge, it should be noted, was unsuccessful, but her study of the ways in which the bureaucratic apparatus as such dealt with that challenge is most instructive. Both essays are being developed for Luxton and Maroney, eds., op. cit. (forthcoming 1984).
43. Dorothy Atkinson, Alexander Dallin and Gail Warshofsky Lapidus, *Women in Russia* (Stanford, Stanford University Press, 1977); Mikhail Stern, *Sex in the USSR* (New York, Times Books, 1979); The Women in Eastern Europe Group, ed., *Women and Russia* (London, Sheba Publishers, 1980); Gail Warshofsky Lapidus, *Women in Soviet Society* (Berkeley, University of California Press, 1978); Barbara Wolfe Jancar, *Women Under Communism* (Baltimore, Johns Hopkins University Press, 1978); Hilda Scott, *Women and Socialism* (London, Allison and Busby, 1976); Marilyn Boxer and Jean Quataert, *Socialist Women* (London, Eslevier, 1978); Vera Broido, *Apostles Into Feminists* (New York, Viking, 1977); Delia Davin, *Women-Work* (Oxford, Oxford University Press, 1976); Julia Kristeva, *About Chinese Women* (New York, Unizen Books, 1977); Agnes Smedley, *Portraits of Chinese Women in Revolution* (New York, The Feminist Press, 1976); Alena Heitlinger, *Women and State Socialism* (Montreal, McGill-Queen's University Press, 1979); Elizabeth Croce, *Feminism and Socialism in China* (New York, Schoken Books, 1978); Kate Curtin, *Women in China* (New York, Pathfinder Press, 1975); Elizabeth Croll, *The Women's Movement in China* (The Anglo-Chinese Educational Institute, 1974); Ruth Sidell, *Women and Child Care in China* (London, Penguin, 1972); Margaret Randall, *Cuban Women Now* (Toronto, Women's Press, 1974); Margaret Randall, *Sandino's Daughter* (London, Crossing Press, 1982); Lovenduski and Hills, op. cit.; see also Alexander Kollontai, *Marxisme et la revolution sexuelle* (Paris, Maspero, 1973); Leon Trotsky, *Women and the Family* (New York, Pathfinder, 1970); William Mandel, *Soviet Women* (New York, Anchor Books, 1975).
44. Wolchick and Lovenduski, in Hill and Lovenduski, op. cit.
45. For recent information on women in Eastern European and Soviet elites, see Lovenduski and Hill, op. cit., ch. 13; for China, see Barbara Wolfe Jancar, op. cit.
46. As the feminist saying goes, 'Women who strive for equality lack ambition'.
47. See Gail Warshofsky, op. cit.
48. Stern, op. cit.; The Women in Eastern Europe Group, op. cit.; Roman Laba, in a paper presented to the Marx Centennial Conference, March 1983, writes,

As in the rest of Eastern Europe, contraceptives and sanitary napkins are produced irregularly. In Poland such devices have been available only in special shops for the last few years. One unforgettable scene of the Solidarity movement was Solidarity and Politbureau member Zofia Glemp being taken to the factory bathroom by the Lodz textile workers who wanted to show her what they used during their menstrual periods. Although Poland had the 11th largest GNP in the world, such devices never made it into the plan. In their place is a very liberal abortion policy. Another aspect of the sexual politics is the disastrous housing situation. An average of 25 years waiting for an apartment. This situation has worsened since the crisis began in 1980. The Sex-Pol movement awaits a reincarnation in Eastern Europe.

49. Ernest Mandel, *Marxist Economic Theory* (London, Merlin Press, 1962).
50. These ideas were first developed in discussions with Judy Rebick in 1975.
51. In addition to Freud's work, see Wilhelm Reich, Herbert Marcuse, Gad Horowitz, Dorothy Dinnerstein, Nancy Choderow, and Juliet Mitchell. See also Mark Poster, *The Critical Theory of the Family* (New York, Seabury Press, 1978); Michael Schneider, *Neurosis and Civilization* (New York, Seabury Press, 1975). For a different approach to sexuality and politics, see Michel Foucault, *The History of Sexuality, Vol. I* (New York, Vintage Books, 1980).
52. The Women in Eastern Europe Group, op. cit.; Tatyana Mamanova, personal communications.
53. For a number of discussions on the 'instrumentality' of the state or lack of it, see, for example, Ralph Miliband, *Marxism and Politics* (Oxford, Oxford University Press, 1977); Nicos Poulantzas, *Political Power and Social Class* (London, Verso, 1978); Nicos Poulantzas, 'The Capitalist State: A Reply to Miliband and Laclau, *New Left Review* 95, January/February, 1976; Corrigan, op. cit.; Ernest Mandel, *Late Capitalism* (New York, Schoken, 1978).
54. Stacey and Price, op. cit.; Hill and Lavenduski, op. cit.
55. See Varda Burstyn, 'Feminism in the Political Arena', part II (CBC Transcripts, Box 500, Station A, Toronto, Ontario, M5W 1E6) for a detailed look at women and political parties in the United States, Canada and Britain; interviews with senior women party activists and parliamentarians, a discussion of party power structures, and other considerations of ways in which masculine programme formulation and norms of comportment and organisation express themselves *across* 'political' (read economic-class) lines from the Centre to the far Left.
56. Hill and Lovenduski, op. cit.; Burstyn, ibid.
57. Burstyn, ibid., Parts II and III, for a discussion of the case of Lise Payette, feminist ex-cabinet minister in the Parti Quebecois government, by her senior political adviser, Lorraine Goddard.
58. Hill and Lovendouski, op. cit.; Stacey and Price, op. cit.; Sheila Rowbotham, Hilary Wainwright and Lynn Segal, *Beyond the Fragments* (London, Merlin Press, 1979); Robin Morgan, 'Goodbye to All That', in *Going Too Far* (New York, Random House, 1977); Varda Burstyn, 'Towards a Socialist Party (Marxist-Feminist)', *Canadian Dimension*, Vol. 15, No. 4, February 1981; for a historical perspective see Dorothy Thompson, op. cit.; Alina Heitlinger, op. cit.; Meredith Fox, *The Rising of the Women* (New York, Monthly Review Press, 1980); Varda Burstyn, 'Feminism in the Political Arena', Part III, op. cit.
59. Burstyn, 'Feminism in the Political Arena', Part II.
60. Ibid., see also Suzanne Findlay, note 41.
61. Alina Heitlinger, op. cit., ch. 18.
62. Tatyana Mamonova and her feminist colleagues were threatened with arrest if they did not cease publication of *Women and Russia*. Some, like Mamonova, chose exile and ongoing solidarity work. Others remained in the USSR and

were harrassed, arrested and eventually imprisoned by the authorities. In Poland too, a group of feminists organised around Warsaw University in 1980–81 — and it too has since been disbanded. In East Germany, a group in Leipzig was also disbanded by the state and its members threatened and harrassed.

63. Livio Maitan, *Party, Army, Masses* (London, New Left Books, 1976).
64. Varda Burstyn, 'Feminism in the Political Arena', Part IV, op. cit.; Mary O'Brien, op. cit.; Dorothy Thompson, ed., *Over Our Dead Bodies* (London, Virago, 1983); Dorothy Dinnerstein, op. cit.; Jon Snodgrass, ed., *For Men Against Sexism* (Crossing Press, 1977).

THE LABOUR PARTY AND THE FUTURE OF THE LEFT

David Coates

In the months to come we will, no doubt, have to argue many times in public that the 1983 general election was not as significant a landslide as Margaret Thatcher will continue to claim. We will need to stress over and again that her popular vote actually fell, and that of those who voted, 57.6 per cent actually voted against her. We might even, to sustain ourselves in difficult times, explain away the Labour Party's dismal performance by remembering the treachery of a Callaghan, the disloyalty of a Chapple, even the vote-splitting impact of a perfidious Alliance. But there will be no getting away from the fact that the election constituted a massive defeat for the Left as a whole, a defeat from which we will have to recover, and a defeat whose origins lie deeper (and whose causes are more structural) than these easier explanations and rationalisations will allow. Indeed if the Left is to recover—if history is not to come on us once as tragedy and twice as farce—we had better be honest now: about the weakness of the Left as a whole; about the problems of the Labour Party in particular; and about the dangers which will face us if we do not draw very radical lessons indeed for strategy and policy from the Thatcherite victory and her 144 seat majority.

To do that, we must begin with the election result—a result which certainly indicated the severity of the crisis now facing the Labour Party as an institution. That party is an electoral body, pure and simple. Its solution to the classic dilemmas of socialist transition is, and always has been, straightforwardly parliamentary in focus. What the election result then indicates is the quite extraordinary extent to which the Labour Party is waning as an electoral force. The average vote per Labour candidate in June 1983 was lower than at any election since 1900. The Party's share of the vote is now lower than at any election since 1918. At under nine million, Labour's absolute vote is lower than at any election since 1935; and in both absolute and percentage terms, the Labour Party's grip on its electorate (which has diminished steadily since 1966, and 1966 apart, consistently since 1951) is now declining at an accelerated rate. The Left was quick to point out in 1979 that the Tories were creating an island of two nations—with their support strong in the South and weak in the North. But we must observe now that it is the Labour Party who in electoral terms are creating two nations. In 1983 the Party was virtually obliterated in the South—outside London, taking only three seats in the area south of the line from Bristol to the Wash. The Labour Party has now been driven back for electoral support into the industrial and urban heartlands of a decaying northern capitalism. It is true that a tiny bedrock of Labour support remains in the South; but its job there is not to win seats but to save deposits, and the arrival of the Alliance has made even that problematic.

Even in the industrial heartlands of northern Britain, the Labour Party is now being challenged by an Alliance vote which has already cost it seats and deposits on an unprecedented scale. In June Labour lost 119 deposits, and came either first or second in only 341 of the 650 seats. Yet it is not enough to blame the Alliance for splitting the progressive vote, tempting as that is in the immediate aftermath of defeat. The Liberals levelled that criticism against Labour itself only three generations ago, and still Labour rose apace. For there is nothing to suggest that the problem of the Alliance will go away. On the contrary, it will stay and no doubt grow, and it will do so because it feeds on widespread electoral scepticism not just about Thatcherism but about Labour too.

Labour's problem (in places like Oxford East and Birmingham North-field no less than in Nottingham and London) is that significant sections of its traditional electorate are sceptical about the ability of the Labour Party to solve unemployment, and are fearful of Labour Party radicalism on defence, Europe and industry. The problem the Labour Party has, in simple electoral terms, is that it faces a population strongly influenced by media presentations of its personalities and policies, and by one easily swayed by Opposition parties that are understandably quick to exploit that media to draw attention to Labour's internal difficulties. It faces an electorate too with sufficient political memory to recall both the failure of Labour Governments in the past and the bitterness of inner-party wrangling to which those failures gave rise. And it faces an electorate large sections of which are profoundly conservative, jingoistic, sexist and racist in their attitudes and practices. Tragic as it is, such an electorate responds more easily to the jingoism and tough-minded realism of an Iron Lady than to the compassionate intellectualism of an old Liberal-Radical; and certainly in 1983 the Labour Party found no solution to electoral in-difference, no matter how hard it fudged its internal disagreements and no matter how far it softened the radicalism of its appeal.

Those outside the Labour Party and to its Left might draw some sectarian comfort from at least part of this. But we delude ourselves if we think that this kind of defeat opens an easy route to political realignment and mass radicalisation on the contemporary Left. It does not. The 1983 election result was not just a defeat for the Labour Party. It was a massive victory for the Right, and we are all going to have to live with the conse-quences of that. We certainly face new government attacks on trade-union rights, on civil liberties and on the position of women. We can certainly expect further significant erosions of welfare provision, rising unemployment and the systematic export of industrial capital. We can certainly expect the arrival of Cruise missiles, and a toughening of police and court handling of civil disobedience in the peace campaign. The Left in general is now definitely on the defensive, facing a government confirmed in its reactionary face by the size of its majority in parliament, and underpinned by its own success as an ideological, even hegemonic, force. There may not be a popular majority for every detail of Thatcherism. Indeed, particularly in the area of welfare provision, there is not; and support for her whole project may well decline as we move out of the middle class proper into the manual working class and the proletarianised and unionised sections of white collar employment. But the ideological sweep of Thatcherism cuts both wide and deep. It cuts wide—in that it sustains a generalised sense of helplessness, inevitability and the absence of an alternative—in strata and classes uncommitted to it. And it cuts deep, because Thatcher's own class allies gain in stridency, self-righteousness and confidence from the size of her electoral victory. The balance of class forces has been shifted, as Thatcher is committed to shifting it, decisively against the Left by four years of recession and by a parliamentary landslide; and the job of the Left is to push that balance back and to stem the tide.

Put that way, it is possible to situate the Labour Party and its problems where they should properly be—on the terrain of class and popular-democratic struggle as a whole, and not just in the arena of parliamentary debate and posturing. At its most obvious, what the election defeat does is to render the Labour Party at national level largely *irrelevant* to the struggles against Thatcherism over the next three or four years (or even indeed over the next seven or eight, given the scale of the electoral swing now required to put Labour back in power at Westminster). In these circumstances the centre of gravity of struggle and resistance must and will shift, to the factories, communities and streets where the daily reality of Tory reaction is experienced and lived. That in its turn will oblige the Labour Party to clarify its policies in relation to these struggles, and not— as in the previous eighteen months—to insist that those struggles subordinate themselves to the emerging rhythm of Labour Party electioneering. One question to be put to the Labour Party, therefore, and something to be discussed in detail a little later, is what the Party's attitude to, and involvement in, these inevitable struggles is going to be. The peace campaign will be its first test here, but it will not be its last. For as, and to the degree to which, industrial recession eases, working-class self-confidence will and must grow again, and the industrial struggle for jobs and wages will be renewed with greater vigour. One test for the Labour Party, and one crucial question facing the Left as a whole, will be its ability to mobilise around those struggles: to give support even to isolated pockets of resistance, to assist in the building of strong working-class industrial organisation, and to link activists in industry and civil society across their separate issue-areas, in an emerging coalition of protest *outside* parliament against Thatcherite excess orchestrated from within.

For even in electoral terms there is a strong Left constituency in this country to be tapped and developed. It is too early yet to give a detailed breakdown on the 1983 vote, and in fact the detail—though intriguing—will probably be less important than the general relationships it will doubtless confirm. For we know already of the existence of well-established left-wing audiences. The peace movement and the women's movement constitute two such: each drawing disproportionately on a middle-class Left entrenched in the bureaucratic structures of the welfare state, and each peopled too by a slightly younger generation of a similar kind, often the product of higher and further education, a generation now largely excluded even from welfare employment and driven back instead into the artisan economy, into domestic production, and into the reserve army of labour. In addition we know of the existence of an activist layer in the trade-union movement, in both the manual and white collar proletariats of Late Capitalism, an activist layer whose members dominate Constituency Labour Parties and who reappear on other nights of the week in peace meetings, union branches and women's caucuses. (It is these people, after all, who most of all aren't deterred from politics by Oscar Wilde's famous complaint that socialism would take a terrible toll of one's evenings.) We know too of the existence of a layer of black activists, and of the potential mass anger of entire ethnic communities locked into urban poverty by racial oppression and capitalist crisis. And we know also of the existence across the working class as a whole not of Thatcherite mendacity but of a mixture of conservative and radical attitudes, an amalgam of ruling-class orthodoxies and anti-system values, there to be burst apart and recast in a left-wing form by a socialist movement as hegemonic in its impact as Thatcher has been since 1979.

It is true that all is not well for the Left in this its traditional constituency, and that the Labour vote slipped more seriously here than anywhere else in 1983. More skilled manual workers voted Tory than voted Labour this time; and even among trade unionists, the Labour vote was apparently only 39 per cent. An overall manual working-class vote of 38 per cent is poor even by recent standards, but is indicative nonetheless of a bedrock of Labour support in the traditional proletariat which Thatcherism has not yet managed to penetrate. The Labour vote held up best—and even then not too well—among council house tenants, ethnic minorities and pensioners; and this reminds us that in other crucial groups (the young unemployed, the less organised sections of the manual working class, women isolated in domestic production, and technicians and lower management) left-wing views are dangerously absent. Yet the very listing of these constituencies gives a first indication of the character and scale of the task ahead for the Left as a whole: and by the Left here I mean not just socialists within the Labour Party, but also the non-aligned Left within the peace and women's movement, and the revolutionary Left most notably in the SWP. It is to aid, encourage, defend and build upon the extra-parliamentary struggles that these groups wage against Thatcherism in its second term, to link together our existing constituencies in common support and struggle, and to consolidate among them a renewed commitment to a democratic socialist alternative which can then be extended out into uncharted social strata whose perspectives now are dominated by cynicism, apathy or Thatcherite dross. That task is, of course, a truly enormous one, but is set for us by the character of the recession and its resulting ruling-class strategy embodied in Thatcherism. What the election result then does in addition is to raise again the question of where the Labour Party fits into such a scenario of extra-parliamentary resistance, left-wing consolidation and potential political radicalisation.

II

The answer to that question is that, unless things inside the Labour Party change dramatically, then it will hardly figure at all. It is already clear that the major response at leadership level within the Labour Party to the 1983 defeat will be grotesquely inadequate. The disease of the Bourbons is rampant again in Parliamentary Labour Party (PLP) circles—an inability to learn anything, to see anything, to break free of the past. Take the Right and Centre of the Labour Party for example. They will, and already are, blaming the defeat on the radicalism of the programme and the assertiveness of the Left, and are hard at it trying to pull the Party's policy commitments back to levels acceptable to the editor of *The Sun* and to their own well-established identification with the logic of private capital accumulation and US imperialism. In response to them, the re-action of the 'soft Left' is even more tragic. The Left is presumably well used to watching Terry Duffy in retreat; but to see Neil Kinnock reducing major political and strategic problems to a series of merely technical issues is particularly galling. He, and others like him, are already saying that the election defeat occurred, not because the programme was too radical, but because the party did not get the message across to its people. For the soft Left, in this age of Saatchi and Saatchi, presentation is all; and they would have us believe that a further debacle can be avoided if more charismatic and articulate leadership is forthcoming, and if the Party can avoid the kind of internal wrangling that put that programme together after 1979. Long experienced in putting the class struggle off until after the next election, the soft Left is now all for putting the party struggle off too; and is joining its Right and Centre 'partners' in the 'broad church' of the Labour coalition in planning to start the *politics of fudge* even earlier this time than is normal in Left Labour circles.

For Kinnock stands in a long tradition of Left Labourism. It is a tradition that, when dealing with questions of tactics and programme within the Labour Party, invariably moves from a correct premise to a false conclusion. It invariably begins with the correct observation that divisions within the party coalition will cost votes if they persist, only to go on to draw the same mistaken conclusion that it is the division and not the coalition which is the problem. Instead of deducing from that premise the recognition that the Labour coalition is too wide to be useful to the Left, that Callaghan and Chapple are not actually on our side, they deduce instead that the problem lies in the fact of public division. If first utterances after the election are any guide, the soft Left is poised to begin even earlier this time a process at which down the years they have become particularly adept, namely that of building a specious unity across the gaping chasms of party division by the generation of clever verbal formulae and the incremental surrender of radical positions. That was always a ludicrous and ultimately tragic process; but if it happens this time it will be close to criminal. For if the 1983 election result proves anything, it is that the politics of fudge have had their day, that there is no longer a constituency to be impressed and held together by the verbal uniting of incompatibles, and that the depth of division that now exists in the Labour Party is sufficiently well known to make 'fudging' so unpopular, so lacking in credibility, as to *cost* the party large numbers of votes. And this is true in spite of the fact that we can now expect Fleet Street to change its line on the Labour Party completely, no longer bewailing its divisions but instead praising the range and diversity of the views represented within its tolerant ranks. It is time for the Left to stop listening to the press, who are not its friends, and to examine instead the difficulties created for its project by trying to hold that cumbersome coalition together.

The attempt to hold the coalition together under Centre-Left leadership can be expected to be self-defeating in two related but different ways. It will fail first because the loyalty of the Right to any programme shaped by left-wing pressure will inevitably and necessarily snap, and in consequence will discredit the unity attempt as a whole in the eyes of the electorate, just when it matters most—in the run up to the general election. Of course the public intervention this time by Jim Callaghan may be dismissable as the product of an old man's bile. But bile is not the party's only problem. The fact that right-wing dissatisfaction surfaced when it did also reflected the incapacity of paper formulae to remove *real* and *profound* disagreements of a basic kind within the party. Those disagreements have always been there, but are made more acute now by the way in which the current crisis in Late Capitalism is also a crisis of social democracy—a crisis of that Keynesian corporatism around which hitherto some apparently credible party unity could be constituted. In years gone by, and when the Right ran the Labour Party, left-wing dissension— though exploited by the Tories to their electoral advantage—was containable and cost few votes because the Left remained marginalised both in the PLP and the country. But with the Left more dominant in the formation of party policy, an enormous gap opens up between the preoccupations of the activists and the attitudes of the electorate as a whole. This is a gap which the Labour Left's weakness outside the party precludes them from bridging; and it is a gap which, as a result, inspires the Right to speak out against the programme as part of their struggle to roll back the Left. The result, of course, is a visible plethora of Labour Party positions laid before the voters, a range of disagreements then picked up and amplified by an unsympathetic media and a hostile set of Opposition politicians, and a range of disagreement which, by its very existence and regardless of its content, drives many voters away from a party which seems too split to govern itself, let alone anybody else.

In seeking to hold together a coalition containing disagreements of that severity, any Centre-Left leadership of the Labour Party in the 1980s will also experience a second blockage on its project—a second impediment even to successful electioneering, let alone to any formation of mass enthusiasm for socialist transformation—a blockage which arises from the necessary inability of that leadership to present the socialist case with sufficient conviction. For Thatcherism's sweep through the popular consciousness is not just a product of good advertising. It has happened only because the general credibility of old style social democracy—of Keynesianism plus welfare corporatism—has been eroded by two long spells of unsuccessful Labour government. And it has happened too because the Labour Party's own reassessment of where its programme should go as a result has been insufficiently radical in its content, insufficiently explanatory in its presentation, and insufficiently honest about the failures of the past—*and necessarily so.* Tony Benn apart perhaps, few leading Labour politicians have been able publicly to break with their own past. They have all had a collective interest in presenting their new policy as but an incremental outgrowth of their old—and that has never been a very credible posture, alienating left-wing voters by suggesting that old habits will in practice die hard, and alienating right-wing ones by implying that the radical new Labour Party is just posed to repeat the disasters of the old one.

Worse than that, the Left in particular within the Labour Party has a real problem in presenting its radical programme with sufficient clarity and enthusiasm to undo the damage of the past and to win sizeable numbers of new converts. For radical programmes need a lot of explaining. They require honesty about past failures. They require detail on what is now to be done, and why more moderate policies will no longer suffice. They require a clear specification of the problems any Left policy will necessarily encounter, any likely oppositions that will arise, and some indication of how those problems and oppositions will be handled. Such honesty is particularly vital too because the radicalism of the programme will leave the Party open to accusations of communism and totalitarianism, accusations whipped up into frenzy by a Tory press able to capitalise on 30 years of Cold War ideology in the popular consciousness, and accusations that have a particularly potent impact on the undecided voter when defence is itself one of the major areas of the new radicalism. In these circumstances it is not enough to reduce Trident to a question of costs, to fudge on Polaris, and to try to sell membership of NATO as compatible with unilateralism. In those circumstances only an honest, regular and full confrontation with the whole set of assumptions and practices of the Cold War can begin to erode the basis in popular consciousness on which the Tory smear tactics of 'gambling with the nation's defences' are so solidly grounded.

But it is just that kind of argument that the Labour Left cannot put in the name of the Labour Party as a whole if it wishes to keep its unity with the Labour Right and Centre. To do so would be to break decisively (and hence to criticise explicitly) the role of the Labour Party itself as the major post-war architect of that very system of alliances, and to jeopardise the ability of a Healey or a Callaghan to remain in the Labour Party at all. The capacity of the Labour Party under Centre-Left leadership to roll back Tory hegemony in an area as vital as defence is thus eroded from the outset, because so much of the Labour coalition is at best a reluctant and silent partner in the new radicalism and at worst actually agrees with Thatcher and the Alliance on the question of Russian expansionism. In such circumstances, to speak out clearly is to threaten the unity of the whole coalition. Yet to be silent is to lose the case by default, and to see the electorate remain sceptical of, or even hostile to, Labour radicalism as Tory propaganda and 30 years of Cold War rhetoric take their inevitable toll. It is also to see the radical constituency beyond the Labour Party grow in despair and disillusionment at the shilly-shallying and backsliding of Labour leaders who were thought to be on our side. As a strategy for winning votes, the politics of fudge got the worst of all worlds in 1983. It didn't stop disunity. It didn't protect even existing levels of Labour voting; and it seriously alienated sections of an already mobilised Left (not least in the peace movement). And now we find that the Labour Left, if Neil Kinnock has his way, is going to start that fudging all over again. But what Kinnock and others like him do not seem to realise is that to unite the Labour Party now on the terms set by Hattersley and Healey will not so much prevent a repetition of 1983 in 1988 as guarantee its certainty.

III

For what the Left actually has to do, if it is ever to win a popular majority again, is not something that the Labour Party can do without driving significant sections of the Labour Party off to the Alliance where they belong. What it has to do is to establish a very different relationship with its entire electorate than that possible or conventional under social democratic parliamentarianism. The politics of the Labour Party hitherto have been the politics of the *carpetbagger*. Wholly preoccupied with the electoral battle, the Labour Party has offered no extra-parliamentary leadership to, or indeed support for, a whole range of struggles that go on outside parliament and between elections. Instead, as a machine and as a presence at grass roots level, it has lain dormant between elections, only to swing into frenetic activity in the three or four weeks before voting is to occur. In those moments it has insisted—always by implication and often quite explicitly—that everything else be put on one side, and that the whole task of the Left be turned into door-knocking and vote catching. Of course the very fact that the Labour Party in the vast majority of constituencies hasn't crossed any door steps since the last election tends to mean that fewer doors open to it, and that doors open to it with increasing indifference, except in circumstances of Tory crisis that the Labour Party can do little itself to precipitate. Not surprisingly then, Labour majorities when they come tend to be accidental rather than created, and invariably prove to be as tenuous as they are fortuitous. And as they slip away, the growing resistance met by canvassers on the door seems only to encourage Labour's inveterate door knockers to knock even more frenetically, as though a better canvassing *technique* could resolve what in fact is a profound *political* weakness in the whole Labour Party strategy.

Door knocking can be a party's main form of contact with its potential constituency only if that party is set on building an inherently intermitent, passive and instrumental relationship with its base. Such a relationship is ideal for conservative parties bent on consolidating mass loyalty to the prevailing order whilst seeking to discourage any mass active participation within it. But it is useless for socialist parties seeking to radicalise a mass base for participation in qualitative social change. The Labour Party down the years has not tried systematically to build a socialist counter-culture around its people. Instead it has left hegemonic politics to its opponents, and then has dashed in periodically to see if its supporters have managed to stay loyal in spite of all the Tory pressures working upon them. Not surprisingly it has found that, in its absence, its electorate, if still loyal at all, has drifted steadily away to the Right. Instead of building a socialist connection with its base, the Labour Party has simply offered itself as a *better* kind of system manager, better at getting economic growth, better at providing national strength, industrial competitiveness and so on. It has even restricted its vocabulary, and its criteria of success and failure, to those given to it by its Tory opponents. Labour's presentation of the 'national interest' is not qualitatively different from that of the Conservatives. Its commitment to a world role within the US alliance is as great as theirs. Its identification with the whole paraphenalia of the modern capitalist state and its dominant symbols (from the monarchy to parliament) is just the same as the pro-capitalist parties it faces across the Despatch Box. And like them, the Labour Party has repeatedly invited its electorate to judge its performance against these conservative criteria: and of course they have, to the Party's immense cost. For its discovery repeatedly in government that you cannot run and reform capitalism at the same time, and that a weak British capitalism cannot be revived by shifting power away from capital to labour, has cost it dear in votes. Having claimed so much and delivered so little, and having consolidated only a voting relationship with its base that invited a purely instrumental reaction to that pattern of failure, the Party has seen its vote drift away, with only itself to blame.

For we are now, and we will remain, in a deep capitalist crisis of a very special kind. Since that crisis is world wide, we can expect no easing of foreign competition. Since it is a crisis of state spending as well as of private profit, we can expect no Keynesian solution. Since it is a crisis of accumulation and not just of realisation, we can expect no industrial recovery without severe curtailments of union rights and welfare provision. And since the British experience of that crisis is so acute, we can expect too that the attack on the working class here will be particularly great. In that context, and with the Alliance here to stay in some form, the Labour Party has no choice but to offer a *radical* programme if it is to avoid slipping away into political oblivion. And if it is to sustain that radicalism effectively, it has to find new ways of penetrating the popular consciousness, and of rolling back powerful tides of Conservative propaganda and prejudice. The intellectual filth of British imperialism has to be cleaned off the beaches of the British mind. Speeches alone will not do that, however charismatic the speaker. Only a party that is capable of building *organic* links with its class base will have a chance of consolidating institutions, attitudes and practices across the entire working class (old and new, manual and white collar) that can act as an effective shield against right-wing pressure; and that organic link can only come through the immersion of the Labour Party, on a daily basis, in the extraparliamentary struggles of its people.

The Labour Party linkage with its base is now so thin that such an organic connection has not so much to be consolidated as created afresh. The Labour Party will not be able to make that fresh connection unless it is willing also to make a qualitative and unambiguously distinct break with the defining features of its whole politics hitherto. The odds against it making that break are, of course, enormous; but at least the break that is now required is starkly obvious. If the Party is ever to build an organic link with its people, if it is ever to make a major contribution to the creation of a mass movement for socialist change in Britain, and if it is ever to re-establish its credibility as a serious political alternative in the eyes of the working class as a whole, it has to throw itself unambiguously into the support and encouragement of factory occupations, peace campaigns, black struggles and women's resistance. It has to so immerse itself in the daily lives of the people it would represent that it will be in a position to recast its policies in ways that link the immediate preoccupations of the dispossessed with the longer term process of shifting class power on a permanent basis. It has to open discussions with its *real* allies—in the movements already in existence to its left and with the revolutionary socialist current—on ways of working together to consolidate a new broad alliance of radical forces. And it has to resist with enthusiasm the hysterical opposition that this will provoke from the Tory press and the Party's own right wing, and live with the internal party divisions and short-term electoral costs that such a radicalisation of its whole politics will involve.

Of course, such a strategy will require enormous courage and extremely strong nerves, for in the short term the Labour Party will look significantly weaker, and the Alliance stronger, as the Right and Centre of the Party defect. But the Labour Party is now so weak that even the short-term costs of such a realignment are not as real as they once appeared. On the contrary, the old argument of the Right (that the party must tailor its policies to the existing preoccupations of the people, because that alone was the route through which a Labour Government could be returned to end the ravages of Toryism) must now be turned back against it. The electoral route to power through policy-moderation is now blocked by the Alliance, and is no longer a short-term solution when Margaret Thatcher has a majority of 144. Nor will the local government enclaves of Left Labourism in London and Sheffield survive easily the attacks now planned upon them by the Thatcher government. In these circumstances, the only effective defence against Tory ravages this side of 1988 will come from the extra-parliamentary struggles waged by workers, ethnic minorities, peace movements and the like; so that if the Right is genuine in its commitment to the protection of its people, it is in those campaigns that it too will immerse itself. The Right will not do that of course, and if left-wing forces inside the Labour Party insist on trying, the internal battles will be fierce, and temporarily costly for *all* the parties involved. But the price will be worthwhile if a clear realignment on the Left is the outcome. For we cannot avoid the fact that realignments of this order do take time. Time however is the one commodity which, after 9 June, the Labour Party now has in abundance. The Labour Party is no longer so close to electoral victory that it needs to worry over-much about short-term marginal adjustments in its popular standing. A 12.8 per cent swing takes one hell of a lot of getting. Far from offering the Labour Party the prospect of political power even in the medium term, the election of 1983 has really put a much more basic strategic choice before the Party: either to go for a new form of politics altogether, or to dwindle away into an even paler shadow of its always inadequate former self.

Now the Labour Party, sadly, is very good at dwindling away; and the odds are that the soft Left's propensity for the politics of fudge will prevent it from undertaking the kinds of changes required. It is much more likely that the bulk of the Labour Left leadership in parliament—no matter who leads the party—will continue to preach the virtues of party unity, will 'hang on in' with the Healeys and the Hattersleys of this world, and will peddle again a programme of radicalised Keynesianism, a sort of Wilsonian modernisation programme Mark II, with appropriate left-wing rhetoric. The fact that such a programme is unlikely to be electorally convincing, and that it would be wholly ineffective if ever applied, is not likely to stop the powerful party pressures for unity from winning the day. And if unity comes on those terms—and it can come on no other given the intransigence of the Labour Party's Right and Centre—then we can guarantee plenty of repetitions of past failures in the years to come— repetitions, that is, not just of 1983, but of the disasters of 1974-9 as well.

However, I suppose this is still just an open question, one for socialists in the Labour Party to explore in the months ahead. Now is the moment for socialists to test the true credentials of the Labour Party against the scale and character of the task before us. For out of the ashes of this enormous defeat we have to consolidate a new Left, by bringing together— first in campaigns of common action and mutual support, and later in a formal political coalition—the three currents of socialist activism that now exist. Two of those are already in place: the revolutionary Left, and the non-aligned Left in the unions, CND and the women's movement. The time of choice for the third—for socialists in the Labour Party—has been brought forward by the result on 9 June. If the Labour Party can be persuaded quickly to make a sharp break with its own past, then socialists within the Labour Party will be able to deliver a vital component to that new grouping on the Left. But if, as seems more likely, the politics of fudge predominate again, then socialists will have to leave the Party and take on the undeniably more difficult task of consolidating a new Left that has no official Labour Party presence within it at all. The future of the Left lies in the consolidation of a new strength outside parliament. The question for socialists inside the Labour Party, now more acutely than ever, is whether and how they can participate in that consolidation, and how they can avoid being drawn instead into yet another attempt to bolster the bankrupt electoral politics of old-style Labourism.

The arguments in this paper derive from, and are developed further in, chapters by Gordon Johnston, Robert Looker and myself in volume 2 of A Socialist Primer *(published by Martin Robertson under the title* Socialist Strategies*). Earlier drafts of this paper were discussed with John Kelly's students at the LSE, and with Gordon, Bob, John Charlton and Ralph Miliband. Arthur Lipow, Sue Thomson, Lewis Minkin, Morris Szeftel and David Beetham also commented on, and often disagreed quite sharply with, an earlier draft. So I must stress that responsibility for the final version is mine alone.*

SOCIALIST ADVANCE IN BRITAIN*

Ralph Miliband

To speak of socialist advance in Britain a short time after the General Election of June 1983 may seem rather strange. For the election was a major defeat not only for the Labour Party but for all socialist forces; and while that defeat may eventually turn out to have had beneficial political effects, in that it may help to break the mould in which the labour movement has long been imprisoned, such a blessing is hypothetical whereas the immediate effects of Labour's defeat are very tangible. The election results have conferred a new legitimacy upon an exceptionally reactionary Conservative government; and they have also served to demoralise further a movement that was already in bad shape well before the election. It may be said—and indeed it should be said—that the Conservative Government only obtained 30.8 per cent of the total vote and 42.2 per cent of those who voted; and that its vote was less than in 1979. But the system is designed to put the main emphasis on the number of seats won rather than on votes cast; and the fact that the Government obtained a majority of 144 seats in the House of Commons makes it possible for it to claim, however spuriously, that it has a 'mandate' for the policies it chooses to put forward.

The extent of Labour's defeat has another long-term consequence which is clearly important, namely that it would require a net gain of well over 100 seats for Labour and a swing from Conservative to Labour of over 12 per cent to bring about a majority Labour Government. This kind of swing (to the Conservatives) has only occurred once in this century, in the exceptional circumstances of 1931, when a former Labour Prime Minister, Ramsay Macdonald, was leading what was in effect a Conservative coalition against the Labour Party. It is useless to speculate on how things will turn out in a General Election which is some years off: but it is nevertheless reasonable to believe that the extent of Labour's defeat, leaving aside all other detrimental factors, greatly reduces Labour's chances of being able to form a majority government for many years to come.

What adds further to the demoralisation of defeat is that the election

*This is a much-revised version of the Second Fred Tonge Memorial Lecture given under the auspices of the Holborn & St Pancras Constituency Labour Party on 29 June 1983. I am grateful to Monty Johnstone and John Saville for their comments on an early version of the article.

results—as is agreed by everybody in the labour movement right, left and centre—are not the product of some extraordinary set of events whose impact will soon be dissipated, at which point the Labour Party will be restored to its former vigour, but rather the most dramatic manifestation of a deep-seated, long-term crisis, for which no immediate remedy is at hand. My purpose here is to discuss the nature of this crisis, in the light of Labour's election defeat; and to link this with the problem of socialist advance in Britain.

Of all the reasons which have been advanced for Labour's defeat, two have obtained the most currency. One of these is that changes in the composition and character of the working class have been such as to erode drastically the support which the Labour Party might expect from its 'natural' constituency; and the other one is that the Labour Party present-ed the image of a party so deeply divided as to inspire no confidence in its capacity to govern. Other reasons which have found favour include the lack of credibility of much of Labour's electoral programme; the dangerously 'extreme' nature of some of its proposals, notably on defence; the mismanagement of the election campaign, to which may be linked the personality of Michael Foot; the 'Falklands factor'; and so on. But it is upon the changes in the character and composition of the working class on the one hand, and the divisions in the Labour Party on the other, that most attention has come to be focused. I will argue that the first of these explanations is misconceived; and that the second is inadequate because it does not explain why divisions, which are nothing new in the Labour Party, have been so much more significant, intractable and damaging than in the past.

It is perfectly true that the Labour Party has suffered a steady loss of electoral support since its peak achievement of nearly fourteen million votes in the General Election of 1951, with 48.8 per cent of the votes cast. By 1983, this had fallen to 27.6 per cent, the lowest percentage share of Labour's vote since 1918, when the Labour Party did not contest over one third of the seats. In 1951, the Labour Party also had an individual membership of around a million: by the early eighties this had dropped to not much more than a quarter of that figure.

It should first be said about the explanations which have found most favour to account for this loss of support that they have a strong ideo-logical purpose: for thirty years now, a shoddy sociology has been invoked by anti-socialist politicians and commentators in the Labour Party and outside as part of an endeavour to rid the Labour Party of those of its commitments which ran counter to their own 'moderate' positions. A certain code language has grown up over the years to obscure the nature of these endeavours. After Labour had lost office in 1951, despite its remarkable electoral performance, it was widely said that the Labour Party must 'rethink' its policies—and who could be against 'rethinking'? After the electoral defeats of 1955 and 1959, it was widely said that the trouble with the Labour Party was that it was saddled with commitments that belonged to an earlier age, and that it must come to terms with a new 'age of affluence': Labour *must* lose, so long as it refused to renew its image and its message, meaning that it must shed what formal socialist commitments it had. After the defeat of 1983, it has been said that the Labour Party must 'learn to listen' to what 'ordinary' people were saying— and who could be so unreasonable as to refuse to listen? When all the verbiage and coded language is cast aside, however, what is left is the insistence that the Labour Party must dilute its policies and programmes, and adopt more 'moderate' positions. This was the whole burden of the battle which Hugh Gaitskell waged in the fifties to change the Labour Party, to 'adapt it to the modern age', to 'bring it up to date', and so forth. The attempt focused on Clause Four of the Labour Party Constitution: unless there was a clear repudiation of this preposterous commitment to nationalise everything in sight, including street corner shops and garages, it was said, the Labour Party was doomed to electoral disaster and annihilation. The attempt failed. Clause Four remained in the Party Constitution (with as little effect as ever before); and notwithstanding the 'age of affluence' which was supposed to have anesthetised the working class, Labour won the election of 1964 on a platform not markedly less 'radical' than previous ones; and it went on to win the election of 1966 with a majority of 97 seats. Nor did the 'radicalism' of Labour's electoral platform in February 1974, with its pledge to bring about 'a fundamental and irreversible·shift in the balance of power and wealth in favour of working people and their families' prevent Labour from winning the election then, or the one in October of that year, again with a much increased majority.

Nothing of this is to suggest that the fact of decline in popular support is not very real: it is simply to note that explanations for it usually advanced by anti-socialist commentators are highly suspect and an intrinsic part of the battle which has been waged against the Left in the Labour Party and outside ever since World War Two—indeed ever since the Labour Party came into being. So too has it been waged since Labour's electoral defeat of May 1979. Once again, it has been said from many quarters that the working class, in so far as it could still be thought of as a class at all, was no longer what it was, and could not be expected to support a Labour Party which obstinately refused to come to terms with these changes (read: 'refused to dilute its policies').

Here too, the point is not to deny that changes in the working class have occurred. 'Traditional' occupations and industrial production have declined, and their decline has been accelerated by the Conservative

Government's policies; white collar and public service employment has grown and those engaged in it form a larger proportion of the working class than heretofore. It is also possible, but by no means certain in the light of the history of the working class, that 'sectionalism' has grown; and it is unquestionably true that unemployment and the fear of unemployment have reduced the willingness of many workers to engage in strike action. The question, however, is what impact these and other changes in the working class may have on its political attitudes and allegiances; and it is here that instant sociology turns into special pleading and bad faith.

To begin with, a very large fact needs to be recalled about the political attitudes of the working class, namely that a very substantial part of it has never supported Labour at all, even in the inter-war years of depression, mass unemployment, the Means Test and Tory retrenchment. Instant sociology often seems to imply that there was a time of depression and poverty when the working class *of course* supported Labour: but that in the age of affluence, of home ownership (a new favourite in the explanation of working-class 'de-radicalisation'), a car in every garage, consumerism, video cassettes and holidays in Spain, no such automatic support could be expected. This conveniently overlooks the fact that, even if one leaves out all general elections from 1918 to 1935, when the Tory and Liberal Parties obtained a vast preponderance of working-class votes against the Labour Party, the General Election of 1935 returned the 'National' Government (in effect a Tory Government) with a majority of well over 200 seats.

This betokens an enduring conservatism in large sections of the working class; and it was this conservatism (which does not necessarily betoken allegiance to the Conservative Party) which was greatly shaken—but not overcome—by the traumas of war. As a result, the Labour Party, after forty-five years of existence, two World Wars and a Great Depression, was at long last able to win a majority of seats in the House of Commons— 146—with 48.3 per cent of the votes cast. Even then, the Conservative Party was still supported by nearly ten million voters (39.8 per cent) and the Liberal Party by nearly two-and-a-half million. Twelve million people had voted for the Labour Party.[1] In other words, the pro-Labour and the anti-Labour votes were more or less evenly divided. Nor can it be assumed that the majority of those who did vote Labour, then and later, were fired by particularly strong radical sentiments. Many perhaps were. But many Labour voters, in 1945, were probably doing no more than expressing a general sentiment that the time had come for a new deal for the working class in Britain, and that the Labour Party was the party to bring it about. Nevertheless, and for all its limitations, the victory of 1945 was a great advance: but instead of being enlarged, that basis was steadily narrowed in subsequent years. I will argue that the main responsibility for this shrinkage lies with Labour leaders and the 'labourism' which provided their ideological and practical framework. But it is at any rate clear, on the historical evidence, that neither the deprivations and sufferings of the 'old' working class, nor the 'affluence' of the 'new' (in any case always grossly exaggerated) provides an adequate explanation for the support or lack of support which Labour has obtained: here is vulgar economic determinism indeed, whose inadequacy is further confirmed by the fact that Labour's loss of support has continued through the last ten years of economic crisis, retrenchment and retreat.

What has sometimes been called 'Labour Socialism'[2] is a loose amalgam of many different strands of thought—Christian ethics, Fabian collectivism, a radical and democratic tradition of reform, based on age-old notions of social justice, equality, cooperation and fellowship. Even so, 'labourism' seems a better label for the ideology which has moved Labour's leaders—and many others in the labour movement—for a hundred years past. Labourism has never been turned into a systematic body of thought; and its adherents and practitioners have frequently made a virtue of their 'practical' sense, their rejection of 'theory', and their freedom from all 'isms' (and they themselves have never adopted 'labourism' as a label for their views). But it is nevertheless ideological promptings suitably called by that name which have guided their practice.

Labourism is above all concerned with the advancement of concrete demands of immediate advantage to the working class and organised labour: wages and conditions of work; trade-union rights; the better provision of services and benefits in the field of health, education, housing, transport, family allowances, unemployment benefits, pensions and so on. These demands may be clad in the garb of 'socialism' but most leaders of the labour movement, however much they might believe in some vague and remote socialist alternative to the present social order, have in practice only had a very weak concern—in so far as they have had any concern at all—with large socialist objectives. The reforms they have sought have never been conceived as part of a strategy for the creation of a fundamentally different kind of society, but rather as specific responses to immediate ills and needs. Their horizons have been narrowly bound by the capitalist environment in which they found themselves, and whose framework they readily took as given; and it is within its framework and the 'rationality' it imposed that they sought reform.

This acceptance of capitalist 'rationality' helps to explain some notable features of their politics: for instance, why the reforms they sought were generally so modest in scope and substance, and so geared to what 'society' could afford; why Labour governments so quickly and so regularly moved from being agents of reform to being agents of conservative retrenchment, more concerned to contain pressure from below than to advance labour's

demands; and also why these leaders were so ready to collaborate with
Labour's class enemies. Trade-union leaders steeped in labourism might
have to fight the class struggle, and occasionally fought it hard; but neither
they nor certainly Labour's political leaders thought of society as a battle-
field upon which the working class was engaged in a permanent and
irrevocable struggle against the domination and exploitation to which it
was subjected by a rapacious ruling class: or if they thought in those
terms, they did not let it affect their political practice. But for the most
part, they thought of 'society' as presented with 'problems' whose solution
mainly required the kind of good will, intelligence, knowledge and com-
passion which their Conservative opponents somehow lacked.

Given these perspectives, labourism readily accepted the political
system that was in existence when the labour movement assumed definite
shape in the second half of the nineteenth century. Labour leaders might
demand some reforms in this realm too—for instance, the extension of the
suffrage, or the reform of the House of Lords or of local government. But
they took the system as a whole more or less for granted and capitalist
democracy on the British model to be the most accomplished form of
democratic government conceivable—hereditary monarchy and hereditary
peers in the House of Lords included. They mainly thought of the political
process in parliamentary terms, and of grassroots activism and extra-
parliamentary activity as party work at local level for the purpose of
supporting local and parliamentary representatives and helping to fight
local and parliamentary elections. The notion that a local party might be a
focus of struggle, agitation and education fell outside their ideological
spectrum. Nor have Labour leaders ever shown much concern to bring
about any large reform in the organisation of the British state so as to
change the closed, oligarchic and profoundly conservative character of its
administrative, judicial, police and military branches.

Finally, Labourism has always had a strong national vocation. The
Labour Party has regularly been accused by its Conservative opponents of
being 'unpatriotic', heedless of British interests abroad, unconcerned with
British 'greatness', etc. Nothing could be further from the truth. Labour
Governments have always pursued foreign and defence policies (and in an
earlier epoch colonial policies) which did not greatly differ from those of
Conservative Governments—not perhaps very surprisingly since Labour
Governments relied on the civil servants and military advisers they
inherited from the Conservatives. Of course, there have been some differences: it may well be, for instance, that a Conservative Government, had
one been elected in 1945, would not have accepted without much bitter
struggle the inevitability of Indian independence; and divergencies between
Labour and Conservative defence policies have widened in recent years and
were manifested in the General Election of 1983. It is permissible to doubt
how far these divergencies would have been maintained, if a Labour

Government had been elected, given the lukewarm support, at best, which senior Labour figures gave to major items of Labour's defence programme; but the divergencies were nevertheless evident. On the other hand, it has to be remembered that, beyond these divergencies, all senior Labour figures, without exception, continued to be committed to the American alliance and NATO, which have been the cornerstones of the defence and foreign policies of *both* the Conservative and Labour Parties since the war years.

These being the main features of labourism, it is reasonable to see it as an ideology of social reform, within the framework of capitalism, with no serious ambition of transcending that framework, whatever ritual obeisances to 'socialism' might be performed by party leaders on suitable occasions, such as Labour Party or trade-union conferences, to appease or defeat their activist critics. Labourism, in other words, is not, like Marxism, an ideology of rupture but an ideology of adaptation.

It is this ideology which has been overwhelmingly dominant in the labour movement for a hundred years and more, whatever 'socialist' label might be given to it. Marxism, as a main alternative to labourism, has not been a negligible strand of thought among activists and its influence has been greater than the proclaimed number of its adherents might suggest. But it has nevertheless been marginal in comparison with labourism. For it is labourism which slowly made its way in the working class and became an acceptable perspective to a substantial part of it; and it is labourism which, from the peak which it reached in 1951, has been losing support in the working class. The question I now turn to is why.

An explanation of this growing alienation has to begin with the long-standing economic decline of the British economy, and with the aggravation and acceleration of this decline by virtue of the world capitalist economic crisis from the early seventies onwards; or rather, an explanation has to begin with the response of the Labour Governments of the sixties and seventies to decline and crisis. The chronic British economic malady and the recurring emergencies which it produced presented these governments with a challenge that they always promised to meet but which they always failed to meet. Instead, and well in line with their labourist ideology, they consistently pursued economic policies which were broadly acceptable to the capitalist forces at home and abroad on whose help and cooperation they relied. In so doing, they were also and naturally compelled to turn themselves, as I noted earlier, into agencies of retrenchment and containment.

The failures, derelictions and betrayals of the Wilson and Callaghan Governments of 1964–70 and 1974–79 have been amply documented and need no retelling here.[3] The point that does need to be made is that these governments did, to a quite remarkable degree, act in ways which were bound to alienate masses of actual or potential Labour supporters in the working class, and not only in the working class. It was the Labour Governments of those decades which inaugurated the 'monetarist' policies which the Conservatives pushed much further after 1979. It was these Labour Governments who launched repeated attacks on public expenditure by central and local government for collective services whose level is of crucial importance to the large majority of people who cannot pay for private health, education, housing, transport and amenities; and it was also they whose budgets turned into tax exercises much more calculated to hit lower incomes than high ones. It was the Wilson and Callaghan Governments which made war on industrial activists, and who persistently sought to curb wages under the guise of income policies, wage norms, social contracts and national agreements. Nor even could these policies claim any measure of success: after a combined period of eleven years of Labour Governments from 1964 until 1979, with a Conservative interruption of only four years, there was no major improvement in the British condition to which Labour could point. Meanwhile, the rich prospered; and so did a Labour state bourgeoisie loud in its denunciation of militants and wreckers who were spoiling their enjoyment of the pleasures of office.

This record alone would be perfectly adequate to account for the progressive alienation of masses of potential Labour voters from the Labour Party. The argument is not, of course, that the working class wanted more socialism and turned away from Labour because Labour Governments did not give it to them. That is indeed nonsense. The point is that Labour supporters wanted, and voted for, programmes of economic and social betterment, but that the betterment they got from Labour Governments was easily overshadowed by the negative side of the record. As a result, many of them abandoned Labour in 1983, as more and more of them had been doing in previous elections, and did so all the more readily as there now appeared to be a plausible alternative to both Labour and Conservatives, namely the Social Democratic and Liberal Parties. Furthermore, many of them simply did not vote: one of the significant facts about the General Election of 1983 is that 47 per cent of unemployed young people between the ages of 18 and 22 did not bother to cast a vote at all.

Even so, eight-and-a-half million people did vote Labour. This is really very remarkable, when account is taken of the relentless and quite unscrupulous assault to which working-class—and other—voters were subjected during the election campaign and for many years before the campaign. The assault had two obvious objectives. One of them was to get voters to overlook the viciously regressive character of the policies of the Thatcher government. The other was to persuade them that the Labour Party had been taken over, or was in imminent danger of being taken over, by political perverts and lunatics. Not the least persuasive element in that assault was the contribution which senior and respected figures in the Labour Party made to it, by joining in the chorus of vilification which united all anti-socialist forces, including of course the ex-Labour renegade leaders and parliamentarians of the Social Democratic Party. In the circumstances, and given the intensity of the assault, the wonder is not that Labour lost, but that so many people resisted the propaganda, overlooked Labour's condition and record, and still voted for it. That so many did constitutes a precious asset, to whose significance I will return later.

The second main reason advanced to account for Labour's defeat, I noted earlier, is that the Labour Party was, and had been for a long time, so obviously and deeply divided. This makes good sense, but needs to be taken a good deal further. For there have always been deep divisions in the Labour Party and the labour movement and they have not stopped the Labour Party from doing a lot better than it did in 1983. The difference is that the more recent divisions have run much deeper than before and that many more activists have opposed their leaders, and also, most significant of all in my view, that the Labour leaders, unlike their predecessors since the Labour Party came into being, have not been able to maintain their ideological and political hegemony over the labour movement. Here lies the root of Labour's troubles.

In this context, too, account has to be taken of the economic decline of Britain and of the Wilson and Callaghan Governments' response to it. For just as the derelictions and betrayals and failures of these governments 'de-aligned' a mass of potential and actual Labour supporters, so did that record 'radicalise' a mass of left activists and give them a new determination to prevent a repetition of past performance. From the early seventies onwards, a new wave of activists emerged, not only more determined but better organised than the Labour Left had been earlier, and less susceptible to manipulation and seduction as well. Also, and not to be under-estimated, they found an articulate and resilient champion in Tony Benn, whose national position and place in the Labour Party gave them added strength. The Labour Left has always had problems with its parliamentary and ministerial standard bearers. Stafford Cripps was a weak and vacillating leader of the Socialist League in the thirties, and Aneurin Bevan in the post-war years was a very erratic and impulsive leader of the Bevanites, in so far as he could be said to have been their leader at all. Bevan soared above his followers, and did not really seek to mobilise support at the grassroots. Benn did. No wonder that he was so bitterly hated and reviled, by his erstwhile ministerial colleagues and fellow parliamentarians no less than by all the forces of conservatism proper.

The new activism was not homogeneous in ideological and political terms. Some small part of it—on which its enemies naturally fastened drew its inspiration from Trotskyism. Some of it proceeded from an unlabelled militant socialist iconoclasm, of which the most representative figure was Ken Livingstone; and most of it was probably the product of a deep but undoctrinal anger at the grassroots on the part of rank-and-file activists who were utterly fed up with the retreat by their leaders into Labour versions of Conservative policies at home and abroad.

Furthermore, the new activists rejected the view traditionally held by Labour leaders (and by much of the traditional Labour Left as well) that the political process must have the House of Commons as its main and all but exclusive focus, with grassroots activism as playing no more than a support role for parliamentarians. On the contrary, the new activists were oriented towards work at the grassroots, and had a strong sense of the political process at local level—hence the importance they attached to what could be achieved in and through local government. Like the women's movement and the peace movement, the new generation of Labour activists (who were in any case often part of the other two movements as well) was strongly committed to extra-parliamentary pressure and did not believe that parliamentary work was so crucial as to dwarf all else: on the contrary, they saw parliamentary work as part of a larger and more important struggle in the country at large.

The new activists were, relatedly, intensely suspicious of all leaders, and notably of parliamentary leaders; and they tended to view most (but not all) left parliamentarians as being part of a 'soft left' that could not be trusted to offer sustained resistance to the retreats and compromises of the leaders of the Labour Party. In so far as this response is unstructured, it may in time fail to protect Labour left activists from appeals stemming from many diverse sources not to rock the boat, make a bad situation worse, and so on. From this point of view, the suspicion which many left activists themselves have of 'theory' is a source of real political weakness, which has very adversely affected many Labour activists in the past.

Nevertheless the General Election defeat of 1979, coming on top of the record of the Wilson and Callaghan Governments, gave a powerful impulse to activist pressures which had been building up throughout the seventies. The left in the Labour Party was able in the following years to force through major innovations in the selection of MPs and in the election of the Leader and Deputy Leader of the Labour Party. Moreover, the left was also able to achieve temporary control of the National Executive Committee and of its important sub-committees; and it was thus well placed to make a marked impact on the programme which eventually presented in the election of 1983.

The most remarkable feature of this pressure from the left is that, even though the Labour leadership bitterly opposed it, with the vociferous encouragement of a virtually united press, it was unable to subdue it. This had in part to do with the strength of the new activism in the Labour Party and in the unions; and also with the much less solid position of that leadership. For another consequence of the failures of the Wilson and Callaghan Governments was to weaken drastically the moral and political authority of the people—drawn overwhelmingly from the Right and the Centre—who had been in charge of these governments. In any case, when one recalls the relative ease with which an earlier Labour Left was brought to heel by expulsion or the threat of expulsion, or was manipulated into submission by the kind of rhetoric and deception of which Harold Wilson was the master, the inability of the Labour leaders to crush or curb their activist opponents stands out as the really new and significant fact in recent Labour history.

However, the new activists, notwithstanding their successes, were just as unable as their predecessors to dislodge the Right and the Centre from their commanding positions in the Labour Party and the trade unions. Even when they had a majority on the NEC, they were confronted by a powerful minority of senior figures (including the Leader and the Deputy Leader) who could marshall considerable resources to block the path of the left. Also, the majority of the Parliamentary Labour Party remained under the control of the Right and the Centre; and the parliamentary left was itself badly split between the 'soft left' and the Bennites. Nor did the left have many reliable allies in the upper echelons of the trade-union hierarchy.

The high point in the activists' campaign after 1979 was the vote for the Deputy Leadership of the Labour Party by the new electoral college at the 1981 Party Conference, when Tony Benn obtained 49.5 per cent of the vote, against Denis Healey's 50.4 per cent. Had Benn won, it is conceivable that the balance of forces in the Labour Party would have shifted considerably to the left, with many more people in the Parliamentary Labour Party moving over to the Social Democratic Party to which many Labour parliamentarians are in any case ideologically well attuned. But Benn did not win, and the Right and Centre remained in command, with a Leader, in the person of Michael Foot, who, for all his past Labour Left record and rhetoric, had long made his peace with the Right and the Centre. Foot had been a main pillar of the Wilson-Callaghan Government between 1974 and 1979 and a chief architect of that Government's alliance with the Liberals, and was a determined enemy of the Bennite Left.

The successes of the new activists, coupled with their failure to win a commanding position in the Labour Party, thus produced the absurd and untenable situation which is at the core of Labour's troubles: the left was able to get major items of policy adopted by Labour Party and trade-union conferences; and these items subsequently found their way into Labour's electoral programme. But the task of defending these policies was left to leaders many of whom—indeed most of whom—did not believe in them, made no secret of the fact and found many opportunities to denounce those who wanted these policies as wreckers or fools.

The full absurdity of this situation became disastrously evident in the General Election campaign. The Labour Manifesto was not the 'extreme' document which the enemies of the left, not least in the Labour Party, found it convenient to claim, then and later. It amounted for the most part to a reiteration of policies which had been put forward in the Labour Party's electoral manifestoes of the seventies and earlier. But, in addition to the pledge that a Labour Government would take Britain out of the European Economic Community, it did include some proposals in the field of defence that had far-reaching implications: thus, it pledged a Labour Government to reject the deployment of Cruise and Pershing missiles on British soil and to 'begin discussions' for the removal of nuclear bases in Britain, 'to be completed within the lifetime of the Labour Government'. The document further proclaimed Labour's commitment 'to establish a non-nuclear defence policy': 'we will, after consultation, carry through in the lifetime of the next parliament our non-nuclear defence policy'. This appeared to commit a Labour Government to unilateral nuclear disarmament. But the document also said that, in addition to cancelling the Trident programme, it would propose that 'Britain's Polaris force be included in the nuclear disarmament negotiations in which Britain must take part'. The obvious question, on which the Conservatives and others naturally pounced, was what would happen if the negotiations failed. On this, the Labour Party spoke with uncertain and divided voices. In other words, the manifesto's attempt to square the circle had failed; and the divisions in the Labour leadership on the issue of defence made it impossible for the Labour Party to proclaim what it was left to Enoch Powell to call the 'transparent absurdity' of the theory of nuclear deterrence, based as it was on the willingness to commit national suicide 'as a last resort'. Mrs Thatcher made the typically reckless and bombastic declaration during the election campaign that she would be perfectly ready to 'press the button': Labour was in no condition to denounce this for the degraded nonsense that it was.

It is very unlikely that any major party in Britain has ever fought so inane a campaign as the Labour Party did in 1983. The basic reason for this was not incompetence and mismanagement, however much there may have been of both. These were only the manifestations of much deeper trouble, namely the division, essentially, between social reformers whose perspectives do not for all practical purposes reach beyond labourism, and socialists whose perspectives do. This age-old division has now reached a point where any attempt at accommodation only produces fudging formulas which neither satisfy nor convince anyone.

Such a situation cannot permanently endure: or at least, no party and movement can be viable in which such a situation endures. Pious references to the Labour Party being a 'broad church' which has always incorporated many different strands of thought fail to take account of a crucial fact, namely that the 'broad church' of Labour only functioned effectively in the past because one side—the Right and Centre—determined the nature of the services that were to be held, and excluded or threatened with exclusion any clergy too deviant in its dissent. Now that this can no longer be done—the clumsy and largely ineffectual attempts to banish the *Militant* Tendency confirm rather than disprove the point— the 'broad church' is unable to do its job.

The question which therefore needs to be asked is what socialists, whether they are in the Labour Party or not, should want to see by way of a resolution of this condition. The answer to that question is best considered by reference to two possible 'scenarios'.

The first of these involves the election of a new Leader of the Labour Party able to combine a vocabulary that would please the left on the one hand with a sufficient degree of flexibility over policy on the other to reassure the Right and the Centre. The task of such a Leader might be eased somewhat by the fact that no major policy decisions have to be incorporated in an election manifesto for some time to come; and a Leader who spoke an adequately left-sounding language might hope to confuse and divide the left sufficiently to isolate its more intractable elements, and thus reduce them to a marginal position.

The realisation of such a 'scenario' would restore a certain degree of coherence to the Labour Party. It would not be quite the party of Clement Attlee and Hugh Gaitskell which Mrs Thatcher was calling for during the election campaign, but it would be a recognisable version of it. Labourism, suitably embellished with some socialist phraseology (but not too much of it) would again predominate. Persuasive appeals would be made to 'unite against the common enemy', and an enticing vision of electoral victory and a Labour Government would be held out as the reward for reasonableness and moderation.

There undoubtedly exists a considerable weight of support for such an outcome: a large majority of parliamentarians would be for it, so would a large number of trade-union leaders; so would the press and the media. It would widely be represented as a welcome sign that the Labour Party was returning to the sensible policies of old, and that it was abjuring the lunatic policies which had brought it to its present pass. Nor is there much doubt that it would meet with the approval of many Labour supporters and Labour Party members.

It is, however, a very difficult 'scenario' to realise. For its realisation would represent a massive defeat for the left in the Labour Party. There is no good reason to suppose that, having got as far as it has, the left would accept such a defeat and desist from their endeavours. Inevitably, however, these endeavours maintain the Labour Party in a state of civil war.

This being the case, a realisation of the 'scenario' in question requires nothing less than a thorough 'purge' of the left in the Labour Party, extending far beyond the *Militant* Tendency; and it would also need a redrawing of the constitutional rules so as to reduce drastically the increased influence which activists have been able to achieve since 1979 on such matters as the re-selection of MPs and the election of the Leader and Deputy Leader of the Labour Party. If this could be done, socialists in the Labour Party would be forced to decide whether the time had finally come to leave the Labour Party to labourism and its devotees, and to seek a realignment of the left by way of a new socialist party. However, this kind of action against the left seems well beyond the powers of any Labour leadership today.

The new activists, for their part, have proceeded from a very different 'scenario', which has not been clearly spelt out, but whose main lines are not difficult to draw. What is involved is a continuation of the struggles in which the left has been engaged, with the purpose of achieving predominance and turning the Labour Party into a socialist party free from the constrictions hitherto imposed upon it by its leaders. It must be presumed that many leading figures in the Labour Party would then want to leave it and seek new political homes elsewhere—in the Social Democratic Party, or the Liberal Party, or even the Conservative Party. In fact, it would be essential that such people *should* leave the Labour Party; for just as the left makes life difficult for a leadership which is opposed to it, so could determined Right and Centre parliamentarians make life difficult for a party in which the left had acquired predominance. No doubt, a good many other Labour Party members, at constituency level, would also leave. But these defections would be compensated by the accretion of strength which would be provided by the many people who are not now minded to join the Labour Party but might then want to do so, and be actively involved in it. It is also very likely that some, perhaps many, trade-union leaders would wish to disaffiliate from a Labour Party that had gone beyond labourism. But any such attempt would meet with stiff resistance from the left in the unions; and though the attempt might succeed in some cases, it would probably be successfully fought in others.

I must enter a personal note at this point. I have for more than ten years written that this hope of the left to transform the Labour Party— which has always been nourished by the Labour Left—was illusory, and that, far from representing a short cut to the creation of a mass socialist party in Britain (which has never existed), it was in fact a dead end in which British socialists had been trapped for many decades—in fact since the Labour Party came into being. It was this view which led me to advocate the formation of a new socialist party able to do all the work of socialist advocacy and agitation which the Labour Party had been prevented by its leaders from doing.[4]

I am far from convinced that I was mistaken. For it is by no means evident that the new activists can realise the 'scenario' I have just outlined: on the most optimistic expectations, they have a long way to go, with many large obstacles on the way. But it is obvious that I underestimated how great was the challenge which the new activists would be able to pose to their leaders; and how limited would be the capacity of these leaders to surmount the challenge. I now take it that the question whether the activists can push matters further and achieve the conquest of the Labour Party is more open than I had believed.

Rather than speculate further upon this, it may be more useful to ask what would be the prospects of a socialist Labour Party, such as the activists seek: and the same considerations would apply to a new socialist party, born from the disintegration of the Labour Party.

Such a party would seek to advance purposes and policies which have long formed part of the aspirations of the socialist left. One of its main concerns would be the democratisation of the whole structure of government; the abolition of anti-trade-union legislation and other repressive legislation, such as the Prevention of Terrorism Act, introduced in 1974 by Roy Jenkins, then Labour Home Secretary; the drastic curbing of police powers and the placing of the police under effective democratic control; and the end of the British military presence in Northern Ireland.

A socialist party would be pledged to the return to public ownership of the industries and services which the Conservative Government has sold off and will further have sold off; and it would take it that a major extension of public ownership under a variety of forms, and with the greatest possible measure of democratic control, was one of the indispensable conditions for the transformation of British capitalism in socialist directions, and for the dissolution of the class structure which would be one of its central aims.

In the realm of defence and foreign policy, such a party would be committed to the nuclear disarmament of Britain, as part of a radical shift in the policies followed by Labour and Conservative Governments since World War Two. A socialist party could not be true to itself if it did not include in its programme an end of British support for the world-wide counter-revolutionary crusade which the United States has been waging across the world ever since the forties, and if it did not support progressive movements throughout the world struggling for national and social liberation. Such defence and foreign policies are clearly incompatible with membership of NATO.

Conventional wisdom has it that such a programme can never be endorsed by a majority of people—indeed, that it dooms the party which propounds it to marginality and irrelevance.

Two points may be made about this. The first is that there is no point in pretending that there exists a ready-made majority in the country for a socialist programme. How could there be? One of the fruits of the long predominance of labourism is precisely that the party of the working class has never carried out any sustained campaign of education and propaganda on behalf of a socialist programme; and that Labour leaders have frequently turned themselves into fierce propagandists *against* the socialist proposals of their critics inside the Labour Party and out, and have bent their best efforts to the task of defeating all attempts to have the Labour Party adopt such proposals. Moreover, a vast array of conservative forces, of the most diverse kind, are always at hand to dissuade the working class from even thinking about the socialist ideas which evil or foolish people are forever trying to foist upon them. This simply means that a ceaseless battle for the 'hearts and minds' of the people is waged by the forces of conservatism, against which have only beem mobilised immeasurably smaller socialist forces. A socialist party would seek to strengthen these forces and to defend socialist perspectives and a socialist programme over an extended period of time, and would accept that more than one election might have to be held before a majority of people came to support it. In any case, a socialist party would not only be concerned with office, but with the creation of the conditions under which office would be more than the management of affairs on capitalist lines. The first of these conditions is precisely a strong measure of popular support; and this support would be all the more essential, given the fierce resistance which a socialist government seeking to apply its programme would encounter from all the conservative forces in the land.

Ever since the Labour Party became a substantial electoral and political force, Labour leaders have taken the view—and have persuaded many of their followers to take the view—that government was all; and that politics is about elections: on one side, there is power, on the other, paralysis. This is a very narrow view of the political process. Elections are important, and no party functioning in a capitalist-democratic context can afford to neglect them, not least at local level. But this is a very different matter from the view that gaining office is the sole and exclusive purpose of politics. For office, however agreeable for those who hold it, has often meant not only impotence, but worse than impotence, namely the power to carry out policies fundamentally at odds with the purposes for which office was obtained. Nor is it necessarily the case that opposition means paralysis. This has never been true of the Conservative Party and the conservative forces; and it has only been true of the Labour Party because of the narrow ideological and political framework in which its leaders have dwelt, and because of their concentration on electoral and parliamentary politics. But it need not be true for a substantial working-class party. It is by no means obvious, for instance, that the Italian Communist Party, in opposition since it was expelled from office in 1947, has, *in socialist terms,* exercised much less influence on Italian life in this period, than the Labour Party has exercised in government. The notion that the Labour Party is either a 'party of government', with all the opportunistic compromises and retreats the formulation carries, or must resign itself to being no more than an 'ineffectual sect' may be useful propaganda for all the 'moderate' forces in the labour movement, but it does not correspond to the real alternatives.

This relates to the second point that, while there is no popular majority for a socialist programme at present, it does not follow that there is no support for such a programme at all, and that more support for it could not be generated. This is where it is necessary to recall the fact that eight-and-a-half million people did vote Labour in 1983. There is obviously no warrant for the view that all of them consciously and deliberately supported all the items in Labour's programme, or even that they supported many of them: many such Labour voters were no doubt simply registering a vote against the Thatcher Government. But among these eight-and-a-half million voters, a large number may be taken to have voted as they did because they approved more or less strongly the general drift and many items of the Labour programme, and were not put off by the massive propaganda to which they were subjected, and which assured them that a vote for Labour was a vote for personal and national disaster. As I noted earlier, they resisted this assault just as millions of Labour voters have resisted such assaults at every election since 1945, when the Labour Party put forward a programme which its leaders had striven very hard to dilute, in the belief that its more radical proposals must inevitably lose them the election. This stubborn popular resistance to the unrelenting campaign of indoctrination to which the working class is subjected at election time and in between elections provides a basis of support on which a socialist party serious about its business can build. Much of the propaganda conducted by anti-socialist forces—Conservative, Liberal, Social Democratic and Labour—seeks to present a picture of the working class as irrevocably opposed to socialist proposals; but the propagandists would have to work much less hard if this was the case. They do have to work as hard as they do precisely because there does exist a vast degree of popular alienation from existing economic, social and political arrangements, which can be turned into support for radically different arrangements. I have called this alienation a 'state of de-subordination', as a result of which 'people who find themselves in subordinate positions, and notably the people who work in factories, mines, offices, shops, schools, hospitals and so on do what they can to mitigate, resist and transform the conditions of their subordination'.[5] Unemployment and the fear of unemployment have undoubtedly had an effect, as they were intended to do, in reducing 'desubordination' at 'the point of production'. But this hardly means that the experience of these years of Tory Government and mass unemployment and the attack on welfare and collective provisions have generated any more popular support for existing arrangements than was previously the case. On the contrary economic decline and crisis, allied to the crying injustices generated by a grossly unequal class system provide the ground on which socialist work can effectively proceed.

Socialist work means something different for a socialist party than the kind of political activity inscribed in the perspectives of labourism. I have noted earlier that political work, for labourism, essentially means short periods of great political activity for local and parliamentary elections, with long periods of more or less routine party activity in between. Socialist work means intervention in all the many different areas of life in which class struggle occurs: for class struggle must be taken to mean not only the permanent struggle between capital and labour, crucial though that remains, but the struggle against racial and sex discrimination, the struggle against arbitrary state and police power, the struggle against the ideological hegemony of the conservative forces, and the struggle for new and radically different defence and foreign policies.

The slogan of the first Marxist organisation in Britain, the Social Democratic Federation, founded in 1884, was 'Educate, Agitate, Organise'. It is also a valid slogan for the 1980s and beyond. A socialist party could, in the coming years, give it more effective meaning than it has ever had in the past.

NOTES

1. The Communist Party, with twenty-one candidates in the field, polled just over 100,000 votes and had two seats, which they lost in the General Election of 1950. Over 100,000 votes were also cast for the Commonwealth Party and under 50,000 for the Independent Labour Party.
2. See e.g., Stuart MacIntyre, *A Proletarian Science. Marxism in Britain. 1917–1933* (1980) Ch. 2.
3. See e.g., L. Panitch, *Social Democracy and Industrial Militancy* (1976); D. Coates, *Labour in Power?* (1980); and K. Coates (ed.) *What Went Wrong?* (1979).
4. See 'Moving On', in *The Socialist Register*, 1976, and 'The Future of Socialism in England', in *The Socialist Register*, 1977.
5. R. Miliband, 'A State of De-Subordination' in *British Journal of Sociology*, vol. xxix, no. 4 (December 1978), p. 402.

THE BRITISH PEACE MOVEMENT AND SOCIALIST CHANGE*

Richard Taylor

In the post-war period the largest, and arguably the most significant, mobilisation of radical forces in Britain has taken place around the issue of nuclear disarmament. From the late-1950s to the mid-1960s, and again from the late-1970s to the time of writing, the peace movement has been a dominant force and has succeeded in bringing together a diverse coalition in opposition to British possession of nuclear weapons.

This paper has two primary purposes: first, to examine the politics of the peace movement of 1958 to 1965 and to analyse the reasons for its ultimate failure; second, to argue, on the basis of the experience of that period, that for the peace movement to succeed in the future there must be a linkage at a number of levels between the movement for peace and the movement for specifically socialist change. The focus is thus upon the various political strategies adopted by the earlier movement, but always within the context of the implications this experience has for the contemporary movement.

The persistent and fundamental problem of the movement since its inception has been its inability to translate its undoubted popular appeal into real, tangible achievement. Although the movement has had a very considerable impact upon public opinion, and thus, arguably, indirectly upon formal political structures and policies, it is quite clear that its central objectives have not been achieved. Moreover, the deterioration of the Cold War climate in the 1980s and the increasing escalation of the arms race both testify to the movement's lack of success. The problem then is essentially political: how to articulate with effect the peace movement's dynamism and strength. The inability to find a solution to this problem was one of the central reasons for the movement's decline and disintegration from the mid-1960s and threatens again to undermine the strength, growth and self-confidence of the movement in the 1980s, both in Britain and elsewhere.

Various 'strategies for advance' have been advocated within the peace movement. In the nature of such movements there is an overlapping and even a confusion among differing groupings and ideological positions.

---

*I am very grateful to David Coates for his detailed and substantial comments on earlier drafts of this paper.

Nevertheless, four main strategies within the 1958 to 1965 period can be identified—and these have influenced considerably the contemporary movement's political profile. These can be described as: the single issue, moral/apolitical; the labourist; the direct actionist; and the New Left.

The single issue, moral/apolitical strategy
Many activists in the earlier movement rejected any political dimension to the movement's aims.[1] And there can be no doubt that much of the movement's appeal rested on entirely moral and humanistic motivations. Those in the CND leadership (and to some extent in the Direct Action Committee (DAC) and the Committee of 100) who accepted the need for political action did so only on the assumption that the essentials of CND's case remained on the moral plane. Moreover, for many, like Canon Collins, the Chairman of the Executive Committee of CND, the task facing CND was confined to the single, central issue of unilateral nuclear disarmament. For the 'moral protester' the movement's strategy was, like the issue itself, a straightforward, simple matter. Protest should be on the moral plane, because the objections to nuclear weapons were fundamentally moral in character, not political. Inasmuch as 'strategy' was important it was assumed that CND policies could be put into effect via the existing political parties with no major implications for other political developments. The 'moral strategy' was simple and direct—and assumed a single-issue orientation. Faced with the enormity of nuclear weapons and their effects, the emotive response was to call for a moral campaign couched in apolitical absolutes.

This was a wholly mistaken perspective. It is true that without this initial moral dynamism the movement would never have arisen. Moreover, that there was an essential moral dimension at the heart of the movement, none (not even the most politically oriented) would deny. However, the *exclusivity* of this moral approach on the part of many supporters, and their refusal to engage in political or strategic planning or action of any sort beyond moral exhortation, was a major contributory factor to the movement's failure. Furthermore, however necessary the moral impetus may have been at the outset of the movement, its continuing dominance rendered the movement static and virtually powerless in the face of the repeated political defeats suffered.

The movement entailed a *new* politics, over and above the specific 'moral lead' argument involved in the central CND case. For the policy of unilateralism to have any real long-term impact it had to be allied to a political programme of commitment which would involve withdrawal from NATO, a commitment *against* both major power blocs and the ideological systems which underpinned them, and a commitment *to* a policy of positive neutralism. A necessary extension of these commitments was the espousal of a radicalised ideological framework: the point here is not to discuss which framework was 'correct', but rather to emphasise that some radical reorientation was a necessary part, by extension, of the unilateralist commitment.

Thus the changes entailed in the unilateralist commitment were so large and so central that it was highly unlikely that the existing governing class[2] would have acquiesced through moral pressure alone, however widely and vociferously articulated. Moreover, the whole historical experience indicates that the governing class in Britain, as elsewhere, responds predominantly to material forces. It is no doubt regrettable, but it remains the fact, that morality has not been a major force in Western politics, and the disarmament movement was unable to make it so. Those pursuing the 'moral' strategy appeared not to have realised the nature of the problem they confronted: there was little if any strategic discussion of how the movement could *persuade* politicians to take note of the moral-force arguments. It may be argued that this underrates the potential power of 'public opinion', which can be important at crucial times of national crisis and which does manifest itself in primarily moral and emotional terms. The undoubtedly large measure of support given by 'the public' in Britain to the Falklands War in 1982 might be held to be just such a case.

This would appear a mistaken argument on at least three counts, however. First, the vested interests, both material and ideological, of the governing class are very strong indeed, as are their reserves of ideological and political power. If the issue is considered important enough, this power will be exercised to whatever degree necessary (*vide* President Allende in Chile). Second, and related to this, the informed and astute political machine can manipulate 'public opinion' (as was the case, quite blatantly, over UN resolution 502 in the Falklands war); moreover, protest based on 'morality' alone can be overcome easily in public debate by seemingly more realistic and sophisticated argument. Emotive 'public opinion' has effect, generally, only when this opinion is being voiced *in support* of the policies of the governing class (as was the case in the Falklands war). Third, the exclusivist moral campaign allows no political compromise, and has no flexibility in making alliances, deals etc. in order to push forward the movement. In that sense such campaigns are sectarian and static, and take no account of the real world in which they operate. More often than not their own 'purity' becomes as important as the cause for which they are campaigning, and the movement becomes increasingly inward-looking and divorced from reality. Paradoxically, therefore, the very universality implied in the moralistic campaign is itself the cause of both narrowness and inflexibility. At the practical common-sense level, it has to be realised too that political change of this radical type can come only through political action. There can be no hope of success for any political movement which does not tap some source of potential political power, as Canon Collins and others in the early CND leadership realised both at the time and subsequently. A political strategy was thus essential if the movement were to become more than what Ian Mikardo has described as 'an annual orgasm every Easter'.[3]

It was within the ideological and political contexts that the real significance of the movement lay. The exclusively 'moral' protesters, necessary and legitimate though their perspective was as a basis for the movement, were ultimately divorced from the real struggle. Their strategy, although it certainly raised the general level of public awareness about nuclear dangers, had no chance of success without embracing a wider political commitment. It is thus within the context of the directly political strategies that the movement must be analysed.

The labourist strategy

Of the explicitly political strategies in the movement there is no doubt that the most orthodox, and probably the most pervasive, has held to the view that success can be achieved only through the labour movement. The strong tradition of 'peace politics', stretching back to the First World War and beyond, made the peace movement inherently appealing to those active on the Labour Left. A labour movement led from the Left, but holding absolutely to both the ideology and practice of democratic, parliamentary socialism would be committed genuinely to the moral and political principles of the peace movement *and* to the wider reform of capitalism. It was only within this latter context, it was argued, that the moral basis of the peace movement could find its real expression. The abolition of nuclear weapons, initially by Britain alone, was seen as a part of the wider moral re-ordering of society that would emanate from a Labour government led from the Left.

Without such a Labour Left leadership, however, the party and the labour movement would continue to be dominated by the pro-Bomb, essentially pro-capitalist right wing (*vide* Gaitskell in the late 1950s). On the other hand, to attempt fundamental change of this type via some formation or coalition *outside* the organised working-class movement was, it was argued, thoroughly unsocialist, and certain to fail. Such a movement, unconnected to the organised working class, would tend towards bourgeois dilettantism or would fade away. In terms of *power* there is, on this argument, no alternative to working in and through the labour movement.

It is thus important to discuss in a little more detail the ways in which such changes—the winning over of the labour movement by the Left and hence the possibility of achieving the peace movement's objectives—might have been accomplished in the 1958 to 1965 period. There were two ways in which the Labour Left saw the struggle for Left power in the labour movement being pushed forward, both in general terms and in the specific case of CND: through winning over major trade unions to Left policies, and through building a strong alternative leadership in the PLP. On the trade-union front there was, superficially, considerable early success—culminating in the 1960 Labour Conference victory, when broadly uni-lateralist resolutions proposed by the AEU and the TGWU, were carried, against the explicit wishes of Gaitskell and the PLP leadership. But this victory was both misleading and short-lived, representing a combination of artificial bloc vote manoeuvring by some of the major trade-union leaders, and a moral, and emotive, rather than a *political,* commitment to unilateralism by the trade-union activists. Thus trade-union support for 'CND style' motions in the 1960s was not the result of a deep under-standing of and commitment to the policies of unilateralism and neutral-ism, but was rather a gesture indicative of the generalised concern of a substantial proportion of trade-union opinion over the whole problem of nuclear armaments, the dangers of nuclear war, and the *immorality* in-volved in the possession and possible use of genocidal weapons.[4] The 1960 victory did not result in closer liaison between the trade-unions and CND: Gaitskell's notorious smear, that CND consisted of pacifists, neutral-ists and fellow-travellers, touched the trade-union leaders, always sensitive to accusations of fellow-travelling, on a raw nerve. Moreover, from late-1960 onwards, trade-union leaders were even more than usually susceptible to leadership appeals for party unity and loyalty to the leader-ship, in view of the perceived dangers of the party splitting irrevocably following the 1960 decision. Given these circumstances, and the ambi-valence of CND itself about its involvement in Labour politics, it was not surprising that Gaitskell and the Campaign for Democratic Socialism were able to reverse the decision at the 1961 Conference. The involvement of the higher reaches of the trade-union movement in the unilateralist move-ment had been a very transitory and almost artificial affair.

Related to this failure within the trade-union section of the labour movement was the nuclear disarmament movement's inability to attract significant levels of working-class support from among the population as a whole. It never managed to attract the support of substantial numbers of ordinary working-class, Labour supporters, let alone the apolitical or Conservative sections of the working class. Paradoxically, such working-class support as there was for the movement tended to be couched in the moral/apolitical perspective. And yet, as has been argued, this was a wholly inadequate vehicle for achieving the movement's objectives. One of the primary objectives, strategically, of the movement should thus have been to devise ways of raising working-class consciousness and of making real links with the industrial labour movement and the wider working class. This would have been a difficult task, but it was an essential one if the movement was to have achieved any long-term success.

There were thus several reasons for the failure of the movement to win over the industrial labour movement on any permanent, genuine basis. But what of the political Labour Left—ground on which the early CND was far more at home and had firm allies? Surely a mass movement led by an elite of predominantly Labourist persuasions would provide exactly the vehicle for the Labour Left to pursue, legitimately, its desire for a change in the leadership and the direction of the party. And, looking at it in reverse, surely the Labour Left offered the movement an ideal opportunity to translate its mass power into political action. Here was a situation where both the interests and the commitment to the single central issue of the two groups coincided. The prospects of this alliance were, of course, considerably enhanced by the Labour Party's third successive General Election defeat in 1959, under Hugh Gaitskell's explicitly right-wing leadership: by late 1959 the unity of the party was looking very precarious indeed. Given all this, how was it that the CND/Labour Left alliance failed to take the Labour Party by storm and sweep away the Gaitskellite leadership?

We need here to look at both the movement and the Labour Left, and analyse their strengths and weaknesses. Although the movement was led by a group that had predominantly Labour sympathies this was by no means true of the whole Executive. The leaders of CND did not see the movement as political in this conventional Labour sense and did not wish to compromise the moral drive and 'purity' of the movement by entanglement in party politics. There was also the disquiet expressed by many, in both leadership and rank-and-file, about close association with what was seen as the committed, politically motivated, socialist Left of the Labour Party. Construing the movement as a moral crusade, they were hostile to, or at best wary of, the 'Labour connection', as was a substantial section of the rank-and-file. However, even for those in the leadership who believed that the only practical way to achieve the objectives of the movement was to work through the Labour Party, there was a less than wholehearted commitment to the Labour Left. The key person here was Canon Collins. There were those on the Executive who were wholly committed to the Labour Left argument—principally Kingsley Martin and Michael Foot— but it was Collins who led the movement and who represented the dominant view of the Executive during the crucial 1959–61 years. And Collins was never wholly committed to the Labour Party, still less to the Labour Left, although he was an astute political operator. Even after the 1960 Conference, many CND activists were unwilling to devote their campaigning energies to securing their position within the Labour Party. Many of them were not politically committed at all, whilst some, like Jacquetta Hawkes, hardly realised the significance of the 1960 Conference.[5] Of those who were politically committed, many feared, with good reason, that an abrupt move to bring the whole movement into the Labour Party would have alienated a large degree of support. Even for those who were ready to undertake this agitation within the Labour Party, the tactics and procedures to adopt were far from clear. All this stood in some contrast to the small, but coherent, cohesive and well financed, Gaitskellite campaign which worked, through 1961, to ensure the reversal of the decision. From the time of the 1960/1 reversal onwards the CND leadership was floundering, strategically speaking. The strategy of winning over the Labour Party via Labour Left and trade-union backing had rather unexpectedly come good in 1960. But the reversal in 1961 and the subsequent burying of the issue in 1962 and the years following, leading up to the election-induced unity under Wilson in 1963–4, left the movement high and dry. Popular support grew dramatically through 1961 and continued strong through 1962 and 1963, but the leadership had nothing else to offer except the now discredited, and increasingly unrealistic, Labour Party strategy. As the years passed so disillusionment with this perspective deepened, and the divisions and cynicism within the movement grew.[6] It was thus unlikely that the leadership of CND could have brought the whole of CND (let alone the DAC and the Committee of 100)[7] into the labour-movement struggle. However, as many realised at the time, as this was the strategy adopted for good or ill by the leadership, it was essential to try to implement it at the most favourable opportunity—that is, following the 1960 Conference victory. The failure to do this was in part the responsibility of the CND leadership, as has been indicated. But it was also due to the inherent weakness of the Labour Left.

This is not the place to enter into the complex (and contentious) debate over the nature and viability of the Labour Left.[8] It must, however, be noted that not only has the Labour Left *in practice* been persistently weak, it has also been bedevilled by all the standard problems of reformism.[9]

The fact that the Labour Left has generally been allied, uneasily and always as the weaker partner, with the Centre and the Right of the party, has greatly exacerbated the problem. This general pattern was certainly confirmed by the political situation in which the Labour Left found itself in the 1958 to 1965 period. By the time of the birth of CND, Aneurin Bevan, the acknowledged leader of the Labour Left, had come out unequivocally against unilateralism and, in the hope of attaining office as a future Labour Foreign Secretary, had reached an 'accommodation' with Gaitskell and the parliamentary leadership. The Left was thus in a very weak position inside the PLP at the time of CND's rise to prominence. Mikardo has summed up the Labour Left view succinctly. 'There wasn't really much hope once Nye had gone.'[10]

In the specific context of the 1958 to 1965 period, then, the Labour Left's ability to achieve power, and bring about the unilateralist objectives of the movement, was severely limited. And yet there can be no doubt that there were socialist dimensions to the movement's demands. There is a strong case[11] for arguing that there have been fundamental connections between the dominant financial and international interests of British capitalism, with its insistence upon sterling as an international currency, and the preoccupation of the governing class, post-1945, with the preservation of Britain's role as an international power, symbolised above all by the independent nuclear deterrent. To achieve unilateral nuclear disarmament, especially in the 1958 to 1965 period, would thus have required a fundamental shift in *economic,* as well as political, position. However, it could be argued that such changes were not necessarily *socialist* in character. A Labour Left government, for example, giving priority to rebuilding the manufacturing base of the British economy and using protectionist measures to ensure that investment was channelled into the domestic economy, could combine unilateralism within an overall programme of a reformed *industrial* capitalism.

Such arguments, however, omit the more fundamental political objectives of the peace movement. For unilateralism to have any real meaning it had to be linked, as CND at leadership level realised,[12] to a commitment to withdrawal from NATO, and to the closure of American bases. The separation of Britain from the Western alliance entails a policy of positive neutralism. Such a change in foreign and defence policy would be unprecedented in twentieth-century British history. However, this again cannot be viewed wholly in policy or ideological terms. Positive neutralism entails not only the development of a distinct and innovative ideological position but also the placing of the whole unilateralist initiative in a progressive *socialist* context. If unilateralism is bound up with the move away from capitalism towards not a communist, totalitarian system, but a distinctive *neutralist* position, then this has implications both for the overall social structure and for the network of international political and economic relationships. The nature of these implications is discussed below in the context of the New Left. Here, it need be noted only that although there is no *necessary* connection between positive neutralism and socialism, the strong implication of the positive neutralist position is the espousal of an ideology which affirms a belief in humanistic socialism. Thus, at this level too, unilateralism has ultimately socialist as well as radical dimensions.

Finally, in a very different sense, unilateralism entails a radical change in attitude, a demand for a change in basic cultural structure. Unilateralism is a symbol, for the whole movement, of deeply felt revulsion against the perceived immorality and insanity of nuclear weapons. It is thus a *rejection, a priori,* of some of the most central of the cultural assumptions and determinants of modern capitalist society—a rejection of violence as a legitimate force in the nuclear age, and of the cluster of concepts ('deterrence', 'defence', 'civil defence' *et al.*) which constitute the military and political establishment orthodoxy.

Given the weaknesses of the Labour Left, as discussed above, and the essentially 'integrated' nature of the Labour Left's ideology and political programme, it is thus unlikely that such major and radical changes in defence and foreign policy could have been instigated—at least in the 1958 to 1965 period—from within a Labour Party led from the Left. And yet, as has been argued, some means of achieving such radical and essentially socialist changes was necessary if the peace movement's objectives were to be attained.

It is thus appropriate at this stage to consider whether there were other, more radical, perspectives in the movement better able than the Labour Left to articulate the political demands and achieve the stated objectives of the movement. The central perspectives to be considered here must be those of the direct actionists and the New Left,[13] both of which, in their different ways, operated on the central assumption that the movement was concerned not with a single issue but with a much wider, more fundamental, and far reaching political struggle.

The direct action strategy

Those within the movement who supported a direct action strategy were in many ways sharply divergent from the orthodox socialist Left—whether mainstream social democratic or Marxian socialist. For the direct actionists the movement for peace was not a part of the wider struggle to achieve a socialist society (still less was it seen as involved with the 'parochial' struggles within the Labour Party). On the contrary, the real struggle was located, so it was argued, within the parameters of the 'warfare state' itself. It was this 'warfare state' and the ideology of violence which underpinned it, which had produced the horrific insanity of nuclear weapons. It was against the military/industrial complex, which was held to dominate the 'warfare state', that the direct actionists directed their protests. Moreover, the orthodox institutions of parliamentary democracy were regarded with suspicion, as an integrated and therefore tainted part of that system— at best, of marginal relevance, and at worst, a snare and delusion which could emasculate the movement. The real struggle, for the direct actionists, lay in the mobilisation of mass, extra-parliamentary, non-violent direct action to immobilise and ultimately to overthrow, the 'warfare state'.

The direct actionists within the movement enjoyed considerable support, articulated at first through the Direct Action Committee from its formation in 1957, and later through the Committee of 100 which was created in late 1960, and into which the DAC merged in 1961. There was a general cynicism and lack of interest in the potential of the Labour Party as an agency for the sort of changes that were desired.[14] Many of the activists who supported the DAC and the Committee of 100 voted Labour, but there was no real involvement or conviction. Moreover, the repeated attempts at mounting alternative electoral outlets—'Voters' Veto', INDEC[15]—testified to the continuing desire to create an alternative formation to the Labour Party, and probably to parliamentary politics *per se.*

The long term commitments of the direct actionists—centrally, to the wholesale transformation, through non-violent revolution, of the 'warfare state'—were broadly adhered to by all those on the direct action wing of the movement. However, the way in which these generalised objectives were brought together varied considerably in the Committee of 100, whilst the more homogeneous DAC always lacked a mass base. Neither organisation had a clear and coherent programme of objectives over and above the central demands of unilateralism and the rest of the CND official policy package.

The DAC, to be sure, had a highly ambitious policy programme which included unilateralism for the West as a whole. But there was no attempt to come to terms with the real nature of the power structure, national or international, or the real possibilities for political change. Indeed, the policy of the DAC was unrealistic at a number of levels. First, it was politically unrealistic, although morally and ideologically consistent with pacifist principles, to call for immediate unilateral nuclear disarmament by both the USA and the USSR. Second, it was strategically unrealistic because its very ambitious policy proposals were wholly out of proportion to its minuscule size and strength. Third, it was ideologically unrealistic because it failed to appreciate the importance of linking-in to the organised working-class movement at both the direct political level, and the more generalised cultural and ideological levels. It made no serious attempt to link its own politics into the more substantial constituencies of radical and socialist opinion that did exist in Britain. Finally, it was psychologically unrealistic in advocating wholesale and immediate changes in the views of the mass of the ordinary people towards war, violence and conflict, with few, if any, intermediate steps.

The DAC's programme was in fact, and despite its genuine radicalism, couched in the traditions of the somewhat esoteric British pacifist movement, whose underlying conceptions had been individualist, almost salvationist, and much opposed to collectivist socialism. The DAC 'purists' did try to change the predominantly individualist ethos of this pacifist tradition, and certainly its Gandhian-influenced, socially oriented pacifism *was* very different. But it produced no central conceptions, in either theoretical or organisational terms, to replace the old individualist creed of pacifism. There was no concerted attempt to bring together the new Gandhian-oriented thinking to create the ideology and the politics of the non-violent society. As Hugh Brock and April Carter, in their different ways the two most important 'Gandhian influences' on the direct action movement, have both testified,[16] no coherent or substantial 'politics of non-violence' was ever evolved by the DAC.

The strategic and ideological perspective of the insurrectionary militants in the Committee of 100 (of whom Ralph Schoenman was the most prominent) was potentially violent, and arguably more unrealistic. However rosy the prospects for the Committee of 100 may have seemed in late 1961 following the mass civil disobedience demonstrations in London and at Holy Loch, there was little, if any, possibility of the insurrectionary scenario envisaged by Schoenman actually developing. It is of course easy to make such judgments with the knowledge of the subsequent historical events. Yet, as Michael Randle and numerous other activists of the time have recalled,[17] the Committee was never in a position to act as the catalyst for a *levée en masse:* it represented a small minority of the population, and, more importantly, had little or no industrial or political power.

Thus, despite its major impact in 1961, the insurrectionary aspirations were never a major threat to the state, whose forces were able to cope with the civil disobedience demonstrations with relative ease. After the September 1961 demonstrations, the peak of the Committee's achievements, the state brought into play its legal and coercive power, and effectively crushed the militant wing of the movement.[18] It seems reasonable to concur with the conclusion of George Clark, who has subsequently argued that this was not really serious politics at any level, but represented rather political 'adventurism'.[19]

The strategy of the libertarian socialists in the Committee—the community-oriented decentralists—was in most cases more realistic. Whilst they placed great emphasis on 'movement power', and the need for control to be firmly in the hands of the movement, they had for the most part no illusions about the enormous problems facing the movement in both its immediate and its long-term objectives. Rejecting both the orthodox anarchist and the orthodox socialist conceptions, assumptions and models, most activists of this tendency concentrated their attention on the immediate task of building a bigger and more radically oriented peace movement. From this involvement in radical peace politics would emerge, they hoped, a more politically conscious and aware movement. Their more long-term objectives and strategies were, however, vague and undefined. Most, in the end, opted for variants of George Clark's community politics —populist, decentralised and radical, with an individualist and 'small group', rather than collectivist, orientation.

Overall, this direct action perspective commanded considerable support in its various guises, within the movement, as has been noted. It is the contention here, however, that such a perspective contained insuperable problems. These were fundamentally twofold: the direct actionists had no coherent and realistic strategy for attaining their objectives (either short- or long-term); equally important, and intimately linked to this, they had no worked-through analysis within which to interpret their involvement in the movement and their more long-term objectives.

There was thus little if any prospect of the direct actionists bringing about either the short-term policy objectives they were aiming for, or the long-term radicalisation which was implicit in their actions. Such a key figure as Michael Randle, chairman of the DAC and secretary of the Committee of 100, has confirmed this, to all intents and purposes. Looking back twenty years to the direct action campaign of the Committee of 100 in 1961, he recalled that even at its height the civil disobedience movement was not within sight of creating a 'revolutionary situation': to achieve this would have required millions rather than thousands of active supporters. The most that could be hoped for, even at this high point in 1961, was to involve direct actionists in ways 'which directly affected the government's ability to carry out the programme of preparation for nuclear war. . .'[20] To claim even that for the direct actionists proved, in the long term, too optimistic. As far as the more ambitious long-term objectives were concerned, these were always unrealistic because of both the essentially weak political position of the DAC and the Committee of 100, and the marginality and incoherence of the direct action position. As noted above, this 'strategic' weakness was linked to political and analytical deficiencies at the very core of the direct actionists' framework. How was the politics of the non-violent society to be defined, let alone achieved? What were the relationships between the direct action perspective and other, arguably wider, frameworks of belief, such as anarchism, libertarian socialism, liberal democracy, etc? These and other central questions remained unanswered: the direct actionists had no coherently articulated overall political framework.

Thus, despite their dramatic early successes the DAC and the Committee of 100 did not offer the prospect of advance towards a structural transformation of society, which would have provided the context for the realisation of unilateralist and wider peace movement objectives. It thus remains, in this section of the analysis, to examine the claims of the New Left to represent some potential agency for both the realisation of unilateralist aims, and a linked but wider socialist restructuring.

*The New Left strategy**
Neither the Labour Left nor the direct action perspectives therefore offered the movement a viable strategy for advance. Both contained elements which were essential if the movement was to succeed. But both were also characterised by inherent and fundamental flaws which

---

*The connections between the New Left and the peace movement have been analysed earlier by Nigel Young in *An Infantile Disorder? The Crisis and Decline of the New Left,* (Routledge and Kegan Paul, 1977) although the conclusions drawn here are somewhat different.

rendered them ultimately inadequate, as has been argued.

It is the contention here that the New Left politics, developing out of the new formations and ideological stances first formulated in the late 1950s, offered in 1958 to 1965, and continues to offer in the 1980s, at least the potential for the creation of a viable political strategy for advance for the peace movement. This is a large and perhaps controversial claim. It rests principally upon two interrelated arguments: first, that the New Left, because of its ideological genesis and profile, had the ability to play the crucial catalyctic role, to bring together the power of the labour movement and the centrally important extra-parliamentary politics of the direct actionists; and, second, that the New Left provided a genuine link with the minority radical tradition in British politics, which has played such an important role in the development of left-wing movements in Britain since the seventeenth century.

To elaborate these arguments it is necessary briefly to discuss the specific politics of the New Left in the 1958 to 1965 period. We will then be in a position to analyse why, despite these advantages, the New Left failed to achieve success, either for itself or for the peace movement.

At the outset it is important to establish that the core of the New Left referred to here is those groups of socialists, and other radical progressives, who were gathered initially around the two journals 'New Reasoner' and 'Universities and Left Review'.

The catalysts which brought into existence these two groups were the dramatic events of 1956: the invasion of Suez and the suppression of the Hungarian uprising. The resultant upsurge of both feeling and intellect against the existing world order, communist East as much as capitalist West, was of profound importance, and had moral and humanistic, as well as political, bases. The predominantly youthful supporters of the New Left thus had in common their broadly humanistic socialist perspective and their commitment to the creation of a new ideological and political formation, distinct from existing orthodoxies. There were several important differences of orientation within the New Left, but on this fundamental approach all were agreed.

It is important to note here, too, that the New Left was an essentially eclectic and open-ended movement. Although predominantly socialist in outlook, there is no doubt that the New Left had strong libertarian sympathies, not in the sense of a formal commitment to anarchism in any form, but rather in the high priority it gave to the preservation and extension of freedom—both at the individual and the societal levels. Moreover, there was, in both theory and practice, a measure of cooperation and integration between the direct actionists and the New Left. (This was particularly the case in the early days of the movement when there was considerable New Left involvement in the 'first'[21] Aldermaston March. Such cooperation was far less marked post 1960/1, when the New Left tended to move more towards an orthodox socialist and strategic critique —*vide* Stuart Hall's 'Steps Towards Peace'—and the Committee of 100 became increasingly anarchistic in orientation.) There was a shared, and unambiguous, commitment to the unilateralist campaign. And there was also a common sympathy with (a broadly defined) libertarian politics. Numerous prominent individual activists spanned the two movements: George Clark and Alan Lovell for example. Moreover, there were links between the DAC and both the syndicalist-oriented tradition within the extra-parliamentary Left, and the ILP Left (e.g. Allen Skinner and Hugh Brock).

There were thus interconnections at a number of levels between the New Left, the direct actionists and, to an extent, the extra-parliamentary wings of the labour movement. And yet it must be emphasised that there were fundamental ideological and political differences between the New Left and the direct actionists. There was a rejection, by the direct action-ists, of one of the basic tenets of Marxist socialism, that politics was at base a process of struggle between social classes whose economic and political interests were inherently different under capitalism. They thus rejected the idea that *conflict* was an inherent part of the political process: indeed, the whole strategy was geared to attaining a *consensus,* ultimately upon a moral basis, on the nuclear issue. The central, defining character-istic of the society for which the DAC was striving would be its non-violence. To be sure, the society would be *socialist* in the sense that an egalitarian and decentralised social structure was envisaged, and a greater equality of both wealth and power, within a context where the coercive power of the state was severely reduced if not abolished, was assumed. But the reference point for the direct actionists of the DAC remained the individual, not the class: and, for the more anarchistic Committee of 100 post 1961/2, the analysis was couched in more conventionally anarchistic categories in which the coercive 'warfare state' was seen as the major adversary. Despite this rhetoric, the direct actionists' fundamental belief was in the *moral* conversion of as many individuals as possible to the cause of nuclear disarmament (and ultimately the wider cause of non-violent politics). Their 'socialism' was thus almost entirely at the level of an emotive commitment to socialist values, and it had little if any compre-hension of socialist analysis, of either Marxist or other varieties.

It would thus be entirely misleading to think of the direct actionists and the New Left as being an integrated entity. Similarly, there were fundamental differences between the New Left and the orthodox labour movement. Not only was a substantial section of the New Left from an explicitly Marxist background (as is discussed below), the whole thrust of the New Left was towards the development of an *extra-parliamentary* politics.

What then were the advantages of the New Left strategy and perspective for the peace movement?

The first, and in some ways the most important, advantage of the New Left lay in its absolute and genuine commitment to the cause of unilateralism, and the movement-style that accompanied it, combined with a coherent and cohesive ideological perspective. This perspective, whilst giving central priority to the peace issue, did not treat it in isolation, and made a realistic assessment of its relationship to other relevant political questions. Thus, unlike the Labour Left which tended to subordinate the unilateralist issue to the wider struggle to achieve a left-wing Labour Party leadership, and viewed the whole movement in terms of the wider struggle within the party, the whole thrust of the New Left was connected intimately with the achievement of the nuclear disarmament movement's objectives.

This is a key point, and thus worth substantiating in more detail. For the New Left, the unilateralist case was in part, but only in part, based upon the moral rejection of nuclear weapons which characterised the overwhelming majority of the movement. This was a genuinely moral commitment, emanating from a perception of the deep immorality of both Eastern and Western systems as exemplified by the events of 1956. The threat of the use of genocidal weapons was held to be the ultimate immorality, and the New Left joined with others in the movement in rejecting this, unequivocally, on moral grounds. However, there was also, for the New Left, a critical political dimension to the movement. If unilateralism were a part of the overall process of the rejection of the values and the structures that underpinned both capitalism and communism, then it must be seen as a part, too, of the wider political attempt to formulate a new politics based upon humanistic, democratic socialist precepts. Such a politics would necessarily evolve its own democratic socialist structures and procedures, but, on the international level, it would crucially involve the adoption of a positive neutralist perspective. To achieve the objectives of international peace, and a reduction of the power of the inherently unacceptable ideological and political systems of capitalism and communism, the formation of an international neutralist movement was essential. Thus, as far as Britain was concerned in the 1958 to 1965 period, the New Left was concerned to show the necessary connections between unilateralism, withdrawal from NATO, the espousal of a foreign policy based upon positive neutralism, and the more general objective of moving towards a democratic socialist society.

In this sense, therefore, the New Left's commitment to unilateralism was both specific and politically coherent. Unlike most of the other radical groupings discussed, it had a coherent ideological stance which did not rely exclusively on emotive moralism. However, equally important was the New Left's commitment to the movement's extra-parliamentary, quasi-libertarian ethos. All the 'orthodox Left' groupings were essentially

ill at ease with the mode of extra-parliamentary politics which characterised the movement (i.e. the Labour Left, the Communist Party, and the
various Trotskyist groups).

However, the whole thrust of the New Left was towards a new politics
centred on the direct participation of ordinary people in the decision-
making process. There was a contrast here between the exclusive concentration of the Trotskyists on the (traditionally defined) 'working class',
and the New Left's more generalised appeal to 'ordinary people'. Whilst
this had certain disadvantages, primarily in relation to the wider movement's lack of appreciation of the political centrality of the working
class and the organised labour movement, the New Left's more eclectic
appeal had the potential to bring together both working-class, labour-
movement activists and the predominantly middle-class supporters of
the disarmament movement. This again was indicative of the catalyctic
role which the New Left had the potential to play.

It was only through this process of involving ordinary people in
decision-making structures, it was argued, that the dangers of an overly
abstract and bureaucratic socialism could be avoided, and a genuinely
humanistic, responsive, and democratic structure be built. In this sense,
therefore, there was, as has been noted earlier, much in common in terms
of fundamental approach between the New Left and the direct actionists.

The commitment to extra-parliamentary politics led to the second
major advantage possessed by the New Left. Potentially, the New Left
had a direct ideological link with the radical tradition in British politics
which, it has been argued by many historians and analysts,[22] has been a
persistent if not continuous element in British society since at least the
mid-seventeenth century.[23] This tradition has been predominantly
humanistic, libertarian and socialist in character. In the nineteenth and
twentieth centuries it has acted as a major focus of protest, sometimes
even rebellion, against the established order. This is not to deny the
importance of other formations and traditions, both within the more
orthodox social democratic mainstream and within the revolutionary
Left, but it *is* to claim that at particular and critical periods there has
been a mobilisation of this popular, political type which has been of
central importance. From the major struggles of the trade-union and
wider labour movement in the nineteenth century to the issue-based
movements of the later twentieth century, this extra-parliamentary,
humanistic tradition has formed an important part of the radical strata
in British society. In two important ways this perspective has acted too
as a link to other central aspects of radical opinion. It has brought together radical intellectual opinion with sections of the organised labour
movement, and has acted as an effective counterforce to the predominant
labourism and parliamentarism. Equally important, it has linked in issue-
based movements to the wider radical and socialist strata of opinion, in

terms of both the labour movement and the more variegated extra-parliamentary, libertarian perspectives.

Alone of the political sections of the movement, therefore, the New Left had the ideological stance and the political position which might, in more favourable circumstances, have enabled some real advances to be made. It was not only that the *policies* that the New Left stood for combined the inherent connection between peace and socialist objectives (e.g. withdrawal from NATO, positive neutralism, etc.) it was also that its overall perspective embodied both peace and socialist conceptions (e.g. emphasis upon people making their own history, and upon the struggle for freedom being inherently linked to the struggle for socialism, etc.).

The New Left was also a rich repository of socialist creativity and intellectual ability. This intellectual power provided the bases for the New Left's creative political ideology: it enabled the New Left to produce qualitatively better—more informed, knowledgeable, and sophisticated—analyses and prescriptions than any other grouping in the movement.

Yet the New Left was fatally flawed in a number of ways. Its very intellectualism was one of the reasons for its failure. Despite all its advantages it never managed to break out of its academic, intellectually elitist constituency. Many people in the movement simply did not understand the New Left's concepts, language, and overall political position. To an extent this was inevitable, given both the strong academic, university background of the New Left's most prominent members, and the relatively low level of intellectual and political awareness in the movement as a whole in the 1958 to 1965 period. It was also the case, however, that the New Left failed to make any significant effort to extend its politics beyond its immediate student/intellectual constituency. In particular, it made very little contact with two key groups, with both of whom, it was argued above, it had considerable common ground. These groups—the direct actionists, and the organised industrial and political labour movement—probably could not have been brought together by any force other than the New Left, for both ideological and organisational reasons. And without their coming together, around both programme commitments and an extra-parliamentary strategy, the movement had little chance of advance.

The New Left's failure to attract significant support in the organised labour movement, however, was not due entirely to its failure to communicate politically. It was the result, too, of a fundamental ideological and political flaw. It was always unable to reach a clear position on its attitude to labourism and parliamentarism. This was not merely a tactical or strategic ambivalence, but was the result of a deep-seated uncertainty about revolutionism or reformism, socialist mobilisation on an extra-parliamentary basis or Left social democracy via the ballot box and the existing institutions. Because it was unable to analyse and resolve satisfactorily these problems, the New Left got the worst of both worlds: it attracted neither the parliamentary Labour Left (which was anyway predominantly antipathetic to the New Left because of its seeming abstraction and intellectualism) nor the (potentially) extra-parliamentary Left in the industrial labour movement and the Constituency Labour Parties. And, of course, the wider socio-economic context of the period was not conducive to the development of a powerful New Left formation. Economic stability—even modest growth—had become the norm by the late 1950s. Capitalism appeared to have solved its inherent problems of instability, and 'boom and slump'. Full employment and relative industrial harmony prevailed. In this climate there was little potential for a radical middle-class movement to grow; and there was certainly a seemingly unbridgeable gulf between the predominantly middle-class New Left and the almost wholly working-class, industrial labour movement.

There was thus little likelihood of the New Left achieving its objectives, or even of its dominating the politics of the peace movement. However, the politics which it represented has subsequently been seen as a far more viable and powerful force. And, as was argued earlier, the politics of the New Left—rather than of the direct actionists or of the orthodox labourists—has formed the basis of the new, and radical, politics which has subsequently developed. In what has this politics consisted, and, more significantly, how can this claim for its importance be justified?

There are several general developments, not related specifically to the politics of the peace movement, which are of contextual importance. First and foremost has been the partial disintegration of the seemingly stable and secure Western economic system. The onset of prolonged crisis and recession in the 1970s, with its concomitant social problems (notably unemployment), has destroyed the political, as well as the economic, self-confidence that hitherto characterised post-war Europe. Within this overall era of crisis, Britain's long-term economic decline has of course been exacerbated, her world role has sharply diminished, and her dependence (economic, military and political) upon both the USA and her Western European allies has increased. Thus, not only has the City's dependence upon the international role of sterling declined, the whole notion of Britain as a 'world power' has all but disappeared. Despite the almost obsessive commitment of the Thatcher government to ever greater stocks of nuclear weapons (both British and American) it remains the case that there is considerable scepticism amongst important sections of the governing class over the viability of the independent deterrent. Prominent military men, for example, from Lord Mountbatten to Lord Carver, have expressed disquiet over British nuclear weapons. Potentially much more significant, however, is the effect of the crisis upon the stability of the socio-economic basis of British society. The material base of the 1950s and 1960s, within which the integration of the working class has been rooted, has been significantly eroded. To date, this has resulted not in radicalisation of the traditional working class, but predominantly in a political demoralisation and disorientation. However, if the crisis persists it would seem likely that the traditional 'quietism' of the bulk of the working class—and equally important, the traditional 'moderation' and adherence to social democratic ideology of the labour movement leadership—may give way to some more radical orientation. Thus the polarisation of British politics, which has already begun in the early 1980s, is very likely to proceed apace as the decade advances. It is not clear, of course, which political *direction* will be taken by the working class in the new context of the recession. But it does seem evident that the old stability of the 1950s and 1960s has disappeared.

A second major development which bears upon the argument has been the rapid growth of the 'middle class' within British society in the period since the 1950s. Whilst major sectors of the class are of course opposed to radical political ideas and remain quite separate from the labour movement, it is also true that there has been a considerable expansion in the number of radical, tertiary educated, professional and intellectual employees, whose public-sector occupations and general background of 'critical thinking', have resulted in an ideological stance opposed to the market individualism of competitive capitalism.[24] Such a disaffected, radical middle-class fraction has of course existed throughout the twentieth century. It has been from within this constituency that most of the impetus for direct action movements in the past has stemmed. The crucial development in the 1970s, however, has been the *expansion* of this social group, as a result, primarily, of the expansion of higher education and public sector employment (and the subsequent rise in unemployment, because of the fiscal crisis of the state as the recession has deepened). There have been three major groupings involved in this radical middle-class growth: trade-union activists in the white-collar unions (white-collar union membership has grown from 1.9m in 1948, to 2.68m in 1964, and 4.26m in 1974);[25] new artisans ('a set of often college trained young people denied access to bureaucratic occupations because of the recession, who have turned instead. . . to petty commodity production—in wood, textiles, paint and so on—')[26] and welfare bureaucrats (those working in schools, hospitals, welfare agencies, etc., who, as Cotgrove and Duff have observed, have rejected, at least to an extent, the ideology and values of industrial capitalism and opted instead for 'careers outside the market place').[27]

What was once a 'marginal constituency' for the Left has thus become a major sub-section of the class structure of contemporary Britain. In this sense, too, therefore, the context for a New Left politics is considerably more favourable in the 1970s and 1980s than was the case in the 1958

to 1965 period. The strength of this radical middle-class Left has manifested itself in numerous ways: most notably through the growth of
ecological/environmentalist politics,[28] and the women's movement.[29]

Finally, the Labour Left has itself undergone profound change since
the 1960s—in part cause and in part effect of the developments already
discussed. This change cannot be measured merely in terms of the adoption of more socialist policies and a more democratic organisational
structure, important though these have been; still less can this change be
identified with the rise to prominence of a particular individual, Tony
Benn, as the media would have us believe. Rather, the change represents
a qualitative move away from the exclusively parliamentarist preoccupations of orthodox labourism and has emphasised far more the concept of
the wider, partially extra-parliamentary, labour movement, giving more
centrality to issue-based campaigns and the need for a broad socialist
alliance. All this has not signified, of course, the collapse of orthodox,
parliamentarist labourism. But it has meant a real advance within the
Labour Left, for the politics espoused by the New Left and its successors.
Thus the specific commitments of the Labour Left, particularly on the
nuclear and NATO issues, have been interpreted, at least to an extent,
within the context of a New Left, extra-parliamentary and positive neutralist politics. The result of these processes has been to remove many of the
barriers and impasses which existed in the 1958 to 1965 period, and
strengthen the potential for creating a genuine alliance between the extra-
parliamentary issue-based movements and the Labour Left.

There has thus been a resurgence of an extra-parliamentary, alternative
Left culture in the 1970s and 1980s, which has been combined with a
structural strengthening of the basis of the radical middle-class Left.
Britain still has, of course, a profoundly conservative political culture,
and a very securely based capitalist socio-economic system. Yet challenges
to this structure and its ideology can and must be made. The original
nuclear disarmament movement of 1958 to 1965 was a major attempt to
challenge an important aspect of this structure. Its politics was deficient,
however, as has been argued. Neither the 'labourists' nor the direct actionists could succeed alone: and the catalyctic force which might have been
provided by the New Left did not materialise. Subsequent developments
have made far more favourable the prospects for a New Left politics,
centred on 'Third Way' concepts of humanistic socialism. The experience
of extra-parliamentary politics in the 1970s and 1980s, combined with the
widespread disillusionment with parliamentarist Labour politics, has
created a new and far more favourable context for the building of a
viable extra-parliamentary, radical movement. Within this process the
peace movement has a crucial role to play: and, equally important, without the creation of such a broader movement the objectives of the peace
movement will remain unfulfilled. 'To build peace', as Raymond Williams

has written in the 1980s, 'now more than ever, it is necessary to build more than peace. To refuse nuclear weapons, we have to refuse much more than nuclear weapons. Unless the refusals can be connected with such building, unless protest can be connected with and surpassed by significant practical construction, our strength will remain insufficient.'[30] It is in this knowledge of the necessary link between the struggle for peace and the struggle for humanistic socialist change that the legacy of the 1958 to 1965 nuclear disarmament movement finds its central articulation.

NOTES

1. See the survey which forms Part II of Richard Taylor and Colin Pritchard, *The Protest Makers, The British Nuclear Disarmament Movement of 1958-1965, Twenty Years on,* (Pergamon Press, 1980). Approximately one-third of the sample in this survey rejected any political dimension of the movement's activities.

2. It is not necessary here to enter into the complex debate over the definition of terms such as 'ruling elite', 'ruling class', etc. The term 'governing class' is used here to denote that cluster of individuals with especial influence over national political decision-making. This comprises chiefly senior government ministers, other leading political figures, senior civil servants and the representatives of the large corporate institutions within particular social, economic, military and industrial spheres. For further discussions of this area see Ralph Miliband, *The State in Capitalist Society,* (Weidenfeld and Nicolson, 1969) eds., John Urry and John Wakeford, *Power in Britain,* (Heinemann, 1973).

3. Ian Mikardo, in conversation with Richard Taylor, April 1978.

4. Still less was such trade-union support indicative of trade-union involvement in CND as an organisation. With some notable exceptions—John Horner of the Fire Brigades Union, for example—trade-union leaders remained purposely aloof from CND *per se.*

5. '. . . many of us were unaware that it (i.e. the campaign within the Labour Party in 1960) was happening. We were absolutely astonished by the 1960 Labour Conference vote.' Jacquetta Hawkes, in conversation with Richard Taylor, January 1978.

6. Significant numbers of disarmament movement supporters, who had joined the Labour Party primarily on the nuclear issue in the late 1950s and early 1960s, resigned their membership in the mid- to late-1960s. This is confirmed by the survey in Taylor and Pritchard, op. cit. Peggy Duff, CND's secretary and one of the most long-standing and committed Labour Party socialists in CND's leadership, resigned from the party in 1967.

7. There was much less ambivalence in relation to the Labour Party amongst the direct actionists of the DAC and the Committee of 100, most of whom, although they may have voted Labour and even in some cases been party members, had little faith in the Labour Party as the agency for achieving the movement's objectives.

8. See, for example: Ralph Miliband, *Parliamentary Socialism,* second edition, (Merlin Press, 1973); David Coates, *The Labour Party and the Struggle for Socialism,* (Cambridge University Press, 1974); David Coates, *Labour in Power? A Study of the Labour Government 1974-1979,* (Longmans, 1980); Tom Nairn, 'The Nature of the Labour Party', in eds. P. Anderson and R. Blackburn, *Towards Socialism,* (Fontana and New Left Books, 1966); David Howell, *British*

Social Democracy, (Croom Helm, 1976); eds. Cook and Taylor, *The Labour Party; an introduction to its history structure and politics,* (Longmans, 1980).

9. The problems of reformism, and the alternative socialist strategies available, are discussed in some detail in eds., David Coates and Gordon Johnston, *A Socialist Primer* Vol. 2, (Martin Robertson, 1983).

10. Mikardo, loc. cit.

11. This argument is pursued in depth in Stephen Blank, 'Britain: the Politics of foreign economic policy, the domestic economy, and the problem of pluralistic stagnation', *International Organization,* Vol. 31, No. 4, Autumn 1977.

12. CND adopted withdrawal from NATO as official policy in 1960. Analyses of defence matters have confirmed that it was the commitment to withdraw from the Western alliance that was the really radical policy: unilateralism *per se* was a relatively minor matter. See, for example, A.J.R. Groom, *British Thinking About Nuclear Weapons,* (Frances Pinter, 1974).

13. The Marxist/Leninist/Trotskyist formations in Britain had little influence within the movement from 1958 to 1965. The Communist Party was the only significant such organisation at the time, and its politics was in tension with that of the movement in two respects. First, it was always suspicious of the movement's neutralist and therefore anti-Soviet tendencies, and it disagreed with the emphasis that was put upon unilateralism *per se* (indeed, the CP withheld full support from CND until 1959/60 on these grounds). Second, the CP neither liked nor really understood the extra-parliamentary, libertarian ethos of the movement as a whole (and of the direct actionists in particular). The CP was thus intent upon re-directing CND *et al.* towards a more conventional labour-movement approach. CP influence in CND remained marginal until the mid 1960s, by which time the movement had ceased, temporarily, to be a major political force.

The Trotskyist groups were tiny and of marginal importance, although the Socialist Labour League (now the WRP) had some contact with the DAC over industrial direct action, and the International Socialists (now the SWP) developed important theoretical analysis of the links between capitalist economic structure and the development of nuclear weapons.

The cumulative total impact of the orthodox Marxist Left on the movement was thus minimal. In conformity with the general history of the Marxist revolutionary Left in Britain since the founding of the Communist Party in 1920, these groupings found themselves unable to mobilise mass support from within the movement, and were equally ineffective in creating any widespread Marxian socialist consciousness. For further analysis of the revolutionary Left in Britain, see Richard Taylor, 'To the Left of Labour: Revolutionary Politics in England, 1920–1980', in eds., Roger Fieldhouse and Richard Taylor, *Revolutionary England 1380s to the 1980s,* forthcoming.

14. However, there was considerable enthusiasm for the potential of industrial working-class action, via the labour movement, on quasi-syndicalist lines. But only in the case of Pat Arrowsmith's series of industrial campaigns was this translated into political *action.* And, however committed and innovative this campaign may have been, its net results in real terms were minimal.

15. 'Voters' Veto' was a campaign to persuade voters to withhold their votes from non-unilateralist candidates at the South-West Norfolk by-election in 1959. Both the CND leadership and those in the Labour Party (especially the PLP), who supported CND, were very opposed to this campaign, and it marked the end of any real cooperation between the DAC and the Labour Party.

The Independent Nuclear Disarmament Election Committee (INDEC) was an attempt by CND radicals (principally New Left activists, with the support initially of Peggy Duff) to mount an independent electoral presence to challenge the Labour Party's reversal, in 1961, of the commitment to unilateralism made at the 1960 Party Conference. INDEC, which was denounced vigorously by Labour Party supporters of CND (Michael Foot referred to the proposal as 'poison'), never received the official backing of CND and by the time it was eventually established (1962) the moment for action had passed.

16.   Hugh Brock and April Carter, in conversation with Richard Taylor, March and January 1978, respectively.

17.   Michael Randle, George Clark and Alan Lovell, in conversation with Richard Taylor, May, January and September 1978, respectively. It is important to note here, however, that neither these activists, nor others, such as Brock and Carter, in the direct action tradition, subscribe to the analysis presented here, and the conclusions drawn.

18.   Principally through the arrest of the Committee of 100's leaders prior to the demonstrations in December at Wethersfield air base and elsewhere, and their subsequent trial and imprisonment under the Official Secrets Act.

19.   George Clark, in conversation with Richard Taylor, January 1978.

20.   Randle, loc. cit.

21.   The first demonstrations at Aldermaston had been organised, on a very small scale, in April 1952 by Hugh Brock and others. However, the first Aldermaston March, *from* London *to* Aldermaston, was organised by the DAC at Easter 1958.

22.   Most notably, E.P. Thompson, *The Making of the English Working Class,* (Penguin, 1963). But see also the works of numerous other historians, Eric Hobsbawm, for example.

23.   See eds., Fieldhouse and Taylor, op. cit.

24.   For further discussion, see David Coates, *An Introduction to the Economic and Social Context of British Politics,* forthcoming.

25.   Coates, op. cit.

26.   Ibid., p. 189.

27.   Steven Cotgrove and Andrew Duff, 'Environmentalism, Middle Class Radicalism and Politics', *Sociological Review,* Vol. 28(2), 1980.

28.   See Cotgrove and Duff, op. cit.

29.   See Sarah Perrigo, in eds., Coates and Johnston, *A Socialist Primer,* Vol. 2, (Martin Robertson, 1983); and Sheila Rowbotham, Lynne Segal and Hilary Wainwright, *Beyond the Fragments,* (Merlin Press, 1979).

30.   Raymond Williams, 'The Politics of Nuclear Disarmament', *New Left Review,* No. 124, 1981. Reprinted in Edward Thompson et al., *Exterminism and Cold War,* (Verso and New Left Books, 1982), pp. 65-85.

C.R. ATTLEE: AN ASSESSMENT

John Saville

The large-scale biography of Attlee by Kenneth Harris,[1] published in 1982 provides a readable but rather superficial account of the man and his times. It has 630 pages of text, notes and index but no detailed or specific references to any matter, or quotation, in the text; and this is not the way to write the history of one of the important figures in the twentieth-century history of Britain. Lists of books and of interviews used for each chapter are given at the end of the book but it is impossible to discover the date of, say, a quotation from *Hansard* except by searching the original source. Naturally we learn a number of things about Attlee that most people will not have known, and Harris is an experienced journalist and has clearly read widely; but a serious evaluation of the most important Labour prime minister so far in office still remains to be written.

Some personal matters first, for Attlee had more positive qualities than the historical fiction of 'the little man' often suggests. He was a unifying influence upon a potentially very divisive leadership in the years after 1945, although his influence was always on the conservative side. As a chairman and a coordinator of difficult colleagues he had an impressive record; and he was very sharp, capable of a political toughness towards his colleagues—except his most senior colleagues, and most of all Ernest Bevin—that is often surprising as it comes through the pages of Harris.

We must begin with an account of Attlee's socialism for it was of a particular kind that explains a great deal of his later political career. He was born in 1883 into a conservatively-minded middle-class family. He left his public school, Haileybury, so Harris writes 'intellectually immature and under-developed' (p. 9) and as with so many of the middle and upper classes in Britain, who never get beyond the emotional cloisters of their public schools, Attlee remained in many ways encapsulated within the language and thought of his own school days.[2] Haileybury was an experience Attlee never recovered from. Sir John Colville, on his first visit to Chequers after the Labour government assumed office in 1945, remarked on the difference between the days of Churchill and the new order: 'Very much stiff collar and starched shirts. I remember Attlee introducing me to his new PPS, Geoffrey de Freitas, and saying, "Old Haileyburian, you know". There never was any Old School Tie talk in Winston's day' (p. 414).

Nor did University College, Oxford, make any difference to the young Attlee. It was 'a social interlude rather than an intellectual adventure' (p. 14) and until he went into the East End of London, Attlee's mind remained closed to any degree of social understanding or conscience. Most of the Attlee family by this time were involved in middle-class social work: Tom, his favourite brother was helping in a working-men's hostel in Hoxton; an aunt was managing a club for factory girls in Wandsworth; his mother was a district visitor in a slum area; and the eldest brother, Robert, was working two nights a week at a mission in Hornsey. Attlee was taken by another brother, Lawrence, to the Haileybury Club in Stepney, and there, within a few months, he was to stay; and this is one of the interesting differences between him and his contemporaries. After the philanthropic 'stint' young middle-class men and women were then expected to return to 'normal' middle-class life. In Attlee's case he went to the Stepney Club every week and gradually was drawn more into its activities; and it was not long before he decided to live in Stepney, and there he remained until the beginning of the First World War. The particular character of the Haileybury Club—of which he became manager—is also important to define. It was a secular, not a religious mission; it aimed to inculcate certain of the attitudes which were thought important at Haileybury, and it did this through military training. The Club was in fact 'D' Company of the First Cadet Battalion of the Queen's (Royal West Surrey) Regiment and joining the Club was joining the junior section of the Territorial Army. The adults who ran the Club took Volunteer Commissions, and were the company officers. Discipline, team work, and a sense of belonging. Attlee, who was physically small, shy and reserved, and always in his younger days at least lacking in confidence, began to find fulfilment in his new responsibilities. But he went much further than administrative and charitable good works. He first joined the Fabians but his education and training in the labour movement began when he became active in the Stepney ILP. Of all the Labour prime ministers of the twentieth century Attlee had the most sustained experience of grass-roots politics. He spoke constantly at street corners, stood at dock-gates collecting money during the Irish Transport Workers strike of 1913, led marches of protest to the local Boards of Guardians and to the mayors, carried banners 'from the Mile End Waste across central London to Hyde Park', and above all, since this was the biggest problem of the London ILP in those days, tried to get closer to the trade unions and their members. Attlee, like so many of the middle class of his generation, was appalled at the waste and the dirt and the misery and the exploited labour that he saw around him. Ruskin and the romantic side of William Morris were his teachers; and in the conditions of the early twentieth century he came to accept the untheoretical labour-socialist rhetoric of mainstream ILP politics. In 1922, in what was to be his most radical period, he expressed his political creed in his address for the general election:

> . . . Like many of you I took part in the Great War in the hope of securing lasting peace and a better life for all. We were promised that wars would end, that. . . the men who fought in the War would be cared for, and that unemployment, slums and poverty would be abolished. I stand for *life against wealth*. I claim the right of every man, woman and child in the land to have the best life that can be provided. Instead of the exploitation of the mass of the people in the interests of a small rich class, I demand the organisation of the country in the interests of all as a co-operative commonwealth in which land and capital will be owned by the nation and used for the benefit of the community.   p.55

These were ideas, sentiments, feelings consonant with the majority of the new-style Labour Party after 1918, and like so many of his time, once living standards improved and biting poverty was abolished, the socialist commonwealth dreamed of in youth became easily identified with the welfare state of the middle decades of the twentieth century. So it was to be with Attlee.[3]

Two days after war was declared in August 1914 Attlee enlisted. His brother Tom was a conscientious objector. Attlee was in the Gallipoli campaign and later in France. He conceived it his duty to fight apparently with no political doubts at all, and he engaged in war with the same un-emotional approach that he brought to his active political life. He ended his Army service as a Major, and as was common in the inter-war years, was often referred to as Major Attlee. When the war ended he returned to Stepney, and to Labour politics. A former member of the Haileybury Club became his batman/valet/housekeeper. Attlee was elected the first Labour Mayor of Stepney (1919–20) and stood successfully for Lime-house in 1922, a constituency he continued to represent until December 1955 when he resigned his seat and went immediately to the House of Lords. In the parliament of 1922 Macdonald made him one of his two parliamentary private secretaries, the other being Jack Lawson of the Durham miners. In the 1924 Labour administration Attlee became Under-Secretary to the War Office, his minister being Stephen Walsh, a miner MP from Lancashire who, so the gossip went at the time, 'was entirely unable to conceal his reverence for generals'.[4] In the 1929–31 Labour government Attlee was not given a post immediately—he was heavily engaged in the report of the Simon Commission on India[5]—but after Oswald Mosley's resignation Attlee became Chancellor of the Duchy of Lancaster and then, five months before the government broke apart, he was transferred to the office of the Postmaster-General. It was his first and only experience of departmental responsibility before he became prime minister in 1945.

A decade before the end of the Labour government in 1931 Attlee had married. His wife was thirteen years younger with no political experience except that derived from a conservative family background. Violet Attlee was never a socialist and later became well-known for her tactless conservative comments on events of the day. It was a notably happy marriage. Clem Attlee had been a lonely young man; his childhood and youth had encouraged little confidence in himself, and he lacked affection and love. Violet was good looking, lively, and she adored him. The marriage provided Attlee with a peace of mind and a happiness which must have been important for his political career. At the same time Violet was undoubtedly something of a liability in his political life. She was unhappy at Downing Street when Attlee became prime minister and resented the time he was away from her. It was understood during Attlee's tenure of No. 10 that work was to be organised, as far as possible, in ways that would allow the Prime Minister to spend as much time as possible with his wife. And she was often a nuisance to the civil servants around Attlee. What is to be said of a woman who spent her adult life with one of the leading Labour politicians of the twentieth century and who, towards the end of their lives, was able to say to her husband's future biographer: 'Most of our friends are Conservatives. Clem was never really a socialist, were you darling?' to which Attlee 'made a mildly dissenting noise. "Well, not a rabid one" she said'.[6] And she was not, of course, too far from the mark.

The fraudulent General Election of 1931 reduced Attlee's majority to under 500. but at least he was returned. The other two Labour members of the Stepney constituency were defeated, as, of course, were all the leading Labour ministers of the 1929 government except George Lansbury. Attlee was the only other member returned who had any experience of office, and it was this 'accident' of electoral history that had profound consequences for his future career. He became deputy leader in the Commons, and with Lansbury and Stafford Cripps, formed the triumvirate who led the forty-six Labour Party MPs in opposition.

These were years of great importance for Attlee. He was exceedingly hard-working and he gained an all-round experience in parliamentary politics that was unusual. Attlee always had a somewhat sharper understanding of social questions than Gaitskell who many years later succeeded him as leader of the Labour Party, but like Gaitskell in the thirties Attlee does not seem to have been politically radicalised by the events of that decade. He went onto a Hunger Marchers' platform in Hyde Park in 1936 and he visited Spain during the Civil War: more than Bevin or Gaitskell or Dalton ever brought themselves to do. But nothing really changed inside him during these difficult years. He became Party leader in 1935 following the resignation of George Lansbury, and was confirmed in the position after the General Election of 1935. The years until the outbreak of war in September 1939 were hardly a shining period in the history of the Labour Party; and Attlee presided over the disavowal of the Unity campaign and then the Popular Front; the dissolution of the Socialist League; the expulsion of Stafford Cripps, Aneurin Bevan and others of the Left. If war had not come and a General Election had been held in 1940 the psephologists calculate that a Tory Government would have been returned again.

The years of war were to shape Attlee's ideas and mould his attitudes in ways that allowed him to make the transition from deputy prime minister in a Conservative-dominated coalition to Labour prime minister in the first peace-time administration without any political or emotional stress or strain. In the 1930s he remained the typical Labour socialist: a moderate, constitutionalist, but anti-capitalist. 'British Socialists' he wrote in his 1937 book, *The Labour Party in Perspective,* 'have always recognised the conflict between classes but have not generally adopted the class war as a theory of society.'[7] Like most of his colleagues at this time he could still envisage degrees of sabotage on the part of the capitalist class against a Labour government, and throughout the thirties Attlee was insisting upon the lesson of 1929–31: 'that Socialists cannot make Capitalism work'.[8]

It was the experience of war-time government, and the working of war-time controls over the economy that convinced Attlee of the practicability of the changes he desired. Since his definition of capitalism was wholly untheoretical, the removal of social evils, or their mitigation, was evidence that capitalist society was capable of transformation.[9] Already at the 1943 Labour Party Conference he was asking delegates to note how much had been achieved:

> I doubt if we all recognise sufficiently the progress our ideas have made. The British never know when they are beaten, and British socialists never know when they have won.

The most explicit statement of what he now believed possible in the future because of what had already occurred during the war years was made in a letter to Harold Laski in 1944. Laski had been arguing for more radical action on the part of Labour ministers during the war itself, and for a more specific commitment to social change when peace came. In a long letter dated 1 May 1944, and typed by himself, Attlee wrote a carefully argued reply in defence of his own position and that of his colleagues. The central argument ran thus:

> Whether the post-war Government is Conservative or Labour it will inevitably have to work a mixed economy. If it is a Labour Government it will be a mixed economy developing towards Socialism.
> . . . Although you are a theorist and I am only a working politician, I think I give more and you give less attention to changes of conception than to legislative achievements.

For instance, I have witnessed now the acceptance by all the leading politicians in this country and all the economists of any account of the conception of the utilisation of abundance. . . It colours all our discussions on home economic policy. There follows from this the doctrine of full employment. . .

Take again the whole conception of State planning and the control of the financial machine by the Government and not by the Bank of England and the City. Here again I see the change since the days of 1931. . .

In my time in our movement, now getting quite long, I have seen a lot of useful legislation, but I count our progress much more by the extent to which what we cried in the wilderness five and thirty years ago has now become part of the assumptions of the ordinary man and woman. The acceptance of these assumptions has its effect both in legislation and administration, but its gradualness tends to hide our appreciation of the facts.[10]

For Attlee, then, the implementation of Labour's programme followed naturally and inevitably from the organisation, and administration, of national resources for war. As he wrote further in the letter to Laski quoted above: 'I find intelligent Service men often of high rank and men in various walks of life who come to me and tell me that they have been converted to Socialism by what they have seen done in wartime. It is therefore in my view mistaken tactics to belittle what has been done.'

This identification of socialism with social welfare and full employment has remained a major source of confusion within the British labour movement to our own day. When the general election of the summer of 1945 produced an overwhelming victory for the Labour Party, and Attlee became prime minister, it was widely accepted that Labour's stated objectives could now be achieved; and indeed nationalisation of the basic economic services and an advanced social welfare programme was put on the Statute book within the first three years of office. It represented a considerable instalment of economic and social reform; the introduction of the National Health Service in particular was the most advanced of any of the major industrial countries and the nationalisation of basic industries offered the opportunity of modernising the economic infrastructure within which private enterprise operated. At the same time full employment continued; the demobilisation of the armed forces and the transition to a peace time economy was carried through with remarkably little friction, and between 1946 and 1950 industrial production increased by fifty per cent. There was also a minor redistribution of income, although the details are still a matter of debate. As Attlee had predicted it was a mixed economy with leanings towards a more equitable society: an advanced liberal state with economic power, measured by the ownership of capital, still in the hands of the capitalists and landlords. By the end of the 1940s there was a clear choice of two roads for the Labour government to follow: either a further extension of state ownership of certain of the commanding heights of the economy in private ownership, with a serious measure of popular control which had so far not taken place, or a standstill on what had so far been achieved. If the latter, which was the inevitable choice accepted, then it could only be a matter of time, given the inherent tendency of capitalist society to generate inequality, for the momentum of change to be reversed.

What complicated, indeed greatly confused the situation was the wholly wrong assessment made by labour intellectuals as to what had taken place since 1945. In *New Fabian Essays*, published in 1952 with a preface by Attlee, there was provided a summing up of the achievements of the Attlee administrations in terms that were both extravagant and wildly beside the mark. Not all the contributors were as naive as C.A.R. Crosland who believed that 'by 1951 Britain had, in all essentials, ceased to be a capitalist society'; but the sense of something fundamental having happened ran through most of the contributions to this volume. John Strachey, for instance, was of the opinion that 'the Labour Government between 1945 and 1951 did in fact appreciably modify the nature of British capitalism' (p. 182); and Roy Jenkins, who continued to exercise considerable political influence within the labour movement for the next quarter of a century, insisted on the political changes that had occurred:

> A staightforward struggle between the capitalists and the proletariat for power over the productive machinery of the nation, there will not be. The capitalists have already surrendered too much power, partly to the State, partly to their own managers, and partly to the trade unions, for a determined stand to be practicable. A classical Marxist clash is not possible in a situation in which, before it takes place, the President of the National Union of Mineworkers is already more powerful than any six capitalists.   p. 72

Multiplication of such politically naive statements would be tedious. They were made, it should be remarked, at a time when Labour had recently lost a general election; when tensions inside the labour movement concerning future polities were developing rapidly; and at the beginning of what was to be thirteen years of Conservative government. By 1964, when the Labour Party came back to power with a tiny majority of three, no one was repeating the Fabian nonsense of the early fifties.

Britain was not, however, an island to itself and even[11] in the *New Fabian Essays* there was one article out of eight entirely devoted to foreign politics. It was a superficial account by Denis Healey that at least recognised the decline of Britain as a world power of the first rank. What the New Fabian essayists in general missed was the central importance of foreign policies and politics to domestic affairs in Britain during the years of war and in its aftermath. The Harris biography gives a fair weighting to foreign affairs, but the discussion and analysis are separated from consideration of domestic issues, and the close intertwining of the two is for the most part missed. And yet it was above all in foreign affairs that consensus was achieved during the Churchill coalition, and carried over unchanged into the era of the Labour administration.

This agreement on foreign politics with the Tories was a new departure —or largely new departure—for the Parliamentary Labour Party as well as for the broader labour movement. The radical tradition in Britain has mostly[12] been critical of the Conservative party and the Establishment generally in foreign policies. In the twentieth century the Boer war, the growth of armaments before 1914, the alliance with Tsarist Russia, the secret diplomacy of the pre-war and war years, the lukewarm attitude to the League of Nations, the failure to oppose Japanese aggression from 1930, the German-Italian intervention in Spain: in all of these matters the greater part of the Labour movement had found itself in sharp opposition. Naturally, the movement has always divided into right and left groupings, but it was only during the Second World War and the years that followed that basic agreement with the Tories was accepted by the Labour leadership, backed by the majority votes of the right-wing trade unions at Party conferences. Whatever the equivocations of the pre-1939 decades—and they were many—there was nothing comparable with the accord on fundamentals that emerged after 1940. As Gaitskell was able to say in the run-up to the general election of 1955:

> I doubt if foreign policy will play a big part in the next election—not because it is not important, but because Mr Eden has, in fact, mostly carried on our policy as developed by Ernest Bevin, in some cases against the views of rank and file Tories.

The inter-relationship between foreign and domestic politics was at least formally understood by Attlee, at least in his pre-war days. In his 1937 book he had written: 'The foreign policy of a Government is the reflection of its internal policy' (p. 226). The present story must begin—although that is not its starting point—with the Anglo-American antagonisms of the war years, themselves a further development of trends that had been growing in earlier years. The crucial fact was the increasing economic weight of the USA in the capitalist world, and the declining position of Britain in relation to the emerging super-powers of Russia and the United States. The British decline was masked, from most of the British public at least, by the political role that Churchill played during the war years, and by the fact that Britain remained the unconquered aircraft carrier off the mainland of Europe. In the chancelleries of the world, however, realities were given their proper place and it was only the sharp division of opinion and approach within the American administration, as well as the immediate problems of the military war, that permitted a somewhat greater power of manoeuvre for Britain than would otherwise have been the case. Very early in the developing Anglo-American relationships—

before America actually entered the war—the conflicts over the phrasing of certain parts of the Atlantic Charter statement emphasised the differences in economic policies that were to become increasingly acute in the years that followed.

Long before the war Cordell Hull, a Wilsonian internationalist who was appointed Secretary of State in 1933, had been campaigning against trade barriers and restrictions as major factors in the development of economic and military tensions between nation states. This was always a central part of Hull's general thinking, and although he made little impact in this context before 1939—his own country's record was hardly a tribute to his crusading zeal—Hull remained single-minded and vehement on the issue. In 1940 he described the Ottawa agreements introduced by Britain from 1932[13] as 'the greatest injury, in a commercial way, that has been inflicted on this country since I have been in public life'.[14] In the spring of 1941 Keynes made a strong statement in Washington that post-war Britain would be troubled by many serious economic problems, and would therefore be forced to resort to bilateral agreements and other forms of discrimination. State Department officials were shocked,[15] and when the Atlantic Charter was on the table for discussion later in the same year, there was fierce discussion and debate, within the American administration and between America and Britain, over the formulation of future economic policies. Sumner Welles, who represented the State Department at the meeting in Placentia Bay, Newfoundland, fought very hard to gain a commitment to end all British discrimination against American goods as a recognition of the aid being given through Lease-lend. Roosevelt had been the original mover for a joint statement on Anglo-American war aims, and he was not especially interested in matters of economic principle. And Roosevelt, prompted by Harry Hopkins, was willing to accept some important British amendments and the fourth and fifth paragraphs, as finally agreed, allowed Britain to avoid any specific commitment inconsistent with imperial preference. At least that was how the British saw it, but inevitably the phrasing was later to be interpreted differently on opposite sides of the Atlantic. In the House of Commons (9 September 1941) Churchill emphasised that the Charter was 'a simple, rough and ready war-time statement of the goals towards which the British Commonwealth and the United States mean to make their way'; but in America the phrases 'equal access' and 'self-determination' were heralded as an important anti-imperialist statement. On commercial policy Sumner Welles said:

The Atlantic declaration means that every nation has a right to expect that its legitimate trade will not be directed and throttled by towering tariffs, preferences, discriminations, or narrowly bilateral practices.

New York Times, 8 October 1941

The rapid growth of the American economy during the war years was greatly to encourage those within the American administration who preached the virtues of a liberalised world economy, and there was increasing recognition among many sections of the business community that only a very high and sustained level of exports would maintain the American economy at anything approaching full stretch. Export surpluses might or would help to avoid the contraction of those sections that were 'over-committed' to the war economy; and the domestic sectors would correspondingly benefit. The vision of an open world market became clearer and more attractive as the end of hostilities approached. Fred Block summed up the American position in relation to the rest of the world:

> The privileged access of imperial countries to their colonies would be eliminated, as would the bilateral payments and trading systems created in the 1930s by Germany, Japan and, to a lesser degree, Great Britain. A multilateral world economy would be one in which trade and capital flowed across national boundaries in response to the law of supply and demand without political interference favouring one nation or another. . .
>
> A world economy organised on these lines would create the markets and investment opportunities needed to assure both a large export surplus and the continued growth of the largest American banks and industrial firms.[16]

Anglo-American antagonisms permeated the close relations between the two countries. The tight restrictions around the Lend Lease arrangements are well-known[17] but what is not so often appreciated was the way in which, during the whole period of Lend-Lease, there was continuous pressure by the Americans to keep British reserves of gold and dollars to a figure of not more than about one billion dollars: reckoned to be around the minimum required.[18] There were two reasons for this policy, apart from a general opposition on principle to Britain and the Empire. The first was what was known as the principle of 'scraping the barrel', a condition for the continuation of Lend-Lease to soothe its critics in Congress. The second was the need to develop as much leverage and bargaining power as possible over the British in order to move towards a greater rather than a lesser dependence upon the USA in the post-war world. This is part of an argument developed by Gabriel Kolko, that there was, inside the American administration in general and within the State Department in particular, an understanding to keep Britain neither too weak nor too strong.[19] Block summarises the situation as it was in the closing years of the war and its immediate aftermath:

> In general, Britain was seen as a kind of bridge between the United States and the rest of the world. If the United States could count on British economic, political and military resource in the pursuit of U.S. global aims, it was thought that it would then be infinitely easier to gain the acquiescence of other countries.

It was precisely U.S. dependence on British co-operation in a variety of areas that made U.S. policy toward Britain so complicated. On the one hand, if Britain were too strong, if she had substantial currency reserves, it would be difficult to force her to act according to American wishes. On the other hand, if Britain were too weak, if her payments position were desperate, she would be of little help in financing European trade, in working to eliminate trade and exchange controls, and in a whole variety of other tasks. The trick, then, was to keep Britain weak and dependent, but not too weak, and debates that took place within the United States government over the proper size of British reserves reflected the subtlety of such an undertaking.[20]

It was, as Block indicates, by no means a straightforward matter for Washington; and the issues involved became more complicated as the end of the war approached. The Treasury, under Morgenthau and Harry Dexter White, was in sharp conflict with the State Department on many aspects of policy. One crucial item of difference that generated bitter conflict was their divergence over Germany and the Soviet Union. The State Department had fought continuously against Morgenthau's plans for a punitive treatment of post-war Germany. The attitude of the State Department favoured German reconstruction—for a mixture of reasons— and the rapid deterioration of relations with the Soviet Union after the end of the war and following the death of Roosevelt, greatly strengthened their position.

Roosevelt's death in April 1945 was critical. It may well have been the case that had he lived, the State Department would have had their way, since the dynamic interests of American imperialism were undoubtedly best served by their approach to world problems. But the timing could well have been different. As it was, the succession of Truman dramatically altered the balance of power within the American administration. Morgenthau, a close personal friend of Roosevelt, very soon left the Treasury, and Dexter White's influence was sharply reduced. Seven days after the end of the war with Japan, Lend-Lease was abruptly discontinued, and the Attlee government was presented with very large problems. Harris (p. 271) argues the common theme—common at the time and since—that 'Truman's precipitate action aroused European fears of an American return to isolationism'. But this was seriously to misjudge the situation, although, as already noted, it was widely accepted at the time. 1945 was not 1919, and the Americans were highly conscious of their role as the most powerful country in the capitalist world, and it was not conceivable that the United States would have relinquished the leadership of the capitalist world order when confronted with the emergence of the Soviet Union as the second major power in the world. Moreover, there were powerful economic interests pushing America into the world economy. It is arguable—and I would wish to argue—that had America retreated into an isolationist position the world in the decades that followed would have been a more peaceful and probably a much happier place; but this is not a matter that can be pursued here. It is necessary to re-iterate, however, that this was not, regrettably, on the historical agenda.

The ending of Lend-Lease confronted the Attlee government with bitter choices; and less than a month later, in early September 1945, Maynard Keynes was sent to Washigton to negotiate large-scale assistance from the Americans. By this time Keynes had shifted away from his earlier arguments for bilateralism and discrimination, and all his exceptional negotiating powers were predicated on the assumption that there was no alternative for Britain but massive aid from America. He was aware of the opposition from the Labour Left in Britain to an open economy and he apparently told the Americans that he would prefer the loan negotiations to take place in Washington, rather than London, since there he would be less constrained by direct ministerial supervision. In all this Keynes seriously misjudged the new temper in Washington which had followed the death of Roosevelt. Keynes began by being highly optimistic concerning the terms on which a loan could be secured, and he was to be disillusioned by the very hard bargain he had to accept. But he had already made his choice. In a memorandum he had presented to the British Cabinet in April 1945 he rejected bilateralism and controls as imposing intolerable burdens upon British society. Independence from the United States would involve, he wrote:

    (a) the continuance of war rationing and war control *more* stringent than at present for (say) three to five years after the war;
    (b) the national planning and direction of foreign trade both imports and exports, somewhat on the Russian model; and
    (c) an indefinite postponement of Colonial Development and Far Eastern rehabilitation and a virtual abandonment of all overseas activities, whether military or diplomatic or by way of developing our trade, wealth and influence, which involved very considerable expenditure.[21]

In this same memorandum Keynes continued to assume that the Americans would make a 'fair offer, not so much generous as just' but he went on to add that if the terms were too onerous the UK should at least consider 'the disagreeable, indeed the disastrous alternative, without, however, disguising from ourselves its true character'. In the event, Keynes was to discover that a 'just' settlement was never possible, given the way the negotiations were conducted; but the alternative, while still appreciated, was not seriously considered. Dalton summed up the course of the negotiations in his 1945 volume:

> So, as the talks went on, we retreated, slowly and with a bad grace and with increasing irritation, from a free gift to an interest-free loan, and from this again to a loan bearing interest; from a larger to a smaller total of aid; and from the

prospect of loose strings, some of which would be only general declarations of intention, to the most unwilling acceptance of strings so tight that they might strangle our trade and, indeed, our whole economic life.   pp. 74–5

The primary concern of the American negotiators was not in fact the size of the loan, or the financial terms on which it was given, but the commitment upon Britain to begin dismantling controls, open up the Sterling Area and accept convertibility. The loan, which was ratified during 1946, offered $3.75 billion dollars at two per cent payable over fifty years starting in 1951. Convertibility, which would come into effect one year after final ratification, would also be accompanied by the ending of discrimination against dollar imports. Harris, who has missed most of the real significance of the Anglo-American conflict of these times, could nevertheless appreciate what was the meaning of the loan: 'For better or worse, she [Britain] had tied her economic future to that of the Americans' (p. 275).

As a postscript, it may be noted that the Labour Government 'chose to mislead the country about what had happened'. These are the words of Harris (p. 274). Dalton, who communicated so much misgiving to his private diary, made a major speech in the Commons advocating acceptance, and Keynes delivered a brilliant defence in the House of Lords. The Left of the Parliamentary Party, and the Left outside Westminster, were, as so often, vindicated in their opposition; and much good it did them.

Fifteen years later Harris asked Attlee if he still thought the decision to accept the loan had been justified. Attlee replied that Britain was in no position to bargain; her needs were desperate, and they had nothing to offer in return. He was always aware, he continued, that the Americans might follow their own example after World War One and pull out of Europe. 'So far as possible' Harris reports him as saying 'nothing should be done to make them feel we were not grateful to them. They had to be humoured' (p. 275). Extraordinary words for a leading politician, of any party, and a further piece of evidence of the loss of nerve of Attlee and the majority of his government. Although Attlee never really understood international finance he was not entirely ignorant of the consequences of the loan. Certainly Dalton was in no doubt but was overwhelmed with the problems of the alternative of rejection. But it is not true that rejection of the American loan, on the terms finally agreed, would have meant stark, unremitting privation. It is agreed that there would have been a continuation, and almost certainly an intensification of austerity in the short run. But a determined national policy, either with the Sterling Area or with Western Europe, or a combination, might well have brought economic improvement and relative prosperity in a few years. The financial interests of the City of London would naturally have been powerfully opposed. They had lost out during the war years and were very anxious to re-establish themselves. But many business interests have always had aims and objectives very different from the banks and finance houses, and the Labour government had large reserves of political support in the country. Moreover, as already indicated above, a tougher bargaining stance from London could have meant that the Americans would have given way, at least temporarily. Britain *was* important to the global perspectives of American imperialism, and a genuinely radical government could have found itself some room for manoeuvre without capitulating to the reactionary foreign policies of the United States.

To argue thus is, however, to miss certain crucial components of the historical record, and in particular the political dimension of anti-communism and anti-Sovietism which affected Attlee and Bevin, his Foreign Secretary, from the earliest days of their administration; by contrast this was not wholly true of the Americans. The Roosevelt tradition lingered on in Washington after Truman took over, although it was certainly declining rapidly by the end of 1945, and Dexter White's vision of a massive loan to the USSR as part of the necessary US-Soviet relationship faded even more quickly. But Bevin and Attlee steadfastly continued the foreign policy directed by Churchill and Eden during the war. Listening to the exchanges between Churchill and Stalin at the first Potsdam meeting in May 1945 Harris records that Attlee 'had soon concluded that there was no possibility of real Anglo-Soviet co-operation' (p. 267). There is a highly revealing letter from Attlee to Fenner Brockway, written in September 1945, a month or so after the abrupt ending of Lend-Lease and just at the beginning of Keynes' negotiations for the American loan; and it is abundantly clear that Attlee could never possibly deviate from the closest possible agreement with the Americans. No man who wrote the words which follow could have rejected the American loan. No doubt Attlee *did* believe that there was no alternative; but his prior acceptance of the politics of American power was a crucial determinant in the formation of his general views on the American connection. The letter which is given below represents a central text for the whole post-war policy of the Labour government:

There is a tendency on the part of some people in the Labour Party to over-simplify foreign affairs. It's partly due to a certain woolly idealism; seeing everything black and white when in fact there are sorts of shades of grey. They mean well but they don't like looking at unpleasant facts. Some of them thought we ought to concentrate all our efforts on building up a Third Force in Europe. Very nice, no doubt. But there wasn't either a material or a spiritual basis for it at that time. What remained of Europe wasn't strong enough to stand up to Russia by itself. You had to have a world force because you were up against a world force. . . Without the stopping power of the Americans, the Russians might easily have tried sweeping right forward. I don't know whether they would, but it wasn't a possibility you could just ignore. It's no good thinking that moral sentiments have any sway with the Russians, there's a good deal of old-fashioned imperialism in their make-up, you know. Their foreign policy has been carried on in much the same way from the days of Queen Catherine the Great. Some of our friends wouldn't see that.   p. 295

It is not wholly clear from Harris' biography when anti-Sovietism became an inflexible postulate of Attlee's thinking, but it must have been sometime during the war years since he emerged as an unyielding opponent of Soviet Russia from the beginning of his own administration. Bevin had long been an anti-communist and he always found it difficult to distinguish his anti-communism, derived largely from his experience of the British Communist Party, from his opposition to the Soviet Union.[22] But what must be insisted on is the continuity with the Churchill coalition. As Eden said in the debate when Bevin made his first speech in the Commons as Foreign Secretary (20 August 1945)—referring to his years in the War Cabinet with Bevin:

Eden.	During that period there were many discussions on foreign affairs I cannot recall one single occasion when there was a difference between us. I hope I do not embarrass the Foreign Secretary when I say that.
Bevin.	No.
Eden.	There were no differences on any important issues of foreign policy.

Nor were there to be throughout the whole period of the Labour administrations. When Churchill made his notorious speech at Fulton, Missouri, on 5 March 1946—an important landmark in the development of the Cold War—Attlee, so Harris reveals 'could not express approval of the speech in public; in private he was delighted with it, and with the impact it had made on the Americans, whom he still considered to be naive in their attitude to Stalin' (p. 298).

This last comment must be taken further. It was Bevin and Attlee who were the front runners in the opposition to the Soviet Union during the second half of 1945. At Potsdam the American Secretary of State, James Byrnes, commented on the aggressive manner that Bevin adopted towards the Russians and 'both the President [Truman] and I wondered how we would get along with this new Foreign Minister' (quoted p. 266). The Americans were not slow to learn and to have an undeviating support from Britain for their Cold War policies was of inestimable value in their world strategy. As Churchill reported in the House of Commons in a foreign affairs debate on 23 January 1948:

On the whole the Government have maintained a continuity in foreign policy with that pursued under the National Coalition Government. . . We have therefore tried to give them all possible help and thus keep the foreign policy of Britain outside the arena of party controversy. . .
[After congratulating the Labour Government on its counter-revolutionary

policy in Greece.]

    I cannot help also feeling content to see that not only the British, but the American Government, have adopted to a very large extent the views which I expressed at Fulton nearly two years ago, and have, indeed, gone in many ways beyond them. . . I was much criticised on both sides of the Atlantic for the Fulton speech, but in almost every detail, and certainly in the spirit and in its moderation, what I there urged has now become the accepted policy of the English-speaking world. The language used by the Prime Minister [Mr Attlee] and the Lord President of the Council [Mr Herbert Morrison] about Soviet Russia and about the dangers of a new war far exceed in gravity and menace anything which I said at that time or indeed have ever said on this subject since the war. The joint use of bases, the maintenance of the common Staff arrangements between Great Britain and the United States, and the close integration of our foreign policies are being pursued throughout the English-speaking world.

Acceptance of the American loan in 1946, and Marshall aid two years later, considerably eased Britain's immediate post-war problems, allowed internal consumption levels to rise, and permitted the enactment of the social welfare legislation for which the Attlee government has become known. In the longer run there was a steady increase in living standards, against the background of a world economy that was rapidly expanding; but the longer run has also made plain the economic and political costs of the attempt in the immediate post-war years to maintain a great power status within a context of subservience to the United States. Convertibility was a disastrous episode that had to be abandoned after seven weeks in the summer of 1947, and little progress had been made towards multi-lateralism by 1950. But the gates towards an open world economy had already been unlatched, and with the return of a Tory government in 1951 the principles the Attlee government had accepted were now increasingly practised. By the end of the decade the shortage of dollars had gone, all the major currencies were convertible, and the physical controls of war and post war had been swept away. The acceptance of a rearmament programme in the closing stages of the Labour administrations of 1950–1 was the end product of the processes of subordination to the global strategy of the United States which Attlee and Bevin had established as the keystone of British policy. Defence expenditure rose to 14 per cent of GNP in 1951, a figure which even the new Tory government found beyond the country's economic and financial capacity; but the burden of armaments has remained as a major factor responsible for the low level of performance of the British economy in the third quarter of the century.

    It has been an incredibly dismal story: a radical movement after 1945 guided by its leaders into a political subservience to the United States with its economic consequences the long-term decline of Britain. But there was one other legacy of the Attlee years for which he himself had almost sole responsibility; and that was the decision, secretly taken, to manufacture an atomic bomb.

The reasons which encouraged the making of an independent British bomb were the product of political misjudgments, muddled and confused estimates of the contemporary world and especially of its future shape, mixed with strong emotional spasms following a more than usually unpleasant example of American bad faith in the matter of atomic information. There was no immediate military threat nor did anyone pretend there was;[23] but because of the secrecy which surrounded the whole matter, there not many who could have argued the case one way or the other. The background of events and personalities out of which the decision appeared was inevitably crowded and complicated, but there are three factors which may be singled out for a brief, and inevitably, simplified discussion.[24]

There was first the delusion that Britain was still capable of maintaining a great power status in the post-war world. Hugh Dalton always argued, when he was Chancellor of the Exchequer, although without serious result, that Britain after 1945 was being seriously over-stretched. On 20 January 1947 Dalton sent Attlee a long memorandum in which he argued powerfully for a serious reduction in the numbers in the Armed Forces and for a general reduction in defence expenditure. January was the same month that the decision was taken about the British bomb; but Dalton was neither consulted nor informed. His memorandum followed a Cabinet meeting which he said was 'a bad failure to face unpleasant facts', and paragraph 8 read:

> What shall it profit Britain to have even 1,500,000 men and women in the Forces and Supply, and to be spending nearly £1000 millions a year on them, if we come an economic and financial cropper two years hence?
>
> And I am told in Cabinet that to have only 1,400,000 Service and Supply personnel and to spend only £750 millions on them is 'unilateral disarmament'.

But among the top elites of the administration and government: politicians, civil servants and not least the Chiefs of Staff, there was a determination to keep the first class power status in more than name. The pressures on Attlee from the many conservative and traditional groups that surrounded him were unremitting. When Attlee, early in 1947 and not for the first time, proposed a military withdrawal from the Middle East, all three Chiefs of Staff said they would resign if it were pressed.[25] So the proposal was dropped. The great power theme was constantly reiterated. Lord Cherwell, a powerful political figure in these years, wrote in 1949 that without its own Bomb Britain would 'rank with other European countries who have to make do with conventional weapons. And, in a nice touch of white imperialist rhetoric, he argued that having to rely on the United States 'for this vital weapon, we shall sink to the rank of a second-class nation, only permitted to supply auxiliary troops, like the native levies who were allowed small arms but not artillery'.[26] Cherwell, who was Churchill's scientific adviser, has not had the critical appraisal he warrants. He was, for example, a strong advocate of mass bombing by the RAF, now widely accepted to have been a serious diversion of economic and military resources; and his acceptance of the great power approach came naturally out of his Conservative politics.

During the years of war, the relations between the British and the Americans on atomic matters generated great mistrust, bitterness and friction. The British had asked, and answered the theoretical questions relating to the making of an atomic bomb; but only the Americans could provide the necessary technology. The Bomb was therefore made in the United States. There were a succession of secret agreements concerning the interchange of information, although their status was not always clear: the Quebec agreement of 1943; the Hyde Park memorandum of 1944; and the Truman–Attlee–King concordat of November 1945. The continued efforts of the British to obtain a more complete channel of atomic information were suddenly brought to a complete halt by the passing of the MacMahon Act of 1946 which prohibited the disclosure of classified atomic information to any foreign country. The reaction on the British side was anger and frustration; and the majority sentiment of those involved on the British side was to press forward to an independent Bomb. This was the 'emotional spasm' noted above. It was an interesting reaction, since the British, like all governments, have been skilled at double-dealing their opponents, yet in these years they seemed so often surprised by American deceit, lack of scruple and general perfidy. Moreover, at this time, the British came back for more, largely of course because they desperately needed American dollars. When, for example General Marshall became Secretary of State in 1947, the British really thought they would be able to reverse in a significant way the trend away from co-operation between the two Atlantic countries. In the first year of Marshall's tenure of office talks on atomic energy produced an agreement which gave the Americans a great deal (including large amounts of uranium) and the British hardly anything.[27]

The decision on the British bomb was not therefore based upon a serious analysis of the British economic situation or upon a sober appreciation of the coming decade or an evaluation of the new world in which there were two, and only two, super-powers. When the Russians exploded their first nuclear bomb in 1949 the British were genuinely surprised; and their own explosion in October 1952 at Monte Bello no longer made any difference to anyone. As an American politician said when there was a poll of Congressmen in Washington, soon after the British bomb had been exploded, on the issue of information exchanges with Britain: 'We would be trading a horse for a rabbit.' Imperialist nostalgia was no substitute for the harsh realities of the contemporary world; and the British after 1945 were singularly lacking in simple realism, with Churchill among the Conservatives leading the vanguard of those who still thought in great power terms.

There ought, of course, to have been a continuing debate on these momentous questions, inside Parliament and in the country; but during the whole period of the Labour government of 1945 to 1950 there was not one single debate on atomic energy. Within the top levels of the administration there were a few who were in possession of the facts, but of those only P.M.S. Blackett seems to have opposed the idea of an independent bomb. Blackett had initially been in favour of the bomb as deterrent, but he soon changed his mind, and by the end of 1945 he wrote to Attlee that an independent British Bomb would not increase our security, but that it would operate the other way. And a year later, after a visit to the United States where talk of a preventive war had shocked him, he produced an internal memorandum which argued for atomic neutrality. Margaret Gowing noted that whatever the merits of the argument, Blackett had produced a closely argued and reasoned thesis, but that it was received either with silence or with contempt. 'He should stick to science' minuted Ernest Bevin, the Foreign Secretary. Sir Henry Tizard, himself an eminent scientist, who was chairman of the Defence Research Committee, knew nothing about the decision to manufacture a Bomb until six months later, but would have opposed it at the time.[28]

Attlee took the decision largely on the advice of two or three close colleagues, the Chiefs of Staff and the chairman of the Advisory Committee on Atomic Power. The full Cabinet was never consulted. During the war years, under Churchill, atomic matters for Cabinet decision had always been muffled and muddled so that only a few members were aware of what was going on; but with the Labour government, secrecy went further. In the Attlee government it was agreed, or understood, that as far as possible atomic matters should be left to the personal decision of the prime minister, guided by the Advisory Committee which Attlee himself had established. The chairman of the Advisory Committee was a prominent Conservative, Sir John Anderson and indeed, the only politician in the Commons, outside a very small group around Attlee, who was capable of making an informed comment on government policy. Harris, who does not fudge this issue in his biography, writes that Attlee

in his readiness to shroud in secrecy what Britain was doing about her bomb, connived at arrangements which were constitutionally dubious. Nearly all his Cabinet ministers were systemetically kept ignorant about a most expensive, and possibly hazardous, national commitment. The Defence Committee never discussed it, and the main committee responsible for atomic energy had only limited facilities for discovering, let alone determining, what was being done.   p. 291

And to help matters along his way, Attlee manipulated the financial estimates to conceal the £100 million expenditure on the Bomb; and this secrecy, and the muddled inefficiency it generated, lasted for the remainder of his administration.

At the general election of February 1950 the Labour Party increased its vote over 1945 by a million and a quarter and won a majority of all votes cast. The national swing to the Tories was 3.3 per cent, and Labour had 315 seats against the Tories and their allies with 298; overall, Labour had a majority of only 5. It was a tired and sick government; Bevin and Cripps died; Attlee had a recurrence of his duodenal ulcer and went into hospital. The most important political issue was the Korean war which broke out at the end of June 1950. Attlee gave immediate support to the American-dominated United Nations and imposed a rearmament programme upon the economy that was far beyond its capabilities. Within a year the government was beginning to fall apart. Bevan resigned in April 1951 followed by Harold Wilson and John Freeman; and Herbert Morrison's mishandling of foreign affairs, especially the Iranian question, all helped to determine Attlee's decision to go to the country again. In the October 1951 general election Labour won slightly more of the total poll than the Tories but with fewer seats; and overall the latter had a majority of 17. Attlee remained leader of the opposition for the next four years: long enough to ensure that Morrison would not follow him as leader of the Parliamentary Labour Party and that Hugh Gaitskell would. His years in opposition did nothing to enhance Attlee's reputation.

Attlee was a highly competent administrator; he worked methodically and efficiently; and he learned much, during his many years as a leading politician, in the way of political management. But he lacked the charisma necessary for a great party leader; he found it difficult to talk even to close colleagues—Ernest Bevin being one of the few exceptions; and there were serious attempts on a number of occasions to displace him as party leader. During the war and after 1945 it was Bevin's support above all which made these attempts fail. Since Attlee's death in 1967, and not least because of the performance of the Labour administrations from 1964 on, his reputation as a party leader and manager has grown. The years after 1945 are looked upon as something of a golden period when the welfare state was established and when a programme of nationalisation of certain key sectors was successfully carried through. There is a haze of nostalgia about the Attlee years; through it Attlee himself has grown in stature and reputation. The myths have begun to gather round him.

In his summing up of Attlee's career, Harris emphasises, as do most historians and politicians, Attlee's 'epoch-making achievement' of Indian independence. 'If any one man can be said to have given India her independence it was Attlee' (p. 568). There is no doubt, of course, that if

Churchill had won the 1945 election India would not have become a sovereign state; and there would have developed, in that sub-continent of hundreds of million of people, a Northern Ireland situation of growing warfare with the foreign occupation. Attlee did not give India her independence: there was no alternative, except a long period of attrition at the end of which Britain would have had to withdraw, bloody and bowed. Attlee believed in Indian independence; it was a central issue for the Labour Party by the time the Second World War ended; and despite opposition even in the Labour Cabinet, he got his way. It was a sensible, rational and thoroughly sane decision; and since politicians only seldom act in this way, Attlee must be given full credit for a wholly proper insistence that there was no other path forward. On the other hand, there are very serious questions to be answered, among them the ways in which power was handed over, and its timing and the imposition of Partition; and half a million dead Hindus and Moslems in the Punjab alone, with probably nearly two million dead in all, point to the need for a comprehensive evaluation of British policy, from which Attlee certainly cannot be excluded.

There are other matters which qualify his record; and these are central to the judgment of historians. What the Attlee administration achieved was the elaboration of a wide-ranging social welfare system; a transition from war to peace that was remarkably smooth and efficient; and by 1950 the economy was in much better shape than could have been anticipated in 1945. Full employment was less the result of government management in the late 1940s than of the beginnings of dynamic growth within the world economy; and that was to remain true for the next twenty years. The Tories could have done none of these things in the same effective way, and certainly the collaboration of the trade unions, so crucial to the return to a peace-time economy, would not have been at the disposal of a Churchill government. The social welfare achievement of the Attlee administration was important, although whether the principle of comprehensiveness, which everyone has assumed since 1946 to be accepted by the great majority of people, will withstand the harsh winds of a rampant Toryism in the 1980s, is now seriously in question. But the establishment of the national welfare schemes after 1946 rested in considerable part upon the acquisition of American dollars, and the terms on which these dollars were obtained effectively removed the possibilities of the continuation of any kind of controlled economy which had been so successful between 1945 and 1950; and the way was thereby opened to the free-enterprise developments of the 1950s when controls were dismantled and unfettered enterprise encouraged. The beneficiaries of the travails and crises of the Attlee government were the profit takers of the 1950s. It was to prove the greatest capitalist bonanza of the century.

In another sector, the programme of nationalisation rebuilt the ill-planned and under-invested national services: coal, gas and electricity, railways. The compensation paid was much too generous, the structures of control established were highly bureaucratic, and workers' control or a minimum of worker-participation was never seriously discussed, let alone implemented. And finally, there is Attlee's personal responsibility for the existence of a British atomic Bomb, and the implications for foreign policy which are central to our concerns today. Moreover, the acceptance by his government of the great power argument encouraged the Tories, when they returned in 1951, to continue the colonial crises foreshadowed by Iran and Egypt in Herbert Morrison's disastrous days at the Foreign Office, and which gave us the crises of Kenya, British Guyana, Aden, Cyprus, and Suez in the 1950s.

The longer term consequences of the Attlee administration were the theory and practice of Butskellism; consensus on all major questions including the acceptance of the gross burden of armaments, and a foreign policy subordinated to that of the United States. Since all effective controls on foreign trade and capital flows had been eliminated by the end of the fifties—the continuation and conclusion of the policies initiated by the Attlee government—deficits on the balance of payments could only be met by what became known as stop-go policies, and these immediately affected domestic investment and welfare services. With the beginning of the world crisis in the early nineteen-seventies the 'cushioning' effect which a world boom had provided very quickly disappeared. Hence the much harsher decisions which the Callaghan–Healey government initiated and which in principle and practice marked a shift towards the monetarism that the Thatcher government accepted as their major articulate premiss after the Conservative election victory of 1979. For the leadership of the British labour movement it was intellectual and political bankruptcy.

NOTES

1. K. Harris, *Attlee* (Weidenfeld and Nicolson, 1982). Except where a specific book is quoted, all page references in the text are to Harris.
2. Attlee commonly talked in cricketing language: a typical upper-class way of expression which inhibits the development of serious dialogue and discussion. See, for an example, the letter from Tony Harman in the *Guardian*, 4 October 1982. Harman was Labour candidate for the Aylesbury constituency in which the Attlees lived and voted. It was the general election of 1951 and Harman asked Attlee why he had cut his period of government short and gone to the country. 'Because I thought it was time to declare' said Attlee. Harman, who clearly had never thought of politics in this way, commented: 'I don't think they play by the same rules.' 'Oh,' replied Attlee, 'we shall get another innings in some day if we don't win this time.' Hayter, the British ambassador in Moscow, told Richard Crossman of a friend of his who had arrived in Brioni sometime during the summer of 1953; and was asked by Attlee who was staying there: 'Have you got the cricket scores? Nobody out here seems to know a think about them.' *The BackBench Diaries of Richard Crossman* (ed. Janet

Morgan, 1981), p. 343.
3. See below, p. 149.
4. *Dictionary of Labour Biography,* vol. 4 (1977), p. 189.
5. Attlee was invited to become a member of the Simon Commission by Ramsay MacDonald who had his own devious reasons for the choice (Harris, p. 77). Vernon Hartshorn, the South Wales miners' leader, became the other Labour representative. Harris writes: 'By becoming a member of the Commission, Attlee became a suspect in the eyes of many Labour Party backbenchers' (ibid.).
6. Harris, p. 56.
7. Attlee, p. 115.
8. Ibid., p. 130.
9. Richard Crossman gave an interesting insight into Attlee's politics in a story of the Labour Party delegation to Moscow in August 1954: 'Attlee was very bad-tempered and tart, discussing Marxism spasmodically. When the Russians had gone, he said to Hayter [British Ambassador to Russia] "Have you read any of this Marxist stuff?. . . I've read none of it, you know".' *Backbench Diaries* (1981), p. 342.
10. K. Martin, *Harold Laski (1893-1950) A Biographical Memoir* (1953), p. 160-2.
11. The Fabian tradition was notably deficient in any serious concern for foreign politics. Hence 'even'.
12. There are, of course, many exceptions, large and small, to the statement in the text: the mass jingoism of the First World War is an obvious example.
13. The Ottawa conference was held 21 July to 20 August 1932. It brought together the UK, and the Dominions of the British Empire, and established a system of Imperial Preference, following the earlier imposition of a tariff by the UK after the General Election of 1931. Imperial Preference was extended to the Crown Colonies in 1933.
14. Quoted in R.N. Gardner, *Sterling-Dollar Diplomacy* (Oxford, 1956), p. 19.
15. Ibid., pp. 41-2.
16. Fred L. Block, *The Origins of International Economic Disorder* (University of California, 1977), p. 36. See also for a similar emphasis upon multilateralism as one of the central factors in the development of American foreign policy: W.A. Williams, *The Tragedy of American Diplomacy* (New York, 1962) and Lloyd C. Gardner, *Economic Aspects of New Deal Diplomacy* (Boston, 1971).
17. See especially R.N. Gardner, op. cit., ch. ix, esp. p. 171 ff.
18. Block, op. cit., p. 55 ff.
19. Ibid., and G. Kolko, *The Politics of War* (New York, 1968).
20. Block, op. cit., p. 59.
21. Quoted in T. Brett, S. Gilliatt and A. Pope, 'Planned Trade, Labour Party Policy and U.S. Intervention: The Successes and Failures of Post-War Reconstruction', *History Workshop,* No. 13 (Spring 1982), p. 134.
22. Dalton reported Bevin as saying that Molotov was just like a communist in a local Labour Party, making the most of grievances if treated badly and putting up his price if treated reasonably. The most extraordinary example of Bevin's megalomania in general, and of his illiterate anti-Sovietism in particular, was his speech to the Bournemouth conference of the Labour Party in 1946. After retailing his exploits as the man who did more than anyone else to defend the Russian Revolution in Britain—these were his words—he continued:
    The thanks that I got was an attempt by the Communists to break up the Union that I had built. I said to Maisky [the Soviet Ambassador] on one occasion: 'You have built the Soviet Union and you have a right to defend it. I have built the Transport Union and if you seek to break it I will fight you'.

That was a proper position to take up. Both were the results of long years of labour. After that there was a slightly greater respect for my view. I think that is fair.

23. Margaret Gowing, 'Britain, America and the Bomb' in *Retreat from Power. Vol. 2 After 1939* (ed. D. Dilks, 1981), p. 129: 'The initial decision in 1947 to make a bomb simply emerged from a body of general assumptions. It was not a response to an immediate military threat but arose rather from a fundamental and instinctive feeling that Britain must possess so climacteric a weapon. It seemed, however, a manifestation of the scientific and technological on which Britain's strength—so deficient in terms of manpower—must depend.' The article from which this quotation is taken is a distillation of the author's official history of atomic energy in the UK. The relevant volume is *Independence and Deterrence. Britain and Atomic Energy 1945-1952. Vol. 1. Policy Making* (1974), chs. 6 and 7.

24. See the reference in the article by Margaret Gowing, cited above; and those in Edward Spiers, 'The British Nuclear Deterrent: Problems and Possibilities' in Dilks, op. cit.

25. Introduction by David Dilks to *Retreat from Power Vol. 2*, p. 21 quoting *The Memoirs of Field Marshal Montgomery* (1960), p. 444.

26. Margaret Gowing, op. cit., p. 131.

27. Harris, p. 289.

28. Blackett's memorandum is reprinted in Margaret Gowing, *Independence and Deterrence* (1974), pp. 194-206.

HIM AND HIS FRIENDS*

Paul Foot

Among the guests of the Shah of Iran during the celebrations in Persepolis of the 2,500th anniversary of the Persian Empire was a right-wing Tory MP now a lord called Jock Bruce-Gardyne. Writing about the occasion in *The Sunday Telegraph* some ten years later, Mr Bruce-Gardyne recalled one of his most convivial companions:

> Several years ago, I enjoyed a memorable junket as the guest of the late Shah of Persia. Dr David Owen was one of that company. As we journeyed to Persepolis, I became more and more worried. For the more we chatted between the helpings of caviar about the state of the world. . . the less we seemed to find to disagree about.
>
> *Sunday Telegraph,* February 1, 1981

Put Bruce-Gardyne in a television studio in Britain with David Owen and there would be instant controversy. They would disagree, passionately, about almost everything. What then made the difference on that sumptuous journey to Persepolis? Mr Bruce-Gardyne gives the clue. The two men were arguing *in between helpings of caviar.* Caviar, as is widely recognised, is a universal healer. It soothes and unites. In particular, it concentrates the minds of party guests on the exceptional kindness, goodness and brilliance of their hosts.

In 1971, when the 'junket' to Persepolis was organised, the Shah of Iran was embarking on one of the twentieth century's most blatant exercises in megalomania and tyranny. The sudden surge in Iran's oil revenues seemed to remove all limits to his two central ambitions: to enrich his own family, and to build the most powerful arsenal on earth, outside the United States and Russia. The following year, United States President Nixon and Secretary of State Kissinger visited the Shah, appropriately enough on their way back from peace talks in Russia. There, as representatives not merely of their country's government but also of its armaments industry, they wrote the Shah a blank cheque for any American arms he wanted to buy. In February 1973, the Pentagon revealed that the Shah had contracted to buy two thousand million pounds worth of arms from the United States, a figure which represented about

---

*P.C. Radji, *In The Service of The Peacock Throne,* Hamish Hamilton, £12.50, 1983.

a quarter of the entire national income of Iran. The American arms manufacturer Grunman spared no pains to win the Shah to the delights of their new jet fighter, the Tomcat. In his book, *The Arms Bazaar*, Anthony Sampson (now a colleague of Dr Owen's in the Social Democratic Party) described the scene near Washington when the Shah was shown the plane by Grunman:

> The Tomcat performed amazing acrobatics touching down in front of the Shah and then shooting up again like a rocket. The Grunman men observed the Shah's delight as he illustrated the swoop with his hands.

The contract was signed, naturally not without a little bit of corruption. Houshang Levi, an 'arms lobbyist', got his cut, a standard 28 million dollars. The Shah's zest for more weapons obliged him to help himself more and more liberally to his country's straining coffers. As opposition grew to his policies, he redoubled his already monstrous power. His secret police, SAVAK, modelled itself on the KGB both for efficiency in detecting dissidents and in ruthlessness in dealing with them. Torture of political and religious dissenters was widespread, and well documented.

Throughout this period, however, and for years after it, the Shah's regime was praised in the West, especially in Britain and the United States, as an example of liberal reformism. This analysis was arrived at partly out of strategic necessity, partly through the work of a highly effective propaganda machine, based in the Iranian Embassies. The Shah, who was a good judge of character within his ruling class, preferred to choose his top civil servants, ministers and diplomats from the liberal intelligentsia, which was renowned across the world for its culture and charm.

From such a background came Amir Abbas Hoveyda, the Shah's most long-serving prime minister, who made a special effort to surround himself with intelligent and cultured young men. Parviz Radji was 29 when he went to work for Hoveyda in 1965. He had a good Economics degree from Cambridge and had been educated exclusively in Britain and America. Unlike many of his colleagues, he was not enormously rich, but he was handsome, charming, intelligent and quickly successful. After ten years in Hoveyda's office, he went to the United Nations, where he worked for the Shah's twin sister, Princess Ashraf. He helped to build up the image of the Iranian Royal family as 'progressive'. The Princess, for instance, became known as a champion of women's rights and sponsored several large initiatives in the field of birth control. The International Planned Parenthood Federation, an impeccably progressive organisation, for instance, got a lot of bounty from the Shah's family. Such cosmetics seen, especially with hindsight, absurdly thin, but they were enough to impress a receptive British and American upper class.

Mr Radji's book is an account of the three years he served as Iranian

Ambassador in London from 1976 to the collapse of the Shah's regime in 1979. It is continuously absorbing, chiefly because it betrays the secrets of the ruling class. It shows what high and important people really say and think. These secrets are made all the more interesting by the tensions in Mr Radji's character. He was no hack of the Shah, at least not in his thoughts. The book constantly slips into self-reproach, which is rare enough in the world of Ambassadors. Deep down, Radji despises the Shah, and hates his own obsequiousness towards the Royal Family. It is as though he knows that his country is plunging to ruin under a corrupt and brutal regime, but steadfastly tells himself that it is his job to stick up for that regime, whatever his private feelings.

By all accounts, not just his own, Mr Radji was very good at this. His first duty was to make himself at home with high society, particularly with Royalty. As a new boy, he made the odd mistake:

> There is an invitation to a Garden Party at Buckingham Palace in the afternoon. The invitation says 'morning dress or lounge suit'. Turn up in the latter, only to discover that in the Queen's tea tent I am a sartorial catastrophe, as everyone else, including the Prime Minister, James Callaghan, is wearing morning dress.

On another occasion, he dared to ask Princess Alexandra, with whom he was dining, to have a drink with him at a fashionable nightclub. 'Angus, being basically tribal, is quite jealous', she replies, rather sadly, in a reference to her husband, the big businessman Angus Ogilvy. Ogilvy himself later impresses on the Ambassador that the Royal Family are a great deal more use to men of money than in purely ceremonial ways:

> He (Ogilvy) mentions more than once that if ever I should wish to see someone in the government through other than my formal diplomatic channels, he would be very pleased to arrange such informal contacts.

All the Royal Family, needless to say, felt a bond of strong solidarity with one of the few really powerful kings left on earth, and so Mr Radji found himself the object of special royal attention. Princess Margaret was a regular guest at the magnificent feasts at the Iranian Embassy. When she came to dinner on one of the Ambassador's first nights in office, she brushed aside his apologies about demonstrators outside who were chanting unseemly slogans such as 'The Shah is a Murderer!' She was used to it, she explained. In America, her official functions were constantly being hampered by demonstrators on Ireland. 'But then, of course, you have torture, and we don't', she added, sympathetically.

This sort of thing shocked the sensitive Mr Radji. But he soon got used to it, particularly as his duties brought him into close contact again and again with the Conservative Party, which was then in opposition. At a dinner party at the home of the Tory MP, Eldon Griffiths, the Ambassador heard Lord Aldington, a former Tory MP and one of Britain's most powerful businessmen, launch a ferocious attack on the American President, Jimmy Carter, for 'introducing human rights as a salient principle of his foreign policy'. He continued:

> It is naive to the point of stupidity to expect the world to comply with a set of moral values that have come to prevail in certain parts of Europe and America, but only as a result of a long process of historical evolution.

The same sophisticated view of human rights was taken at another dinner, thrown by another Tory MP, at which Mr Radji, who had by then rehearsed a rather moving speech defending human rights, denounced the practice of torture. 'Perry' Worsthorne, the elegant *Sunday Telegraph* columnist, took him to task:

> He says he is surprised to hear me applying 19th century English liberal standards in my defence of Iran, when *no* defence is necessary. Quite the contrary, praise is due.

At Mr Radji's first meeting with Mrs Thatcher, she reminded him, at first sight, of a 'priest's wife'. Almost at once, she was ranting on about the need to bring back the rope for terrorists ('not very priest-like' Radji comments). He noticed, too, how solidarity with the Shah was instinctive in *all* Conservatives, whether supporters of Mrs Thatcher or supporters of Edward Heath (who went out of his way to be kind to the Ambassador, and to impress on him how much he admired the Shah). From time to time, Mr Radji expressed his irritation that there was so little criticism among the Tories of the Shah's excesses. At a 'stag dinner' for bright young Tory gentlemen at the Turf Club, thrown by Peter Walker, a former senior Cabinet Minister under Heath, the conversation was 'fast-paced'. 'Peter Walker', Mr Radji comments, 'strikes me as a bit too strongly pro-Shah'.

Mr Radji was more at ease among politicians of the social democratic stamp. Among them, to his intense surprise and relief, he found support for the Shah even more gushing and generous. An early guest at the Embassy was Lady Falkender, Rasputine to the former Labour prime minister Harold Wilson, who had left office only a few months before Mr Radji arrived. Lady Falkender hated caviar—so the first course had to be changed. But she made up for it by saying how much Harold Wilson admired the Shah, and she also told the Ambassador that Martin Ennals (the Secretary of Amnesty, which was relentlessly pursuing charges of torture in Iran), and his brothers were 'Trotskyites'. 'You shouldn't have anything to do with them', the Labour peeress told the Ambassador.

Later, Mr Radji met Harold Wilson himself, inevitably at another dinner party, this one thrown by the publisher, Lord Weidenfeld (ennobled, of course, thanks to Wilson and Falkender's patronage). Wilson recalled one of his 'great sayings' for the Ambassador's benefit: 'I once described the Shah', he said, 'as one of the world's great redistributive leaders'.

Lord Weidenfeld also showed himself to be the last in a long line of British radical publishers when he dined alone with the Ambassador at the Iranian Embassy. He suggested a book on the Shah—'A kind of *Red Star over China* that would put across the Shah's point of view in the same way as Edgar Snow's had done for Mao.' Only someone with Lord Weidenfeld's intense commitment to socialism could bracket the multi-millionaire dynast and hereditary autocrat with the Chinese revolutionary leader.

Again and again, Mr Radji was obliged to his fellow Cambridge graduate and friend, David Owen. The sensitive doctor had not forgotten his journey to Persepolis at the beginning of the decade. He and the entire Labour Government were, throughout the period, unequivocally loyal to the Shah and his regime. When the Ambassador complained to David Owen that the BBC broadcasts to Iran were unduly hostile to the regime, Owen agreed at once, complaining that he did not have the power to stop the broadcasts. Even at the end, when the Shah's regime was toppling, the enthusiasm of David Owen for the dictator did not waver. When Radji complimented him on making a pro-Shah speech in opposition to Labour Party policy, Owen smiled a supercilious smile and said that the National Executive of the Labour Party 'should be told to shut up from time to time'. But then the smile vanished and he admitted he was worried by the hostility to his remarks on Iran. Never since Persepolis had he imagined that opposition to the Shah might consist of anything more than a handful of saboteurs and Russian agents.

Two striking pictures painted by the Ambassador symbolise the attitude of the Labour Government and its supporters towards the Iranian dictatorship. At yet another dinner (the whole book is one long banquet), he found himself next to Judith Hart, champion of the Movement for Colonial Freedom, who was then Minister for Overseas Development. Mr Radji remonstrated with her about her sponsorship of the Committee Against Repression in Iran:

> To my delight she blushes visibly, and asks whether her name *still* appears on the letterhead. When I confirm that it does, she says: 'It is wrong for a government Minister's name to be there, and it must be removed.'

And removed it was. With its removal, the principle was firmly established that for a Labour Minister to be seen to be against repression is a clear breach of the basic tenets of the Constitution and parliamentary democracy.

The other story concerns the philosopher Stuart Hampshire, author of a book on Spinoza and of books and articles championing a more democratic society. Dr Hampshire was Warden of Wadham College, Oxford, when Ambassador Radji and Princess Ashraf arrived to inspect a library which the Princess, in her role as intellectual and reformer had financed. The place was thronged with demonstrators, some in hoods in case they were recognised as Iranian students and deported into the care of SAVAK. The royal car was stuck in an alley and pelted with eggs. Even inside the college, the chants of the demonstrators completely ruined the occasion. Mr Radji wrote:

> Warden Hampshire looked distinctly unhappy, afflicted as it were, with a social responsibility from which he couldn't rid himself soon enough.

Spinoza, no doubt, would have enjoyed the Warden's discomfiture, and might perhaps have asked why he had allowed himself to be compromised in this way; and why the whole academic community had not risen in protest against accepting money from so hideously tainted a source.

Ambassador Radji's job was not completely taken up with royalty and politicians. His main aim was to improve the image of his country and its dictator, and therefore most of his business was with the press. The tremendous care and concern afforded to every word written or broadcast about his country was astonishing. The smallest article, even in *Private Eye,* was a matter for long telegrams between London and Teheran. Indeed, on one of the two audiences granted to Mr Radji in the course of this book, the Shah himself was asked to give judgment on how to react to a snippet of gossip in *Private Eye.*

The most frequent guests at the Ambassador's table at Princes Gate, then, were journalists, usually 'friendly' journalists, but often ostensibly 'hostile' journalists as well. Lord Chalfont and Lord George-Brown had written often in support of the Shah before, and they were always welcome friends. Frank Giles, of *The Sunday Times,* was another reliable lunch guest. A typical entry about another great fan of the Shah reads like this:

> Go to Homayoun Mazandi's for dinner. Simon Fraser and his pretty wife, David Frost and Lady Milford Haven are among the faces I recognise. An enormous house, opulently decorated, tons of caviar and rivers of Dom Perignon. At dinner, David Frost speaks to me about his love for Iran and admiration for HIM.

The word 'HIM' is printed like this throughout the book to designate the Shah. Missing a short note at the beginning, I read two thirds of the book believing this 'HIM' to be an exercise in disrespectful satire by the

Ambassador. Then I found the real reason for it: HIM stands for His Imperial Majesty.

Anthony Howard, then editor of the *New Statesman,* accepted invitations to lunch at the Iranian Embassy during this period, and boasted to Parviz Radji that he would not have accepted such an invitation to the South African Embassy. Even more surprisingly, David Pallister, one of the *Guardian*'s more challenging journalists, was also to be found there. He gave as good as he got at lunch, it is true, but the thrust of the public relations approach was to gain a journalist's confidence through *hospitality.* However hard a journalist tries, it is very hard to remain independent, let alone hostile, to anyone after you have waded through 'tons of caviar and rivers of Dom Perignon' at that person's expense. Indeed, the discussion and angst about *Private Eye* in the Ambassador's diaries are caused by puzzlement about how to proceed. *Who* could be asked to lunch, for instance? Who could be approached for a civilised argument? When the Ambassador told the Shah that he didn't think *Private Eye* could be 'bought', he was not speaking literally. Except in rare cases, journalists were not *bought* by cash offers, or even with freebees to Persepolis. They were, however, available for agreeable lunches and civilised parties at which questions such as corruption or torture could be discussed in a civilised manner. More often than not, this approach paid off handsomely, to the Ambassador's huge delight:

> A favourable article in the *Guardian, not* by Liz Thurgood, entitled: The Shah shoves Iran towards Freedom. There are references to improvements in the condition of political prisoners, an end to torture, and a greater climate of political freedom all of which puts me in a good frame of mind when Parviz Mina takes me to the BP tent at Wimbledon for lunch, and then to watch the men's finals. In four thrilling sets, Borg obliterates Connors.

That entry, for July 8, 1978, perfectly symbolises the life to which Mr Radji was growing accustomed, when suddenly and unannounced, the people, who had played no part in any of his dramas, crudely pushed onto the stage. They toppled the Shah, killed Hoveyda, and would certainly have killed Parviz Radji if he had returned to Iran. This impertinent intervention forced Mr Radji to reflect on the end of 'the aura of elitist authority and importance which has glimmered, as if by divine light, round the heads of those of us who represented Iran's ruling classes for as long as I can remember'. He himself had lost that aura and was forced to contemplate life as a 'stateless refugee'.

But in Britain and the other countries whose governments sustained the Shah through the most corrupt and brutal years of his dictatorship the aura persists, almost unaffected by its grisly end in Iran. There are those who seriously argue that the British ruling class, worn down by long years of democracy, parliamentary questions, trade unions, national councils for civil liberties and the like, have lost a lot of their arrogance, confidence, and self-importance. Certainly, if their official statements are anything to go by, they seem to have developed a sensitivity which would have shocked their ancestors.

The great value of this book is that it banishes such myths. The ruling class is quoted as its members talk to themselves and their fellow rulers overseas without the slightest fear that anything they say will be repeated. The old prejudices and the old arrogance strides out of their cages as confident, as corrupt and as barbaric as ever. Of course the British ruling class is against torture, but there are times when it must be defended. Of course the British ruling class does not like dictators who rely on one-party states. But there are times when they must be singled out for praise.

There are those, too, much more numerous, who argue that these prejudices can be changed and the havoc they cause averted by the existing institutions: that a free Parliament, a free press, and all the lobbying organisations which go with them are themselves powerful enough to roll back the tide of reaction.

Such people should read Mr Radji's book and reflect on the role played in it by the Labour Government. It was, curiously enough, not Old Corrupt Labour upon which the forces of reaction in Iran relied. It was the new, sensitive, 'civil libertarians' who bowed to tyranny. As David Owen inveighed against the BBC for daring to broadcast critical reports to the Iranian people, and Judith Hart ripped her name off the letterhead of the Committee Against Repression in Iran, the government which they represented became, as Mr Radji graphically describes, a bastion against the people of Iran and, a haven in which the shipwrecked agents of the Shah could shelter from the storm. Just as the Labour Government could so swiftly jettison so many of its principles and resolutions, so too could the press which is meant to safeguard freedoms be used again and again to ditch them.

Parviz Radji's riveting diaries show that very little has changed up top. The loss of empire has, if anything, made the British ruling class more greedy and cunning. As long as its opponents play the game by the book, it remains as confident as ever that it can hang on to its property and its power. That may seem a pessimistic conclusion, but curiously the end of the book is not pessimistic at all. By then, the Iranian masses had taken to the streets, breaking every rule that was ever made. The ruling class, in Iran, and in Britain and the United States as well, lost both cunning and confidence and blundered about in blind despair. Perhaps the most hopeful quotation comes from no less a person than HMQ (Her Majesty the Queen). Shaking hands sadly with Mr Radji at the time when the Shah was preparing to leave Iran, she murmured, perhaps with a trace of foreboding: 'It all happened so *suddenly*.'

THE SOVIET UNION AT THE BEGINNING OF A NEW ERA: STAGES IN THE DEVELOPMENT OF SOCIETY AND THE POLITICAL LEADERSHIP IN THE USSR

Roy Medvedev

It has become obvious to everyone that with the autumn of 1982 the Soviet Union entered into a new phase in its development, a phase which will differ substantially from the dreary Brezhnev era which has just concluded. We stand on the threshold of a new era, and this gives rise to a national desire to take a look back, even if only a cursory one, at the past and to review the main features of the path our country has traversed during the last few decades.

The periodisation of Soviet history can be based on various principles, because, depending on the purpose of the study, we can put in the forefront either this or that one from among the most important indicators of Soviet society. But it will not be a mistake to say, also, that, under the conditions of so highly centralised and authoritarian a state as the Soviet Union, each lasting administration creates its own era. From this standpoint we can, looking back, speak of four main stages in the development of our society, namely, the eras of Lenin, Stalin, Khrushchev and Brezhnev. It is important to make clear that what is involved here is a series of really different periods, which are distinguished one from another not only by the personal qualities and names of the Soviet leaders but also in respect of economic and social reality, the state of social well-being, the methods of political and economic government, the nature and characteristics of the ruling elite, the international situation the country was in and the priorities of its domestic and foreign policy, the predominant conception of military strategy, the level of technical equipment and the role assigned to the armed forces, the importance of these on those social and political institutions, the prevailing mood and world-outlook, the level of general culture, the style of behaviour and even the outward appearance and habits of both ordinary citizens and leaders, the character of art, architecture and literature, and many other values and phenomena of social life.

The idea that the Soviet Communist system is eternally immutable is false. If we consider only the most important changes in the nature of society we can perceive that each of the eras listed above was in many ways the negation of that which preceded it, while in other ways no less significant, it retained a link of continuity with the past, basing itself on the achievements of that past and the previously established social and

176

political institutions. Each successive administration solved numerous acute problems and contradictions inherited from its predecessor. At the same time, however, a heap of new problems and contradictions accumulated which it was difficult to solve within the framework of the given stage of development, for both objective and subjective reasons.

The few transitions which have occurred in our history from one administration to another have not been smooth and even but painful and difficult, and in this connexion it is fully appropriate to employ the concept of 'crisis'. Not only the development of capitalism but also that of socialism, in all the socialist countries, has proceeded up to now from crisis to crisis, although the character, circumstances and chief factors creating the socio-political crisis situations in a given country were, of course, different as between the 'camp' of capitalism and the 'camp' of socialism.

In the Soviet Union, as everyone knows, we do not have a sufficiently clearly-defined constitutional mechanism, determining the procedure for one administration to succeed another. A considerable accidental element often enters into this very important political process. And yet we see that the advancement of each new leader to the summit of the Soviet pyramid of power is to be explained not simply by the role of accidents or of personal ambitions, but also by a complex combination of social forces and socio-political moods, the influence of which proves to be stronger than the will of the outgoing leader. Lenin fervently opposed the promotion of Stalin as his successor. Yet all Lenin's letters and appeals on this matter were ignored. And it was the same, even though in different form, with the other successions in the Party and state administrations of the USSR.

The view exists that in our country the 'apparatus' itself, the establishment or ruling 'elite' decide upon and bring forward new leaders, in accordance with the interest and requirements of a system of government that suits the 'apparatus'. This view contains a considerable measure of truth. We have not yet seen an example of the advancement of a 'chief' who did not himself belong to the highest circles of the existing governmental machinery, or who was antagonistic to the prevailing interests and expectations in those circles. From this circumstance, however, it does not follow at all that the role of the leader in the Soviet system of government is insignificant. In the first place, the composition of the ruling 'elite' in the Soviet Union is heterogeneous: it does not constitute in any way a 'new class' the members of which are bound together by a sort of mutual responsibility. Second, the moods and expectations of the 'apparatus' may not coincide with those of the broad masses of the Soviet population, from which this 'apparatus' is not separated by any legal barriers or the distinctions that mask off one social estate from another, or by any other walls that are hard to surmount. These circumstances

may be made use of by the new leader—especially under the conditions
of an authoritarian system of government. The new Soviet leader may
gradually alter not just the style and methods of government, or the make-
up of his immediate entourage, but also the entire composition of the
ruling elite. He may create new institutions of government and exert
influence on all spheres of social and cultural life, on the tempos and forms
of development of the economy, and on the character of foreign and
domestic policy. This circumstance, too, helps historians and political
scientists to 'personify' the eras through which our country has passed.
But historians cannot ignore such leaders, also, as, for example, Malenkov
or Zinoviev, who were able to stay in power for only one or two years
and turned out to be merely transient figures in a period of transition
between two different eras. It is just such a transition period that has
begun at the present time in our country. This is a time of hopes and
fears, and I shall discuss it later.

The Lenin Era

It is not possible to discuss here in detail the comparatively brief but
infinitely complex era of Lenin, with which the history of the Soviet
state began. It was, in the first place, a time of revolution, of that twentieth-
century revolution which has been more important in its consequences
than any other. It was comparable only to the eruption of a mighty
volcano, accompanied by a tremendous earthquake, which destroyed
everywhere not only structures that were decrepit but also quite solid
ones, and saw thrown up from the bowels of the earth red-hot rocks
and thousands of millions of tons of volcanic ash that burned down or
overwhelmed in their course many towns and villages reduced to ruin,
creating in our country within a mere few weeks or months, a completely
new social and political landscape!

It was, secondly, a time of cruel civil war lasting several years, a war of
classes and parties that gave no quarter to each other and were prepared
to use any means in order to gain victory over their opponents. Across
the huge expanse of Russia battled armies of 'whites' and 'reds', 'greens'
and 'blacks', nationalists and interventionists, leaving behind or ahead
of them devastated towns and villages, and hundreds of thousands of
people dying of disease or hunger. Even before the revolution, Lenin
warned that revolution is 'a period in the life of a people when the anger
accumulated during centuries. . . breaks forth into actions, not merely
into words; and into the actions of *millions of people,* not merely
individuals'.[1]

Notions of violent revolution as 'festivals of the oppressed', notions
of how only in open armed conflict between hostile classes and in prolonged civil war can the proletariat rid itself of 'all the old muck' and be
morally reborn in order to create a new society—these romantic notions

of the young Marx and Engels were far from being confirmed by actual historical experience. It was found that revolutions not only 'clarify' the social atmosphere, they also 'darken' it. The protracted and cruel civil war that they engender not only pulverises the best element of the proletariat but also sanctions in a fight to the death the application of such methods of terror and coercion the employment of which does not so much elevate as morally pervert those who take part in the revolutionary struggle. The total ruin of the old society and the introduction everywhere of iron discipline does not only prepare the ground for the building of a new socialist society, it also creates the conditions for the appearance of a new despotism and a new 'revolutionary tyranny', to get rid of which sometimes proves still harder than to get rid of the vices of the previous society. This has been shown not only by the history of the French Revolution of the eighteenth century but also by that of the October Revolution, which brought to the peoples of Russia, along with social and national liberation, also the ordeals of Stalin's dictatorship.

It was not given to Lenin to see all the consequences of the revolution that he led. But even what he saw in 1921 did not inspire any particular optimism. Before the victors lay a country with a new social and political system, but also with a ruined economy and with a hungry and discontented population. The cities were deserted and the villages were disaffected. Lenin saw more clearly than anyone else the danger and instability of the situation that had come about. 'Our proletariat', he wrote at that time, 'has been largely declassed. . . The terrible crises and the closing-down of the factories have compelled people to flee from starvation. The workers have simply abandoned the factories—they have had to settle down in the country and have ceased to be workers. . . We must admit that at the present time the proletarian policy of the Party is not determined by the character of its membership but by the enormous undivided prestige enjoyed by the small group which might be called the old guard of the Party. A slight conflict within this group will be enough. . . to rob it of its power to determine policy.'[2]

Lenin saw the way out of this very grave crisis, the first and most dangerous socio-political and economic crisis of Soviet power, as consisting in a system of concession and retreats which should have the effect of reducing tension, reassuring the peasant masses, cooling the atmosphere of hatred and intolerance, creating stumuli for economic growth and gradually consolidate the social basis and the political institutions of the new regime. But at the same time it was necessary to consolidate the Party to an even greater degree, binding it with hoops of discipline, forbidding the formation within it of any factions, or any discussion that might weaken Party unity. Lenin understood the danger of degeneration that threatened a party which had acquired enormous power and was deprived of the possibility of freely discussing its own problems. He tried to create some forms of supervision of the activity of the Party's leaders, but was unable to find any effective solution to this problem. Thanks to Lenin's proclamation of the new economic policy (NEP), the crisis of the Soviet power was basically overcome, but Lenin died in January 1924 very well aware of the imperfection and incompleteness of the new state and the new society which had been created under his leadership.

The Stalin Era

The period when Stalin ruled was the longest and the most contradictory era of Soviet history to date. It had its own different phases, and Stalin himself, an experienced politician and actor, assumed different guises in the course of his struggle for unrestricted power.

Stalin came to power in the Party under the conditions of NEP, which enjoyed the support of the overwhelming majority of the population of the USSR. It was natural, therefore, that Stalin at first supported NEP and even enlarged its scope, while at the same time increasing and strengthening all the organs of Party and state authority.

In doing this, Stalin gradually altered the relation between the organs of Party and of state leadership. It is well known that Lenin was the chief creator of one-party dictatorship and spoke more than once of 'dictatorship of the Party'. However, after the February Revolution the Bolshevik Party had to struggle with other parties for majority in the Soviets, which were organs of power elected at open meetings of workers (both blue-collar and white-collar) and peasants. Down to October 1917 this struggle was carried on mainly by political methods, but in 1918–1919 administrative and repressive methods were also used in order to oust other parties from the Soviets. To the slogans of creating 'soviets without Bolsheviks' the latter counterposed tacitly, the implicit slogan of 'Soviets without Mensheviks, Socialist-Revolutionaries and Anarchists', and this aim was gradually achieved. Already at the beginning of the 1920s we see operating in the Soviets only the Bolshevik Party, together with groups of non-party deputies. At first the Party exercised its dictatorship through the Soviets. In this phase the Soviets were not just formally but also in fact the principal organ of state power, with the Party as their political and ideological guide. Lenin assumed no official position in the Party—he was the head of the Council of People's Commissars of the RSFSR (later of the USSR). In the provinces and districts the chairman of the provincial or district executive committee of the local soviet summoned to his presence, when necessary, the leaders of the Party organisation of that province or district, just as Lenin could summon to his office, the office of the chairman of the Council of People's Commissars, any of the executives of the Central Committee of the Russian Communist Party. After Lenin's death the situation changed. Now it was not A.I. Rykov, chairman of the Council of People's Commissars of the RSFSR, who summoned Stalin to his presence, but J.V. Stalin, General Secretary of the Central Committee of the Party, who summoned Rykov. Similarly, in the localities, the First Secretary of the Party's provincial or district committee summoned to his presence any of the leaders of the local soviets. Stalin transformed the Party apparatus into the focus of power. The soviets now became just one of the 'transmission belts' of the Communist Party's dictatorship. The Central Committee of the Party finally became the chief directing and legislative organ of the proletarian dictatorship.

Freedom of trade, freedom of private enterprise in small and medium industry and also in agriculture, together with great efforts by the Party and economic organs to restore large-scale industry led comparatively quickly to improvement in the country's economic situation. Despite many difficulties and disproportions, by 1926–27 the pre-war level of industrial and agricultural production had been recovered and even exceeded in the USSR. The Red Army had been reduced in numbers but strengthened qualitatively, and the same was true of the Cheka-GPU. In the mid-1920s Stalin resolutely abstained from the revolutionary experiments that the Left Opposition was demanding. The country needed to heal its wounds, to rest, to enjoy a period of relative stability. This period of NEP and NEP-economy, which was to be remembered later by many as the best and most liberal phase in the history of Soviet power, lasted a comparatively short time. In the 1920s, in the towns, private industry could not develop to any significant degree, because it was confronted by large-scale state-owned industry and trade. The state also controlled the entire financial system. In the countryside, however, socialist relations and socialist enterprises were still very feebly developed. What predominated there was the spontaneous development of small private farms, among which the leading position was held by relatively rich farms of the 'kulak' type. State regulation, and also the state system of procurement and purchase of grain, which was unfavourable to the rich farms, encountered increasing resistance in the rural areas. When he found himself in serious difficulties, Stalin was unable to find a compromise policy and take the path of manoeuvring and concessions. Relying on the full might of the state and Party apparatus, on the Army, the GPU and the poorest section of the peasantry, Stalin undertook a radical reorganisation of the countryside, which consisted in liquidating the well-to-do section of the peasantry and evicting millions of peasant families to the North and East of the USSR. What remained of the peasantry was grouped not so much willingly as forcibly in collective farms (kolkhozy), which were intended to take responsibility for the production of all the main forms of agricultural produce, employing the most up-to-date methods of mechanised agriculture.

This 'revolution from above' was accompanied at first by a decline in agricultural production and a mass-scale famine in most of the producing areas, which carried off millions of lives. The standard of living of the town population was also lowered, but this did not prevent a relatively rapid development of all branches of industry, and especially of engineering, heavy industry and defence industry. The feeble private industry in the towns was liquidated, along with private trade, and measures of repression were taken not only against various groups of traders and 'industrialists' but also against considerable sections of the old Russian intelligentsia—engineers, specialists, scientists and scholars. They were replaced by 'Red' specialists who had been trained in the numerous institutions of secondary and higher education. Throughout the country not only was illiteracy successfully abolished but universal primary schooling was introduced, soon to be followed by seven-year education. Thanks to an influx of people from the villages and from other strata of the population, the working class quickly grew in size. However, these were mostly first generation workers, who differed substantially from that nucleus of hereditary proletarians who had served as the Bolsheviks' chief support in 1917.

Serious economic difficulties and discontent among the masses of working people, on the one hand, and, on the other, an increase in bureaucratism, centralisation and the cult of Stalin's personality gave rise to criticism from that section of the Party and state cadres who had been formed under Lenin's leadership before the revolution and in the first years after it. This opposition that was beginning to take shape constituted a potential threat to Stalin's power. He did not wait for it to develop into a real force. Slanderously accusing the Party's Old Guard of 'treachery', Stalin carried out in 1936–8 an unprecedented campaign of bloody terror directed against the Communist Party itself and its cadres. Only in the first stages of this campaign of repression was it directed against all who had participated in the inner-Party oppositions of the 1920s. Later on, the organs of the GPU-NKVD, increased to the dimensions of a large army, rained their blows on the basic cadres of the Communist Party, the Red Army, the Soviet and economic organs, the Young Communist League and the Comintern, on all workers in science, culture and art who were displeasing to Stalin, and also on the cadres of the punitive organs themselves. Hundreds of thousands of Communists were physically destroyed, millions of Communists and non-Party people were put in prison or sent to forced-labour camps. To replace the Soviet and Party leaders thus eliminated, Stalin promoted representatives of the younger generation of Party and State cadres: they carried out unquestioningly the will of the dictator, whose power became practically unlimited. The combination of ideological demagogy, unrestrained cult of the leader, lawlessness, terror and forced labour, on the one hand, and particular institutions of socialist society on the other, constituted the main features of the phenomenon which came to be called Stalinism.

The cruel terror of 1936–8 weakened all the organs of the Party and State and slowed down the country's economic progress. This was, though not the sole, yet one of the chief causes of the defeats suffered by the USSR in the first phase of the Patriotic war. By the autumn of 1942 the Hitlerite armies were in the foothills of the Caucasus, on the banks of the Volga and at the walls of Moscow and Leningrad: they had occupied territory inhabited by almost half of the population of the USSR and including about half of its industrial potential. Danger of annihilation hung not only over Stalin's dictatorship but also over the national existence of all the peoples of the USSR, their statehood and their culture, their lives and history. All the peoples of the USSR rose up to defend their country, the Army's losses were quickly replaced, and in the Eastern regions industry expanded on an immense scale the production of all kinds of modern weapons and war materials. During the fight against the aggressor thousands of talented military leaders and commanders came to the forefront in the Army, and the ranks of the Communist Party were reinforced by millions of patriotic young people. All this altered the course of the war. And the further westward the divisions and armies of the Soviet armed forces advanced the more powerful were the blows they struck and the more marked their superiority in military skill and techniques over the armies of Hitler, which had behind them the war-industry potential of almost all Western Europe. The United States and Great Britain, too, recovered from their initial setbacks and considerably increased their machinery of war and their pressure on the aggressive alliance of Germany, Japan and Italy. The resistance movement also grew in strength in nearly all the enslaved countries of Europe and Asia.

The Second World War ended quite otherwise than had been desired by those who began it and those who had long been encouraging Fascist aggression. Western Europe was devastated and weakened. The immense colonial empires created by the European countries began to break up, and many large countries in Asia were able, so early as the 1940s, to achieve political independence. In the capitalist, or Western world, unprecedented power and influence was acquired by the United States, which now possessed the strongest war machines. There were American military and air-force bases in every continent and the American navy dominated every ocean. The USA alone possessed the atomic bomb, the new super-power whose power had already been demonstrated in the destruction of the Japanese cities of Hiroshima and Nagasaki. However, the Soviet Union, too, despite all the losses and destruction suffered, had been transformed from a great power into a 'super-power' whose military might lagged not far behind that of the Western countries. The USSR wielded effective control over the countries of Eastern and South-Eastern Europe and the eastern part of Germany. The influence of left-wing movements had increased in many parts of the world and especially in

Western Europe. In Italy and France Communists were included in the first post-war governments.

Such an outcome of the war as this did not suit the leaders of the capitalist world. However, the 'cold war' against the USSR which was soon proclaimed by Churchill and Truman did not bring great successes for the West. The Communists were ousted from the governments of the Western countries, NATO formed, which was joined by the West German state created soon afterward. The Western countries recovered economically in a relatively short time. The Soviet Union was obliged to relax its pressure on Iran and Turkey. Some of the Western countries even tried to get back their colonies in Asia. France, for example, began its first war to recover Indo-China.

Nevertheless, on the whole, the policy of 'rolling back Communism' did not give the results its initiators wanted. In the countries of Eastern and South-Eastern Europe the power of the Communist Parties was strengthened. A new, Communist government was formed in East Germany. Yugoslavia alone, which had thrown down a challenge to Stalin's tyranny, remained outside the Soviet bloc. In Asia, the changes were even more remarkable. Victorious after a civil war lasting twenty years, the Chinese Communists established effective control over the entire territory of mainland China and set up there in 1949 a new state, the Chinese People's Republic. American forces and the remnants of the Kuomintang armies maintained control, with considerable difficulty, only in the island of Taiwan. In order to keep control over South Korea the United States had to wage a bloody war lasting four years. By the end of 1949 the USSR had succeeded in making its own atomic bomb. Although the USSR had also managed to restore its industry, our country was still far from attaining the level of the USA: industrial production in the USSR in 1950 was about 10 per cent of industrial production in the USA. But it was in these post-war years that began that competition and rivalry between the USSR and the USA which largely determined the history of international relations in the succeeding decades.

The internal situation in the USSR in the post-war years was difficult and complex. The political and patriotic upsurge called forth by victory in the war was accompanied by a strengthening of Stalin's despotic regime. Already in 1941 Stalin had made himself head of the Soviet state not only de facto but also formally. The personal dictatorship of Stalin became more and more sharply defined. He hardly ever convened not only plenums of the Party's Central Committee but even sessions of the Political Bureau of the Council of Ministers of the USSR or else convened them without all their members being present. The holding of the Party's next congress was continually postponed. The Party's organs, including the apparatus of its Central Committee, all fell even further under the control of the punitive organisations, losing their guiding role in society. In the last years of the war Stalin already began to resume 'selective' terror. Several nationalities of the Volga region, Northern Caucasia and the Crimea were deported to eastern parts of the country. (All persons of German nationality had been arrested or deported in 1941–2.) An anti-semitic campaign gathered force and led in 1948–50 to the destruction of all Jewish national organisations, the elimination of most Jews from the ruling apparatus and the ideological organisations, and then to mass arrests among the Jewish intellectuals. Certain sections of the Party and state apparatus were also subjected to harsh repression (the case of N. Voznesensky and A. Kuznetsov, the 'Leningrad affair', and so on).

Industrial production was restored in the post-war years with comparative speed: the experience acquired during the war helped here. As early as 1952 the USSR's total industrial production was twice what it had been in 1940. Agriculture, however, progressed extremely slowly, even though the country's demand for agricultural produce had markedly increased. The gross production of agriculture in 1946–50 in annual averages was less than in 1940 and only a little more than before the revolution, in 1913. The system of requisitioning was, in practice, introduced into the countryside, and the collective farmers were bound to the soil and deprived of incentives to develop production. Most of the rural population lived in conditions of extreme poverty, economic and political pressure on the peasantry was intensified, and the work done by the collective farmers was practically not paid for. Extreme poverty was also characteristic of the life of most of the workers, blue-collar and white-collar alike. Very little was done to build houses in the towns. The workers were not allowed to change their place of work as they liked. Food supplies for the towns were poor, wages were low, and pensions were insufficient to cover the minimum needs of their recipients. All over the country, and especially in the North and East, there was a huge network of forced-labour camps. The very harsh conditions of life and work in these camps resulted every year in the death of hundreds of thousands, even millions, of prisoners. In the post-war years the ranks of the political prisoners of the 1930s—the once-rich peasants, the former commanders of the Red Army, the representatives of the technical intelligentsia—had thinned out: their places were taken in the camps by former prisoners of war, 'displaced persons', Jews and members of other national minorities, and Party and military executives of a new generation. Among this influx of innocent victims there was, of course, a streamlet of persons who really were guilty—not only ordinary criminals but also persons who had collaborated with the occupying forces during the war.

Altogether, at the beginning of the 1950s the Soviet Union was entering into a period of severe economic and political crisis, which Stalin's administration tried to resolve through intensifying its methods of pressure and terror. While the people were living in poverty, the privileges and salaries of the leading executives of the state and Party administration were enormously increased. The gap between state and society widened. The executives of the apparatus of power, intimidated and bribed, were ready to carry out any orders Stalin cared to give. Nevertheless, although the driver's whip whistled ever more sharply, the enfeebled horses dragged the overloaded cart forward more and more slowly.

The Khrushchev Era

Stalin came to power not only thanks to his skill at political intrigue, but also through the feelings and expectations of a considerable part of the Party and Soviet apparatus in the 1920s, especially at its middle and lower levels. He did not, of course, leave this apparatus unchanged, but constantly chopped off one bit after another. Even persons who had always served Stalin with the utmost devotion could expect as 'reward' either a bullet in the back of the head or a bunk in a concentration camp. Nevertheless, Stalin sought to retain the backing and support of the main part of the apparatus of government which he renewed or refashioned, and the bureaucratisation of which took a big step forward under his rule.

But even this Stalinist apparatus grew tired, towards the end of his era, of the constant tensions and fears of repression. By giving Stalin false, embellished ideas of the real situation the bureaucratic apparatus set a trap for itself, as Stalin's ever-increasing demands in the last years of his life resulted from the false idea of reality which had become firmly fixed in his mind. This mutual self-deception could not go on for ever. Consequently, a considerable section of the huge Stalinist apparatus received the news of his death not only with sincere sorrow but also with carefully concealed relief.

We know that Stalin's accession to power was accompanied by a fierce struggle, at first with the 'Left' and then with the 'Right' opposition. But Khrushchev's accession to power, too, was preceded by a hard fight, in the first phase of which Khrushchev, supported by most of the leading men in Party and state and by the Army, smashed the top leadership of Stalin's punitive apparatus and gave back supreme power in the country to the Party leadership and, in particular, to the Party's Central Committee. In the second phase of this struggle Khrushchev, supported by the Army, by the renewed apparatus of the KGB and by a considerable section of the Party apparatus, ousted from power most of those who had formed Stalin's Political Bureau, that is, the men who were most seriously compromised by participation in Stalin's crimes. However, Khrushchev was not in a position to change completely the composition of the governing apparatus, and he was surrounded by people who had, in the previous era, held important posts in Stalin's bureaucratic hierarchy. This circumstance, together with the contradictory nature of Khrushchev himself, determined many of the contradictions in the activity of the new leader.

Khrushchev's activity was developed in several directions at once. He saw as one of his tasks the cessation of the Stalin terror and the liquidation of the monstrous machinery of terror which Stalin had created. Working towards that end, he curtailed considerably, already in 1953-4, the size, power and scope of the supreme organs of state security. Subsequently, he took steps to bring about a decisive change in the personal composition of the security organs. Cautious and selective rehabilitations began already in 1953 and were extended and continued in 1954-5. The decisive turning-point came after Khrushchev's famous secret speech at the Twentieth Congress of the CPSU, when he denounced many of Stalin's crimes and mistakes. Following that congress nearly all the political prisoners who were still alive were released and rehabilitated. To many millions rehabilitation came posthumously. Hundreds of forced-labour camps were closed down. In 1957 the Moslem and Buddhist nationalities of the Volga region and Northern Caucasia were rehabilitated and allowed to return to their homelands. The rehabilitation of the Volga Germans and the Crimean Tartars, however, was delayed, without reason, for several years, and even then they were not given the right to live where they had lived before and recover their former national autonomy.

The Twenty-Second Congress of the CPSU, held in 1961, took a further step in the fight against Stalinism. At this congress the crimes of Stalin and of many of his henchmen were talked about not in secret but in open sessions. The congress resolved to remove Stalin's body from the Lenin mausoleum and at the same time to do away with all monuments to Stalin and to rename all towns, villages and enterprises which had been named after him. Criticism of Stalin and Stalinism began to be heard in literature, in films, in historical works and in the other social sciences. This deepening and broadening of the front of struggle against Stalinism and the attempts being made to find new, democratic forms of government had already evoked protest and alarm among a large section of the bureaucracy and the apparatus on which Khrushchev himself relied. Under the influence of these groups, the criticism of Stalin began to be played down even while Khrushchev was still in charge. Even the work of rehabilitating Party members was not carried to completion, and many prominent figures in the October Revolution and the civil war, Lenin's comrades-in-arms, remained un-rehabilitated. The men around Khrushchev feared that, even so, he had gone too far in his criticism of Stalin. Khrushchev himself was not sufficiently staunch where this matter was concerned and did not exploit all the opportunities inherent in the position he held. Employing the terminology of earlier epochs, one could say that the period when Khrushchev ruled was something half-way between enlightened absolutism and moderate liberalism. It was still far from being socialist democracy. Khrushchev's occasional impulses in the direction of developing greater democracy were effectively doused by the bureaucrats around him.

Another line taken by Khrushchev's activity was his vigorous effort to overcome the crisis in the Soviet economy, and especially in the sphere of agricultural production. Reduction, and later abolition of a number of taxes which bore too heavily not only on the personal plots of the country-folk but also on the collective farms, and substantial increase in the procurement prices paid for agricultural produce—all this increased the incomes of the collective farmers and created new economic incentives for the development of farming. Within a short space of time Khrushchev broke up the collective-farm system in its Stalinist form though he failed to sweep away completely many of its vestiges. At the same time he made considerable efforts to bring under cultivation tens of millions of hectares of new land in the East and South-East of the Soviet Union. During Khrushchev's ascendency several measures were adopted to speed up the development of industry and transport, including the production of consumer goods. Particular attention was given to rapid expansion of house-building and lowering of its cost. Tens of millions of people were at last able to obtain flats of their own. Pensions for the elderly and the disabled were increased several times and wage-rises given to many categories of workers, both blue-collar and white-collar. On the whole, the material situation and food-supply of the broad masses had improved markedly before the end of the 1950s.

Many of Khrushchev's economic reforms and initiatives, however, were too hasty and poorly thought-out, and so remained ineffective. Some of them caused more loss than gain to the Soviet economy. Khrushchev's measures to decentralise the management of industry, abolish the ministries in charge of particular industries and create provincial and regional economic councils did not fulfil his hope. The hasty abolition of the state-owned machine-tractor stations (MTS) and sale of all agricultural equipment to the collective farms resulted in most cases only in worsening the financial position of the collective farms and collective farmers, while failing to improve the use made of agricultural equipment in the USSR. The enormous plantations of maize which were established, on Khrushchev's personal orders, in all parts of the country proved in most cases to be highly unprofitable investments of labour and capital. As a result of incorrect agricultural technique, millions of hectares of land in the virgin-soil regions became subject to erosion. Utter failure was the fate, too, of Khrushchev's widely-proclaimed campaign under the slogan: 'Within three or four years, catch up with the USA in production of meat per head of population.' Khrushchev was inexhaustible as a source of proposals for more and more reforms and initiatives. After a brief acceleration, however, the huge flywheel of the Soviet economy began, once more, to turn slower and slower.

Already in the 1950s Khrushchev made substantial changes in the

USSR's foreign policy. Under Stalin even the leaders of the new India, Gandhi and Nehru, were declared to be 'stooges of imperialism'. Khrushchev altered decisively the Soviet attitude to the independent countries of Asia and Africa which had been given, in world geopolitics, the collective name of 'the Third World', and whose number continually increased during the 1950s. As a result, the influence of the Soviet Union among these countries grew to a notable extent. Among the Arab countries the USSR's chief ally was the new Egypt. With the revolution in Cuba the USSR obtained a reliable ally in the Western hemisphere as well.

The year 1955 saw a decisive change for the better in relations between the USSR and Yugoslavia. In that year, also, the socialist countries of Eastern Europe formed a defensive military alliance, the Warsaw Pact Organisation, counterposed to NATO. The inter-state organisation of socialist countries called the Council for Mutual Economic Aid (Comecon) which had been set up in 1949 was strengthened: its members were the USSR, Albania, Romania, Bulgaria, Mongolia, the German Democratic Republic, Hungary, Poland and Czechoslovakia. In the Khrushchev era Soviet control over the external and internal policies of the European socialist countries was considerably slackened. However, the troubles in Poland in October 1956, which it proved possible to bring to order by mainly political means, and the revolt in Budapest, which was put down mainly by the Soviet troops stationed in Hungary, showed that the USSR's liberalism in relation to its allies in Eastern Europe had definite limits.

Soon after it came to power, Khrushchev's administration took energetic steps to relax the strained relations between the USSR and the USA and other advanced Western countries and put an end to the 'cold war'. These steps resulted in a weakening of that barrier between East and West which had been called 'the iron curtain' and which, in the past, had been erected by the efforts of both sides. But both the USSR's policy towards the Western countries and their policy towards the USSR and its allies were still full of contradictions. Consequently, short periods of improved relations alternated constantly with periods when these relations again deteriorated. Thus, for example, after the first 'summit' meeting attended by Khrushchev and the heads of Western great powers, which took place in 1955 and gave rise to great hopes, not only the events in Poland and Hungary but also the Anglo-French attack on Egypt led to renewed tension between East and West. Soon after Khrushchev's lengthy visit to the United States, which set in train a fruitful dialogue between the two countries, a fresh acute crisis arose, connected with the flight of American spy-planes over the USSR, one of which was shot down over the Urals by a Soviet missile. In Western Europe, after the establishment of diplomatic relations between the USSR and the Federal Republic of Germany and the confirmation of a new status for Austria, and also the release of all German prisoners-of-war and the signing of a series of economic and trade agreements, a new Berlin crisis arose and the notorious Berlin Wall was erected. The Caribbean crisis, which was extremely threatening to the whole world, and was caused both by American menaces to Cuba and by the USSR's attempt to install on Cuban territory missiles with nuclear warheads, was succeeded by negotiations and the conclusion of an agreement on prohibiting nuclear weapon tests in three areas.

Few could doubt Khrushchev's sincerity in striving for peace. He really did try to end the arms race. On his initiative the Soviet Union in the 1950s substantially reduced the size of its army and ceased work on certain projects to expand its navy. But Khrushchev also strove to push ahead the development of Soviet missiles and nuclear weapons, because in that sphere the USSR was still well behind the USA. Although the Soviet Union had begun work on the creation of a hydrogen bomb later than the Americans, our country was the first to explode a nuclear device in the atmosphere. From the technical standpoint Soviet missiles were less perfect than their American counterparts. But the USSR was the first country to succeed in putting an artificial earth-satellite into space, and the first man to circumnavigate the earth in a space-ship was a Soviet citizen, Yuri Gagarin.

At the beginning of the 1960s, despite successes in some fields of foreign and domestic policy, a situation of socio-economic and political crisis began to take shape once more the the USSR. The currency reform of 1961, together with an increase in prices for many foodstuffs and some manufactured goods, led to a fall in the real wages of the workers. On Khrushchev's initiative a number of supplements to wages in the East and Northern parts of the country were abolished. Certain indicators of the economic efficiency of production started to decline and the rate of industrial progress to slow down. All this gave rise to discontent among the workers. Strikes took place in some big enterprises.

An especially bad situation came about in agriculture, which almost ceased to progress, in spite of the tremendous efforts made by the administration and of substantial investments. In 1963 the Soviet Union was for the first time in its history obliged to buy large quantities of grain abroad. In numerous cities people were having to queue even for bread and flour. The real incomes of the peasants shrank. Particular irritation was caused in the countryside by a fresh drive on the part of the authorities against the personal plots of the collective farmers, the workers on state farms and the workers in small towns. The creative intelligentsia, who had recently hailed the Twenty-Second Congress of the CPSU, were upset by intensified censorship and ideological pressure in 1963 and new 'worked-up' campaigns.

While the country at large was unhappy over Khrushchev's attempts to effect a further cut in the armed forces by about one-third, the regimental officers were angered by the abolition of a number of their privileges and reduction in the amounts of pensions for servicemen. The salaries of officers of the militia were also reduced. The apparatus of the Party and the state was also extremely discontented with several of Khrushchev's reforms. Already some time before this Khrushchev had done away with many privileges and unjustifiably large payments enjoyed by the executives of this apparatus. The new Rules of the CPSU, adopted at the Twenty-Second Congress, swept away the principle of professionalism in Party work and limited the periods for which elective Party posts could be held. Highly unpopular also was the reform which split the Party organs into 'industrial' and 'agricultural' sections—a reform which merely brought confusion into the whole system of Party and state leadership. The number of executives employed in the apparatus rapidly increased, but their salaries and privileges were reduced.

The USSR economy experienced no small difficulties also through the excessive obligations which Khrushchev undertook abroad, as for example, in Egypt and other Arab countries. The conservative elements in the Party apparatus likewise blamed Khrushchev for the difficulties that appeared in the early 1960s in the international Communist movement and in consequence of the split with China. They were unhappy about the fresh denunciations of Stalin at the Twenty-Second Congress of the CPSU and about the enlivening of social and cultural activity in the country which this congress stimulated. By and large, Khrushchev lost his popularity and the social basis for his personal rule. He was able to rule only with the support of his colleagues in the Presidium (the Political Bureau) and the Central Committee of the Party. And when the majority of the Central Committee's members turned against Khrushchev he was easily ousted from power and sent into retirement.

The Brezhnev Era

The promotion of L.I. Brezhnev and consolidation of his influence and authority was accompanied by hardly any inner-Party conflict. In the first year of the 'Brezhnev era' there did occur, of course, both in the Political Bureau and the Central Committee and in the Council of Ministers, some contradictions and disputes between individual members of the leadership and Brezhnev. But these did not at all amount to the sort of struggle for power that Khrushchev or Stalin had to wage. Our country's Party and state apparatus backed Brezhnev almost unquestioningly, and potential rivals were left without hope. This apparatus was tired of strong leaders who would not let Soviet bureaucrats lead a quiet life. But Brezhnev, though vainglorious, was a weak and characterless man and lacked any distinct intellectual capacities. He did not try to raise himself above the apparatus, as Stalin had, nor did he wage that constant struggle against the bureaucratic apparatus which Khrushchev had waged. On the contrary, Brezhnev gave his complete confidence to that apparatus and, it can be said, transferred to it a large share of the functions of governing society and the state, only rarely displaying some sort of initiative. Never had the grey and faceless mediocrity of bureaucratic government achieved such triumphs in our country as in Brezhnev's time. But never, either, had the sterility of the Soviet bureaucracy as a social stratum been manifested so completely. Naturally, during the eighteen years of Brezhnev's leadership our society and state made notable progress in some spheres. But when we draw the balance of an era we must speak not only of its successes but also of its omissions, and these were extremely big—bigger, perhaps, than the successes achieved under Brezhnev's leadership.

The Brezhnev era can for convenience be divided into three periods. The first of these cover the middle and last years of the 1960s. First and foremost, the new leadership tried to put right everything that it thought mistaken in the activities and reforms of Khrushchev. For example, his splitting of the Party organisations between industry and agriculture was cancelled and the old system of Party and soviet administration on a district and regional basis restored. The economic councils were wound up and the ministries, at all-Union and republic levels, which had been in charge of particular industries were revived. Many of Khrushchev's reforms in the sphere of education were gradually abolished. The new leadership took a series of cautious steps towards a partial rehabilitation of Stalin. Simultaneously with these 'counter-reforms', the leadership of Brezhnev and Kosygin tried to alter the previous ways of administering industry and agriculture, enlarging the role of economic incentive and management factors. This was the intended purpose of the decision taken at the March 1965 Plenum of the Central Committee with regard to agriculture, and those of subsequent Plenums concerning the implementation of what was called 'the economic reform'. The protracted period of stagnation was replaced by a quickening in both industry and agriculture. Between 1966 and 1970 gross industrial output increased by nearly 50 per cent and that of agriculture (calculated in annual averages) by about 20 per cent. However, this economic reform was itself put into operation by bureaucratic methods, and its effect on the country's economy, far from deepening, grew weaker and weaker and had almost vanished by 1970.

The international situation of the USSR worsened markedly in the 1960s. From the outset of the 'cultural revolution' in China Soviet-Chinese relations became extremely strained. In 1969 armed clashes began to occur on the border between the two countries, and their scale became greater in 1970. China started to make extensive military preparations in the northern parts of her territory, and pressed ahead with the creation of nuclear weapons and missiles. In place of an ally there had suddenly appeared on the eastern and southern borders of the USSR a new adversary of strategic importance. This called for a review of Soviet military plans and the taking of costly measures for strengthening defence in the East of the country. The situation in Asia became further complicated as a result of the escalation of the war between the USA and North Vietnam. The USSR steadily increased its military aid to the latter.

Awkward problems also arose for the USSR in Eastern Europe. After adopting a pro-Chinese attitude, Romania was only in a formal sense a member of the Warsaw Pact. The liberal-socialist movement in Czechoslovakia brought to power in that country a group of Communist reformers headed by A. Dubcek. Frightened by the scale of the changes being made in Czechoslovakia, the conservative leadership in the USSR, Poland and the GDR resolved to send the forces of the Warsaw Pact into that country. This occupation of a neighbouring country against the clearly-expressed will of its people and government was a gross violation of the fundamental norms of international law and socialist internationalism. The USSR's actions strained relations with the Western countries and evoked condemnation from almost all the Communist Parties of Western Europe. The defeat suffered by the Arab countries in the 'Six-Day War' complicated the position of the USSR in the Middle East. It had to incur very heavy expense in order to restore the armed forces of Egypt and Syria. During the 1960s the USSR's relations with several countries of the 'Third World' took a turn for the worse. A number of regimes in Asia and Africa that were friendly to the Soviet Union were overthrown in military coups. Relations with Cuba deteriorated. The number of active and sincere friends of the USSR throughout the world decreased markedly during the 1960s, with a simultaneous growth, in all parts, of anti-Soviet and anti-American sentiments. An acute political crisis arose in 1970 in Poland, leading to the fall of Gomulka's government. The worsening of the USSR's international position was accompanied by a considerable increase in Soviet military expenditure. It was decided to carry out a series of new, large-scale arms programmes.

So far as internal affairs were concerned, the Brezhnev leadership had to reckon with the appearance and development of the 'dissident' movement, which gained strength during the 1960s in spite of repression. For the first time in many years, a public opinion independent of the state began to form and an opposition to emerge. This opposition movement was variegated: reformist-socialist and radical-communist, religious and nationalist, liberal-democratic and so on. All these different groups were at one, however, in protesting against the rehabilitation of Stalin. Although the opposition groups in the USSR had a relatively insignificant number of active participants, they found many sympathisers among the intelligentsia and produced a significant echo abroad.

The years 1971–9 must be seen as the second period of 'the Brezhnev era'. In many respects this was the calmest decade in our country's twentieth-century history. The chief watchword of this period was:

'stability'—stability in foreign and domestic policy, stability where Party and state cadres were concerned, stability in economic development. To a large extent this watchword was fulfilled, though stability often meant stagnation, with the country's leaders refusing for the sake of a quiet life and 'stability', to implement many wise innovations or to replace executives who were obviously useless or senile.

During the 1970s the USSR's industry made notable progress, and the inhabitants began to receive more goods and services. However, the rate of growth of industrial production declined considerably, first to 5 per cent per year, and then by the end of the decade to 3.5 per cent. Neither the ninth (1971–5) nor the tenth (1976–80) five-year plan was fulfilled.

By the end of the 1970s the Soviet Union had outstripped the USA in production of coal, iron ore, cement, diesel locomotives, tractors, combines, iron and steel, mineral fertilisers, steel tubes, metal-cutting machine-tools, woollen and cotton fabrics, leather footwear, industrial timber and many other products. The USSR led the world in the peaceful use of atomic energy, in the technique of constructions for the use of water-power, in electric welding, in the technology of blast-furnaces and open-hearth furnaces, in space research, in the transmission of electric power over long distances, in the amount of medical services provided for the population and in many other fields.

Of enormous importance was the fact that it was in the 1970s that the Soviet Union drew level with the USA in all the main types of strategic weaponry. The USSR substantially enlarged its navy and created some new types of weapon which were not inferior to the best Western examples.

Nevertheless, the USSR lagged well behind the USA in productivity of labour and in gross national product. Not only the USA but also Japan and West Germany were still ahead of the USSR in such key branches of industry as electronics, instrument-making, oil-technology, the production of programme-controlled machine-tools and the production of up-to-date means of communication, and also in the quality of most machines and consumer goods.

Investment in agriculture increased markedly during the 1970s. In those ten years agriculture received nearly 230 milliard roubles in investments—more than in all the previous five-year plan periods put together. Yet the annual increase in agricultural production stuck at about 1.5 per cent, and exceeded only slightly the increase in the country's population. Consequently, the cost of production of agricultural produce increased considerably while the food supplies reaching the towns worsened to a notable extent. The population's total money income increased in the last ten years faster than the volume of production of consumer goods, including agricultural produce. This resulted, on the one hand, in inflation, which attained a rate of between 2 and 3 per cent per year, and, on the other, in an increase to not less than 250 milliard roubles in the population's unsatisfied demand (as expressed in deposits in savings-banks and other forms of monetary accumulation). The quantity of grain purchased abroad also increased greatly. Other foodstuffs as well were purchased in large quantities—e.g. meat and butter.

During the 1970s the Soviet Union escaped from that state of international isolation in which it had found itself towards the end of the 1960s. The basis of Soviet foreign policy in this period was 'détente', which was also backed by influential circles in the West. The USSR's relations gradually improved with all the major countries of Western Europe, especially France and West Germany. Relations with the USA also improved to a considerable degree. American Presidents visited the Soviet Union on three occasions and Brezhnev visited the USA. Numerous political and economic agreements were concluded with Western countries. Of particular importance was the agreement on limiting strategic weapons —SALT I. Negotiation for the signing of another such pact—SALT II— went forward successfully. The USSR's trade turnover with the developed capitalist countries increased seven times during the 1970s, and in 1980 exceeded 31 milliard roubles. The culmination of 'détente' was the agreement on security and cooperation in Europe signed in 1975 in Helsinki, in which the leaders of 36 countries of Europe and North America took part. The outcome of this agreement was the Final Act, in which a number of important principles of international relations were proclaimed.

The influence of the Soviet Union in the Third World was strengthened. The only major success achieved by the USA in the Third World was probably an improvement in relations with Egypt and the Camp David agreement. But the USA suffered defeat in Vietnam. A serious blow to all the Western countries was the substantial increase in oil prices effected by the organisation of petrol-exporting countries (OPEC). The USA's position in the Middle East was markedly weakened by the fall of the Shah's regime in Iran, and its position in Central America by the defeat of Somoza's regime in Nicaragua. Meanwhile, the Soviet Union strengthened its friendship with Vietnam and the other countries of Indo-China. In Africa the USSR acquired new allies—Ethiopia, Angola, Mozambique. Relations were strengthened with India, Libya, South Yemen, Benin and a number of other countries, big and small, in Asia, Africa and Latin America.

Whereas in the first half of the 1970s the 'dissident' movement in the USSR grew in strength, while assuming a variety of new forms, by the end of the decade we observed a definite decline in this movement. This was due to several causes. There was the mass emigration of Jews from the USSR and also the emigration or deportation from our country of most of the active members of the Soviet opposition at the end of the 1960s and the early 1970s. Repressive measures taken by the authorities also had their effect, of course, together with weariness and disappointment on the part of a section of the oppositionist intelligentsia. Nevertheless, the dissident movement continued, even though on a smaller scale, in all its chief manifestations.

Brezhnev's personal authority and influence notably increased during the 1970s. An apparatus serving this personal power gradually came into being. Brezhnev united in himself the posts of General Secretary of the Party's Central Committee, Chairman of the Presidium of the Supreme Soviet and Chairman of the Supreme War Council of the USSR. However, the administration of the country became more and more bureaucratic, and the glorifying and eulogising of Brezhnev himself grew more and more grotesque, without finding any echo among the mass of the population. Official propaganda became less and less effectual and the gap between state and society widened. In the sphere of culture the 1970s were a period of patent stagnation. All the same, if Brezhnev had departed from leadership of the USSR in 1979, he could have had grounds enough to speak of many important achievements by his administration.

Alas, we now have to speak of the third period of 'the Brezhnev era', which began at the end of 1979, and which was undoubtedly a period of renewed social and economic crisis.

None of the plans of economic development drawn up in 1979–82 was fulfilled. The rate of growth of industrial production fell once more, to between 2.5 and 3 per cent per year. The Soviet economy had exhausted the principal factors of extensive development and had not proved able to utilise effectively enough the factors of intensive development. Productivity of labour in the last year hardly increased, while at the same time a shortage of labour-power began to make itself felt. Great difficulties arose in the power and fuel industries. After 1979 the output of coal and production of iron and steel began to decline. An extremely acute situation came about in transport. With the small growth in goods-turnover in 1979–83, all the main indicators of utilisation of rolling-stock on the railways deteriorated. Particularly great difficulties were experienced in agriculture, with harvest-failure in all four of the last years of the era. According to plan, the average annual production of grain was to have amounted to not less than 230 million tons, but in fact it amounted in 1979–82 to no more than 180 million tons. The yield of all the principal crops except cotton declined. The annual average production of meat fell in the last few years and that of butter and milk in the last five years. In the majority of the country's industrial centres, various forms of rationing had to be introduced in the distribution of foodstuffs and the system of commercial trade at higher prices had to be extended.

The USSR's international position worsened again. The decision by NATO to 'arm up', the American Senate's refusal to ratify the SALT II agreement and the attempts by the Carter administration to form a

military and political alliance between the USA and China were all factors
which in 1979–80 led to a definite deterioration in relations between the
USSR and the West. When the more conservative Reagan administration
came to power in the USA, this made relations still worse. America
announced the deployment of new systems of nuclear-missile weaponry
and a substantial increase in military expenditure. To the East of the
USSR there appeared the intractable problem of Afghanistan, and to the
West the no less intractable problem of Poland. The Sino-Vietnamese
conflict, the problem of Cambodia, the Western countries' boycott of the
Moscow Olympics, the economic crisis in Romania, the accession of a
more conservative government in West Germany—all these events
complicated the conduct of Soviet foreign policy in 1979–82. In one
sphere alone did Brezhnev accomplish some 'big successes' in the last few
years, namely that of struggle against the dissidents inside the country. By
the end of 1982 this movement had practically ceased to exist as a noteworthy factor in domestic and foreign policy. However, while showing
'strength and firmness' in the fight against the dissidents, Brezhnev's
administration showed increasing feebleness in the solution of other
problems. During the last year a number of resolutions were adopted
which nobody thought of carrying out. All the symptoms of bureaucratism and corruption in the state organs became more marked.
Dissidents were fewer and fewer, but discontent among the masses
increased rapidly and the prestige of the supreme governmental
institutions decreased. Such ulcers of Soviet society as criminality and
alcoholism grew worse. Of course, if we speak not just of the last years of
Brezhnev's administration but of its entire activity over eighteen years, we
can point to considerable improvements both in the standard of living of
the Soviet people and in the international situation of the USSR. But
people usually compare their position not with how it was twenty years
earlier but with how it was five or six years earlier. This was one reason
why many citizens of our country received the news that 'the Brezhnev
era' had ended not only with apprehension but also with a certain feeling
of relief and hope.

The Changing of the Guard in the Kremlin
The end of the Brezhnev era, like that of any other era in the history of
our country, provides plenty of opportunities for forecasts and prophecies
of one kind or another. What can we expect of the new era now
beginning? What will our country be like in the year 2,000?

It is possible to say a lot about the changes that would be *desirable* for
our country in the next few years. Although viewpoints on this subject
vary widely, most observers are probably agreed that it would be highly
desirable for the Soviet Union to make a turn towards a broad and deep
democratisation of social and political life and the creation of conditions

for normal activity by the different oppositional groups and tendencies. It is a mistake to say that the population of the USSR has no possibilities of participating in the country's political life. Such possibilities exist, but they are offered exclusively to those who *agree* with the ideology and policy of the Communist Party, if only so far as its most important aspects are concerned. There is no possibility of participation in the country's political life for those who *disagree* with the policy and ideology of the Communist Party, either as a whole or in some of its principal aspects. In our country there are no facilities for political activity by an opposition or by political minorities. We usually talk of democracy for the majority—although we have no completely reliable mechanism for determining this majority. But the authorities in our country are against democracy for the minority, even though respect for the rights of the minority is essential in determining the quality of any true democracy. In the last analysis this is the most important knot that needs to be untied if health is to be restored to all sides of Soviet life. It is not very probable, though, that this will be understood in the years immediately ahead. Any prognosis has to take account of the actual state of things, the possibilities, the capacities and even the interest of the already existing hierarchy and its most influential groups, the country's traditions and the level of political consciousness and culture of the bulk of its population. It is not only the fifteen or twenty members of the Political Bureau and the Secretariat of the Party's Central Committee, and not only the 500 members and candidates for membership of that Central Committee who take a hand in the government of the Soviet Union, but also millions of people at all levels. These people possess not only power but also political influence over the tens of millions who constitute the political activists of the Soviet order. When solving any acute problem of domestic or external policy one cannot ignore the feelings, views and abilities of this entire hierarchy and this entire body of activists. Without the participation of these people it is not now possible to overcome the political and economic crisis in which Soviet society has found itself in recent years. But the overwhelming majority of persons at all levels of leadership fail to appreciate the value of democracy: they cannot, they do not know how to work under democratic conditions. These persons are therefore capable of supporting only very small steps in the direction of democracy. It may be supposed that Andropov and his circle will not be so petty in their dealings with the intelligentsia and the heterodox as their predecessors were. But it will not be problems of democratisation that will be given priority in the near future.

We may expect, however, that the new leadership will wage a resolute struggle against the corruption which in the last 15 or 20 years had pene-trated so deeply into the ruling apparatus, and constitutes one of the chief causes of discontent among the people. Covering himself with the watchword: 'stability', Brezhnev notoriously winked at many abuses of power, even in his own immediate entourage.

We may expect, further, that the new leadership will wage a struggle against the *nepotism* which in the last 15 to 20 years has also deeply penetrated the ruling apparatus and has become a serious obstacle to effective leadership of the state and society. Unfortunately, in the course of the last few years an ever-greater number of persons have been appointed to the highest posts in the Party and state apparatus, not on practical or political grounds, but because of their family connexions, their acquaintances, their devotion to certain individuals and so on. Brezhnev acted here in accordance with that rule of which Famusov spoke long ago, in Griboydev's comedy *Woe From Wit*:

> Each time one must present a post or decoration,
> Well, how can one neglect the man that's a relation!

We may expect that in the next few years there will be a weakening of that bureaucratisation of the whole system of government which has gone so far in our country. This will not mean democratisation. But it can be hoped that the near future will see the giving of a bigger role to specialists, experts and scientists in the solving of fundamental political and economic problems. The leadership that was formed in the 1970s often lacked mere competence, as well as vigour and persistence. The bureaucratic leaders were interested not so much in seeing that things were going well as in maintaining an appearance of well-being. For them, reports were more important than reality. The numberless good decisions and resolutions taken were not backed by vigorous activity to ensure their fulfilment. There were so many promises and decisions that Brezhnev's last offspring, the so-called 'Foodstuffs Programme' was received by the population of the USSR with indifference or even mockery rather than with enthusiasm. The new leadership will be able to win prestige among the people not by adopting fresh resolutions but by real measures to alleviate the position of the country and the people.

The Brezhnev leadership lacked firmness, especially in the last years of its career. The weakness of the central leadership facilitated weakness and even lack of discipline in many departments of local government. Discipline grew slack in the state apparatus, in the factories, on the building sites and on the farms. Any work that is done for the benefit of society should be done well and diligently. Otherwise, it is not possible to improve the living conditions of the people and solve urgent problems. In recent years the demand for *order* has become one of the most popular demands among persons who are concerned about the interests of society. This demand finds expression even in the distorted forms of praise for Stalin— frequently uttered by individuals who never lived under him. 'Why have you stuck Stalin's portrait on the windscreen of your car?' I asked a young driver recently. 'Under Stalin there was order', he replied. There can be no doubt that the new leadership, if it reckons to overcome the present crisis, will have to take measures to restore discipline and order in all parts of the state and economic mechanism. Their success in this campaign will depend on the methods used.

Especially difficult tasks confront the leadership in the sphere of the country's economy. Without doubt, the basic principles of centralised leadership and planning will be retained. Within this framework, however, attempts will continue to be made to find new schemes and methods of management. It can be supposed that the new leadership will refrain from carrying out any radical reforms in the sphere of economic administration but that it will encourage some important changes and experiments aimed at greater decentralisation of the management of secondary branches of production, by enlarging the role and scope of the heads of enterprises and big production units as well as those of provincial and regional administrations. The market cannot serve as the principal regulator of the functioning of the Soviet economy. Nevertheless, we may suppose that some experiment in expanding the role of the market will again be undertaken, in the spirit of the economic reform of 1965. Something that is increasingly necessary from the economic standpoint is a decision to widen the opportunities for individual and cooperative initiative in the sphere of services and small-scale production. The taking of such a decision has been held up until now only by fears of a political character, but the pressure of economic factors is becoming more and more powerful. In the last analysis it is upon intelligent decisions in this sphere that depend not only improvement in important branches of the economy immediately connected with the needs of the population, but also the mood of the population itself.

The new leadership will naturally show vigour in seeking ways, methods and incentives for decisive improvement in the condition of agriculture. One 'Foodstuffs Programme' is not enough for that purpose.

I do not think that there will be any changes in the main lines of Soviet foreign policy. We may only assume that this policy will become more flexible and that some fresh opportunities will be found for bettering relations both with the USA and other Western countries and with China. That depends on both sides. One can repeat back to Mr Reagan his own recent maxim: 'It takes two to tango'. Concessions are needed, but these concessions can only be reciprocal.

The watchword of 'stability' in cadres policy cannot be a watchword for the new leadership. Even apart from the question of nepotism, bureaucratism and corruption, it is impossible not to notice that in many of the most important branches of state and Party leadership the cadres are now too old and no longer capable of energetic work—and still less of solving any new and unusual problems. It is therefore to be hoped that in the next few years there will be a serious renewal in all the leading departments of government, and that younger, more intelligent, more highly qualified and bolder persons will be promoted to the leading posts. If this is not done, the crisis which our country is now experiencing will not only not be overcome, it will grow deeper. This renewal of cadres must be accompanied by broader and more profound discussion of many painful problems of our political and economic reality. This will not yet be democracy in the generally accepted sense of the word, but it will be the first step towards that democracy.

I am writing here, of course, only of what Soviet people expect as a result of the changes of administration in the USSR. Moreover, these are only the absolute minimum of expectations. One cannot forget how many of the expectations of Soviet people have not been met during the last 65 years or whenever a new era began in the development of Soviet society. Will the coming decades prove an exception to this not too reassuring experience? Stern reality demands that all statesmen throughout the world now show greater responsibility and greater ability to cooperate. Otherwise there will be no future for anyone on this Earth.

Translated by Brian Pearce

NOTES

1. Lenin, *Collected Works,* 4th edition, English version, Vol. 10, p. 247.
2. Ibid., Vol. 32, p. 199 and Vol. 33, p. 257.

NUCLEAR STRATEGIES AND AMERICAN FOREIGN POLICY

Paul Joseph

Amid great controversy, the Reagan administration has undertaken an ambitious programme of modernising the US strategic forces. Some of the new weapons are offensive in character. They include the land-based MX, the submarine-launched Trident II, cruise missiles, and two new bombers—the B-1 and the 'Stealth'—to carry them. In addition, new ground-launched cruise missiles are to be stationed in Europe along with a medium-range land-based missile, the Pershing II. These are all counter-force weapons. They threaten Soviet retaliatory forces. The new systems enhance the possibility of striking first and raise the possibility—at least in theory—of limiting the damage that the Soviet Union will be able to inflict on the US in response.[1]

The Reagan administration is also attempting to improve its defence capacity. Civil defence programmes are receiving more money. T.K. Jones, an Assistant Secretary of Defense, argues that the US can rebound from a full-scale nuclear attack within two to four years. The MX may be deployed with a ballistic missile defensive system that some claim can be expanded into a full scale ABM. After a March speech promising that new exotic technologies have become feasible, Reagan established an office that will accelerate development of space-based lasers and particle beam weapons designed to intercept Soviet missiles before they can strike the US. Administration officials believe that this commitment to an effective defence permits political leaders to act more forcefully. A commitment to improving defence capacity demonstrates a resolve that can be translated into negotiating advantages.

Members of the Reagan administration have also been quite forthcoming in their discussion of fighting and winning both limited and protracted nuclear wars.[2] A commitment to developing warfighting capabilities can be seen in the renewed concern of the Pentagon with preparing command, control and communication facilities (C^3) against the effects of blast, radiation, and electromagnetic pulse. Actually to fight a nuclear war, a political leader must be able to contact the military forces at his command. Assessment of damage, determining the opponent's intentions, deciding on a proper response, communicating that decision reliably, and maintaining control over military forces so that the actual response matches the original decision are all notoriously difficult to achieve in war. The unique conditions of nuclear war make reliable C^3 even more difficult to achieve.[3] Yet, the Reagan administration has plunged ahead with efforts to protect communication lines, computers, and command stations from interruption. It has been called the most important priority of the recently announced strategic modernisation package.

The Reagan administration has begun arms control talks with Moscow, but argues that progress is dependent on modified Soviet behaviour in other areas of foreign policy such as Poland, Afghanistan and Central America. The strategists associated with the Reagan administration believe that the deployment of weapon systems will lead to greater political influence over Moscow. For them, arms negotiations are not a process of mutual concession with the aim of preserving rough parity. Nor is arms control *per se* held to be in the national security interest of the US. Negotiations are, instead, a strategy to mould Soviet behaviour. In the meantime, the specific proposals advanced by the President under START are geared to achieving superiority or forcing Soviet rejection.[4]

In pursuit of these goals, the Reagan administration is willing to spend vast sums of money. The total obligational authority of the Pentagon for 1984 is more than two hundred and fifty billion dollars. Over the next five years defence spending will total 1.8 trillion dollars. Some administration members argue in private that it will be necessary to spend an additional 750 billion dollars over the same time period. Military spending will rise from 24 to 37 per cent of the defence budget.

The Reagan administration's wholesale adoption of a nuclear warfighting posture has developed in parallel with foreign policy commitments predicated on unremitting hostility towards the Soviet Union. Before examining the connection between Reagan's nuclear strategy and his foreign policy, let me outline in more detail the main features of the debate over the use of nuclear weapons.

Deterrence versus Warfighting Postures

Strategic doctrines are usually divided into two groups. The first, called deterrence, recognises that nuclear war would inevitably end in holocaust. To talk of winners and losers in this context is nonsense. The only purpose of nuclear weapons is to deter, or prevent, war between the US and the Soviet Union from breaking out. Bernard Brodie, an early deterrence theorist, recognised that the bomb changed the very way in which we think about war. He argued that 'thus far the chief purpose of our military establishment has been to win wars. From now on its chief purpose must be to prevent them. It can have almost no other useful purpose'.[5] Brodie anticipated the fact that nuclear weapons would make war irrational for either side.

The second group, advocates of warfighting doctrines (or what is sometimes called 'extended deterrence'), admits that the level of destruction may be great in a conflict involving nuclear weapons. But, as in all other wars, there will still be winners and losers. There are two purposes for weapons. The first is to win the war between the US and the Soviet Union. The second is to threaten war so that the US can exert greater influence on other issues of foreign policy. Colin Gray, a supporter of warfighting and a consultant to the Reagan administration, argues that if 'American nuclear power is to support US foreign policy objectives, the United States must possess the ability to wage nuclear war rationally.'[6] It is this view that now dominates governing circles in the US.

Those associated with the deterrence position include former Secretary of Defense Robert McNamara, former head of the Arms Control and Disarmament Agency Paul Warnke, former CIA director William Colby, and former National Security Advisor McGeorge Bundy. Prominent members of the warfighting camp include Assistant Secretary of Defense Richard Perle, Assistant Secretary of State Richard Burt, former National Security Council staffer Richard Pipes and Reagan administration advisors Colin Gray, Scott Thompson, and William Van Cleave.

Let us look a little more closely at the arguments of each group.

The first contrast between the deterrence and warfighting schools concerns the posture that strategists and decision makers should adopt towards nuclear weapons. Those in the deterrence camp believe that the development of nuclear weapons and their use in Hiroshima and Nagasaki was a qualitative break in the history of war. They recognised that nuclear weapons carry enormous destructive power and that the impact of even a few bombs would be catastrophic. As military instruments, nuclear bombs are unique.

The advocates of the warfighting position strongly disagree. Nuclear weapons are more destructive than other weapons, but they are not qualitatively different. Our thinking about nuclear wars, they argue, should not be different from our thinking about previous wars. For example, any past introduction of a new weapon has been in combination with existing weapons. There is no reason to think that nuclear weapons are any different in this respect from the machine gun, the spear, the rifle, or a tank.[7] The bomb can be used alongside the existing arsenal. There is no great divide between nuclear and conventional weapons.

The second contrast concerns the connection between nuclear weapons and 'unacceptable damage'. The deterrence position recognises that it is comparatively easy for one side to inflict a level of damage that the other side considers unacceptable. The warfighters disagree. Critical to the exchange is the precise definition of what constitutes 'acceptable' and 'unacceptable' damage. Most readers of the *Socialist Register* would no doubt consider the dropping of just one bomb on one city 'unacceptable' and would, as a result, be deterred from starting a war with this as a consequence. On the other hand, American militarists have argued that the Soviet Union would accept the loss of some thirty million people since that was the approximate level of damage that they suffered in World War II.[8] American policy makers have, for the most part, followed former Secretary of Defense Robert McNamara's definition of unacceptable damage as twenty-five per cent of the civilian population and seventy five per cent of the industrial capacity. This official conception of 'unacceptable' can be achieved by delivering as few as 400 bombs. Those in the deterrence camp feared nuclear war because they believed that any exchange of hostilities would inevitably escalate to at least this level of destruction. For them, nuclear weapons obviated the Clausewitz dictum that war was the extension of politics by other means. Nuclear war, they argued, could only be the continuation of madness.

Those in the warfighting position are not so sure. They believe that nuclear wars can be kept limited in the sense that they involve levels of destruction that do not threaten the existence of the other state. Nuclear wars can also be protracted. They can take days, weeks, even months. They reject the belief of the deterrence school that wars involving nuclear weapons will inevitably escalate to an all-out exchange leading to the destruction of both sides. Clausewitz has not been transcended. The warfighters believe that it is still possible to think of war as the extension of politics.

A third contrast concerns the targeting of nuclear weapons. Under deterrence, the main purpose of nuclear forces is to prevent war by threatening unacceptable damage to the other side. To do this most effectively, American bombs should be aimed at Soviet cities and the industrial base. This is called counter-city targeting. The supporters of warfighting doctrines favour counterforce targeting or aiming at the military forces and command centres of the other side. Counterforce raises the possibility of striking the other side so that they will not be able to retaliate. The logical extension of counterforce is a first-strike capability or the ability to strike at the other side's retaliatory forces so that they are either unable to reply, or can reply only at a level that the attacking country considers 'acceptable'.

Since many targets, especially missile silos and command bunkers, are 'hardened' with steel and concrete, destroying them requires fantastic accuracies—as close as a tenth-of-a-mile. (Many of the new weapon systems are achieving these levels of accuracy—at least in testing carried out under optimum conditions.)

A fourth comparison concerns the possibility of erecting an effective defence against nuclear attack. The deterrence position has always been sceptical and has respected the weight of the scientific community which has argued that the difficulties associated with intercepting warheads travelling at close to eighteen thousand miles an hour are virtually impossible to overcome. Some in the warfighting camp, on the other hand, believe in the possibility of erecting a 'layered' defence. This includes the so-called exotic, space-based systems such as lasers and particle-beam weapons designed to intercept Soviet missiles shortly after they leave their silos; exo-atmospheric systems that are supposed to intercept warheads before they re-enter the atmosphere; endo-atmosphere defences that will intercept warheads before they explode on the earth's surface; and, finally, a programme of civil defence that properly conceived and carried out can save the lives of millions. The technical evidence stands against them. Yet advocates of warfighting argue that their support for counterforce targeting and erecting a defence against nuclear attack is morally superior to deterrence which would target civilian populations and, by denying the possibilities of defence, leave oneself open to attack.

Those in the deterrence camp recognise that the Soviet Union has had, at least since the late-sixties, the capacity to inflict unacceptable damage against the US. No matter what the US does, no matter how effective the first blow, the Soviet Union will be able to retaliate. The ability of the US and the Soviet Union to inflict unacceptable damage on the other is called mutually assured destruction or MAD. MAD is a fact of life in a world afflicted with nuclear weapons.

But those supporting the warfighting posture are concerned with another question: what if deterrence fails. Their answer is that there will be war and the US must be prepared to fight it. After the hostilities end, one side will be in a better position than the other to organise whatever remains. The victor will be in a position to issue orders to the loser. To maximise the possibility of winning, the US should demonstrate its superiority at every possible step in a 'ladder of escalation'. Political and military leaders should enjoy the flexibility of selecting from a 'menu of options', both nuclear and conventional. In particular the US should never, in their view, be in a position where it would be deterred from using nuclear weapons first.

Another contrast concerns Soviet intentions. The deterrence camp thinks that Moscow accepts the inevitability of holocaust should a war start. Basing its analysis on statements from government officials and the more recent pronouncements of military officers, those in the first school argue that Moscow accepts the reality of MAD, does not really have a serious civil defence programme, and wants to reduce the risk of nuclear war. The warfighting camp argues that Soviet 'strategic culture' does not reject the idea of fighting and winning a nuclear war. Basing their analysis on military manuals they argue that Moscow plans for nuclear war in much the same terms as they have previous wars. The implication is that the US fails to do likewise at its own peril.

The final issue dividing the two positions is the stance taken towards arms control efforts. The logical result of deterrence is support for talks designed to regulate the competition between the two superpowers.

Supporters of deterrence hope to use arms treaties to isolate nuclear weapons from the inevitable tension between Washington and Moscow. Negotiations are seen in the direct national security interests of the US.

Warfighting advocates may reject arms negotiations entirely or, more commonly, see these talks within the context of all relations with the Soviet Union. A clever negotiating stance may enhance superiority, or elicit compliant behaviour from Moscow on other crucial issues. The prospect of arms control should be used as leverage. If Moscow wants arms control, it should be willing to pay for it. The implication is that nuclear weapons can be used in pursuit of other defence interests and foreign policy goals.

The Instability of Deterrence

Clearly the actual history of US strategic policy is much more complicated than a simple comparison between deterrence and warfighting would imply. As outlined above, deterrence and warfighting doctrines should be seen as ideal types, with the actual behaviour of a particular policy maker or even an administration falling somewhere between the two poles.

A further complication is that governments present different policies to different audiences. It is necessary to make a distinction among *declaratory policy,* that which is announced publicly; *internal policy,* that which is actually believed by government officials; and *operational policy,* that which the actual force structure is capable of carrying out. In general, declaratory policy tends to focus on deterrence. The internal, or actual policy, is more a warfighting doctrine. (In fact, actual policy has been more a warfighting position than one of deterrence since the mid-fifties.)[9] The operational forces tend, for a variety of technical and bureaucratic reasons, to lag behind internal policy.

Given all this, it is still important to realise that as a doctrine, deterrence is, by itself, unstable. Pressures generated within the ideology and structure of deterrence have produced significant dangers even without considering the perils offered by the warfighting position. For example, a 'pure' or minimal deterrence position requires a limited arsenal; certainly no more than several hundred bombs. Yet the United States has more than ten thousand strategic bombs and another twenty thousand tactical warheads. One reason for this instability is the paradox built within the concept of deterrence itself. Under deterrence, nuclear weapons are not to be used because to do so will produce unacceptable levels of destruction on both sides. The arms race is a rough standoff. Stability comes from a balance of terror. Yet the stability implied in deterrence is based on threatened destruction. To make this threat credible, decision makers approve the construction of powerful offensive weapons systems, and engage in various acts of sabre-rattling.[10] Political leaders who do not seriously believe in the possibility of actually fighting a nuclear war will nonetheless procure better weapons and make threats to use them because the doctrine of deterrence requires them to do so. The weapons and threats acquire a history. Organisations establish a vested interest in maintaining 'their' weapons. Or they lobby for new ones. The threats become institutionalised. The result is an environment of brinkmanship within which supporters of warfighting doctrines can operate to their own advantage.

There are other important elements of instability within the deterrence position. The advocates of deterrence find nuclear weapons politically useful, even if they are not to be used. In actual battle, it may be recognised that the level of destruction obviates Clausewitz's dictum regarding war as the extension of politics. But in the *preparation for battle*, nuclear forces certainly remain political. For example, nuclear weapons not only preserve the balance between Moscow and Washington, but are instrumental in preserving a bipolar world. The respective nuclear umbrellas have a significant impact on the structure and politics of NATO and the Warsaw Pact. Private messages can be exchanged with the Soviet Union through the medium of nuclear forces. All American presidents have threatened to use nuclear weapons, in part to maintain a commitment to Europe, in part to lower the chances of a Soviet response to US conventional intervention in regional conflicts. Strategic war between the US and USSR may be rejected. Yet the structure of forces required to sustain the threatened use of nuclear weapons go far beyond the requirements of minimal deterrence. Domestically, a president can support certain types of weapons to protect himself from his political opponents. The specific configuration of nuclear weapons is a valuable way of managing Pentagon politics. The secrecy and command procedures accompanying nuclear weapons sustain the authority of a president within the governmental structure. And his virtual control over public pronouncements regarding strategic policy make it possible to influence and even manipulate the electorate. Nuclear forces, in other words, are 'politically useful'. It is hard for a president, for both international and domestic reasons, to give them up, even if he doesn't expect to use them in a war. Additional breaks with the pure deterrent posture are the result.

Deterrence has been further undermined by technical advances in weapon systems. The accuracy of ballistic missiles has improved—at least in tests—and now sustain counterforce arguments regarding the possibility of limited strikes against the other side's land-based missiles. Computers and surveillance techniques have also improved to the point where some supporters of the warfighting position are able to argue that it will be possible to detect and track Soviet submarines. Technical advances are also occurring in defensive systems. Accurate land-based and cruise missiles, in combination with anti-submarine warfare and an effective defence, raise the prospect of achieving a disarming first-strike. In reality, a first-strike remains impossible. But changes in technology are enabling advocates of warfighting to argue that a first-strike and more limited counterforce scenarios may be possible to execute in the near future. In the meantime, no president, including those believing in deterrence, has been able to block these technical developments.

Another factor that drives the arms race forward and makes deterrence unstable is the pattern of inter-service rivalries that exist within the US military. For example, an almost unchallengeable component of American strategic thinking is that each leg of a triad that includes bombers, submarines, and land-based missiles must be capable of independently delivering unacceptable damage.[11] The result, at a minimum, is a tripling of the four hundred equivalent megaton bombs that are necessary to deliver the prevailing definition of unacceptable damage. In addition, presidents are often forced to compromise and bargain with various military interests. Even a president who enjoyed such impeccable anti-communist credentials as Richard Nixon found a price tag attached to his desire to sign a SALT agreement that had the approval of the Joint Chiefs of Staff. There was a trade-off. In exchange for Congressional testimony from the Joint Chiefs that SALT I would not undermine US national security, Nixon approved construction of a new submarine—the Trident.[12] The Trident boat is larger and has longer range. But most importantly, it will carry a new missile, the Trident D-5 that is capable of counterforce levels of accuracy. In effect, a political bargain that was made in the early seventies to stabilise deterrence created the conditions that may undermine deterrence in the late 1980s. There are other examples of this trade-off dynamic. When Carter cancelled the B-1 bomber—temporarily as it turned out— the Air Force was given permission to develop cruise missiles. The MX was in part a price for military support for SALT II. This pattern of trade-offs has less to do with relations between the Soviet Union and the United States than with politics inside the Pentagon. Presidents have been loath to tamper with the Pentagon for their only other choice would be the deliberate mobilisation of public opinion against the arms race. Instead they have chosen a series of accommodations. These have preserved political niches that have been exploited by opponents of deterrence.

The implication of these factors—the paradox embedded in deterrence, presidential interests, improvements in technology, and trade-offs with the Pentagon—is that, left to their own devices, the deterrence camp will be defeated by the warfighting camp. Only popular movements can rescue the minimal deterrence position yet also create movement towards genuine disarmament.

Nuclear Weapons and Foreign Policy

Let us now return to the issue of foreign policy and its connection to the development of nuclear weapons. The most important reason driving up the number of nuclear weapons is that the bombs have been harnessed to Washington's foreign policy goals *even by those who did not expect to use them in actual combat.* Those former American government officials who are currently quite visible in their opposition to Reagan's strategic policy, approved, *while in office,* of quantitative and qualitative improvements in the nuclear arsenal. In effect, they recognised that a nuclear war with the Soviet Union would be terrible. But they maintained that if the US could stay ahead in numbers of warheads, accuracy and other measures those advantages could be translated into political leverage on other issues. For example, it was felt that the USSR would be much less likely to aid their third world allies if the US held nuclear superiority. If the US intervened in the Middle East, Moscow would be less likely to respond. If Washington attempted to destabilise a revolutionary government, the Soviet Union would be reluctant to develop a counter response, all for fear of taking the first step in a scenario in which the US held the winning hand.[13] Thus nuclear weapons proved useful for American international interests.

By and large, this thinking has been followed by both the deterrence and warfighting supporters. The difference is that the former thought it was important to stop short of war, and the latter took more seriously the task of preparing for a war that would use nuclear weapons. In addition, to further the political influence of nuclear weapons, *every* post-war US administration has ruled out a declaration of no first use. Washington has deliberately preserved uncertainty concerning the policy of the US towards the initiation of nuclear war. Closely coupled to the refusal to rule out no first use is the practice of American presidents of threatening to use these weapons in crisis situations. Dan Ellsberg has listed twelve cases where the US had used nuclear weapons, not in the literal sense, but as a deliberate threat on behalf of American interests.[14]

On the other hand, every president has *not* made a concerted effort to improve the operational forces—the actual warheads, delivery systems, and communications—in a way that enhanced their capacity to fight a nuclear war with the Soviet Union. In other words, while the actual policy regarding nuclear weapons has consistently been one of warfighting, the effort to bring the operational forces more in line with actual policy has been more episodic. In fact, such an effort has only happened in four distinct periods: between 1948 and 1950 while Truman was President; in 1961 and 1962, the first two years of the Kennedy administration; the last two years of the Nixon administration; and, finally, from the last year of the Carter presidency to the present. (Note that in the last case the dividing line is not between Carter and Reagan. Reagan has merely continued—albeit with a substantial boost—the commitment to prepare to fight a nuclear war that was initiated by Carter.)[15]

From the point of view of establishing a link between nuclear weapons and foreign policy, it is useful to remember that in each of these four periods major debates took place in the US foreign policy establishment. The most important was specifying the main international threat to American capitalism. Was it more important to preserve the economic and political structures of Western Europe and Japan or prevent the expansion of Soviet influence and power? A second disagreement concerned the origins of revolutions in the third world. Were they the product of local conditions or the inspiration of the Soviet Union? A third disagreement revolved around the methods of responding to those revolutions. Should the US use a combination of modest reforms coupled with comparatively small counterinsurgency operations, or a large, more conventional, military response?

These intra-elite conflicts are all linked to different perspectives regarding the conflict between East and West. On one side is the more pragmatic view. Its main assertion is that the Soviet Union is a great power and, as such, enjoys certain entitlements. Ideology does not drive the Soviet Union forward. In fact, the proper diplomacy can make Moscow behave as a junior partner in the task of world management. The other half of this disagreement is based on the premise that the Soviet Union is inherently expansionist, that it seeks world domination and that the stakes between East and West are global.[16] The Soviet Union is the devil and the West represents a higher moral code. Good and evil must inevitably collide. The Soviet Union is an illegitimate state. Scratch the surface and you will find festering underneath the roots of internal revolt. Ethnic groups are against the Russians. Eastern Europe is on the verge of rebellion. All of the religious minorities want to rise up. And the proper policy can act as a catalyst in undermining the very brittle forms of social control exercised by the Kremlin. The Soviet Union, in short, is vulnerable.

It is at this point that the nuclear issue returns. One motivation on the part of Reagan is to force Moscow to compete in an arms race that it cannot afford. The US economy is larger. If the Soviet Union is forced to match US military spending, the level of resources that Moscow will have available for investment in agriculture, consumer goods, and industry will be severely reduced. Reagan has been understood to support a technology embargo on the grounds that it will hasten the process of internal crumbling. The connection between this ideological view of the Soviet Union and nuclear warfighting postures can be seen as well in the emergence of so-called decapitation strategies. In this scenario a few well-placed bombs would destroy the KGB, the Kremlin, and other political command posts. In this view, power in the Soviet Union is over-centralised. With the political head lopped off, the commanding officers of the local missile silos and submarines will not respond. The military forces would be indecisive and the US will be able to dictate terms. The Pershing II missile, due to be deployed in Germany, is crucial for this strategy since it has a flight time of only eight minutes to Moscow.

The influence of this distorted view of the Soviet Union in the Reagan administration has enormous significance. The implication is that the issue raised by the Bolshevik revolution in 1917 has yet to be resolved in American ruling circles. Does the US want 'merely' to contain socialism, or should the US attempt actually to roll back revolutions that have established communist or socialist parties in power?

Containment or Rollback

Many representatives of the Reagan administration have called for a return to Truman's policy of containment.[17] The most influential presentation of containment during that period was offered by George Kennan who argued in his 'Mr X' telegram:

> The main element of any United States policy towards the Soviet Union must be that of a long term patient but firm and vigilant containment of Russian expansive tendencies. Soviet pressure against the free institutions of the western world is something that can be contained by the adroit and vigilant application of counter force at a series of constantly shifting geographical and political points, corresponding to the shifts and manoeuvres of Soviet policy, but which cannot be charmed or talked out of existence.[18]

For Kennan the measures necessary to prevent Soviet expansion included military force, or at least the threat of military force. But the main counter-pressures were economic and political. Kennan, for example, saw the West's economic strength as its best weapon. He pointed out that of the five key industrial regions in the world—the United States, the United Kingdom, the Rhine valley, the Soviet Union and Japan—only one was a threat. Kennan also advocated the exploitation of actual and potential splits between Soviet leadership and the international communist movement. A non-communist government was of course preferable, but a communist government independent of Moscow presented possibilities that were worth exploring.[19] Yugoslavia offered the best opportunities in this regard.

Containment is usually thought to be the policy of enforcing the existing dividing line between East and West. Yet, some policy-makers defined containment more as a policy of rollback or liberation. The overthrow of communist governments would not be accomplished directly, that is by military action. Instead, internal instability in the East was to be promoted through economic and political pressures and by the *threat* of military attack. Containment was redefined as a more moderate version of rollback which included economic warfare, convert operations against Eastern Europe, and political isolation. For both Truman and Reagan this conception of containment was accompanied by the development of war-fighting doctrines.

The reflection of containment-as-rollback in the Truman administration can be clearly detected in National Security Council-68, a lengthy planning document approved by the President in April 1950. NSC-68 called for a significant commitment to rearming the US. As set out by its authors, containment was defined as 'all means short of war to block further expansion of Soviet power' (so far consistent with normal usage), but also as 'a retraction of the Kremlin's control and influence' and 'fostering the seeds of destruction within the Soviet system' (which is more a roll-back position).[20]

It is worth pausing for a moment to examine the image of Soviet society embedded within NSC-68 and the parallels that exist between that document and the views of the Reagan administration. NSC-68 makes an important distinction between the Soviet government and the Soviet people. The problem is not with the Soviet Union as a whole, only with the Kremlin which is 'inescapably militant' because it is 'possessed by a world-wide revolutionary movement, because it inherits the traditional Russian drive for imperialism and because it is a totalitarian dictatorship'. The fundamental design of the Kremlin is to gain the 'complete subversion or forcible destruction of the machinery of government and structure of societies of the non-Soviet world'. The conflict between the United States and the Soviet Union is total; no compromise or 'peaceful coexistence' is possible. The stakes are civilisation itself. In this battle, the Soviet Union enjoys two organisational sources of strength: the Communist Party and the secret police. Each is capable of imposing 'ideological uniformity' at home and 'propaganda, subversion, and espionage' abroad. The Soviet Union's ideological 'pretensions', or promises of a society with equal justice and a fairer distribution of resources, are another source of strength. So is an 'utterly amoral and opportunistic conduct of foreign policy' that gives the Kremlin great tactical flexibility. By contrast, the goals of the US are completely benign. According to the authors of NSC-68 they are '. . . to form a more perfect union, establish Justice, insure domestic tranquility, provide for the common defence, promote the general Welfare, and secure the Blessings of Liberty to ourselves and our Posterity'.

The weaknesses of the Soviet Union are also important. The greatest vulnerability of the Kremlin is the nature of its basic relations with the Soviet people. These are 'characterised by universal suspicion, fear and denunciation'. The Kremlin is also vulnerable with regard to its relations with its satellites and their peoples. Nationalism (on the side of the Eastern European nations) remains the most potent emotional-political force. Here Soviet 'ideas and practices run counter to the best and potentially strongest instincts of men, and deny their most fundamental aspirations'. The authors of NSC-68 speculate on the possibilities of making the Soviet people allies of the West (if successful 'we will obviously have made our task easier and victory more certain'). The final weakness of the Soviet system is the necessity continually to expand. Efforts to prevent or contain this expansion, either through meetings with the 'superior force' or a 'superior counterpressure' will lead to stagnation. In short, willingness on the part of the United States to counter Soviet expansion will create a situation in which 'the seeds of decay within the Soviet system would begin to flourish and fructify'. In this view containment becomes a catalyst to the 'rot' spreading within the Soviet system itself.

There is a link between this conception of containment-as-rollback and plans to fight a nuclear war. The war plans of the Truman administration included DROPSHOT which was based less on deterrence than on delivering an initial disabling blow. Another plan, code named BROILER, reflected on the possibility of liberating Eastern Europe and Russia 'immediately following the initial bomb campaign'.[21] The drafters of the plan urged that 'preparations should be made early. . . to enable the Allies to take quick action in case of an early Soviet collapse'. The bomb was the key factor in the hope of inducing this early surrender. Air Force plan TROJAN provided for a total of 300 atomic bombs in an initial attack on Russia and expected the political and economic system to collapse as a result.[22]

The expectation that the threatened use of the bomb could catalyse internal weaknesses in the Eastern bloc, especially to the point of collapse, was hopelessly optimistic. Yet the identical view can be found some thirty-odd years later among many members of the Reagan administration. As in the 1948–50 period, policy makers continue to hold open the possibility that some combination of economic pressure, political isolation and military threat involving atomic weapons will hasten internal crumbling.

As in NSC-68, members of the Reagan administration believed that Russian history displays an inherent militarism and drive for expansion. For example, Richard Perle, the current Assistant Secretary of Defence for International Security Policy, thinks that the Soviet Union is much like Hitler's Germany—both driven toward world control unless the West responds. Perle believes that nuclear warfighting plans are necessary to counter the threat. He is not as worried about nuclear escalation as he is about appeasement.

> I've always worried less about what would happen in an actual nuclear exchange than about the effect that the nuclear balance has on our willingness to take risks in local situations. It is not that I am worried about the Soviets' attacking the United States with nuclear weapons confident that they will win that nuclear war. It is that I worry about an American President's feelings he cannot afford to take action in a crisis because Soviet nuclear forces are such that, if escalation took place, they are better poised than we are to move up the escalation ladder.[23]

At the same time, the Reagan administration believes that Russia is weak because it is over-centralised and its policy is brittle. As argued above, these features, for some members of the Reagan administration, leave the Soviet Union open to a decapitation strike (an attack on the Moscow political command posts). Destruction of the 'brain' in combination with the Soviet tendency to refuse to delegate authority, will, in this thinking, prevent the land-based retaliatory missile force from responding—at least before the European-based cruise missiles and US-based ICBMs hit their silos. The new five-year defence plan explicitly bases nuclear war strategy on decapitation. American forces are to 'render ineffective the total Soviet (and Soviet-allied) military and political power structure'.[24] The five-year plan also calls for 'investment on weapon systems that render the accumulated Soviet equipment stocks obsolescent'. 'Costs on the Soviets' are to be imposed, 'by raising uncertainty regarding their ability to accomplish some of their higher-priority missions'.[25] The expectation is that the effort of the Soviet Union to keep up with the US in the arms race will be so exacting that their civilian economy will collapse.

On this view the US must prepare itself to gain victory over the Soviet Union. Eugene Rostow believes that we are living in 'a pre-war and not a post-war world'.[26] Before his appointment to the staff of the National Security Council, Harvard historian Richard Pipes had criticised the nuclear war plans of previous administrations because 'deeply embedded in all our plans is the notion of punishing the aggressor rather than defeating him'. Pipes now makes explicit the connection between the arms buildup and the goal of transforming Soviet society. 'Soviet leaders would have to choose,' Pipes has said, 'between peacefully changing their communist system. . . or going to war'.[27]

The plans of the Reagan administration for conducting war with the East include special operations, or guerrilla warfare, sabotage, and psychological warfare. The five-year Pentagon plan calls for 'revitalising and enhancing special operation forces to project United States power where the use of conventional forces would be premature, inappropriate, or infeasible'.[28] As with NSC-68, the goals are total. A senior White House official has stated that Reagan has 'approved an 8-page national security document that "undertakes a campaign aimed at internal reform in the Soviet Union and shrinkage of the Soviet empire" '.[29]

The strategic doctrines and operational programme of the Reagan administration essentially return us to Truman, NSC-68 and the other war plans of the 1948–50 period. But what of the Kennedy and Nixon administrations, the other two periods in which a concerted effort was made to develop an operational warfighting capacity using nuclear weapons? The continuity among all four periods is empire. In each case, Washington decision makers found it necessary to develop and implement new programmes taken in defence of American interests. Passage of these programmes involved a major effort and a review of the traditional issues that divided the foreign policy elite. For Washington decision makers these changes constituted a 'project', a redefinition of the role of the US as the guarantor of the world order. Accompanying the project was an ambitious modernisation programme.

Between 1948 and 1950, Truman took the steps that transformed the US into the active leader in creating and protecting an international system. By 1950, the US had given economic and military assistance to Europe, and made a substantial military effort in Korea. From a post-war low the defence budget had more than tripled. An atomic arsenal had been created that could be used in a war with the Soviet Union. Domestic opposition to an active international role had been swept aside.

By 1960 new tensions appeared in the system, tensions that seemed to require different military capabilities. Kennedy was concerned with the spread of revolutionary movements in underdeveloped countries, particularly in the case of Cuba. Using methods ranging from assassination to full-scale invasion, Kennedy tried to overthrow the Castro government. American foreign policy and defence interests seemed threatened in Indochina as well. During the first two years of his administration, Kennedy defined revolutionary movements and accompanying regional instability as grave threats to the US, and yet found Washington's capacity to respond quite inadequate. Something had to be done. The answer was 'flexible response' or the development of capabilities against national liberation movements as well as preparing the nuclear force structure for use in a variety of situations short of all-out war. By 1962 Kennedy had created a defence posture that permitted a more active programme of intervention and at least the illusion of being able to fight a limited war.[30] Because of the more adequate defence preparations, Moscow, it was thought, would be deterred from responding to American actions in underdeveloped countries.

By the early-seventies the world order that the US had organised was beginning to unravel. Control could no longer be exercised through the comparatively simple management of a system. Bretton Woods was defunct. International financial adjustments, such as the convertibility of the dollar, were necessary. Inter-capitalist competition increased. After making a major commitment in Southeast Asia, the US was all but defeated. The Nixon Doctrine, pledging support to allies capable of helping themselves, but avoiding a direct US commitment, was one kind of evidence demonstrating the limits of American military power in the third world. Another was the use of the 'China card', a more determined effort to take advantage of tensions existing inside the Communist bloc. Domestically, the political situation, especially in the Watergate atmosphere, weighed against a sustained remilitarism. In this context, Nixon and Kissinger felt it was important to demonstrate American power. Increased strength in nuclear weapons was seen as providing additional leverage for American policy makers.[31]

By 1980 the process of deterioration had proceeded still further. Summit meetings among the leading capitalist nations had become no more than rhetorical exercises. The structure of US alliances was more volatile and opportunist. Iran demonstrated the impotence of the US to control political developments in a region of central interest. While the contours of the empire could still be seen, the substance of the system was more precarious. Nuclear warfighting scenarios and operational improvements appeared again.

In each of the four periods, the executive branch reoriented the global position of the US, often against domestic as well as international opposition. Under Truman, the main structures of the post-war order were put into place. Under Kennedy, a new focus on revolutionary movements in the third world was adopted. Under Nixon, the US began the difficult adjustment to the limits that had been placed on American power. Under Reagan, the US is continuing to act as an imperial power, but after the structures set up for maintaining orderly economic growth and political control have been severely weakened—in some cases to the point of collapse. Nuclear warfighting strategies were instrumental in this process. By contrast, the years 1950–60, 1963–8 and 1976–8 did not call for such major adjustments in the world role for the US. And the strategic doctrines of this period have been closer to deterrence. Over the post-war years Washington retained its commitment to containment. Yet, its ability to secure this policy through economic, political and conventional military means has gradually diminished. A tendency to redefine containment as rollback, focused either on the Soviet Union and Eastern Europe or against successful revolutions in the third world, has proved remarkably persistent. There has also been an increased reliance on nuclear weapons and atomic diplomacy as substitutes for control through economic and political organisations. The post-war order is over. The US must adjust. Failure to do so will only lead to desperation. And the danger is that, in this desperation, nuclear weapons will be used.

NOTES

1. See Robert Aldridge, *First-Strike* (Boston, South End Press, 1983).
2. See especially Richard Halloran, 'Pentagon Draws Up First Strategy for Fighting a Long Nuclear War', *New York Times,* May 30, 1982, pp. 1, 12.
3. See William Broad, 'Nuclear Pulse: Awakening to the Chaos Factor', *Science,* Vol. 212, May 29, 1981; pp. 1009–1012.
4. Christopher Paine, 'A False START', *The Bulletin of Atomic Scientists,* August/ September 1982.
5. Bernard Brodie, *The Absolute Weapon,* 1946.
6. 'Victory is Possible', *Foreign Policy,* Summer, 1980.

7. Colin Gray, 'Across the Nuclear Divide', *International Security*, Summer 1977.
8. Richard Pipes, 'Why the Soviet Union Thinks it Could Fight and Win a Nuclear War', *Commentary*, March 1977.
9. See David Alan Rosenberg, 'A Smoking Radiating Ruin at the End of Two Hours": Documents on American Plans for a Nuclear War with the Soviet Union', *International Security*, Winter 1981/82, p. 13.
10. On this point see Anders Boserup, 'Deterrence and Defence', *Bulletin of Atomic Scientists*, December 1981.
11. See Fred Kaplan, *Wizards of Armageddon*, (New York, Simon and Schuster, 1983).
12. John Newhouse, *Cold Dawn: The Story of SALT*, (New York, Holt, Rinehart and Winston, 1973).
13. For an assessment of the successes and failures of this strategy see Barry Blechman, *Force Without War*, (Washington, Brookings, 1979).
14. 'Call to Mutiny', E.P. Thompson and Dan Smith, eds., *Protest and Survive*, (New York, Monthly Review Press, 1981).
15. On the deterioration of Carter's commitment to a minimal deterrence position see Thomas Powers, 'Thinking About World War III', *Atlantic*, November 1982.
16. For an analysis of the impact of this dispute on the early history of the cold war see Daniel Yergin, *Shattered Peace*, (Boston, Houghton Mifflin Company, 1977).
17. For an example see the testimony of Eugene Rostow quoted in *Aviation Week and Space Technology*, June 29, 1981, p. 24; or Norman Podhoretz' sympathetic commentary in *The Present Danger*, (New York, Simon and Schuster, 1980).
18. 'The Sources of Soviet Conduct', *Foreign Affairs*, July 1947, pp. 576-86.
19. See NSC-20/1 ('US Objectives With Respect to Russia'), August 18, 1948 included in Thomas Etzold and John Lewis Gaddis, *Containment Documents on American Policy and Strategy: 1945-1950*, (New York, Columbia University Press, 1978). NSC-20/1 was drafted by Kennan.
20. NSC-68 ('United States Objectives and Programs for National Security'), April 14, 1959, in Etzold and Gaddis, op. cit.
21. See Gregg Herken, *The Winning Weapon: The Atomic Bomb in the Cold War, 1945-50*, (New York, Vintage, 1982), p. 228.
22. Ibid., p. 286.
23. Robert Scheer, 'With Enough Shovels', *Playboy*, December 1982, p. 154.
24. Halloren, op. cit.
25. Ibid.
26. Scheer, op. cit., p. 120.
27. Ibid., p. 122.
28. Halloren, op. cit.
29. Scheer, op. cit., p. 122.
30. Desmond Ball, *Politics and Force Structure in the Kennedy Administration*, (Berkeley, University of California Press, 1981).
31. See Desmond Ball, 'Déjà Vu: The Return to Counterforce in the Nixon Administration', California Seminar on Arms Control and Foreign Policy, occasional paper, December 1974.

IMPERIALISM AND INTERVENTION IN THE THIRD WORLD: US FOREIGN POLICY AND CENTRAL AMERICA

James F. Petras and Morris H. Morley

Introduction: Imperial State and Imperial Economy

To understand US foreign policy, and in particular its interventionist character in Central America, the Caribbean and South America, it is necessary to examine the relationship between the state and the banking, trade and investment interests that operate abroad. The central factor which has enabled the massive growth of US capital overseas has been the emergence and consolidation of the US state as an imperial state. The latter can be defined as those executive bodies or agencies charged with promoting and protecting the expansion of capital across state boundaries by the multinational corporations. The US imperial state exercises inter-related economic, coercive and ideological functions which operate to facilitate capital accumulation and reproduction on a worldwide scale. The economic apparatus includes both agencies serving particular forms of capital (e.g. Department of Agriculture) and agencies performing specific tasks that cut across the different forms of capital (e.g. Treasury and Commerce Departments) promoting investment, loans and trade. The Department of the Treasury also pursues the larger objective in the multilateral development banks (e.g. World Bank, Inter-American Development Bank, International Monetary Fund) through its responsibility for the appointment of US representatives to these 'international' institutions. The coercive apparatus includes the armed forces, the Central Intelligence Agency and other specialised intelligence bodies. The ideological apparatus serves to promote the legitimacy of imperial activities directly through the United States Information Agency and related propaganda arms of the state or through 'sub-contracted' activities related to the practices of un-official groups.[1]

The imperial state provided the 'shell' within which multinational corporations moved around the globe after World War Two. Through military aid programmes, the coercive apparatus built up the repressive institutions while the economic agencies created the necessary infra-structure to facilitate profitable opportunities for the private sector. In other words, while US multinationals now increasingly dominate economic relations between states, the universe in which they operate was created, and is sustained, by the imperial state. Nationalist or socialist threats to the interests of these transnational enterprises have evoked different

219

forms of imperial state intervention (depending on the historical context) to restabilise or reconstitute the conditions for capital accumulation in the target country.

Forms of Imperial State Intervention
The activities of the imperial state and the multinational corporations have polarised societies, fueled the growth of national and social liberation movements and, not infrequently, led to the assumption of political and state power by regimes opposed to exploitative capitalist development. The imperial state has typically responded to such regimes with policies of outright confrontation. This hostility has been operationalised through a combination of interventionist measures to destabilise and overthrow these antagonists of imperial policy.

(a)*Direct and indirect military intervention.* The former through the sending in of American armed forces to occupy a country in order to put in place a collaborator regime and secure US corporate interests (e.g. the Dominican Republic invasion of 1965); the latter, much more common-place but no less destructive of national political institutions, has involved efforts by US policy makers to manipulate non-US military forces to oust nationalist and anti-capitalist regimes. Indirect military intervention has involved one or a combination of approaches: (i) *internal subversion* in the form of CIA inducements to local military officials to organise a coup (e.g. Brazil 1964, Chile 1973); (ii) *external subversion* or the training, financing and directing of former regime collaborators based outside the country to invade and overthrow the regime (e.g. Guatemala 1954, Cuba 1961, Nicaragua 1981 to present); and (iii) *surrogates* such as 'third countries' covertly recruited to train, and supply arms to, counter-revolutionary forces and US client regimes (e.g. the role of the Argentine, Honduras and Israeli governments in Central America over the last decade).

(b)*Economic intervention.* The imperial state intervenes in the 'international' banks to halt loans and other forms of economic assistance to the target country and, where necessary, pressures multinational corporations to take similar actions in the areas of trade, investment, spare parts and technology transfers (e.g. Chile 1970–73, Cuba 1961–68). The intent of this economic warfare is to create internal hardships, stimulate popular discontent and tarnish the international appeal of the regime. Not infrequently, an additional Washington goal is to drive the regime into closer relations with the Soviet Union and the socialist bloc and then trumpet the 'fact' in its propaganda efforts to cast the leadership in the role of 'totalitarians'.

(c)*Political and diplomatic intervention.* The CIA and other intelligence agencies of the imperial state intervene through the channeling of funds to local political, economic and cultural organisations in the target country. Frequently, the recipients include strategic groups in the mass media and the transportation sector, and influential business figures in the export industry sector. External funds are also directed into the coffers of local elites to encourage them to disinvest in order to sabotage production or funneled to complicit labour unions willing to press exorbitant salary demands to provoke social disorder and undermine government economic planning (e.g. Brazil 1962–64, British Guiana 1962–64). By financial internal subversion, the CIA hopes to undermine the economy and set in motion conditions favouring the regime's demise—from the inside, outside, or both. If the effort is thwarted, the imperial state can propagandise the repression of the opposition as an indication of the coercive nature of the regime and encourage its international isolation. A second form of political intervention is the concerted effort by the State Department to control and pressure representatives of other governments in international or regional forums to act in concert with Washington's destabilisation purposes. The Organization of American States has been one arena within which the imperial state has attempted to fashion a regional bloc to intervene against dissident countries attempting to fashion independent economic and foreign policies.[2]

While policy makers representing the imperial state have utilised a variety of policy instruments to defend corporate interests, the selection and effective application of interventionist policies depends on the *historical context* within which they operate. It would be a serious mistake (made by critics as well as proponents of imperial policy) to assume that what policy makers 'will' they can 'realise'—that Washington has an omniscience which allows it to pull whatever trigger, whenever it so chooses.

Contextual Factors Shaping Interventionist Policies
The capacity of imperial-state policy makers to intervene (the scope and depth, as well as the type of intervention) depends on at least four factors: (a) domestic public opinion; (b) international and regional opinion; (c) the strength of the targeted regime; and (d) the condition of the American armed forces.

The United States is an imperial democracy which means that while the state is organised to promote accumulation on a world scale, it is also accountable to an electorate. In many cases the forms of intervention—especially covert operations against popularly-based regimes—are shaped by the need to pursue imperial goals without public awareness, presumably because an informed populace might not authorise such interventions. The capacity to engage in direct military intervention, the ultimate guarantor of US imperial interests, requires the acquiescence (if not support) of the majority of the population. Where deep cleavages extend throughout the body politic, severe constraints develop in the capacity to finance the war, recruit combatants and sustain morale. For intervention of this magnitude, especially where it is prolonged and costly in human and economic terms, is conditioned by the degree of public cohesion and institutional support.

Interventionary capacities also depend on the degree to which international or regional allies can be mobilised to provide political, diplomatic and material support. Where such policies lead to political isolation, retaliatory economic reactions and diplomatic denunciations, they defeat the purpose of the imperial state—which is to extend the terrain for capital accumulation. Regarding the armed forces directly involved in the intervention and occupation, it is imperative that they retain a loyalty to the imperial state or at least to their commanding officers which represent it. When, as in Indochina, the US armed forces became deeply divided over the policies of intervention, there was no recourse but to withdraw from the conflict.

The question of the imperial state's pursuit of an interventionist policy hence is not merely or even most importantly a question of 'will' or 'strong leadership'. Before direct intervention is politically possible, there are essential 'foundations' that must be brought into place. Without these necessary conditions, the imperial state must rely on forms of indirect intervention, and attempt to recreate political circumstances that build up the capacity for direct intervention.

One of the most serious problems facing US imperial-state policy makers since World War Two was the disarticulation of the state as a consequence of the massive military involvement in Vietnam and the equally massive anti-war movement that it spawned on the home front. The successful effort to oust the democratic socialist Allende government in Chile in 1973 was achieved by resort to more indirect means of intervention precisely because there no longer existed a domestic social constituency that would support further imperial military adventures. By the mid-1970s, an enormous 'gap' had developed between the dominant and still growing imperial economic stake and the shrinking imperial state designed to protect and promote it. In this context, where Washington lacked the political and military capacity to intervene (and where such intervention was not perceived as a credible threat by revolutionary forces in the Third World), US multinationals became increasingly vulnerable to the new upsurge in revolutionary struggles throughout the periphery: Ethiopia, Angola, Iran and Nicaragua experienced far-reaching socio-political revolutions that overthrew US collaborator regimes and challenged the power and prerogatives of US corporate interests in the regions in which they occurred.

Washington's interim response to this conjunctural challenge took the form of a multitrack strategy which emphasised (i) reliance on indirect (covert) modes of operation, (ii) promotion of regional policemen, (iii) renewed encouragement of detente and efforts to secure Soviet support in controlling insurgent forces, and (iv) the search for both the means and manner to reconstruct the political basis for new direct interventionary actions.

The dependence on covert operations yielded very limited positive results and, in some cases, provoked at least temporary public and congressional opposition. The most notable instance involved Angola where the Ford White House approved a CIA 'Action Plan' in July 1975 to provide large-scale arms and personnel assistance to the FNLA and UNITA forces in a last ditch effort (supported by South Africa) to prevent the socialist MPLA from taking political power following the withdrawal of the Portuguese colonial regime.[3] Although the clandestine actions failed to achieve their objective, due to the major military participation of the Cubans whose troops guaranteed the MPLA victory, it induced Congress to pass the Clark Amendment in 1976 which placed a complete ban on covert or overt assistance to anti-regime forces in Angola.

The imperial state's reliance on 'regional policemen' such as Brazil, Iran, Israel and South Africa also produced minimal results. In the case of Iran, the overdevelopment of the repressive capacity of the Shah's regime to the complete neglect of the construction of any consequential social base produced the worst possible outcome for Washington.[4] The overthrow of the Shah at the end of 1978 was a key precipitating factor in the Carter administration's decision to launch a New Cold War, replete with an expanded programme of rearmament at home and abroad and increased expenditures for a new interventionist armed forces (the Rapid Deployment Force). In other instances, regional powers such as Israel and South Africa have not infrequently sought to extend their own influence rather than merely serving to defend US interests—sometimes in opposition to Washington policy in the particular region.

The Ford-Kissinger and Carter efforts to secure Soviet cooperation in controlling Third World insurgency was doomed to failure from the beginning, largely due to an exaggerated perception among US policy makers of Moscow's leverage over revolutionary forces in Africa and other parts of the periphery which in practice has been, and remains, quite limited. Notions such as 'trading' global arms agreements in exchange for Soviet acquiescence in suppressing national and socialist armed struggles were thus based on faulty assumptions. The revolutions that took place in Iran, Nicaragua, Ethiopia and Angola between 1975 and 1979 owed nothing to the local pro-Soviet Communist Parties or the Soviet Union.

Unable to secure an adequate substitute for direct intervention and confronted by a spreading challenge to the historic growth of US multinational corporations and banks—exemplified most clearly in Iran—Washington's brief flirtation with a moralising human rights policy was soon overtaken by White House–National Security Council forces intent on global confrontation and the remilitarisation of foreign policy. What followed was an accelerated arms buildup, using the Embassy takeover in Iran as the initial pretext and then improvising Soviet threats as the need arose (e.g. the 'discovery' of a Soviet military brigade in Cuba in September 1979) for further military escalation.

The essential issue that policy makers faced was once again how to increase the capacity of the imperial state commensurate with the world-wide economic interests of the multinational corporations. The military buildup begun in the late Carter administration was accompanied by the need to create the 'political will' to use the renewed capacity to inter-vene—that was provided by the Reagan White House, with its concerted effort to enclose all conflicts within a global East-West confrontation straightjacket. It is within this larger context of the revival of the Cold War and the now predominant military definition of reality that the current policy toward Central America should be examined.

US Foreign Policy and Central America: Confronting the Imperial Presence
Historically, Central America has been within the sphere of US domina-tion: frequent military invasions and occupations, economic and political interventions, and the routine manipulation of elected officials and army generals to suit overseas investors have been recurring themes in the relationship during the twentieth century. Prior to World War Two, US economic interests mainly centred on the agro-export business and trading companies operating within the region; the metropole's geopolitical interests centred on the control and operation of the Panama Canal, a colonial enclave seized in an earlier period.

In the post-1945 era, the rapid and massive expansion of US multi-national capital around the world relegated Central America to a second-ary position in Washington's global concerns—except on those occasions when political forces in area countries (e.g. Guatemala 1950–5) sought to alter the status quo. While the rest of the Third World was experiencing political and social upheavals, US policy makers continued to support the entrenched landed oligarchies and military regimes. Capitalist develop-ment and the expansion of markets for American products and services, according to Washington, would best be promoted through the appro-priately dubbed 'modernising oligarchies' or 'technocratic military'. The notion was to promote large-scale commercial agriculture and manu-facturing based on cheap labour, major infusions of US and international bank economic assistance for infrastructure development, the attraction of foreign investment and the conversion of local oligarchs and generals to 'entrepreneurial behaviour'.

Beginning in the mid-1950s, US policy makers became increasingly linked with those sectors of the Central American ruling class involved in financial and industrial institutions and less tied to the direct ownership of land. The shift in economic activity did not, however, lead to any change in policy toward those forces seeking to change the political and social status quo. The convergence of the interests of the US imperial state and its investor interests with those of the area's ruling class led to an historic compromise in which successive US governments sacrificed democratic rights in exchange for capitalist economic opportunities and US strategic interests.

The imperial state's support for Central American dictatorships has been manifested through a vast programme of bilateral and multilateral economic aid and various forms of military assistance. Between 1953 and 1979, Washington provided the ruling classes in El Salvador with $218.4 million in economic aid and $16.8 million in military loans and credits. This sum was more than matched by the World Bank, Inter-American Development Bank and other US-influenced multilateral banks to the tune of $479.2 million. The Guatemalan oligarchy received $526.0 million in US economic aid and $41.9 million in military assistance, as well as some $593.0 million from the 'international' banks. The Somoza clan in Nicaragua was the recipient of $345.8 million in US economic aid and $32.6 million in military assistance, while the 'international' financial agencies channeled $469.5 into its pockets. In Honduras, the ruling groups during this quarter century also benefited significantly from these same sources: $305.1 million in US economic and, $28.4 million in US military assistance, and $688.0 million from the multilateral banking corporations.[5]

Decades of American financial assistance and military aid were geared essentially to promoting and supporting capitalist development programmes and the repressive regimes prepared to implement them. Through public and private loans and investments, direct governmental programmes and its influence in shaping the policies of the so-called international banks, Washington promoted economic infrastructures, financial institutions and industries in Central America consonant with the interests of its own overseas capitalist class. At the same time, US military assistance, arms sales and training programmes were directly linked to the maintenance of these very dictatorial regimes that supported imperial-state political, economic and strategic goals in the region.

The geopolitical importance of Central America continues to lie in its role as a staging ground for US military intervention into the Caribbean Basin countries, a training base for US and Latin American military forces, and a testing area for counterinsurgency and counterrevolutionary methods. The invasion and overthrow of the Arbenz government in Guatemala in 1954 was organised from across its border; the 1961 Bay of Pigs invasion forces were trained and organised in Guatemala and Nicaragua; Central American dictatorships provided troops during the invasion sponsored by the US of the Dominican Republic of 1965; Honduras, El Salvador and Guatemala currently provide training areas for Somocista counterrevolutionaries sowing terror in Nicaragua; and US armed forces personnel, at an array of military training bases in Panama, continue to prepare the future hemisphere counterinsurgency officers who will head up repressive forces in their home countries.

The watershed in US-Central American relations was the Nicaraguan revolution of July 1979 which directly and fundamentally challenged long-standing imperial-state policy in the region—its alliances with the oligarchy and the generals, and the assumption that Central America was and will always be a subordinate element in Washington's global and regional design. More important, revolutionary processes were developing in the neighbouring countries of El Salvador and Guatemala. The growth of mass popular peasant trade-union movements, the activation of Indian communities and the growing effectiveness of the guerrilla movements initially caused the Carter administration to pursue a combined 'repression and reform' policy with the military regime in Guatemala, pressuring the generals in the form of cutbacks in military credits to be more selective in their coercive policies. In El Salvador, Washington attempted to forge an alliance between reformist civilians and rightist military officials. In the subsequent period, the Carter administration escalated its military aid to El Salvador and began to expand its military assistance programmes to Honduras. During 1979 and 1980, economic aid, military sales and private financing continued to flow to the repressive regimes, to the accompaniment of White House human rights sermons. The proposed land reforms in El Salvador disintegrated as the potential beneficiaries were slaughtered by the regime's paramilitary forces and death squads. Failing to implement their original programme, the reformist civilian and military officials abandoned the government to be replaced by right-wing Christian Democrats who had no compunction about collaborating with the organisers of the death squads.

The Carter administration's short-lived effort to develop a reformist alternative to revolution in Central America failed in the wake of its over-riding concern with strengthening the military forces in the area and simultaneously repressing nationally-based popular movements allied with guerrilla forces in pursuit of political and state power. Thus, even before Reagan entered the White House, the logic of a military solution to the basic socioeconomic problems was established; the increase in military assistance and the introduction of military advisers to the region, together with the invention of Soviet-Cuban conspirators, were taken over from the Democrats and further embellished by the Reagan presidency.

The Reagan Presidency: Intervention and Terror in Central America
The whole thrust of Reagan's global foreign policy rests on the twin assumptions that revolutions in the Third World are products of Soviet expansionism and that military force is the only means to successfully

defeat them. Based on these assumptions, the Reagan imperial state developed a programme of massive military buildup and escalating military aid and sales to right-wing military regimes throughout Latin America and the Third World. But Central America was chosen to be the testing ground to 'prove' the effectiveness of the new policy.

Nicaragua: The 'Outsider' Strategy. The structure and nature of US imperialism, the forms of intervention and the evolving global historical position of the United States are essential to understanding contemporary interventionist policy whether in South America during the 1970s or Central America in the 1980s. Yet, while there is a common structural and institutional base that formulates and designs US interventionist policy, it is important to identify clear differences that exist regarding each targeted country and the particular international context. Some brief observations on US intervention against Allende's Chile offer an instructive comparison and contrast with Washington's efforts to overthrow the Sandinista government in Nicaragua.

Chile was the region's largest recipient, on a per capita basis, of US Alliance for Progress economic assistance and a major destination for international bank loans and grants during the 1960s—dictated in no small part by Washington's determination to prevent socialist political forces from gaining power via the electoral process. The Kennedy and Johnson administrations, for instance, channelled millions of dollars into the 1964 presidential campaign of the Christian Democratic candidate Eduardo Frei and dispatched hundreds of State Department and CIA operatives to promote Frei's candidacy against a major left-wing challenge under the leadership of Salvador Allende. In 1970, Washington attempted to replicate this successful strategy but this time failed to prevent the Allende forces from winning a plurality of the popular vote.

The Nixon-Kissinger response to the election result was to organise a covert two-track effort to subvert Allende's victory, hoping through either bribing members of Congress or the organisation of a military coup to block the popular will. In both areas, the CIA was the designated instrumentality for achieving this objective. The failure to prevent Allende's inauguration confronted the Nixon White House with a serious problem: how to destabilise the socialist regime in Chile in a context where it lacked a domestic social base of support for direct military intervention. This problem was resolved in the form of a multitrack 'insider/outsider' strategy. Two key pressure points were identified: the Chilean economy's enormous dependence on external sources of financing, spare parts and markets, and the state apparatus which remained firmly under the control of forces opposed to the new regime.

The insider strategy of covert intervention through strategically located groups in the Chilean state and society was facilitated by the persistence of an open bargaining political system which provided the CIA with in-

numerable opportunities for disrupting the economy and polity: it subsidised truckers' strikes which blocked the flow of goods; financed copper
employees' strikes which reduced foreign exchange earnings, financed a
series of political strikes by taxi drivers, bus owners, small businessmen,
lawyers, doctors, etc. with attendant losses in production; funded various
private sector organisations which acted as conduits for channelling monies
to anti-government strikers; subsidised *El Mercurio* and provided funds to
the opposition Christian Democratic and National Parties to purchase their
own radio stations and newspapers. In the electoral arena, a report prepared by the US Senate Intelligence Committee pointed out that 'Covert
American activity was a factor in almost every major election in Chile in
the decade between 1963 and 1973'. In discussing the specifics of the
Allende period, it noted: 'Money provided to political parties not only
supported opposition candidates in the various elections, but enabled the
parties to maintain an anti-government campaign throughout the Allende
years. . .'[6]

In the military sphere, following the abortive CIA supported and
financed coups of October 1970, the Agency was forced to develop an
entirely new network of contacts within the Chilean armed forces. 'By
September 1971', the Senate Study reported, 'a new network of agents
were in place and the [CIA Santiago] Station was receiving almost daily
reports of new coup plotting.'[7] The CIA's new 'assets' were spread
throughout all three branches of the armed forces and the military plotters
willingly accepted Agency leadership and direction. Meanwhile, the
Chilean military also received continuous infusions of grant aid and
weaponry from the Nixon administration and its generals were in constant
communication and consultation with their American counterparts.

Beyond the immediate terrain of the conflict, the imperial state moved
to maximise external pressures against the socialist regime. Washington's
economic blockade against Allende's Chile focused on four main areas:
the termination of all US economic assistance and spare parts exports,
mobilisation of support for its position in the international banking
institutions which resulted in no loans from the World Bank and only
two small loans to opposition educational centres from the Inter-American
Development Bank during Allende's tenure in office; a dramatic fall in
available lines of short-term US private commercial bank credits compared
with the prior period; and a refusal on Washington's part to renegotiate
Chile's enormous public debt to the United States, most of which was
accumulated in the 1960s under the Alessandri and Frei regimes. The
continuing process of escalating economic warfare and covert subversion
mediated through key groups and forces in the state and society opposed
to the socialist experiment allowed the imperial state to work its will:
paralyse the economy, provoke social disorder and promote the conditions
for a military coup.[8]

Just as successive US administrations had for an extended period of time provided military and economic assistance to the pro-capitalist regimes that preceded Allende, the Somoza family dictatorship in Nicaragua was also on the receiving end of imperial-state largess to the tune of almost $380 million in economic and military aid and $32.6 million in military assistance between 1953 and 1979. At the same time, US representatives in the international banks supported loans totalling nearly $470 million for the Nicaraguan regime. As the Sandinista forces gained political and military support during 1977 and 1978, and as it became obvious that his regime was collapsing, Washington sought to dump Somoza and forge an alliance between conservative civilians and the Somocista armed forces. This alliance, however, failed to stem the advance of the Sandinista forces. Washington then sought to activate the military intervention option in the form of an inter-hemispheric military force operating under the aegis of the Organization of American States. The opposition of a number of important Latin American countries, supported by the European Social Democratic movement, prevented this proposal from being passed by the regional body.

Like Nixon and Allende's Chile, the historical conjuncture—the continuing hostility among the population and within Congress to new direct military interventions in the aftermath of Vietnam—limited the capacity of the Carter administration to take any such unilateral action against the Sandinista-dominated government in Nicaragua after July 1979. A further constraint was the virtual certainty that direct US military involvement in a prolonged guerrilla war would have resulted in substantial loss of American lives—accompanied by a resurgence of the anti-war movement.

Lacking this interventionist capacity, the Carter White House attempted to intervene within post-revolutionary Nicaraguan society through the manipulation of economic aid—channelling funds to conservative business people and other antisocialist groups among the middle class supporters of Sandinismo. Unlike Allende's Chile, however, the Sandinista-dominated political system provided much fewer opportunities for covert intervention. The old Somocista state apparatus with its longstanding liaisons to US military intelligence and the CIA was destroyed and replaced with a revolutionary army and popular militias. The top revolutionary leadership controlled the key executive and legislative institutions, blocking efforts to paralyse government through bribery and collusion. In civic society, the Sandinist trade unions and peasant associations presented formidable challenges to Washington efforts to foment disorder and political strikes. The small AFL–CIA promoted trade-union centre had few followers and no influence due to its collaboration with the Somoza dictatorship. The only sectors toward which Carter policy makers could direct their attention and resources were located in the media and among private business. *La Prensa,* like its CIA-funded counterpart in Chile

(*El Mercurio*), published virulent anti-government propaganda until the revolutionary government's security laws forced it to tone down its incendiary message. The business groups, faced with a mobilised labour force and an uncorruptable regime, have been unable to paralyse production as they did in Chile: if they organise a lockout, they will be the principal parties 'locked out' of the participating firms.

An analysis of the impact of Washington's economic blockade against the Sandinistas reveals that it has been far less effective in the case of Nicaragua than it was in Chile under Allende. A number of allied countries, bilaterally and within the international banks (despite some Washington successes in these latter arenas), have been unwilling to follow the White House lead. Credits and loans from Western Europe, and particularly the Social Democratic governments, have been augmented in some cases (e.g. France) by the provision of military assistance. Furthermore, some of the oil-rich countries such as Libya have made available substantial amounts of economic aid.[9] Finally, the Cubans have provided technical and military assistance which probably acts as a deterrent to those in Washington who might risk a direct invasion under the illusion of a 'quick low cost' victory. Thus, while US economic warfare has indeed had a serious impact on the Nicaraguan economy, it has not been able to destabilise the society as the internal organisation of the revolution has been able to contain internal sources of subversion and as sufficient alternative sources of trade and finance have emerged to compensate for losses due to the blockade gains. Even US private banks who hold most of the accumulated Nicaraguan debt have resisted Washington's pressures and agreed to renegotiate the debt—rather than enter into a no-win confrontation.[10]

In the absence of a viable counterrevolutionary vehicle for overthrowing the Sandinista government and limited by its external economic leverage, Washington has now turned toward an externally based military solution: organising an invasion army of ex-Somocistas; building up the military capabilities of the Honduran, Guatemalan and Salvadoran armed forces for interventionary action; and encouraging surrogate forces, principally Argentina and Israel, to share the responsibility for training and arming these hostile regional opponents of socialist Nicaragua.[11] A massive buildup of military forces currently underway in Honduras is being supervised by the biggest contingent of CIA forces in a Latin American operation since the overthrow of Allende in 1973. The imperial state's reliance on a military approach to the Sandinista revolution coincides with the massive militarisation of US foreign policy in general and its increasing rapprochment with rightist military regimes throughout the hemisphere in particular.[12]

During 1979 and 1980, the Carter administration revitalised and expanded US covert intelligence gathering activities in Central America, and clandestinely provided funds and other supports to anti-regime individuals and groups (e.g. media, labour unions) in socialist Nicaragua. The advent of the Reagan presidency set the stage for an accelerated covert and military involvement in Central America, focused largely on Nicaragua and El Salvador. In a verbal message relayed to Managua in February 1981, and supposedly originating from a staff member of the National Security Council, the American Embassy was informed that 'the question is not whether US–Nicaraguan relations were good or bad, but whether there will be any relations at all'.[13] The hardliners in the State Department, especially Secretary Alexander Haig and Assistant Secretary for Inter-American Affairs Thomas Enders, were convinced that the Sandinistas were playing a key role in both extending Cuban influence in the area and providing arms for the guerrillas in El Salvador. At a number of high-level foreign policy meetings early in the administration, Enders spoke of the need to 'get rid of the Sandinistas'.[14] Meanwhile, Secretary Haig's Ambassador-at-Large, General Vernon Walters, and other imperial state officials conferred with members of the governments of Argentina, Guatemala and Honduras regarding possible joint covert operations against Nicaragua.[15]

By late 1981, Reagan policy makers were declaring that the Sandinista government had 'very nearly become intolerable. . .'[16] Laying the groundwork for possible intervention, one official opined that it may ultimately be necessary to take direct action: 'Something has to be done and done soon. . .'[17] In testimony before the House Foreign Affairs Committee in mid-November, Haig refused to exclude the possibility of US efforts to overthrow the social revolutionary regime in Managua.[18] However, while there was a consensus determination within the highest echelons of the imperial state to prevent Nicaragua from becoming 'another Cuba',[19] bureaucratic disagreements developed over the efficacy of the military option.[20] Secretary Haig emerged as the leading advocate of using military force in opposition to senior Pentagon officials and the Joint Chiefs of Staff who feared the consequences of a protracted military involvement in the absence of domestic social support and were also concerned over any interventionist adventure that might endanger the administration's plans to modernise the US armed forces.[21] 'Haig used to say that he wanted to do more, but it was the Defence Department that was always opposing military moves,' a State Department official recalled. 'They didn't like doing anything', he would say. Whenever he proposed something they had a thousand and one reasons why it couldn't be done. "We don't have the ships, we don't have the men, we don't have this or that".'[22] The outcome was a decision to forego direct military intervention in favour of an extensive complementary programme of indirect military intervention and covert subversion.

In December 1981, President Reagan formally authorised a covert action programme developed by the CIA and first presented in detail by

Director William Casey at a mid-November meeting of the National Security Council. With the concurrence of Secretary of State Haig and Secretary of Defence Caspar Weinberger, Reagan approved the largest paramilitary and political action operation mounted by the CIA in almost a decade with a first stage operating budget of almost $20 million. The programme or planning efforts included the following: encouragement of political and paramilitary activity by foreign governments; contingency planning (naval quarantine, air actions, etc.) against Cuba; an estimated $250 million to $300 million in additional economic assistance for the countries of Central America and the Caribbean; training Salvadoran military forces in the United States and El Salvador; increased US intelligence activity in the region; maintenance of trade and credit to the private sector in Nicaragua; upgrading the American military posture in the Caribbean through military exercises, expanded intelligence work, the establishment of a new command communications network, etc.; a major propaganda effort in the United States to mobilise domestic support for the new covert intervention policy; and tightened economic sanctions against Cuba.[23]

Much of the focus of this programme was directed toward Nicaragua as Reagan gave the CIA 'marching orders' to increase its liaisons among the anti-Sandinista exiles and conduct paramilitary raids to halt the so-called flow of weapons from the revolutionary regime to the insurgents in El Salvador. Specifically, the White House directed the CIA to put together and finance a paramilitary force of 500 Latin Americans to be based along the Nicaraguan-Honduras border for the purpose of commando raids into Nicaragua to destroy key economic targets such as power plants and bridges. The plan projected an additional 1,000 man force trained and financed in Honduras, largely by Argentine military forces, for participation at a later date.[24] Argentina's involvement dates from the inception of the programme. Reagan administration officials state that the military dictatorship in Buenos Aires agreed to take primary responsibility for financing and training the anti-Sandinista exiles to intercept arms shipments from Nicaragua to El Salvador and Guatemala—an arrangement interrupted for a time by the falling out between Washington and Buenos Aires over the Argentine invasion of the Falkland Islands in April–June 1982 which forced the US to assume direct control over the entire clandestine paramilitary operation.[25]

In April 1982, Reagan convened his senior foreign policy advisers in a meeting at which the goals of the December 1981 covert action plan were reaffirmed and a complementary policy programme for Central America was approved. This new National Security Council document expressed the determination of the White House to prevent a 'proliferation of Cuba-model states' in the region and authorised the use of covert and political action plans to stop Nicaragua from 'exporting revolution' to

El Salvador. It further asserted that the Sandinista government was 'under increased pressure as a result of our covert efforts. . .' and suggested that the CIA operating budget be increased by $2.5 million for use in expanding the Agency's operations in Guatemala.[26]

Since early 1982, Honduras has been the centre of CIA operations against Nicaragua. Following the 'green light' for the CIA action plan in December 1981, the size of the CIA Station in Tegucigalpa almost immediately doubled to about 50 operatives.[27] By the end of the year, more than 150 agents were based in Honduras providing intelligence data and military advice to the paramilitary units engaged in clandestine operations against the Sandinista regime.[28] A significant proportion of the $31.3 million US military assistance package to Honduras for fiscal year 1982 was indirectly rechannelled to facilitate the activities of these groups.[29] A Honduran participant in the planning and execution of US covert operations at the time provides some interesting detail: Agency officials provided intelligence reports regarding troop movements inside Nicaragua and the location of tanks and artillery; they shipped planeloads of arms and ammunition to the Moskito Indian units in eastern Honduras in August 1982; and they provided underwater equipment and explosives to Argentine-trained sabotage teams that destroyed port installations in Puerto Cabezas, Nicaragua, in early 1983.[30] According to US intelligence officials, Argentine involvement in the training of the paramilitary forces resumed in late 1982. During this period, the CIA also worked in liaison with the intelligence and military services in Colombia and Venezuela.[31]

The US covert and military presence in Honduras was augmented and reinforced by a series of joint US-Honduran military manoeuvres held near the Nicaraguan border with the express objective of 'intimidating' the Sandinista government.[32] The most recent, notable for the unprecedented number of participants, took place in February 1983 and involved 1,600 American military personnel and 4,000 Honduran troops backed by an array of sophisticated weaponry and communications equipment.[33]

El Salvador: The 'Insider' Strategy Continued. Beyond the planning of policies to reverse established revolutionary governments, the core strategic goal of the Reagan administration is to prevent any other popular nationalist or revolutionary movements from gaining political power in the Third World. To contain revolutions in the periphery, the US has been willing to maximise the use of force to sustain repressive regimes, even at the cost of massive loss of civilian lives, even in the absence of support from its senior partners in the Western Alliance.

As the struggle against imperial-state client regimes gained momentum in Central America, the Reagan White House escalated its commitment to the dictatorial cliques in the region, in particular pouring millions of dollars of economic and military aid to a faltering regime in El Salvador.

Combined US economic, financial and military assistance, and loans and grants from the US-influenced multilateral development banks to El Salvador increased from $174.5 million during the last year of the Carter presidency to $266.8 million in 1981, rising dramatically to an estimated $468 million in 1982.[34] The massive US state commitment, completely out of proportion to any political, economic or strategic advantage that could be obtained from the Salvadoran regime can only be understood in terms of the stake which the Reaganites have invested in a military victory to vindicate the militarisation of US foreign policy on a global scale. A defeat in El Salvador would call into question all the assumptions about Soviet involvement and the centrality of military power in confronting Third World revolutions. The escalation of military aid to El Salvador, and the massive slaughter which has resulted from a government waging war on its own people, is the price the Salvadoran population is being made to pay in order to uphold and justify imperial policy.

As the opposition to US policy in El Salvador began to multiply at home while the guerrilla movement was gaining political and military support in its struggle against the Washington-backed regime, the Reagan administration began to accelerate the shipment of arms and expand training facilities for recruits and officers in early 1982.[35] Additionally, it decided to borrow a page from the Carter period: in March, the imperial state literally staged an election to legitimate its war against the Salvadoran people. Midst the systematic destruction of all the most basic freedoms necessary to make elections meaningful (freedom of speech, assembly, press, etc.) an 'election' was held which produced the biggest gains for the most revanchest rightist forces under the leadership of Roberto D'Aubuisson—under conditions of mass terror those who were most active in the organisation of the death squads demonstrated the greatest capacity to secure votes. Despite the absence of the most elementary conditions of personal security, the election was heralded in Washington as the basis for transforming the terrorist regime into a 'representative government'. Yet, apart from the context within which the elections actually took place, two studies conducted by El Salvador's largest university, the Jose Simeon Canas University of Central America further charged 'massive fraud' in the number of reported votes.[36] The Reagan administration, however, had no problem increasing its economic and military aid to the now predominantly ultra-rightist dominated regime which in the months immediately following the election proceeded to increase the overall level of state violence directed against the Salvadoran people and evicted thousands of peasant families from the land they were entitled to purchase under the much vaunted agrarian reform programme.[37]

In February 1983, the White House proposed a foreign military assistance programme for fiscal year 1984 totalling $9.2 billion (an increase of $400 million over 1983). El Salvador's allocation was increased from

$165 million in 1983 to a projected $205 million in 1984.[38] Within weeks, administration officials were testifying before Congress in support of an additional $60 million in emergency military assistance to the Salvadoran regime.[39] Secretary of State George Shultz, in language reminiscent of his supposedly more confrontationist predecessor Alexander Haig, justified the request to the legislators on the grounds that 'the problem is far broader than a simple American problem; it's a problem of our contest with the Soviet system, the Soviet military power, and the exertion of that power'.[40] A comprehensive review of Central American policy undertaken at this time 'in the light of the Soviet threat' also led Reagan to seriously consider increasing the number of US military advisers in El Salvador beyond the current limit of 55.[41] In mid-March, the White House made plain its intent to, if possible, further militarise Salvadoran civil society to combat and destroy the revolutionary movement. Reagan proposed that an emergency $298 million economic and military assistance package be authorised for Central America, with approximately 60 per cent of the total—$110 million in arms aid and $67 million in economic aid—being earmarked for the government in El Salvador.[42] In April, administration officials acknowledged that negotiations were in progress with the Honduran regime to establish a military base inside the country, staffed by approximately 100 US military advisers, for the purpose of training Salvadoran troops.[43]

Conclusion

During its first two years in office, Reagan White House requests totalling more than $50 million to construct an intelligence-gathering network in Central America have been approved by the Congressional intelligence committees.[44] By early 1983, covert intelligence operatives and technicians in the region were more numerous than US military advisers. The administration is now seeking to correct this imbalance through projected major increases in military aid and Pentagon personnel to bolster its clients and defeat its antagonists in the area.

The open-ended nature of US support, no matter how terrorist the regime is, indicates that much more is involved than 'defending' El Salvador or destabilising Nicaragua: the basic issue is the Reagan imperial state's determination to demonstrate that its militarist policy 'works'—it defeats revolutionaries, it defends US allies. The 'reconstruction' and recovery of US domination in Central America through projections of military power reflects the attempt by Washington to recreate the 'golden age' of the 1950s—the era of virtually unquestioned US domination.

The Reaganites engage in a wilful disregard of the fundamental objective changes which have taken place in the world since the 1950s: an increasingly independent and competitive Western Europe; the growth of economic ties between Western Europe, the Third World and the Soviet bloc; Latin America's declining trade dependence on the US and parallel expansion of commercial links with Western Europe, Japan and the non-capitalist countries; regional organisations and cartels which define new sets of relationships, etc. Recognition of these objective changes and the development of diverse interests would certainly temper the Reagan foreign policy makers' efforts to 'impose' an East-West confrontational straightjacket and to solve problems through military escalation.

Rather than face the constraints, the Reaganites prefer to cling to their 1950s vision and try to 'create facts' through an ultra-voluntarist approach: the belief that by sheer acts of 'will', by escalating the bellicose rhetoric, by increasing US military commitments, they can bring about a change in the 'objective world'. In many ways, the voluntarism of the Reagan Right in the 1980s resembles the ultra-left 'foco' practitioners so numerous in Latin America during the 1960s: both subsitute(d) subjective wishes for objective realities.

NOTES

1. For an extended discussion, see James F. Petras and Morris H. Morley, 'The US Imperial State', *Review* (Journal of the Fernand Braudel Centre, Vol. IV, No. 2, Fall 1980, pp. 171-222.
2. Detailed analyses of the different forms of US imperial state interventions are found in the following literature: James Petras and Morris Morley, *The United States and Chile: Imperialism and the Overthrow of the Allende Government* (Monthly Review Press, New York, 1975); US Congress, Senate, Select Committee on Intelligence, *Covert Action in Chile 1963-1973*, 94th Congress, 1st Session, December 18, 1975 (US Government Printing Office, Washington, 1975); US Congress, Senate, Select Committee on Intelligence, *Alleged Assassination Plots Involving Foreign Leaders*, 94th Congress, 1st Session, Report No. 94-465, November 20, 1975 (US Government Printing Office, Washington, 1975); Stephen Schlesinger and Stephen Kinzer, *Bitter Fruit: The Untold Story of the American Coup in Guatemala* (Doubleday & Company, New York, 1982); 'How the CIA got rid of Jagan', *Sunday Times,* London, April 16, 1967, p. 1, 3; Phyllis R. Parker, *Brazil and the Quiet Intervention, 1964* (University of Texas Press, Austin and London, 1979).
3. See Nathaniel, 'The Angola Decision of 1975: A Personal Memoir', *Foreign Affairs,* Vol. 56, No. 1, Fall 1978, pp. 109-124.
4. The contradiction between economic growth and dictatorial rule in Iran under the Shah is discussed in James F. Petras and Morris H. Morley, 'Development and Revolution: Contradictions in the Advanced Third World Countries— Brazil, South Africa, and Iran', *Studies in Comparative International Development,* Vol. XVI, No. 1, Spring 1981, pp. 3-43.
5. US Agency for International Development, Statistics and Research Division Office of Program and Information Analysis Services, *US Overseas Loans and Grants and Assistance from International Organizations, July 1, 1945–September 30, 1975* (Washington, D.C., 1977), pp. 43, 47-48, 53-5, 183-5; US Agency for International Development, Office of Planning and Budgeting, Bureau for Program and Policy Coordination, *U.S. Overseas Loans and Grants and Assistance from International Organizations, July 1, 1945–September 30, 1979* (Washington, D.C., 1980), pp. 45, 49-50, 53, 55-7, 218-22.

6. US Congress, Senate, *Covert Action in Chile 1963–1973*, op. cit., pp. 9, 28–29.
7. Ibid., p. 37.
8. A detailed analysis of the Chilean case is found in James Petras and Morris Morley, *The United States and Chile*, op. cit.
9. See 'Nicaragua: Widening the search for credit', *Latin America Weekly Report* WR-82-44, November 12, 1982, p. 10; Sabine Mabouche, 'France to Complete Arms Sale to Managua', *Washington Post*, July 10, 1982, p. A18; 'French Arms Go to Nicaragua', *New York Times*, July 13, 1982, p. 6.
10. The White House continues to pursue its economic warfare against the Sandinista regime. At the time this manuscript was completed (April 1983), the Reagan administration was drawing up plans that would drastically cut back on the amount of sugar that US firms could purchase from Nicaragua. These exports represent a major source of Managua's badly needed hard currency earnings. See Patrick E. Tyler, 'Nicaragua's Sugar Sales May Be Cut', *Washington Post*, April 5, 1983, p. A11; Seth S. King, 'US Study of Sugar Imports Set', *New York Times*, April 6, 1983, p. D9.
11. On the role of Argentina and Israel, see, for example, Leslie H. Gelb, 'Argentina Linked to Rise in Covert US Actions Against Sandinists', *New York Times*, April 8, 1983, p. 10; John Rettie, 'Israeli arms help Guatemala's fight against guerrillas', *The Guardian* (UK), January 10, 1982, p. 9; Ignacio Klich, 'Caribbean boomerang returns to sender', *The Guardian* (UK), September 5, 1982, p. 8; Edward Cody, 'Sharon to Discuss Arms Sales in Honduras', *Washington Post*, December 7, 1982, p. A19.
12. Despite Congressional restrictions on military aid to Guatemala, the Reagan administration has taken advantage of loopholes in the legislation to provide the Guatemalan armed forces with materials, instruction and expert advice since the Rios Montt coup of March 1982. In January 1983, it formally lifted the embargo on arms sales, paving the way for the military dictatorship to purchase $6.3 million worth of spare parts and other equipment for its air force—primarily for US-made helicopters which play a major role in the regime's war against the guerrilla movement. See Alan Riding, 'US Is Said to Plan Aid to Guatemala to Battle Leftists', *New York Times*, April 25, 1982, pp. 1, 21; Richard J. Meislin, 'US Military Aid for Guetamala Continuing Despite Official Curbs', *New York Times*, December 19, 1982, pp. 1, 18; Bernard Gwertzman, 'US Lifts Embargo on Military Sales to Guatemalans', *New York Times*, January 8, 1983, pp. 1, 4.
13. Quoted in Alan Riding, 'Nicaragua Seeking Accord in El Salvador', *New York Times*, February 12, 1981, p. 11.
14. Quoted in 'A Secret War for Nicaragua', *Newsweek*, November 8, 1982, p. 44.
15. Ibid.
16. Quoted in James Nelson Goodsell, 'Nicaragua Drift to Left Stirs Washington Warning', *Christian Science Monitor*, November 4, 1981, p. 1.
17. Ibid.
18. See John M. Goshko, 'Haig Won't Rule Out Anti-Nicaragua Action', *Washington Post*, November 13, 1981, p. A13.
19. Quoted in Michael Getler and Don Oberdorfer, 'US Nearing Decision on Nicaragua: Pressure to "Do Something" Grows', *Washington Post*, November 22, 1981, P. A1.
20. Ibid., p. A33. Also see Don Oberdorfer, 'Haig and Seese Vent Impatience with Nicaragua', *Washington Post*, November 23, 1981, p. A1, A16; Bernard Gwertzman, 'Haig Warns Time is Growing Short on Nicaragua', *New York Times*, November 23, 1981, p. 15.
21. See Richard Halloran, 'Nicaragua Arms Called Peril to Area', *New York Times*, December 3, 1981, p. 12.

22. Quoted in Bernard Weinraub, 'Reagan Policy in Central America: After 2 Years, Tough Tone Softens', *New York Times*, January 25, 1983, p. 12.
23. See Don Oberdorfer and Patrick E. Tyler, 'Reagan Backs Action Plan for Central America', *Washington Post*, February 14, 1982, pp. A1, A4; Patrick E. Tyler and Bob Woodward, 'US Approves Covert Plan in Nicaragua', *Washington Post*, March 10, 1982, pp. A1, A16.
24. Ibid.; Leslie H. Gelb, op. cit., p. 10.
25. Ibid.
26. Quoted in 'National Security Council Document on Policy in Central America and Cuba', reprinted in *New York Times*, April 7, 1983, p. 16. Also see Raymond Bonner, 'President Approved Policy of Preventing "Cuba-Model States" ', *New York Times*, April 7, 1983, pp. 1, 16.
27. See 'A Secret War for Nicaragua', op. cit., p. 44.
28. See Philip Taubman, 'CIA is Making a Special Target of Latin Region', *New York Times*, December 4, 1982, p. 1.
29. Ibid.
30. See Raymond Bonner, 'US Ties to Anti-Sandinists are Reported to be Extensive', *New York Times*, April 3, 1983, pp. 1, 14. The Honduran informant has close ties to the Honduran military as well as American diplomatic and military officials in Tegucigalpa, and was directly involved in joint military planning activities until early 1983. Also see Philip Taubman, 'US Backing Raids Against Nicaragua', *New York Times*, November 2, 1982, p. 6.
31. See Philip Taubman, 'CIA Is Making a Special Target of Latin Region', op. cit., p. 7.
32. Christopher Dickey, 'US Presses Honduran War Games', *Washington Post*, October 17, 1982, pp. A1, A12.
33. See Michael Wright, 'GI's Join Honduran Soldiers in Manoeuvres on Nicaraguan Border', *New York Times*, February 2, 1983, p. 4. Also see Christopher Dickey, 'US-Honduran Exercise is Held near Nicaragua', *Washington Post*, February 3, 1983, p. A25.
34. See John Eisendrath and Jim Morrell, *Arming El Salvador* (Center for International Policy, Washington, D.C., 1982), p. 2.
35. See Michael Getler, 'US Pumps in Arms, Widens Training to Rescue El Salvador', *Washington Post*, March 5, 1982, pp. A1, A20.
36. See Raymond Bonner, 'Fraud is Reported in Salvador Vote', *New York Times*, June 4, 1982, p. 5; Raymond Bonner, 'New Doubt Cast on Salvadoran Vote', *New York Times*, June 14, 1982, p. 2.
37. See Raymond Bonner, 'Salvador Evicts Peasants from Land', *New York Times*, May 30, 1982, p. 3; Raymond Bonner, 'Peasant Leader in El Salvador Asserts 25 Are Evicted Daily', *New York Times*, June 5, 1982, p. 21; Raymond Bonner, 'Salvador Killing is Said to Increase', *New York Times*, June 1, 1982, p. 3.
38. Bernard Weinraub, 'Reagan Asks $9.2 Billion in Foreign Military Aid for Next Year', *New York Times*, February 5, 1983, p. 3.
39. See Bernard Gwertzman, 'A New Focus on Salvador', *New York Times*, March 1, 1983, pp. 1, 10.
40. Quoted in Bernard Gwertzman, 'Shultz Says US Told Salvadorans to "Clean Up" their Rights Record', *New York Times*, March 23, 1983, p. 3.
41. Quoted in Bernard Weinraub, 'Reagan Weighing More US Advisers for El Salvador', *New York Times*, March 1, 1983, p. 1. As of March 1983, there were almost three times as many CIA personnel (150) as Pentagon officials in El Salvador. See Philip Taubman, 'US Said to Have Large Spy Network in Latin America', *New York Times*, March 20, 1983, p. 16.

MARXISM WITHOUT CLASS STRUGGLE?

Ellen Meiksins Wood

A distinguishing characteristic of 'Western Marxism', it is said, has been a separation of theory and practice which has followed inevitably upon the separation of Marxist intellectuals from a revolutionary mass movement.[1] The result has been a Marxism more at home in the Academy than in the arenas of political struggle. Nevertheless, to say that theory has become divorced from revolutionary practice and from the realities of working-class politics is not necessarily to say that theory has no implications for practice. In fact, many theoretical innovations in contemporary Marxism, for all their philosophical abstraction, have been intended precisely as political statements. In some cases, the theoretical divorce from working-class politics represents a deliberate writing-off of the working class, which is in itself a significant political stance. The most interesting case, however, is the connection between Althusserian, or post-Althusserian, theory with Eurocommunist practice. Some of the most important and influential theoretical developments of contemporary Marxism have emerged as theorisations of Eurocommunist strategy. The political objectives of these innovations have been obscured by their formal abstraction and academicism and their claim to theoretical autonomy and universality. But if people have failed to note their political intentions and consequences, it is probably less because the evidence is obscure—since the theorists themselves are often quite explicit about their practical objectives—than because we have come to take for granted the dissociation of Marxist theory from political practice.

In what follows, it will be argued that the effect of this new unity of theory and practice has been a substantial transformation of Marxist theory which goes to its very foundations. Specifically, class struggle and the self-emancipation of the working class have been displaced from the centre of Marxism.

The Displacement of Class Struggle and the Working Class

Class struggle is the nucleus of Marxism. This is so in two inseparable senses: it is class struggle that for Marxism explains the dynamic of history, and it is the abolition of classes, the obverse or end-product of class struggle, that is the ultimate objective of the revolutionary process. The particular importance for Marxism of the working class in capitalist society

239

is that this is the only class whose own class interests require, and whose own conditions make possible, the abolition of class itself. The inseparable unity of this view of history and this revolutionary objective is what above all distinguishes Marxism from other conceptions of social transformation, and without it there is no Marxism. These propositions may seem so obvious as to be trivial; yet it can be argued that the history of Marxism in the twentieth century has been marked by a gradual shift away from these principles. The perspectives of Marxism have increasingly come to be dominated by the *struggle for power.* Where the achievement of political power was originally conceived by Marxism as an aspect or instrument of class struggle, whose object is its own abolition, class struggle has increasingly tended to appear as a means toward the achievement of political power—and sometimes not even as a primary or essential means.

Such changes in the Marxist tradition have not been confined to movements whose clear objective has been the attainment of power by 'democratic' or electoral means. Equally important divergences have occurred in revolutionary movements which have accepted insurrectionary action as a possible, even necessary, expedient in the struggle for power. The major revolutionary movements of the twentieth century—in Russia and China—have in a sense been forced by historical circumstances to place the struggle for power above all else, and even to some extent to place the 'people' or 'masses' before class as the principal agents of struggle. In these cases, such developments have been determined by the immediate necessity of seizing power, of taking an opportunity that could not be rejected, and doing so without a large and well-developed working class. The principles of 'popular struggle' and the primacy of the contest for power have, however, taken root in advanced capitalist countries in very different conditions and with very different consequences. Here, the struggle for power has increasingly meant electoral contests; the working class has been large and even preponderant; and the 'people' or 'masses' have ceased to mean primarily an alliance of exploited classes, notably workers and peasants. Electoral strength has become the principal criterion of alliance, with little concern for whether the constituents of the 'popular' alliance can have as their objective the abolition of classes or even, more specifically, the abolition of capitalist exploitation and whether they possess the strategic social power to achieve these objectives. The implications have been far from revolutionary and far more conducive to displacing class struggle and the working class altogether from the centre of Marxism.

These historical developments have had profound effects on Marxist theory. It might have been possible for theory to serve as a guiding thread through the complexities of historical change and the compromises of political struggle, a means of illuminating these processes in the constant light of class struggle and its ultimate goal, analysing changes in class structure and especially the development of new formations within the working class, laying a foundation for new modalities of struggle while keeping the revolutionary objective constantly in sight. Instead, Marxist theory, when it has concerned itself with matters of practice at all, has increasingly adapted itself to the immediate demands of the contest for political power, whether in the form of revolutionary action or electoral alliance.

In the most recent major developments in Western Marxism, theory has become in many respects a theorisation of Eurocommunist strategy and especially its electoral strategy of 'popular alliances'. While the ultimate objective of Eurocommunism is still the construction of socialism, presumably a classless society without exploitation, this objective seems no longer to illuminate the whole process of revolutionary change. Instead, the process is coloured by the immediate needs of political strategy and the attainment of political power. So, for example, Marxist theory seems no longer designed to enhance working-class unity by dispelling the capitalist mystifications that stand in its way. Instead, as we shall see in our discussion of Nicos Poulantzas and Ernesto Laclau, these mystifications have in effect been incorporated into the Marxist theory of class, which is now largely devoted not to illuminating the process of class formation or the path of class struggle, but rather to establishing a ground for alliances within and between classes as they are here and now, for the purpose of attaining political power.

This reconceptualisation of the revolutionary project has served to reinforce a tendency which has come from other directions as well: the displacement of the working class from the centre of Marxist theory and practice. Whether that displacement has been determined by the exigencies of the power struggle, by despair in the face of a consistently non-revolutionary working class in the West, or simply by conservative and anti-democratic impulses, the search for revolutionary surrogates has been a hallmark of contemporary socialism. Whatever the reasons for this tendency and whether or not it is accompanied by an explicit reformulation of Marxism and its whole conception of the revolutionary process, to dislodge the working class is necessarily to redefine the socialist project, both its means and its ends.

Revolutionary socialism has traditionally placed the working class and its struggles at the heart of social transformation and the building of socialism, not simply as an act of faith but as a conclusion based upon a comprehensive analysis of social relations and power. In the first place, this conclusion is based on the historical-materialist principle which places the relations of production at the centre of social life and regards their exploitative character as the root of social and political oppression. The proposition that the working class is potentially *the* revolutionary class is not some metaphysical abstraction but an extension of these materialist principles, suggesting that, given the centrality of production and exploitation in human social life, and given the particular nature of production and exploitation in capitalist society, certain other propositions follow: 1) the working class is the social group with the most direct objective interest in bringing about the transition to socialism; 2) the working class, as the direct object of the most fundamental and determinative—though certainly not the only—form of oppression, and the one class whose interests do not rest on the oppression of other classes, can create the conditions for liberating all human beings in the struggle to liberate itself; 3) given the fundamental and ultimately unresolvable opposition between exploiting and exploited classes which lies at the heart of the structure of oppression, *class struggle* must be the principal motor of this emancipatory transformation; and 4) the working class is the one social force that has a strategic social power sufficient to permit its development into a revolutionary force. Underlying this analysis is an emancipatory vision which looks forward to the *disalienation of power* at every level of human endeavour, from the creative power of labour to the political power of the state.

To displace the working class from its position in the struggle for socialism is either to make a gross strategic error or to challenge this analysis of social relations and power, and at least implicitly to redefine the nature of the liberation which socialism offers. It is significant, however, that the traditional view of the working class as the primary agent of revolution has never been effectively challenged by an alternative analysis of social power and interest in capitalist society. This is, of course, not to deny that many people have questioned the revolutionary potential of the working class and offered other revolutionary agents in its place: students, women, practitioners of various alternative 'life styles', and popular alliances of one kind or another. The point is simply that none of these alternatives has been supported by a systematic reassessment of the social forces that constitute capitalism and its critical strategic targets. The typical mode of these alternative visions is voluntaristic utopia or counsel of despair—or, as is often the case, both at once: a vision of a transformed society without real hope for a process of transformation.

The most recent, and perhaps the single most systematic, attack on the traditional Marxist view of the working class is symptomatic and worth a brief consideration to illustrate the strategic bankruptcy of these alternative visions to date. André Gorz's *Farewell to the Working Class* is both utopian vision and counsel of despair. Gorz proceeds from the premise that, since the future of society must lie in the abolition of work, it must be the objective of the socialist project to determine the particular form in which work will be abolished—whether, for example, as the degradation of mass unemployment or as an emancipatory 'liberation of time'. The goal he proposes is the creation of a 'discontinuous social space made up of two distinct spheres':[2] the realm of necessity, constituted by the demands of necessary material production to satisfy primary needs—a sphere that can never be fully escaped—and a realm of freedom outside the constraints of necessary social production, a sphere of autonomy which must be enlarged and to which the necessarily 'heteronomous' sphere of material production must be subordinated. The working class cannot by its very nature be the agent of this transformation because the abolition of work cannot be its objective. A class 'called into being' by capitalism,[3] the working class identifies itself with its work and with the productivist logic of capital. It is itself a *replica* of capital, a class 'whose interests, capacities and skills are functional to the existing productive forces, which are functional solely to the rationality of capital'. It is also a class whose power has been broken by the form and structure of the labour-process itself. The transformative impulse must, therefore, come from a 'non-class of non-workers' not 'marked by the insignia of capitalist relations of production',[4] made up of people who, because they experience work as 'an externally imposed obligation' in which life is wasted, are capable of having as their goal 'the abolition of workers and work rather than their appropriation'.[5] This group includes all those whom the system has rendered actually or potentially unemployed or underemployed, all the 'supernumeraries' of contemporary social production.

Countless questions can and certainly will be raised about Gorz's analysis of the labour-process in contemporary capitalism and its effects on the working class. One critical point stands out: his whole argument is based on a kind of inverted technologism, a fetishism of the *labour-process,* and a tendency to find the essence of a mode of production in the technical process of work rather than in the relations of production, the specific mode of *exploitation.* (This, as we shall see, is something that he shares with post-Althusserian theorists like Poulantzas. In both cases, the tendency to define *class* less in terms of exploitative relations than in terms of the technical process of work may help to account for a very restrictive conception of the 'working class', which appears to include only industrial manual workers.) This tendency also affects his perception of the working class and its revolutionary potential, since in his account the experience of exploitation, of antagonistic relations of production, and of the struggles surrounding them—i.e. the experience of class and class struggle—play little part in the formation of working-class consciousness, which seems to be entirely shaped and absorbed by the technical process of work. Gorz is undoubtedly pointing to important changes in the structure of the working class which must be seriously confronted, but, in the end his is a metaphysical, not an historical or sociological, definition of the working class and its limitations, which has little to do with its interests, experiences, and struggles as an exploited class.

Questions could also be raised about his utopian vision itself. What is important from our point of view, however, is not simply this or that objectionable characteristic of Gorz's utopia, but the very fact that it *is* a utopia without grounding in a process of transformation—indeed, a vision ultimately grounded in despair. (It is no accident that Gorz's account of the utopia begins with citizens waking up one morning and finding their world already transformed.) In the final analysis, Gorz offers no revolutionary agent to replace the working class. It turns out that the 'non-class of non-workers', this new revolutionary lumpen-proletariat which apparently 'prefigures' a new society, holds that promise only in principle, notionally, perhaps metaphysically; it has, by his own testimony, no strategic social power and no possibility of action. In the end, we are left with little more than the shop-worn vision of the 'counter-culture', bearing witness against the 'system' in an enclave of the capitalist wilderness. This is revolution by example as proposed in various forms from the fatuous 'socialism' of John Stuart Mill to the pipe-dreams (joint-dreams?) of bourgeois flower-children growing pot in communal window-boxes (while Papa-le-bourgeois sends occasional remittances from home).

Even if the objective of the Left were to be perceived as the abolition of work—and not as the abolition of classes and exploitation—it would be the destruction of capitalism and capitalist exploitation, and their replacement by socialism, that would determine the form in which the abolition of work would take place. What is significant about Gorz's argument is that, like other alternative visions, his rejection of the working class as the agent of transformation depends upon wishing away the *need* for transformation, the need to destroy capitalism. It is a monumental act of wishful (or hopeless?) thinking, a giant leap over and beyond the barrier of capitalism, bypassing the structure of power and interest that stands in the way of his utopia. We have yet to be offered a consistent and plausible alternative to the working class as a means of shifting that barrier. Even for Gorz the question is not, in the final analysis: who else will make the revolution? He is effectively telling us: if not the working class then no one. The question then is whether the failure of the working class so far to bring about a revolutionary transformation is final, insurmountable, and inherent in its very nature. His own grounds for despair—based as they are on an almost metaphysical technologism which denies the working class its experiences, interests, and struggles as an exploited class—are simply not convincing. Much the same can be said about other proposals for revolutionary surrogates, including those implicit in the Eurocommunist doctrine of popular alliances.

The Theoretical Requirements of Eurocommunism

The single most influential school of Western Marxism in recent years has been a theoretical current that derives its principle inspiration from Louis Althusser. The innovations of Althusser himself have been located by Perry Anderson in the general tendency of Western Marxism toward the 'rupture of political unity between Marxist theory and mass practice' occasioned by both 'the deficit of mass revolutionary practice in the West' and the repressions of Stalinism.[6] Hence the 'obsessive methodologism' that Althusser shared with other Western Marxists as questions of theoretical form displaced issues of political substance; hence the pre-occupation with bourgeois culture and the 'retroactive assimilation' into Marxism of pre-Marxist philosophy, notably in its idealist forms, (in Althusser's case, especially the philosophy of Spinoza)[7] as 'bourgeois thought regained a relative vitality and superiority'[8] in the face of a retreating socialism in the West; hence, too, Althusser's linguistic obscurity. Althusser's theoretical academicism has existed in uneasy tandem with his active political involvement in the PCF, and the precise connection between his theory has been a matter of hot dispute. There is in any case a certain incoherence in attempts to combine political practice, especially revolutionary practice, with a theory that acknowledges no *subjects* in history. The theoretical work of Althusser's pupils and successors has been no less prone to scholastic abstractionism, 'obsessive methodologism', philosophical idealism, and obscurity of language; but their development has been much more clearly and concretely tied to the political move-ments of the West in the sixties and seventies and specifically to the shifting programmes of Eurocommunism. Whatever the motivations of Althusser himself, the theoretical products of post-Althusserian Marxism have answered directly, albeit often critically, to the demands of Euro-communist strategy.

Eurocommunists insist that their objective, unlike that of social demo-cracy, is not merely to manage capitalism but to transform it and to establish socialism. Their strategy for achieving that objective is, essential-ly, to use and extend bourgeois-democratic forms, to build socialism by constitutional means within the legal and political framework of bourgeois democracy. Eurocommunist theoreticians generally reject strategies of 'dual power' which, they argue, treat the bourgeois democratic state as if it were impenetrable to popular struggles and vulnerable only to attack and destruction from without, from an oppositional base in alternative political institutions. Eurocommunist parties, therefore, offer themselves both as 'parties of struggle' and as 'parties of government' which, by achieving electoral victories, can penetrate the bourgeois-democratic state, transform it, and implant the conditions for socialism. This strategy is based on the conviction that, in the 'monopoly phase' of capitalism, a new opposition has emerged alongside—and even overtaking—the old class opposition between exploiters and exploited, capital and labour. In 'state monopoly capitalism', there is a new opposition between monopolistic forces, united and organised by the state, and the 'people' or 'popular masses'. An absolutely crucial, indeed the central, principle of Eurocommunist strategy is the 'popular alliance', a cross-class alliance based on the assumption that a substantial majority of the population including the petty bourgeoisie and even elements of the bourgeoisie, not just the traditional working class, can be won over to the cause of socialism. It is precisely this new reality that makes possible a 'peaceful and democratic' transition to socialism. Communist parties, therefore, cannot be *working class* parties in any 'sectarian' sense; they cannot even merely open themselves to alliances with, or concessions to, other parties or groups. They must themselves directly represent the multiple interests of the 'people'.

The general strategy of Eurocommunism, then, seems at least implicitly to be built upon a conflict other than the direct opposition between capital and labour and a moving force other than class struggle. Its first object is to rally the 'popular' forces against 'state monopoly capitalism', to create the broadest possible mass alliance, and then to establish an 'advanced democracy' on the basis of this popular alliance, from which base some kind of socialism can be gradually constructed. The force that drives the movement forward is not the tension between capital and labour; in fact, the strategy appears to proceed from the necessity—and the possibility—of avoiding a confrontation between capital and labour. Insofar as the strategy is aimed at anti-capitalist goals, it cannot simply be guided by the interests of those who are directly exploited by capital but must take its direction from the varied and often contradictory ways in which different elements of the alliance are opposed to monopoly capitalism. It can be argued, then, that the movement need not, indeed cannot, in the first instance be motivated by specifically socialist objectives.

The doctrine of cross-class alliance proposed by Eurocommunism is, therefore, something more than simply an electoral strategy. It embodies a particular judgment about the source of the impulse for historical transformation. There are two ways of looking at the extension to other classes of the historic role formerly assigned to the working class. One is to stress the optimism of Eurocommunism concerning the revolutionary potential of the 'people'. The other is to stress their pessimism concerning the revolutionary potential of the working class. There can be little doubt that, however optimistic its claims, Eurocommunist strategy is ultimately grounded in the same historical reality that has so profoundly shaped Western Marxist theory and practice in general: the disinclination of the working class for revolutionary politics. It must be added that the Eurocommunist solution has been deeply affected by the experience of the Popular Front. It is even possible that there is more in this political strategy than simply pessimism about the working class. For example, the strategy for transforming the capitalist state by a simple extension of the bourgeois democratic forms, by the proliferation of representative institutions as against a system of direct council democracy, may reflect a more profound lack of interest in, or suspicion of, popular power.[9] At any rate, though the recoil of the working class from revolutionary politics is a reality which any socialist strategy must confront, there are different ways of confronting it (about which more later); and the Eurocommunist choice is a very specific one which tells a great deal about the nature of the movement. However the doctrine of popular alliances is conceived and explained, the effect is the same: it displaces the working class from its privileged role as the agent of revolutionary change and diminishes the function of class struggle as the principal motor of social transformation.

Here is the crux of Eurocommunism. We cannot get to the heart of the matter simply by equating Eurocommunism with social democracy. It is unhelpful merely to dismiss the professions of Eurocommunists that their objective is to transform, not to manage, capitalism. To do this is to avoid the real challenge of Eurocommunism. Nor can the issue be reduced simply to the choice of *means*—revolutionary insurrection versus constitutionalism, electoral politics, and the extension of bourgeois-democratic institutions. The critical question concerns the source and agency of revolutionary change. It is this question that, finally, determines not only the means of socialist strategy but also its ends; for to locate the impulse of socialist transformation is, as we have seen, also and at the same time to define the character and limits of socialism itself and its promise of human emancipation.

No socialist organisation can afford to neglect the implications of the working class recoil from revolutionary politics. Nor should socialists deny the necessity of establishing broader alliances in various political and social struggles. It is, however, quite another matter to suggest that other groups or combinations of groups, even 'popular alliances' in which the working class is 'hegemonic', can assume the historic revolutionary role formerly assigned to the working class. To do so may be to redefine the socialist project altogether, to limit its objectives, and to circumscribe socialism itself. To put it simply, however disadvantaged the petty bourgeoisie or 'small' and 'medium' capital may be in the conditions of 'state monopoly capitalism', their self-emancipation cannot be the same, in its means or in its ends, as the self-emancipation of the working class. A socialism that addresses itself to the kinds of oppression they all share, whatever else it may be, is a very different thing from the socialism whose immediate and essential impulse comes from the exploitation of one class by another.

There may or may not be a different emancipatory vision at the heart of this modified socialist project, but it certainly entails a different assessment of social relations and power. The strategic judgments of Eurocommunism have required more than just an evaluation of the political forces in the field at a particular historical 'conjuncture'. They have demanded a more thorough-going reassessment of capitalism, its dominant social relations and its structure of power. Such a reassessment has been provided not only by party strategists but by academic theoreticians; and

in the process, there has occurred an even more fundamental reformulation of Marxist theoretical principles. In the final analysis, the doctrine of
cross-class alliances and the political strategy of Eurocommunism have, it
can be argued, demanded nothing less than a redefinition of *class* itself and
of the whole conceptual apparatus on which the traditional Marxist
theory of class and class struggle has rested, a redefinition of historical
agency, a displacement of production relations and exploitation from the
core of social structure and process, and much else besides.

The Journey to Eurocommunism: A Case Study

The case of Nicos Poulantzas best exemplifies the new union of Marxist
theory with Eurocommunist practice. Poulantzas deserves special attention
not only because he is perhaps the most important theorist of the post-
Althusserian tradition, the one who has done most to ground that tradition, with its philosophical preoccupations, more firmly in the immediate
political problems of contemporary socialism, but also because he has
made a major contribution to directing Marxists generally to long neglected theoretical problems. The extent of his influence on the present generation of Marxist political theorists, which is the more impressive for the
tragic brevity of his career, would be reason enough for singling him out as
an exemplary case. But he is exemplary also in a more general, historical
sense. The course of his political and theoretical evolution traces the
trajectory of a major trend in the European Left, reflecting the political
odyssey of a whole generation.

    When Poulantzas wrote his first major theoretical work, *Political
Power and Social Classes,* published—significantly—in 1968, like many
others he was seeking a ground for socialist politics that was neither
Stalinist nor Social Democratic. There was then, on the eve of the Eurocommunist era, no obvious alternative in Europe. Poulantzas' theoretical
exploration of the political ground was still abstractly critical, negative,
chipping away at the theoretical foundations of the main available options
without a clear positive commitment to any party line. Like many of his
contemporaries, however, he seems to have leaned towards the ultra-left,
more or less Maoist, option. At least, his theoretical apparatus, deeply
indebted to Althusser whose own Maoist sympathies were then quite
explicit, bears significant traces of that commitment. The attack on
'economism', which is the hallmark of Poulantzas' work and the basis of
his stress on the specificity and autonomy of the political, was essential
to Maoism and constituted one of its chief attractions for people like
Althusser. The concept of 'cultural revolution' also held a strong fascina-
tion for Poulantzas, as for the many others who claimed it as the operative
principle of 'revolutions' like that of May '68. Whatever this concept
meant to the Chinese, it was adopted by students and intellectuals in the
West to cover revolutionary movements without specific points of concen-

tration or focused political targets, characterised instead by a diffusion of struggle throughout the social 'system' and all its instruments of ideological and cultural integration. The theoretical implications of this conception are suggested by Poulantzas himself, for example, in his debate with Ralph Miliband. In this exchange, Poulantzas adopted the Althusserian notion of 'ideological state apparatuses', according to which various ideological institutions within civil society which function to maintain the hegemony of the dominant class—such as the Church, schools, even trade-unions—are treated as belonging to the system of the state.[10] He went on to suggest a connection between the idea of 'cultural revolution' and the strategic necessity of 'breaking' these ideological apparatuses. It is not difficult to see why advocates of 'cultural revolution' might be attracted to the notion of conceiving these 'apparatuses' as part of the state and thus theoretically legitimising the shift to 'cultural' and ideological revolt and the diffusion of struggle. Indeed, the centrality of *ideology* in post-Althusserian politics and theory, whatever modifications it has since undergone, may be rooted in a conception of social transformation as 'cultural revolution'—if not in its original Chinese form, at least in the specifically Western idiom of May '68. There is also in the earlier Poulantzas, as in many of his contemporaries, much that is reminiscent (as Miliband pointed out in the debate with Poulantzas) of the 'ultra-left deviation' according to which there is little difference among various forms of capitalist state, whether fascist or liberal-democratic, and bourgeois-democratic forms are little more than sham and mystification. Strong traces of this view can be found, for example, in Poulantzas' conception of Bonapartism as an essential characteristic of *all* capitalist states.

Many of these notions were abandoned or modified by Poulantzas in the course of debate and in his later work. As his earlier political stance, with its ultra-left and Maoist admixtures, gave way to Eurocommunism, he moved away from his earlier views on Bonapartism, 'ideological state apparatuses', and so on. Most notably, his theory of the state as well as his explicit political pronouncements shifted from an apparent depreciation of liberal democratic forms toward an albeit cautious acceptance—especially in his last book, *State, Power, Socialism*—of the Eurocommunist view of the transition to socialism as the extension of existing bourgeois democratic forms. From 'smashing' the state, he moved to 'transforming' it. From the unstructured voluntarism of the '68 'cultural revolution', he moved to the highly structured organisation of Communist Party politics.

The shifts, both political and theoretical are substantial; but there is nevertheless a continuity, a unity of underlying premises, that says a great deal not only about Poulantzas himself but about the logic running through the evolution of the European Left, or an important segment of it, since the 1960s. On the one hand, Poulantzas' work is informed by a consistent anti-statism and a forthright assault on the deformations of Stalinism, as well as on the statism of Social Democracy. On the other hand, there is a characteristic ambiguity in his own conception of democratic socialism and the means by which it is to be achieved, an ambiguity that persists throughout the journey from 'Maoism' to Eurocommunism and tends toward the displacement of class struggle and the working class.

To understand the logic of that journey and the ambiguous conception of democracy and popular struggle that informs it, something more needs to be said about the attractions which the Maoist doctrines of 'cultural revolution', the 'mass line', and anti-economism have held for many people, especially students and intellectuals, in the European Left, something that explains the unlikely transposition of these doctrines from China to be very different conditions of Western Europe. Faced with the 'backwardness' of the Chinese people and an undeveloped working class, the CPC asserted the possibility of 'great leaps forward' in the absence of appropriate revolutionary conditions—i.e. *class* conditions—by dissociating revolution from *class* struggle in various ways. Not only did the *masses*—a more or less undifferentiated mass of workers and peasants—replace *class* as the transformative force, but the rejection of 'economism' meant specifically that the material conditions of production relations and class could be regarded as less significant in determining the possibilities of revolution. It became possible to conceive of political action and ideology as largely autonomous from material relations and class, and to shift the terrain of revolution to largely autonomous political and cultural struggles. The later Cultural Revolution was the ultimate expression of this view, and of the extreme voluntarism which necessarily followed from this autonomisation of political action and ideological struggle.

This conception of revolution inevitably entailed an ambiguous relation to the masses and to democracy. On the one hand, there was an insistence upon the necessity of massive popular involvement; on the other hand, the Maoist revolution was necessarily a revolution conducted by party cadres for whom popular involvement meant not popular democratic organisation but rather 'keeping in touch' with the masses and constructing the 'mass line' out of the 'raw material' of ideas and opinions emanating from them. The revolution was no longer conceived as emerging directly out of the struggles of a class guided and unified by its own class interests. Instead of a class with an identity, interests, and struggles of its own, the popular base of the revolution was a more or less shapeless mass (What identity do the 'people' or the 'masses' have? What would be the content of a revolution made by them 'in their own name'?) to be harnessed by the party and deriving its unity, its direction, and its very identity from autonomous party cadres.

The transportation of these principles to the advanced capitalist countries of the West, to be adopted especially by students and intellectuals, was clearly no easy matter and required significant modifications—given the existence of well-developed and large working classes with long histories of struggle, not to mention the less than ideal conditions of intellectuals in China itself. Nevertheless, it is not difficult to see the attractions exercised by this view of revolution, with its delicately ambiguous synthesis of democratic and anti-democratic elements. On the one hand, Maoist doctrine, with its insistence on keeping in touch with the masses, its attack on bureaucratic ossification, its mass line, and its Cultural Revolution seemed to satisfy the deepest anti-statist and democratic impulses. On the other hand, (whatever its actual implications in China) it could be interpreted as doing so without relegating declassed intellectuals to the periphery of the revolution. The dissociation of revolution from class struggle, the autonomisation of ideological and cultural struggles, could be interpreted as an invitation to them to act as the revolutionary consciousness of the people, to put themselves in the place of intrinsic class impulses and interests as the guiding light of popular struggles. After all, if there is any kind of revolution that intellectuals can lead, surely it must be a 'cultural' one.

Maoism, never more than a marginal and incoherent phenomenon in the context of advanced capitalism, could not long survive transportation; but the themes of cultural revolution, the autonomy of political and especially ideological struggles, and in particular the displacement of struggle from *class* to *popular masses* did survive in forms more appropriate to a Western setting. At least, some of those who had been attracted to Maoism for its adherence to these doctrines seem to have found in Eurocommunism a reasonable substitute: an alternative to Stalinism which promised both democracy or popular involvement and a special place for elite party cadres and declassed intellectuals. In particular, here, too, *class* was increasingly displaced by the more flexible 'popular masses'—though, of course, in a very different form. And here, too, political and ideological struggles were rendered more or less autonomous from material relations and class. Direct Maoist influences need not, of course, be invoked to explain Eurocommunist doctrine. European Communism has traditions of its own on which to draw—the legacy of the Popular Front with its cross-class alliances, suitably modified versions of Gramsci's theory of hegemony with its stress on ideological and cultural domination, etc. But for one important segment of the European Left, the transition from 'Maoism' (in its Western variant) to Eurocommunism had a certain comfortable logic. It is therefore not surprising to find certain continuous themes figuring prominently in the academic theoretical systems that have grown up side by side with Eurocommunism. Poulantzas, who wrote from the standpoint of *left* Eurocommunism, had a stronger commitment to the democratic side of the ambiguous synthesis than did many others; and he did not, therefore, go nearly as far as, say, Ernesto Laclau has done in dislodging class and class struggle from the centre of Marxism or detaching politics and ideology from class. Nevertheless, his theoreitcal system is, as we shall see, deeply coloured by these themes.

Poulantzas on the State
Two aspects of Eurocommunist doctrine have figured most prominently in post-Althusserian theory: the conception of the transition to socialism as an extention of bourgeois-democratic forms and, more fundamentally, the doctrine of the cross-class 'popular' alliance. Accordingly, the chief theoretical innovations of this Marxism have occurred in the theory of the *state* and the theory of *class*, in which the question of *ideology* has assumed an increasingly pivotal role. The most important contributions have been Nicos Poulantzas' theory of the state, his theory of class in general and of the 'new petty bourgeoisie' in particular, and Ernesto Laclau's theory of ideology.

Poulantzas' theory of the state, for all its scholasticism, was from the beginning motivated by strategic considerations and the need to provide a theoretical base from which 'scientifically' to criticise some political programmes and support others. In his first major work on the state, *Political Power and Social Classes,* Poulantzas constructed an elaborate theoretical argument largely to demonstrate and explicate two principal characteristics of the capitalist state: the unitary character of its institutionalised power, and its 'relative autonomy' *vis-à-vis* the dominant classes. Paradoxically, argued Poulantzas, the dominant classes in capitalism do not derive their 'unambiguous and exclusive' political power from actual participation in or possession of 'parcels' of institutionalised state power, but rather from the 'relative autonomy' which permits the state to provide them with the political unity they otherwise lack.[11]

The question underlying these theoretical arguments is fundamentally a strategic one: 'Can the state have such an autonomy *vis-à-vis* the dominant classes that it can accomplish the passage to socialism without the state apparatus being broken by conquest of a class power?'[12] Poulantzas' answer is aimed at specific targets. He attacks 'instrumentalist' arguments which treat the state as a mere tool of the dominant classes. He also rejects the other side of the 'instrumentalist' coin, the view that the instrument can easily change hands and that, as an inert and neutral tool, it can be wielded as easily in the interests of socialism as it was formerly wielded in the interests of capital.[13] In short, Poulantzas is explicitly attacking not only the conventions of Stalinist political doctrine but also the theoretical foundations of 'reformism' and the political strategy of social democracy. This strategy in effect shares the bourgeois pluralist view that the state can belong to various countervailing interests, and proceeds from there to the conviction that, once representatives of the working class predominate, revolution can be achieved 'from above', quietly and gradually with no transformation of the state itself. Indeed, to social democrats, today's state monopoly capitalism may appear as already a transitional phase between capitalism and socialism. Political and juridical forms, which are in advance of the economy, will simply pull the latter behind them, allowing a piece-meal transition to socialism without class struggle.

Poulantzas' theory of the state means that the reformist strategy is mistaken in its very premises. The question then is what political strategy would be appropriate to the realities of the contemporary capitalist state, its 'relative autonomy' *and* its 'profound relations' with the 'hegemonic fraction' of monopoly capital?   Poulantzas does not explicitly outline his strategic proposals until his later work, and then there appear at first to be certain similarities to the reformist programme he has attacked.[14] He too accepts that the state is open to penetration by popular forces and that there is no need for a strategy of 'dual power' which is based on the assumption that the state is a 'monolithic bloc without cracks of any kind'.[15] The state need not be attacked and destroyed from without. Since it is 'traversed' by internal contradictions—the contradictions inherent in intra- and inter-class conflicts—the state itself can be the major terrain of struggle, as popular struggles are brought to bear on the state's internal contradictions. Like the social democratic strategy, this one too seems confident that the state can lead the transition to socialism without encountering insurmountable class barriers along the way. The critical difference between the two strategies, however, is that for Poulantzas, the state cannot be simply *occupied;* it must be transformed. There must be a 'decisive shift in the relationship of forces' within the state—not simply within representative institutions through electoral victory, but within the administrative and repressive organs of the state, the civil service, the judiciary, the police and the military. This project is arguably even more optimistic than the social democratic programme about the possibilities of transforming the capitalist state into an agent of socialism with a minimal degree of class struggle; but the difference between the two strategies is a real one.

At first glance, then, Poulantzas appears to accept the orthodox Euro-communist theory of 'state monopoly capitalism', its strategy of popular alliances and the transition to socialism by the extension of democracy within the framework of the bourgeois-democratic state. Yet much of his work, especially *Classes in Contemporary Capitalism,* has been devoted to criticism of both the PCF 'anti-monopoly alliance' strategy and the theory of 'state monopoly capitalism' that underlies it. PCF doctrine, according to Poulantzas, contains several fundamental errors. It treats the relation between the state and monopoly capital as if it were a simple *fusion,* ignoring the fact that the state represents a 'power bloc' of several classes or class fractions and not the 'hegemonic' fraction of monopoly capital alone; it treats all non-monopoly interests as belonging equally to the 'popular masses', including elements of the bourgeoisie, without acknowledging the class barriers that separate the whole bourgeoisie from the truly 'popular' forces; and, in much the same way as the social democrats, it treats the state as in principle a class-neutral instrument, responding primarily to the *technical* imperatives of economic development, so that there appears to be nothing in the inherent nature of the capitalist state that prevents it from being merely *taken over* and turned to popular interests.

So Poulantzas appears to be undermining the foundations of PCF and Eurocommunist strategy. And yet, though it is certainly true that his own position is to the left of the PCF mainstream, it nevertheless represents a criticism from within, proceeding from basic principles held in common—notably, the transfer of revolutionary agency to the 'people' or 'popular alliances', the transition to socialism via 'transformation' of the bourgeois state or 'advanced democracy', and hence the displacement of class struggle. In the final analysis, Poulantzas' theory is intended not to undermine Eurocommunist strategy but to set it on a sounder foundation. He does not fundamentally reject the notion of 'state monopoly capitalism' but rather *rescues* it. He reformulates the idea to correct its own contradictions, taking account of the incontrovertible fact that the state represents interests other than those of the hegemonic monopoly fraction. This has the added advantage of making it clear why and how the state is vulnerable to penetration by popular struggles, as Eurocommunist strategy requires. More fundamentally, though Poulantzas questions the unconditional inclusion of non-monopoly capital in the 'people', he retains the conception of 'popular alliance' and the focus of struggle on the political opposition between 'power bloc' and 'people' instead of the direct class antagonism between capital and labour. Poulantzas' 'left Eurocommunism' certainly diverges in significant respects from its parent-doctrine, but the shared premises are more fundamental than the divergences and have substantial consequences for Marxist theory.

Here we come to the crux of the matter and Poulantzas' contribution to the displacement of class struggle. The critical transformation in Marxist theory and practice, the pivot on which Eurocommunist strategy turns, is a displacement of the principal opposition from the class relations between labour and capital to the political relations between the 'people' and a dominant force or power bloc organised by the state. This critical shift requires a number of preparatory moves. Both *state* and *class* must be relocated in the struggle for socialism, and this requires a redefinition of both state and class. If the opposition between people, or popular alliance, and power bloc *cum* state is to become the dominant one, it is not enough simply to show how the state reflects, maintains, or reproduces the exploitative relation between capital and labour. It must be shown

how the political conflict between two political organisations—the power
bloc organised by the state and the popular alliance which organises the
people—can effectively *displace* the class conflict between capital and
labour.

Poulantzas accomplishes this by ascribing a special and predominant
role to the political sphere and the state in state monopoly capitalism:
'. . . monopoly capitalism is characterised by the displacement of dominance within the capitalist mode of production from the economic to the
political, i.e. to the state, while the competitive stage is marked by the fact
that the economic played the dominant role in addition to being determinant.'[16] In other words, despite the separation of the economic and the
political which is uniquely characteristic of capitalism and which survives
in the monopoly phase, because of the expansion of the domain of state
intervention the political sphere acquires a position analogous to the
'dominance' of the political sphere in pre-capitalist modes of production.
Poulantzas even draws an analogy between state monopoly capitalism and
the 'Asiatic mode of production' in this respect.[17]

This analogy and Poulantzas' conception of the 'dominance' of the
political in state monopoly capitalism reveals a great deal about his point
of view. His argument is based on the Althusserian principle that, while
the economic always 'determines in the last instance', other 'instances'
of the social structure may occupy a 'determinant' or 'dominant' place.
In fact, the economic 'determines' simply by determining which instance
will be determinant or dominant. This is at best an awkward and problematic idea (the merits of which I do not propose to debate here); but it
makes some kind of sense insofar as it is intended to convey that in some
modes of production—indeed typically, in pre-capitalist societies—the
relations of production and exploitation may themselves be organised in
'extra-economic' ways. So, for example, in feudalism surplus-extraction
occurs by extra-economic means since the exploitative powers of the lord
are inextricably bound up with his political powers, his possession of a
'parcel' of the state. Similarly, in the 'Asiatic mode of production' the
'political' may be said to be dominant, not in the sense that political
relations take precedence over relations of exploitation, but rather in the
sense that exploitative relations themselves assume a political form to the
extent that the state itself is the principal direct appropriator of surplus
labour. It is precisely this fusion of 'political' and 'economic' that distinguishes these cases from capitalism where exploitation, based on the
complete expropriation of direct producers and not on their juridical
or political dependence or subjection, takes a purely 'economic' form.
This is more or less the sense in which Althusser and Balibar elaborate
the principle of 'determination in the last instance'. In Poulantzas' hands,
however, the idea undergoes a subtle but highly significant transformation.[18]

In the original formula, the relations of exploitation are always central, though they may take 'extra-economic' forms. In Poulantzas' formulation, relations of exploitation cease to be decisive. For him, relations of exploitation belong to the *economic* sphere; and the 'economic' in pre-capitalist societies, and apparently also in monopoly capitalism, may be subordinated to a separate political sphere, with its own distinct structure of domination. It would, of course, be perfectly reasonable for Poulantzas to point out that the role and the centrality of the 'political' vary according to whether it plays a direct or indirect role in surplus extraction and whether it is differentiated from the 'economic'. It would also be reasonable to suggest that the expansion of the state's role in contemporary capitalism is likely to make it increasingly a target of class struggle. But Poulantzas goes considerably beyond these propositions. He suggests not only that the nature of exploitative relations can vary in different modes of production according to whether they assume 'economic' or 'extra-economic' forms, but also that modes of production—or even phases of modes of production—may vary according to whether the relations of exploitation are themselves 'dominant' at all. When he argues, therefore, that the 'political' and not the 'economic' is 'dominant' in monopoly capitalism, he is in effect arguing that the *relations of exploitation* (though no doubt 'determinant in the last instance') no longer 'reign supreme'.

What all this amounts to is the displacement of exploitative relations to a secondary role, which is a radical departure from Marxist theory (and practice); but it is arguably essential to the Eurocommunist doctrine of state monopoly capitalism and popular alliances. As we shall see, a similar displacement is carried out in Poulantzas' theory of class. The immediate effect is to transform class struggle into—or rather, replace it with—a political confrontation between the power bloc organised by the state, and the popular alliance. One might say that class struggle remains only as a 'structural' flaw, a 'contradiction', rather than an active practice. As Poulantzas points out, the state, together with bourgeois political parties, plays the same organising and unifying role for the power bloc as a 'working class' party plays for the popular masses.[19] Thus, the chief antagonists are no longer classes engaged in class struggle but pluralistic political organisations engaged in party-political contests.

Poulantzas on Class
This new theory of the state in contemporary capitalism goes a long way toward establishing a theoretical foundation for Eurocommunist strategy, but even more important to the doctrine of 'popular alliances' is a comparable transformation in the concept of *class*. If *class* and *class struggle* are to be made compatible with a strategy that displaces the opposition between capital and labour from its pivotal role, it is necessary to re-define class itself in such a way that the relations of exploitation cease to

be 'dominant' in the determination of class. Poulantzas achieves this re-formulation, and in the process succeeds by definition in reducing the *working class* to such minute proportions that any strategy *not* based on 'popular alliances' appears recklessly irresponsible.

The most important element in Poulantzas' theory of class is his discussion of the 'new petty bourgeoisie'. The question of the petty bourgeoisie, as Poulantzas points out, 'stands at the centre of current debates' on class structure and is of critical strategic importance.[20] It is certainly the issue that most concerns Eurocommunist strategists. Considerable debate has surrounded not only the class situation of 'traditional' petty bourgeois traders, shopkeepers, craftsmen, but most particularly the 'new middle classes' or 'intermediate strata', wage-earning commercial and bank employees, office and service workers, certain professional groups—that is, 'white collar' or 'tertiary sector' workers. These two 'petty bourgeoisies' are the main constituents of the popular alliance with the working class, those which together with the working class constitute the 'people' or 'popular masses'. To locate them correctly in the class structure of contemporary capitalism has been a major pre-occupation of Eurocommunist strategists and theoreticians. Poulantzas stresses the strategic importance of the theoretical debate, the necessity of accurately identifying the class position of these groups 'in order to establish a correct basis for the popular alliance. . .'[21]

Poulantzas begins by attacking two general approaches to the question of these 'new wage-earning groups', lumping together some very disparate arguments in each of the two categories. The first approach is that which dissolves these groups into either the proletariat or the bourgeoisie, or both. The second general 'tendency' is what Poulantzas calls 'the theory of the middle class', a politically motivated theory according to which both bourgeoisie and proletariat are being mixed together in the 'stew' of an increasingly dominant middle group, 'the region where the class struggle is dissolved'.[22] Most of these theories are intended to dilute the concepts of class and class struggle altogether. From the point of view of Marxist theory and socialist strategy, there is only one theory, among the several included in these two categories, which represents a serious challenge to Poulantzas' own: the theory which assimilates the new wage-earning groups to the working class, arguing that white collar workers have been increasingly 'proletarianised'. We shall return in a moment to Poulantzas' reasons for dismissing this approach.

Poulantzas then turns to the solution proposed by the PCF in its political strategy of the 'anti-monopoly' alliance. Like Poulantzas himself, the PCF line rejects the 'dissolution of the wage-earning groups into the working class';[23] but it denies their class-specificity altogether and allows them to remain in a classless grey area as 'intermediate strata'. Poulantzas attacks this refusal to identify the class situation of the new wage-earning 'strata'. It is, he suggests, an abdication to bourgeois stratification theory and is inconsistent with the fundamental Marxist proposition that 'the division into class forms [is] the frame of reference for every social stratification'. The principle that 'classes are the basic groups in the "historic process" ' is incompatible with 'the possibility that other groups exist parallel and external to classes. . .'[24]

It should be noted immediately that Poulantzas' criticism of the PCF line on the 'new wage-earning groups' does not strike at its roots either theoretically or practically. In fact, his argument proceeds not as a rejection of PCF principles but, again, as an attempt to supply them with a sounder theoretical foundation, albeit somewhat to the left of the main party line. A truly Marxist theorisation of popular alliances must, he argues, be based on a definition of class which allows these 'strata' their own class position instead of allowing them to stand outside class. The significant point, however, is that this class position is *not* to be found within the working class. In other words, Poulantzas is seeking a more clearly Marxist theoretical support for the Eurocommunist conception of an alliance between a *narrowly defined* working-class and non-working-class popular forces.

Why, then does Poulantzas, in common with the PCF, refuse to accept the theory which 'dissolves' these 'strata' into the working class? This theory, which he attributes primarily to C. Wright Mills, has been developed more recently in unambiguously Marxist ways by Harry Braverman and others. Poulantzas, however, apparently regards it as a departure from Marxism—for example, on the grounds that it makes the *wage* the relevant criterion of the working class, thereby making the mode of *distribution* the central determinant of class.[25] (It is perhaps significant that Poulantzas focuses on the wage as a mode of distribution and not as a mode of exploitation—as we shall see in a moment.) He argues further that by assimilating these groups to the working class, this view promotes reformist and social democratic tendencies. To identify the interests of 'intermediate strata' with those of the working class is to distort working-class interests, accommodating them to more backward, less revolutionary elements.[26] A political strategy based on the hegemony of the working class and its revolutionary interests, he maintains, demands the exclusion of these backward elements from the ranks of the working class.

On the face of it, then, Poulantzas' refusal to accept the proletarianisation of white-collar workers appears to be directed in favour of a revolutionary stance and the hegemony of the working class which alone is 'revolutionary to the end'.[27] He even criticises the PCF analysis on the grounds that, despite its refusal to accept this dissolution, it courts the same danger by neglecting to identify the specific class interests of the new wage-earning strata and hence their divergences from working-class interests. It is true that he fails to explain how these dangers will be averted by a 'working-class' party whose object is precisely to dilute its working-class character by directly representing other class interests, but let us leave aside this question for the moment. Let us pursue the implications of his own theory of the 'new petty bourgeoisie' to see whether it does, in fact, represent an attempt to keep exploitative class relations, class struggle, and the interests of the working class at the centre of Marxist class analysis and socialist practice.

For Poulantzas, the primary structural criterion for distinguishing between the working class and the new petty bourgeoisie at first seems to be the distinction between productive and unproductive labour. The 'unproductive' character of white-collar work separates these groups from the 'productive' working class. Poulantzas proceeds on the assumption that Marx himself applied this criterion and marked off the 'essential boundaries' of the working class by confining it to productive labour. Now it can be shown convincingly that Marx never intended the distinction to be used in this way.[28] In any case, Marx never said that he did so intend it, and Poulantzas never demonstrates that this is what he *meant*. He bases his argument on a misreading of Marx. He quotes Marx as saying 'Every productive worker is a wage-earner, but it does not follow that every wage-earner is a productive worker.'[29] Poulantzas takes this to mean something rather different: 'as Marx puts it,' he says, putting words into Marx's mouth, 'if every agent belonging to the working class is a wage-earner, this does not necessarily mean that every wage-earner belongs to the working class.' The two propositions are, of course, not at all the same, nor does Poulantzas *argue* that the one entails the other. He simply *assumes* it—i.e. he assumes precisely what needs to be proved, that 'agent belonging to the working class' is synonymous with 'productive worker'. He can then go on to demonstrate that various groups do not belong to the working class simply by demonstrating that they are not, according to Marx's definition (at least as he interprets that definition), productive workers.

Why this distinction—as important as it may be for other reasons— should be regarded as the basis of a *class* division is never made clear. It is not clear why this distinction should override the fact that, like the 'blue-collar' working class, these groups are completely separated from the means of production; that they are exploited (which he concedes), that they perform surplus labour whose nature is determined by capitalist relations of production—the wage-relationship in which expropriated workers are compelled to sell their labour-power; or even that the same compulsions of capital accumulation that operate in the organisation of labour for the working class—its 'rationalisation', fragmentation, discipline, etc.—operate in these cases too. Indeed, the same conditions—the compulsory sale of labour-power and an organisation of work derived from the exploitative logic of capital accumulation—apply even to workers not directly exploited by capital but employed, say, by the state or by 'non-profit' institutions. Whatever the complexities of class in contemporary capitalism—and they are many, as new formations arise and old ones change—it is difficult to see why exploitative social relations of production should now be regarded as secondary in the determination of class. Poulantzas' use of the distinction between productive and unproductive labour to separate white-collar workers from the working class seems to be largely arbitrary and circular, with no clear implications for our under-standing of how classes and class interests are actually constituted in the real world.

In fact, it soon turns out that this 'specifically economic' determination is not sufficient—or even necessary—to define the new petty bourgeoisie. It cannot account for all the groups that Poulantzas wants to include in this class. Not only, he suggests, can it not account for certain groups which *are* involved in the process of material production (e.g. engineers, technicians, and supervisory staff), it cannot explain the overriding unity which binds these heterogeneous elements into a single class set off from the working class. Now, *political* and *ideological* factors must be regarded as decisive. These factors are decisive even for those groups who are already marked off by the productive/unproductive labour distinction,[30] and in some cases even override that division. In the final analysis, once these groups have been separated out from the bourgeoisie by the fact that they are exploited, the decisive unifying factor that separates them from the working class is *ideological,* in particular the distinction between mental and manual labour. This distinction cannot be defined in 'technicist' or 'empiricist' terms, argues Poulantzas—for example, by empirically distinguishing 'dirty' and 'clean' jobs, or those who work with their hands and those who work with their brains, or those who are in direct contact with machines and those who are not. It is essentially a 'politico-ideological' division. Although this division cannot be entirely clear-cut and contains complexities which create fractions within the new petty bourgeoisie itself, it is the one determinant that both distinguishes these groups from the working class *and* overrides the various differences within the class, *including* the division between productive and un-productive labour with which it does not coincide. In other words, this *ideological* division is the decisive factor in constituting the new petty bourgeoisie as a class at all.

It is not at all clear to what reality this ideological division corresponds, or why it should override the structural similarities among workers. What *is* true is that the organisation of production in industrial capitalism establishes various divisions among workers within the labour process which are determined not by the technical demands of the labour-process itself but by its *capitalist* character. These divisions often con-stitute obstacles to the formation of a unified class—even in the case of workers who belong to the same class by virtue of their relation to capital and exploitation. But it is not clear why the divisions cited by Poulantzas should be more decisive than any others that divide workers in the labour-process or disunite them in the process of class formation and organisation. It is not clear why such divisions should be regarded *not* simply as obstacles to unity or roadblocks in the difficult process of class-formation —a process riddled with obstacles even for blue-collar workers—but rather as definitive class barriers dividing members from non-members of the working class.[31] In fact, Poulantzas' theory seems unable to accommodate any *process* of *class-formation* at all. There seems to be only a string of static, sometimes overlapping, class situations (locations? boxes?). This is a view which in itself would seem to have significant political implications.

If the ideological division between mental and manual workers within the exploited wage-earning groups does not correspond to any objective barrier directly determined by the relations of production between capital and labour, neither does it correspond to a real and insurmountable division of interest between these workers. The class interests of both groups are determined by the fact that they are directly exploited through the sale of their labour-power, these interests have to do in the first instance with the terms and conditions of that sale, and in the last with the elimination of capitalist relations of production altogether, both the 'formal' and the 'real' subjection of labour to capital. The different functions of these workers in the labour-process may create divisions among them, based in some cases on differences in their responsibilities, education, income, and so on;[32] but these differences cannot be regarded as *class* divisions by any standard having to do with relations of production and exploitation—and in any case, the organisation of production in contemporary capitalism has increasingly tended to homogenise workers in the labour-process by subjecting them to the same principles of 'rationalisation' and 'productivity'. The ideological divisions between them are constituted less from the point of view of their own class interests than from the point of view of capital, which has an interest in keeping them apart. The imposition of capitalist ideology can certainly operate to discourage unity within the working class and interfere with the processes of class formation and organisation, but it can hardly be accepted as an absolute class barrier between different kinds of workers.

Poulantzas has thus presented a class analysis in which relations of exploitation are no longer decisive. This is in keeping with the fundamental principles of his theory. The relations of production and exploitation, according to him, belong to the 'economic' sphere which, as we have seen, though it 'determines in the last instance' may not be *dominant* in any given mode of production or social formation. This notion is carried over into the analysis of class. It now becomes clear that there are cases in which political or ideological factors 'reign supreme' in determining class.[33] Poulantzas is saying more than simply that the formation of classes is always a political, ideological, and cultural process as well as an economic one, or that relations between classes are not only economic but also political and ideological. Nor, again, is he simply pointing to the special role of the 'political' where relations of production are themselves 'politically' organised. He is suggesting that ideological and political relations may actually take precedence over the relations of exploitation in the 'objective' constitution of classes, and that political or ideological divisions may represent essential class barriers. Again the relations of exploitation have been displaced.[34]

What, then, are the practical consequences of Poulantzas' views on class? Why is it a matter of such critical importance whether or not white collar workers are theoretically included in the working class? Poulantzas himself, as we have seen, maintains that it is strategically important to separate out the 'new petty bourgeoisie' in order to protect the revolutionary integrity and hegemony of the working class. There is, however, another way of looking at it. We have seen that for Poulantzas the relations of production are not decisive in determining the class situation of white-collar workers. The 'new petty bourgeoisie' is distinguished as a class on the basis of ideological divisions defined from the point of view of capital. In other words, they constitute a class insofar as they are absorbed into the hegemonic ideology of capitalism; and that absorption seems to be definitive: the new petty bourgeoisie can be made to adopt certain working-class positions—that is, their political attitudes can 'polarise toward' the proletariat; but they cannot be made part of the working class. These propositions are very different from the observation that the inclinations of white-collar workers to accept capitalist ideology may be stronger than those of blue-collar workers; that these inclinations constitute a problem for class organisation, for the development of class consciousness, and for the building of class unity; and that they must be taken into account by any socialist strategy. For Poulantzas, it would appear that these inclinations represent a decisive class boundary; and this has significant strategic implications.

Despite Poulantzas' criticism of PCF theory and strategy, his theory of class belongs to the '. . . attempt of the theoreticians of Eurocommunism to reduce the weight of the Western proletariat to that of a minority within society. . .'[35] At a stroke of the pen, the proletariat is reduced from a comfortable majority in advanced capitalist countries to a rump group which must inevitably place class alliances at the top of its agenda. Poulantzas' very definition of class in general and the 'new petty bourgeoisie' in particular displaces the focus of socialist strategy from creating a united working class to constructing 'popular alliances' based on class differences, even based on divisions imposed by capital. Any appeal to the 'new petty bourgeoisie', for example, must be directed not to its working-class interests but to its specific interests as a petty bourgeoisie. The strategic implications become even clearer when this view of alliances is embodied in a particular view of 'working class' parties as organisations which do not simply form alliances with other groups and parties but directly *represent* other class interests. Poulantzas insists that 'the polarisation of the petty bourgeoisie towards proletarian class positions depends on the petty bourgeoisie being *represented* by the class-struggle organisations of the working class themselves. . . This means, firstly, that popular unity under the hegemony of the working class can only be based on the class difference between the classes and fractions that form part of the alliance. . .'[36] This notion turns out to be a two-edged sword. On the one hand, it suggests that the popular forces should themselves be transformed in the process of struggle. That is why, argues Poulantzas, the alliance should be established 'not by way of concessions, in the strict sense, by the working class to its allies taken as they are, but rather by the establishment of objectives which can transform these allies in the course of uninterrupted struggle and its stages, account being taken of their specific class determination and the specific polarisation that affects them'.[37] On the other hand, the very idea that alliances must not be based merely on 'concessions' to allies 'taken as they are' also entails that working-class organisations must cease to be organisations of the working class. It now appears that it is not just the integrity of working-class interests that these organisations must protect, but also that of the petty bourgeoisie. Poulantzas now seems to be criticising the PCF for taking the 'popular masses' too much for granted, instead of acknowledging the specificity of their various class interests. A 'working-class' party cannot simply make 'concessions' to elements outside itself from a vantage point consistently determined by working-class interests, it must actually *represent* other class interests—and this means establishing objectives addressed to these other class interests. This inevitably raises the question of the degree to which the ultimate objectives of socialism itself must be tailored to the measurements of cross-class alliances.

Paradoxically, if Poulantzas' approach—and that of Eurocommunism generally—places unnecessary obstacles in the way of the struggle for socialism by erecting artificial class barriers *within* the working class, the same approach tends to underplay the real difficulties of the struggle by underestimating the barriers *between* classes. Poulantzas' analysis, for example, creates a gradual continuum of classes which blurs the sharp divisions between the working class and clearly non-working-class elements of the 'popular alliance'; but even more fundamentally, the incorporation of a wide range of class interests within the popular alliance, together with the relegation of exploitative relations to a secondary position, tends even to narrow the gap between capitalist and socialist forces. This may help to account for the Eurocommunist tendency 'to understate the problems of

[the] transition'[38] and underestimate the necessity of direct class confrontation and struggle. The whole approach is compounded of a
pessimism based on the assumption that the real (potentially revolutionary) working class represents a minority, and an optimism based on the
assumption that the mass constituency for a (modified) socialist programme represents a vast majority. Both assumptions have significant
practical consequences which, taken together, circumscribe the socialist
project: optimism limits the means, pessimism curtails the ends.

Laclau on Ideology
Viewed from this Eurocommunist perspective, the chief task of the
'working-class' movement is to win the hearts and minds of the 'middle
sectors'. Since this battle must be fought on the ideological and political
terrain, the strategy of popular alliances places a particularly heavy burden
on ideological struggle and attaches a very special theoretical importance
to the question of ideology. Ernesto Laclau has clearly formulated the
theoretical demands imposed by the strategy of class alliances: 'Today,
when the European working class is increasing its influence and must
conceive its struggle more and more as a contest for the ideological and
political hegemony of middle sectors, it is more necessary than ever for
Marxism to develop a rigorous theory of ideological practice which
eliminates the last taints of class reductionism.'[39] Accordingly, Laclau
introduces important innovations into Marxist theories of ideology, with
the specific purpose of meeting these strategic needs. To lay the foundation, however, he must first tie up certain loose ends in the theories of
class presented by both Eurocommunist strategists and Poulantzas. Again
the question is where to locate the 'middle sectors'. Laclau, too, is dis-
satisfied with the standard PCF notion of 'intermediate wage-earning
strata' as fundamentally classless, but he concludes that this position may
be less mistaken than Poulantzas supposes.[40] The difficulty with
Poulantzas' position, suggests Laclau, is that by making *ideological* factors
the primary determinant of class in these cases, he effectively denies the
very basis of Marxism because he defines class apart from production
relations.[41] The problem for Laclau, then, is to acknowledge and explain
the ideological unity of these groups (which he accepts) *and* to give that
ideological unity the priority it deserves, without contradicting the fundamental premises of Marxist class analysis. In his analysis, class retains its
theoretical purity but loses its historical significance. Laclau concedes,
in contrast to Poulantzas, that the 'new petty bourgeoisie' is a fraction
of the working class; he simply goes on to argue that, whatever the objective class situation of these groups in terms of production relations, that
situation is secondary in determining their position. For them, the primary
'contradiction' with the 'dominant bloc' is not a *class* contradiction. In
their case, the important contradictions 'are posed, not at the level of the

dominant relations of production, but at the level of political and ideological relations. . .'[42] In other words, their 'identity as *the people* plays a much more important role than their identity as *class*.'[43] The fact that Poulantzas' old and new petty bourgeoisies are two different classes, and that the latter technically belongs to the working class, is overridden by the political and ideological unity which binds them together and separates them from other classes; and their location between the two principal classes allows them to 'polarise' either way. The class struggle between bourgeoisie and proletariat, then, is increasingly an ideological battle over these groups as the two contenders seek to win them over by ideological means.

This clearly represents an important innovation in the Marxist conception of class and class struggle. It should be emphasised, however, that all three attempts to revise Marxist theory to accommodate the 'middle sectors'—the PCF theory of classless intermediate wage-earning strata, Poulantzas' theory of the new petty bourgeoisie, and Laclau's displacement of class contradictions by ideological divisions—represent an in-house debate, a dispute about which theory of class is best suited to support the strategy of popular alliance and the 'power bloc versus people' opposition on which that strategy rests. All three depend in one way or another on displacing the relations of production and exploitation and the direct opposition between capital and labour from the centre of Marxist theory and practice.

Laclau then presents a theory of ideology that extends the *autonomy* of ideology by dissociating it as much as possible from class relations. To summarise his argument very briefly:[44] There are ideological 'interpellations' which are generated not by class contradictions and struggles, but by other contradictions, notably that between 'people' and 'power bloc'. The latter ideological elements, though 'articulated' with class ideologies, are in principle neutral, autonomous, not class-specific, and therefore detachable from their class associations. These become the central arena of class struggle, 'the domain of class struggles par excellence',[45] as one class struggles to detach them from the other in order to establish hegemony over the 'people'. The argument applies specifically to 'popular democratic interpellations' which have tended to be associated with the bourgeoisie. The working class can achieve hegemony by 'disarticulating' these 'interpellations' from bourgeois class interests and claiming them for itself. Laclau thus (as I argued on another occasion) 'makes class struggle appear to be in large part an "autonomous" intellectual exercise in which the "autonomous" intellectual champions of each class compete in a tug-of-war over non-class ideological elements, victory going to that class whose intellectuals can most convincingly redefine these elements to match its own particular interests'.[46]

It should be noted that Laclau goes beyond the argument that not all social conflicts are class struggles and that not all ideologies are class ideologies, even when they are implicated in class struggle. He also goes beyond the observation that a particular class ideology—such as bourgeois-democratic ideology—can achieve a certain appearance of *universality*, and that it is precisely this appearnace of universality that constitutes class *hegemony*. He is not even saying simply that such claims to universality must contain an important element of truth in order to be hegemonic. All this would be true, and would correctly characterise bourgeois democracy—which is both a *class* ideology and a plausible claimant to universality to the extent that it has captured the allegiance of other classes not simply by mystification but also by bringing them real benefits. Laclau, however, is saying something else. Instead of arguing that an ideology that is class-determined in origin and meaning may acquire an appearance of generality and thus contribute to the hegemony of its parent-class, he argues essentially the reverse: that such an ideology should be recognised as having 'no precise class connotations',[47] and that class hegemony depends upon claiming and seizing these essentially class-neutral 'interpellations'. To judge the 'democratic' aspects of bourgeois democracy in these terms, for example, is quite different from acknowledging that bourgeois-democratic forms, however 'bourgeois' they may be, cannot be dismissed as mere sham and mystification. It is, in effect, to argue instead that they are not 'bourgeois' at all. Laclau insists in a footnote that by 'democratic interpellations' he has more in mind than the ideology of liberalism and parliamentary democracy;[48] but it is clear that his argument is calculated to bridge the gap between bourgeois and socialist democracy and to conceptualise away the radical break between them. The strategic implication of this argument seems to be that socialism can be built simply by extending these essentially class-neutral democratic forms. Again we encounter no class barriers along the way. If, in contrast, we were to look upon these forms as class-specific, we could acknowledge their value and even the plausibility of their claims to a certain generality; but we should also have to acknowledge the break, the 'river of fire', between bourgeois and socialist democracy, as well as the difficulty of proceeding from one to the other. For Laclau, the appropriate strategy is not to stress the specificity of socialism, not to reclaim democracy for socialism by challenging the limits of bourgeois democracy with alternative socialist forms, and, finally, not to pursue the specific interests of the working class but to dilute them in an intermediate 'stew'. We now have a theory of ideology to accompany the theories of class and the state which are needed to underpin the strategy of popular alliance and the building of socialism by the extension of bourgeois-democratic forms, all by-passing the direct opposition between capital and labour.

Conclusion

Because for Laclau the chief task of socialist strategy is to forge a popular alliance, the chief enemy is 'class reductionism' and 'sectarianism'. Yet in the final analysis, this is a mystification. The issue is not whether socialists should remain wedded to a dogma of revolutionary purity and 'class-reductionism' which precludes alliances with other forces and dismisses bourgeois democracy as mere sham. The issue is whether the dominant parties or organisations of the Left can be anything else but essentially working-class parties or organisations. It is a mystification to pose the question as if it were a matter of alliances or no alliances, democracy or no democracy, as if the only choice were between, on the one hand, the Eurocommunist strategy of class alliances and, on the other, 'ultra-left' sectarianism which dismisses democratic ideology as simply bourgeois, perceives no difference between liberal democracy and fascism, and rejects any and all alliances. It is, in short, a mystification to transform a case against 'class-reductionism' and 'sectarianism' into an indictment of *any* working-class politics and into a conception of socialist struggle in which the chief task is to win the allegiance of the 'middle sectors'. It is possible to acknowledge the value of bourgeois democracy without reducing socialism to a mere extension of it, without ignoring its role in absorbing and containing class struggle, and without understating the obstacles it places in the way of socialism and, indeed, in the way of democracy itself.[49] It is also possible to conceive of alliances that do not dilute the specificity of socialism or curtail its objectives.

There is, in fact, a sense in which the political doctrines espoused by Laclau and his colleagues themselves converge with the undemocratic and reductionist principles of the 'sectarian' left, as described, for example, in the following sharp characterisation of the socialist sects:

> . . . sectism involves the tendency to counterpose socialism as a Good Idea to the class movement as a defective reality. . . This. . . indicates the source of the close association in socialist history between intellectuals and sectism: firstly, predilection for the primacy of ideas over material interests; and secondly, elitist fear of a mass movement which is not under the control of Superior Minds. This intellectualist fear of self-moving masses is transmuted into programmatic terms by the ultimatistic requirement that a class movement must measure up to intellectually established political standards before it can be accepted without contamination. . . To put it still another way: sectists saw socialism primarily as a *concept to convince people of*. . . Marx saw socialism as the necessary outcome of the proletariat's struggle. . .[50]

What has characterised these forms of sectarianism above all is the shift away from the interests and struggles of the working class. The linchpin of traditional Marxism has always been the *interests* of the working class—*both* their short-term material interests and their long-term revolutionary interests. The chief and most delicate problem for socialist strategy has been to serve the one without betraying the other. If working-class movements have consistently refused to adopt a revolutionary stance, a commitment to socialism and its democratic values allows no simple contempt for working-class 'economism', 'reformism', or 'false consciousness', no easy escape to an elitist vanguard which embodies the *true* consciousness of the working class and will achieve its emancipation by proxy.

Solutions of this 'ultimatistic' kind have, however, appeared in various 'Western Marxist' incarnations which go even beyond the most elitist vanguardism and substitutism—for example, in the idealism of Lukács which completely separates revolutionary class consciousness from the working-class itself and constructs a disembodied ideal consciousness. The post-Althusserian theories of Poulantzas and Laclau have introduced a new and paradoxical variant to this tendency. The essence of this approach is a replacement of class interest by ideology, either in the sense that class itself is conceived as determined by ideological factors or in the sense that class divisions based on class interests are subordinated to ideological 'contradictions' which cut across class. In either case, 'ideas' take precedence over material interests, and the working class is judged inadequate to the degree that it fails to measure up to the Idea of a true working class. In fact, certain 'backward' elements are in danger of being altogether excommunicated from the working class by definition. In effect, we are being told yet again that the ideological hegemony of capitalism is so complete—at least as it concerns a large proportion of the 'popular masses'—that it has overcome class determinations; and the impulse for revolutionary change can no longer be sought in class interests and class struggle.

It is typical of this mentality that, while it rails against the anti-revolutionary restrictions of working-class politics or trade unionism, it leaps over the heads of the working class to even more restricted forms of cross-class politics. The paradox of this view is that, in practice, to separate the socialist 'idea' from the interests and struggles of the real working class, no matter how deficient in revolutionary consciousness, is to dilute and curtail the socialist idea itself. The quantitative and qualitative inadequacies of the working class must be compensated for by alliances or substitutions which place their own demands and limits on the socialist project—and *these* limits are absolute and final. In the end, the question is a very practical one. If the socialist movement is to consist of 'popular alliances' in which a narrowly defined working-class minority, whose interests are (as Poulantzas puts it) alone 'revolutionary to the end', combines with a non-revolutionary majority, how are we to envisage the process of transition? At what point will socialists come up against the insurmountable differences between the revolutionary interests of some and the non-revolutionary interests of others? When the latter's interest in change is exhausted, will they simply be jettisoned along the way? How will capitalist opposition be overcome, especially when the unity of the 'people' has reached its limit? Or will the socialist project have to be curtailed to stop short of these obstacles? The strategy of Euro-communism never faces up to these questions. The issue is evaded by its programme for building socialism through the extension of bourgeois democratic forms. This programme seems never to encounter any real class barriers, by-passing both the oppositions between capital and labour and the barriers within the popular alliance. It is a very different matter to conceive the chief task of the socialist movement in the first instance as an effort to build a united working class by organising its disparate elements in the full recognition of their common class situation, always keeping in view the revolutionary objectives of socialism but never evading the difficulties of reaching them.

The question of how and under what circumstances a working-class movement should establish alliances remains a critical one. The socialist movement has much to gain from association with other popular move-ments and protests and much to learn from them. It has much to learn not only about the dimensions of human emancipation—here the women's movement is especially important—but even about overcoming the barriers to working-class unity itself—notably the barriers of gender and race. And of course there are many important objectives short of revolution that require alliances of one kind or another. The dangers of nuclear annihila-tion and ecological disaster have no doubt added a whole new dimension to the problem. But if at the root of these dangers there still lies the capitalist imperative which is able to impose its competitive pressures of accumulation not only on its own people but on the whole world, if that drive has transformed 'life-forms and land-forms' (as Raymond Williams has recently put it) into 'a range of opportunities for their profitable exploitation, which at certain definite technical stages becomes, on a rising scale, a form, not only of production, but of destruction and self-destruction'[51] —then it is simply an evasion to say that the terrain of struggle has irrevocably shifted, requiring new visions of social trans-formation and new agents to achieve it. The structure of power and interest that constitutes capitalism is still in the way, and the class barriers to its destruction are still there. They cannot simply be dissolved in alliances or theorised out of existence. Marxist theory must certainly develop to apprehend the changing structure of capitalism, the trans-formations in the working class, and the new divisions within it. No one, however in theory or practice, has offered a plausible and realistic substitute for class struggle and its abolition as the form and substance of the revolutionary, emancipatory process, or for the working class as its principal agent.

NOTES

1. See in particular Perry Anderson, *Considerations on Western Marxism* (London, New Left Books, 1976).
2. André Gorz, *Farewell to the Working Class: An Essay on Post-Industrial Socialism* Boston, South End Press, 1982, p. 96.
3. Ibid., p. 15.
4. Ibid., p. 68.
5. Ibid., p. 7.
6. Anderson, op. cit., p. 55.
7. Ibid., p. 64-5.
8. Ibid., p. 55.
9. Cf. Ralph Miliband, 'Constitutionalism and Revolution: Notes on Euro-communism', *Socialist Register 1978*, pp. 165-7.
10. See R. Blackburn (ed.) *Ideology in Social Science* (1972) Ch. 11.
11. Nicos Poulantzas, *Political Power and Social Classes* (London, New Left Books and Sheed and Ward, 1973), p. 288.
12. Ibid., p. 271.
13. Ibid., pp. 273, 288.
14. See in particular *State, Power, Socialism* (London, Verso, 1980), especially the last chapter.
15. Ibid., p. 254.
16. *Classes in Contemporary Capitalism* (London, New Left Books, 1975), p. 101.
17. Ibid., p. 55.
18. It is worth noting that Poulantzas finds Balibar's approach too 'economistic'. (*Classes in Contemporary Capitalism*, p. 13, n. 1.)
19. *Classes in Contemporary Capitalism*, p. 98.
20. Ibid., p. 193.
21. Ibid., p. 204.
22. Ibid., p. 197.
23. Ibid., p. 198.
24. Ibid., p. 199.
25. Ibid., p. 194.
26. Ibid., p. 204.
27. Ibid.
28. See Peter Meiksins, 'Productive and Unproductive Labour and Marx's Theory of Class', *Review of Radical Political Economics*, Vol. 13, No. 3, Fall 1981, pp. 32-42.
29. *Classes in Contemporary Capitalism*, op. cit., p. 210.
30. Ibid., p. 224.
31. For a discussion of this distinction between class divisions and obstacles to class formation as it applies, for example, to the case of engineers, see Peter Meiksins, 'Scientific Management: A Dissenting View', forthcoming in *Theory and Society*.
32. Some of these factors—e.g. education—may even be purely 'conjunctural', varying in different capitalist countries at different times. Poulantzas may, for example, be generalising from certain European cases—notably France? —in which the education of white-collar workers differs from that of blue-collar workers more markedly than is the case, say, in the United States or Canada. This would not be the first time that the historical particulars of French experience have been transformed into theoretical universals by Althusserian theory.
33. See, for example, *Political Power and Social Classes*, op. cit., p. 57.
34. It is worth adding that Poulantzas appears to have difficulty keeping his focus on relations of exploitation even in cases where the 'economic' is clearly 'domi-

nant', that is, social formations where the capitalist mode of production (in its simple or 'competitive' form) prevails. For example, in his statement of basic principles, where he defines the determining characteristics of modes of production, he suggests that *property relations* in all class societies are characterised by a separation of the producer from the means of labour. The particular separation from the means of production which uniquely characterises capitalism takes place in the labour process, in the relations of 'real appropriation'. *This* separation 'occurs at the stage of heavy industry' (*Political Power and Social Classes,* op. cit., p. 27). Poulantzas again attributes this view to Marx. For Marx, however, the critical factor is *wage-labour;* the crucial separation occurs long before the 'stage of heavy industry', not merely with the reorganisation of the labour-process in the 'real' subjection of labour to capital, but in the earlier transformation of the *expolitative relationship* in the 'formal' subjection. This is the essential boundary between capitalist relations and other modes of production, even though transformations in the labour-process have followed in its train and have had profound effects on class formation. Poulantzas has shifted the focus away from the relations of exploitation to the labour-process, which then appears as the distinctive and essential characteristic of the mode of production at the 'economic' level. This may help to account for certain peculiarities we have already noted in his analysis of white-collar workers: for example, his refusal to regard their status as wage-labourers—i.e. their exploitation through the sale of their labour-power—as decisive in determining their class, on the rather curious grounds that wages are simply a mode of distribution; and his tendency instead to accord a critical role to the position of these workers in the organisation of the labour-process and its ideological expression in the division between mental and manual labour.

35. Ernest Mandel, *From Stalinism to Eurocommunism* (London, New Left Books, 1978), p. 209.
36. *Classes in Contemporary Capitalism,* op. cit., pp. 334–5.
37. Ibid., p. 335.
38. Miliband, op. cit., p. 170.
39. Ernesto Laclau, *Politics and Ideology in Marxist Theory* (London, NLB Verso, 1979), pp. 141–2.
40. Ibid., p. 114.
41. Ibid., p. 113.
42. Ibid., p. 114.
43. Ibid.
44. I have discussed Laclau's argument in another context in 'Liberal Democracy and Capitalist Hegemony: A Reply to Leo Panitch on the Task of Socialist Political Theory', *Socialist Register 1981,* pp. 183–6.
45. Laclau, op. cit., p. 109.
46. Wood, op. cit., p. 184.
47. Laclau, op. cit., p. 111.
48. Ibid., p. 107, n. 36.
49. The ways in which the liberal democratic state can function in 'managing' class conflict have been explored by Ralph Miliband in *Capitalist Democracy in Britain* (Oxford, Oxford University Press, 1982).
50. Hal Draper, *Karl Marx's Theory of Revolution, Volume II: The Politics of Social Classes* (New York, Monthly Review Press, 1978), p. 526.
51. Raymond Williams, 'The Red and the Green', *London Review of Books,* 3–16 February, 1983, p. 3.

ANDRE GORZ AND HIS DISAPPEARING PROLETARIAT

Richard Hyman

Farewell to the Working Class: an apposite text to review in election week 1983?[1] The erosion of traditional Labour loyalties—first through the relative or even absolute decline in the staple industries and occupations in which Labourism was rooted, second through a switch from political support and identity as an inbuilt reflex to more calculative and volatile electoral behaviour—has been a topic of analysis and debate for a quarter of a century. Three successive defeats for Labour in the 1950s provoked influential assertions that the party's working-class identification had become a fatal handicap,[2] as well as pleas for a dilution of the state socialist objectives enshrined in the 1918 party constitution.[3] Though apparent electoral recovery under Wilson largely stilled such controversies, mass unemployment and the rise of Thatcherism have brought renewed attention to the political implications of the changing composition and structure of the working class.[4]

In the agonisings which will inevitably follow Labour's new disaster, what can British socialists learn from experience and analysis elsewhere? André Gorz is well known among the British Left (and even better in the United States) as a prolific essayist and polemicist. In his early years profoundly influenced by Sartre, he has been a member of the editorial committee of *Les Temps Modernes* since its formation in 1961;[5] and has shown a distinctive capacity to apply a humanistic Marxism to the contemporary predicament and struggles of workers both nationally and internationally. His writings during these years have revealed an uncanny aptitude to crystallise, and at times anticipate, innovatory concerns among socialists: shop-floor union rebellions, demands for workers' control, the growth and seeming radicalisation of technical employment, the nature of capitalist control of the labour process, the connections between work, consumption and the environment.[6]

Farewell to the Working Class (first published in French in 1980) was written after the defeat of the French Left in 1978; and though no overt reference is made to the immediate political context, the demoralisation and recrimination of the period must have influenced the writing of this book—accentuating its relevance for socialists in Britain today. It is a work characteristic of Gorz's perceptive and rigorously (if often selectively) critical intelligence; and characteristic also in its limited overall

272

integration. In its 152 pages the book provides a preface, an introduction, nine main chapters, a postscript and two appendices, in the course of which a variety of themes emerge, combine, diverge, disappear and re-appear. Rarely can so brief a work have been so discursively fashioned. Rather than attempting to impose my own structure, however, I propose to set out Gorz's arguments according to his own format before offering a critical assessment of what I regard as the central themes.

For the English reader, Gorz offers his own initial summary: 'Nine Theses for a Future Left'. First, he defines his objectives as 'the liberation of time and the abolition of work', insisting that within capitalism work is always an externally imposed obligation rather than self-determined activity. Second, he relates the contrast between work and autonomous activity to that between exchange-value and use-value. Thus the pro-gressive abolition of waged work implies the reciprocal liberation of productive activity from the domination of commodity relations. Third, he argues that the abolition of work is already in process, as a result of mass unemployment. Current trends offer the alternatives of a society sharply divided between a mass of unemployed or those in casual and marginalised work, and an advantaged minority in relatively secure employ-ment; or one in which socially necessary labour is spread thinly among all who are available to work, freeing the bulk of people's time for self-defined activities. Fourth, Gorz stresses the inadequacy of the 'right to work' as a political slogan. Full-time employment for all is no longer possible, nor necessary or desirable. A guaranteed income for all, as commonly demanded by the Left, would merely represent 'a wage system without work': exploitation by capital would give way to dependence on the state, perpetuating the 'impotence and subordination of individuals to centralised authority' (p. 4). Instead, the aim should be 'the right to autonomous production': access to means of production (in the form defined by Illich as 'tools for conviviality')[7] so that individuals and grass-roots communities can produce directly for their own use. One conse-quence would be to break down the division between social production and domestic labour.

Gorz turns to the question of agency. His fifth thesis is that the abolition of work is not a demand of immediate appeal to the minority of skilled workers still able to take pride in their occupation and exert some control over the labour process; their response to changing technology is typically negative and defensive. But the abolition of work could win the support of routine employees in boring jobs, whom he describes as 'a non-class of non-workers' (p. 7). Restoring skill and creativity to the bulk of work, he insists as his sixth thesis, is not an option. While some aspects of capital-ist work organisation and its application of high technology may be rejected, the rapid production of use-values which is the precondition of a major reduction in working time requires 'a standardisation and formalisation of tools, procedures, tasks and knowledge. . . The socialisation of production inevitably implies that microprocessors or ball-bearings, sheet metals or fuels are interchangeable wherever they are produced, so that both the work and the machinery involved have the same interchangeable characteristic everywhere' (p. 8). Seventh, the socialisation of production also limits the scope for self-management. Autonomous collective decisions within productive units can do no more than adjust the details of each unit's integration within the overall social division of labour. Such forms of decentralised democracy 'may eliminate the degrading character of work, but they cannot endow it with the characteristics of personal creativity' (p. 9). In his eighth thesis Gorz distinguishes his view of the 'non-class of non-workers' from the classic Marxist conception of the working class as historical actor. They are a 'non-class' because they share 'no transcendent unity or mission, and hence no overall conception of history and society' (p. 11). Their concerns are parochial and individualistic; but because of their tendency to reject 'law and order, power and authority' they are the potential vehicles of a libertarian social movement. The final thesis is that such a movement is 'fragmented and composite. . . by nature refractory towards organisation,' and suspicious of large-scale political projects. A possible consequence is that 'spaces of autonomy from the existing social order will be marginalised, subordinated or ghettoised' (pp. 11–12). What is required is a synthesis of autonomous movement and political struggle, of a form which Gorz does not attempt to predict or prescribe.

The main text of *Farewell to the Working Class* begins with a critique of Marx, challenging two fundamental principles: that the development of productive forces within capitalism creates the material basis for a socialist society; and that the working class engendered by capital is the inevitable agent of its overthrow. On the contrary, insists Gorz: the productive forces functional to the capitalist mode of production are antagonistic to an alternative socialist rationality; while 'capitalism has called into being a working class (or, more loosely, a mass of wage earners) whose interests, capacities and skills are functional to the existing productive forces and not directly consonant with a socialist project' (pp. 14–15). Marx's theory of the proletariat was essentially metaphysical: the working class as historical subject transcended the concrete reality of empirical workers, its revolutionary essence deduced from a critical engagement with Hegelian philosophy. 'It is not a question of what this or that proletarian, or even the whole proletariat, at the moment *regards* as its aim. It is a question of *what the proletariat is,* and what, in accordance with this *being,* it will historically be compelled to do': in this famous passage from *The Holy Family,*[8] argues Gorz, are the roots of Marxist substitutionism. The philosophers of revolution best understand the proletariat's essential nature; this revolutionary essence cannot be contradicted by historical experience, which at most is evidence of temporary deviation from the inevitable path; the question how workers *might become* revolutionary does not require serious attention.

Gorz adds that a mystical vision of the proletariat does not merely pervade the writings of the 1840s, but frames the analysis of *Capital* itself. The possibility of communist revolution is located in the destruction of the artisan character of work, in the transformation of concrete into general abstract labour, in the submersion of workers' limited particularistic interests within an overarching class identity. Reduced by capital itself to interchangeable components of labour in general, workers have no possibility of redemption short of appropriation of 'the totality of productive forces'. But does this mean that they *can* and *will* embrace such a mission? This was unproblematic for Marx, says Gorz, because he already *knew* that the proletariat was revolutionary.

Yet the account of factory labour presented at length in the first volume of *Capital* is a catalogue of degradation: the destruction of creative ability, the suppression of intelligence, the habituation to servility. Was this the agent of revolution? Gorz argues that, from the *Grundrisse* onwards, Marx envisaged the re-emergence of the confident and assertive artisan within capitalist industry itself.

> He anticipated a process in which the development of the productive forces would result in the replacement of the army of unskilled workers and labourers—and the conditions of military discipline in which they worked—by a class of polytechnic, manually and intellectually skilled workers who would have a comprehensive understanding of the entire work process, control complex technical systems and move with ease from one type of work to another. . . He was convinced that the figure of the polytechnic worker embodied the reconciliation of the individual proletarian with the proletariat, a flesh-and-blood incarnation of the historical subject.
>
> (pp. 27–8)

But modern capitalism has followed the opposite path: not only manual workers, but also technicians and supervisors, have increasingly lost control over the production process; expansion of the power of the collective worker has been associated with the destruction of the power of individuals and work groups.

Only when viewed *from above*, Gorz continues, does the working class possess an organic unity. Hence the collective appropriation of the productive forces cannot reflect workers' own initiative: it can only be undertaken from above in their name. A system in which a 'workers' state' sustains and amplifies the productive forces developed by capitalism cannot avoid 'a quasi-military hierarchical set of relationships and a substantial body of staff officers and quartermasters', workers' continued subordination being underpinned by a set of principles 'akin to the ideology of the bee-hive' (pp. 32–3).

If one aspect of proletarianisation is the destruction of creativity and autonomy within work, another is the worker's definitive status as wage-labourer.

> As long as workers own a set of tools enabling them to produce for their own needs, or a plot of land to grow some vegetables, and keep a few chickens, the fact of proletarianisation will be felt to be accidental and reversible. For ordinary experience will continue to suggest the possibility of independence: workers will continue to dream of setting themselves up on their own, of buying an old farm with their savings or of making things for their own needs after they retire. In short, 'real life' lies outside your life as a worker, and being a proletarian is but a temporary misfortune to be endured until something better turns up.
>
> (p. 35)

Perceptive bourgeois rulers may indeed seek to preserve such fragments of autonomy for workers, precisely because they inhibit identification with a general class of dispossessed proletarians. For the same reason, the labour movement has traditionally proved hostile to workers' attempts to preserve or construct areas of individual autonomy, seeing these as detrimental to the broader class struggle. But in fact, says Gorz, the alienation of the 'pure' wage-slave is not expressed in a generalised challenge to capitalist relations of production; at most, conflict with capital is normally manifest in routinism, passive sabotage, impotent resentment; and in a politics which focuses on the state as provider of satisfactions and resources for workers' passive acceptance. The culture of proletarianisation generates no vision of the collective negation of workers' subordination to capital.

Gorz directs this argument specifically at strategies based on the demand for workers' control. 'The factories to the workers' was a slogan which could appeal to an artisan elite, to whom capitalist managers represented arrogant usurpers of workers' legitimate autonomy and culture. No such response is to be anticipated from a more fully proletarianised labour force. Moreover: traditional notions of workers' control (and associated movements to form revolutionary workers' councils) flourished when capitalist industry was relatively decentralised, when 'the site of production was also the site of power' (p. 48). But economic concentration and technological interdependence entail that today, workers' control at factory level can involve at best a limited power of veto, not directive control. Similarly, such bodies as factory councils may succeed in modifying aspects of management policy and practice, but cannot impose a major shift in priorities and strategies; hence their real function is to provide a representative mechanism accommodating workers to the dictates of capitalist production. Indeed, the same type of limitation applies at higher levels of aggregation:

The obstacle standing in the way of workers' control, power and autonomy is not merely legal or institutional. It is also a material obstacle, which derives from the design, size and functioning of factories. It ultimately derives from the 'collective capitalist' responsible for the management of all factories. For the great secret of large-scale industry, as of any vast bureaucratic or military machine, is that *nobody holds power.* Power in such organisms does not have a subject; it is not the property of individuals freely defining the rules and goals of their collective actions. Instead, all that can be found—from the bottom right up to the top of an industrial or administrative hierarchy—are agents obeying the categorical imperatives and inertias of the material system they serve. The personal power of capitalists, directors and managers of every kind is an optical illusion. It is a power that exists only in the eyes of those lower down the hierarchy who receive orders from 'those above' and are personally at their mercy.

(p. 52)

To 'capture' the productive system without transforming its structural dynamics would permit no alteration of substance.

Gorz reiterates this contention in a chapter which contrasts 'personal' and 'functional' power. The former is associated with superior skill, aptitude, training; those who deploy such power must be ready to demonstrate these qualities in order to establish the legitimacy of their position. Anarcho-syndicalist challenges to management prerogatives were typically associated with craftsmen who denied the superior competence of their appointed supervisors. But power today is characteristically bureaucratic: authority is legitimated by the position occupied rather than the personal qualities of the occupant. When power is personal, a change of personnel may permit far-reaching practical consequences; when it is functional, little can be expected from a change of office-holders. As a result,

the concept of seizure of power needs to be fundamentally revised. Power can only be seized by an already *existing* dominant class. Taking power implies taking it away from its holders, not by occupying their posts but by making it permanently impossible for them to keep their machinery of domination running. Revolution is first and foremost the irreversible destruction of this machinery. It implies a form of collective practice capable of bypassing and superseding it through the development of an alternative network of relations.

(p. 64)

Such an institutional transformation can in turn transform the nature of functional power; but it cannot abolish such power altogether, for a new institutional order will necessarily contain positions of authority. Gorz's prescription is thus to impose strict bounds upon functional power, and 'to dissociate power from domination' (p. 65).

From the elusiveness of the ruling class, Gorz returns to the ambiguities of the working class. In complete proletarianisation, the reduction of all specialised competencies to the level of generalised, homogeneous abstract labour, Marx premissed the growth of working-class unity. Yet the aspiration to displace capitalist management of production requires workers committed to their own productive identity and confident of their ability to take control: a commitment and confidence destroyed by proletarianisation.

> Loss of the ability to identify with one's work is tantamount to the disappearance of any sense of belonging to a class. Just as work remains external to the individual, so too does class being. Just as work has become a nondescript task carried out without any personal involvement, which one may quit for another, equally contingent job, so too has class membership come to be lived as a contingent and meaningless fact.
>
> For workers, it is no longer a question of freeing themselves *within* work, putting themselves in control of work, or seizing power within the framework of their work. The point now is to free oneself *from* work by rejecting its nature, content, necessity and modalities. But to reject work is also to reject the traditional strategy and organisational forms of the working-class movement. It is no longer a question of winning power as a worker, but of winning the power no longer to function as a worker. The power at issue is not at all the same as before. The class itself has entered into crisis.
>
> (p. 67)

Just as the rise of capitalist production created the working class, so its crisis and decay are creating the 'non-class of non-workers', encompassing 'all those who have been expelled from production by the abolition of work. . . It includes all the supernumeraries of present-day social production, who are potentially or actually unemployed, whether permanently or temporarily, partially or completely (p. 68).

Transient, marginal, insecure, 'they do not feel that they belong to the working class, *or to any other class*' (p. 70). For the post-industrial proletariat, work is simply 'the contingent form of social oppression in general' (p. 71). The microprocessor revolution will accelerate this process of marginalisation, multiplying both unemployment and those employments designed simply to 'provide work'.

What Marx referred to as production for production's sake, accumulation for accumulation's sake, Gorz defines as 'productivism'. The advance of capitalist technology has largely eliminated the *need* to work, but within capitalism it results in an ever more desperate drive to produce more, and more destructively. 'The forward march of productivism now brings the advance of barbarism and oppression' (p. 73). 'The threshold of liberation,' Gorz continues, 'can only be crossed at the price of a radical break, in which productivism is replaced by a different rationality. This rupture can only come from individuals themselves' (p. 74).

More specifically, the break can only come from those who are driven to reject the work ethic. Gorz regards the social aspirations of his 'non-class' as essentially negative: 'to regain power over their own lives by disengaging from the market rationality of productivism' (p. 75). They hold no common or coherent vision of the type of society in which this aim might be realised; their aspirations are essentially individualist, closer to traditional bourgeois thought than to orthodox socialism. The socialist ideal, as articulated by Marx, assumed that individual fulfilment could be unproblematically achieved within collectivised production; and conversely, that the free association of producers would be the sufficient foundation of a socialised economy. Gorz denies this. Small-scale communities may be able to function on the basis of spontaneous collaboration, but grassroots collaboration alone will not sustain a complex large-scale economy with an elaborate social and geographical division of labour.

Under socialism, he insists, economic planning directed towards the attainment of collectively defined goals cannot be the unmediated expression of aggregated individual preferences.

> However open and sincerely democratic the process of consultation, the plan schedule and objectives will never be the expression of a common civic will or of grass-roots preferences. The mediations which made it possible to coordinate broad social options with grass-roots preferences will be so complex and so numerous that the local community will be unable to recognise itself in the final result. This result—the plan—will inevitably be the work of a state technocracy obliged to make use of mathematical models and statistical materials which in itself can only imperfectly control because of the very large number of inputs, variables and unforeseeable elements. Thus the plan will never be a 'photograph' of everyone's preferences, but will have to adjust each sub-set of preferences in the light of all the other sub-sets and of the technico-economic constraints upon their coherence. In the last analysis, 'democratic elaboration' of the plan does not allow each and all to become the subject of that voluntary social cooperation through which 'the associated producers' are supposed to impose their common will upon the society they seek to create. Instead, the plan remains an 'autonomised result', intended by no one and experienced by all as a set of external constraints.
>
> (p. 78)

If a socialist economy required workers' unconditional commitment to the plan *because* it embodied their collective interests and wishes, the experience would indeed be even more oppressive than under capitalist market relations. This is the crucial weakness of contemporary socialist ideology: bourgeois apologists have learned to appeal successfully, through their emphasis on the need for individual choice, 'to the lived experience and aspirations of the post-industrial proletariat, as well as the major part of the traditional working class' (p. 79). Most reject the authoritarian connotations of socialism in favour of 'a private niche protecting one's personal life against all pressures and external social obligations' (p. 80). Rejecting the work ethic, seeking satisfaction in a realm of (at least apparent) autonomy from the world of work, the 'post-industrial neo-proletariat' is repelled by conventional models of socialism and does not fully recognise that its demands are incompatible with capitalism.

What alternative social order might capture their imagination? Marx himself at times bespoke the diminution of work as the externally directed component of social production, and the enlargement of creative activity outside the domain of economic rationality. Ending the equation of work with full-time wage-labour would enlarge the scope for all to engage in 'raising children, looking after and decorating a house, repairing or making things, cooking good meals, entertaining guests, listening to or performing music' (p. 82);[9] not least among the consequences would be a possible abolition of the traditional sexual division of labour.

In elaborating this vision, Gorz draws explicitly on both Illich and Bahro.

> The priority task of a post-industrial left must therefore be to extend self-motivated, self-rewarding activity within, and above all, outside the family, and to limit as much as possible all waged or market-based activity carried out on behalf of third parties (even the state). A reduction in work time is a necessary but not a sufficient condition. For it will not help to enlarge the sphere of individual autonomy if the resulting free time remains empty 'leisure time', filled for better or worse by the programmed distractions of the mass media and the oblivion merchants, and if everyone is thereby driven back into the solitude of their private sphere.
>
> More than upon free time, the expansion of the sphere of autonomy depends upon a freely available supply of convivial tools that allow individuals to do or make anything whose aesthetic or use-value is enhanced by doing it oneself. Repair and do-it-yourself workshops in blocks of flats, neighbourhood centres or rural communities should enable everyone to make or invent things as they wish. Similarly, libraries, places to make music or movies, 'free' radio and television stations, open spaces for communication, circulation and exchange, and so on need to be accessible to everyone.
>
> (p. 87)

The interrelationship of work and autonomous activity is crystallised in the concept of a 'dual society', premissed in turn on the insistence that 'contrary to what Marx thought, it is impossible that individuals should coincide with their social being, or that social being should encompass all the dimensions of individual existence' (p. 90). Emotional, affective and aesthetic experiences are essentially subjective; their subordination to impersonal social norms spells oppression. In this realm of individual choice, Gorz adds, is the only terrain for morality.

The obverse of this argument Gorz has already presented: individual autonomy is impossible within the area of social production governed by scarcity and necessity. The much quoted passage from the third volume of *Capital*,[10] he suggests, is often misunderstood:

> The actual wealth of society, and the possibility of constantly expanding its reproduction process. . . do not depend upon the duration of surplus-labour,

but upon its productivity and the more or less copious conditions of production under which it is performed. In fact, the realm of freedom actually begins only where labour which is determined by necessity and mundane considerations ceases; thus in the very nature of things it lies beyond the sphere of actual material production. Just as the savage must wrestle with Nature to satisfy his wants, to maintain and reproduce life, so must civilised man, and he must do so in all social formations and under all possible modes of production. With his development this realm of physical necessity expands as a result of his wants; but, at the same time, the forces of production which satisfy these wants also increase. Freedom in this field can only consist in socialised man, the associated producers, rationally regulating their interchange with Nature, bringing it under their common control, instead of being ruled by it as by the blind forces of Nature; and achieving this with the least expenditure of energy and under conditions most favourable to, and worthy of, their human nature. But it nonetheless still remains a realm of necessity. Beyond it begins that development of human energy which is an end in itself, the true realm of freedom, which, however, can blossom forth only with this realm of necessity as its basis. The shortening of the working-day is its basic prerequisite.

Within the 'realm of necessity', freedom can be only partial and restricted, even given the most democratic social and economic arrangements; real freedom is possible only in the context of activities not directed to sheer subsistence. Gorz links Marx's distinction to that made by Illich between manipulative institutions and conviviality. Unless socialism is conceived in terms of self-sufficient small-scale communities with pre-industrial technology (a recipe for back-breaking toil, restricted culture and suffocating interpersonal relationships) much social production (telephones, bicycles, computers) will remain standardised, depersonalised and intrinsically unsatisfying. Such other-directed work cannot be eliminated; but ideally its extent can be minimised; it can be distributed equitably; and it can be utilised to produce goods and services which genuinely enhance the quality of life.

The final chapter in the main body of the book takes issue with another established doctrine of the Left: the withering away of the state. In bourgeois society, the expansion of state functions is in part a necessary socialisation of costs evaded by individual capitals, in part a repressive guarantee of social order. But as with other-directed work, argues Gorz, the functions of the state cannot be abolished under socialism even though they can and must be reduced. If it *were* possible to do away with the state, then the conflation of state and civil society would paradoxically diminish individual autonomy; for social order could be maintained only through an inflexible adherence to standardised norms and obligations.[11] Echoing his earlier discussion of 'functional power', Gorz defines the socialist objective as 'the abolition not of the state but of domination' (p. 115). The role of the state can diminish only as *other* sources of social and economic dominance are neutralised. This depends in turn on the mobilisation of struggle from below.

The state can only cease to be an apparatus of domination over society and become an instrument enabling society to exercise power over itself with a view to its own restructuring, if society is already permeated by social struggles that open up areas of autonomy keeping both the dominant class and the power of the state apparatus in check. The establishment of new types of social relations, new ways of producing, associating, working and consuming is the fundamental precondition of any political transformation. The dynamic of social struggles is the lever by which society can act upon itself and establish a range of freedoms, a new state and a new system of law.

(p. 116)

Such struggles constitute the domain of politics: an essential mediation between the spheres of autonomy and necessity—before, during, and also after a transition to socialism.

In a postscript and appendices, Gorz explores further the connections between work, politics, technology and ecology. In capitalism, consumption is subordinated to the dictates of profitable production; and waste, destruction and triviality are built into both. Were the principle of accumulation to be replaced by that of sufficiency, existing technical resources would permit the satisfaction of needs though a small expenditure of labour, opening a substantial space for autonomous creativity. The application of microelectronics could in principle greatly accelerate the opportunity to 'work less, live more' (p. 134). (In a concluding 'utopia', Gorz specifies three pivotal principles: work less, consume better, and re-integrate culture with everyday life.) Enhanced choice by individuals of their expenditure of social labour (and corresponding income), and its phasing over the week, year, and even lifetime, is immediately feasible and increasingly reflects workers' own express wishes. A 'politics of time' could thus represent the key to a realistic socialist programme with genuine popular appeal.

Farewell to the Working Class is provocative in both senses of the word: it stimulates fresh perspectives on a range of vital issues for socialist theory and practice; but is often over-anxious to stress the novelty of the positions adopted in opposition to 'orthodox Marxism'. Its structural looseness is allied with a journalistic breathlessness of style, often at the expense of precision and analytical acuity. Thus it is perplexing that Gorz defines his objective as the abolition of work, before going on to insist that work *cannot* be abolished; the revised (and less dramatic) goal must be to overcome the dominance of other-directed labour in social existence. It is equally bewildering that, having argued at the outset that the present forces of production are adapted specifically to capitalist priorities and hence inappropriate for socialism, he appears in all subsequent discussion to assume that current technology will be applied largely unaltered within the sphere of necessity in a socialist economy. Likewise it is frustrating, given the emphasis on the need to differentiate power from domination, that the criteria for this distinction are nowhere defined.

Gorz as *prestidigitateur:* seemingly striving to make his thesis *appear* more daring than is actually the case. The illusion is helped along by a tendency to straw mannerism in the presentation of 'orthodoxy' as a foil to his own analysis. The treatment of 'Saint Marx', as Gorz terms him in the opening chapter,[12] arguably trivialises the evolution of his arguments over the four decades of his writing, suppresses many of the nuances of his theories, and neglects the extent to which he can be associated with contradictory positions on many key issues. I shall pursue these questions while focusing on what I see as the four main themes of the book: the critique of Marx's theory of the proletariat; Gorz's own conception of the 'neo-proletariat'; the case against 'oversocialised' conceptions of socialism; and the alternative model based on a 'dual organisation of social space'.

Gorz reiterates a now familiar argument in insisting on the idealism of Marx's vision of the revolutionary proletariat.[13] Bahro has recently offered a cautious statement of the case: in the writings and actions of Marx and Engels 'it seems to me that their entire concept of the proletariat was never completely free from the Hegelian antithesis between (rational, essential) reality and (merely empirical, accidental) existence'.[14] Gorz is more forthright: 'Marx's theory of the proletariat is not based upon either empirical observation of class conflict or practical involvement in proletarian struggle' (p. 16). This is, to say the least, an undialectical interpretation: Marx and Engels were surely profoundly influenced by their involvement with the empirical working class, but their vision of the proletariat was refracted by their philosophical polemic with the young-Hegelians. Marx philosophically discovers the proletariat as agent of world revolution (in the *Introduction to the Critique of Hegel's Philosophy of Right*) only *after* moving to Paris in the autumn of 1843 and experiencing a working class which 'pulsed with all the political and social movements from liberal reform to revolutionary communism'.[15] Engels, in England from the end of 1842, was caught up in the ferment of militant Chartism.

Thus it is incorrect to regard Marx's theory as without empirical foundation. What *can* plausibly be argued is that the time and place in which Marx and Engels encountered the working class were exceptional; and that they were encouraged to treat the militant socialist worker as prototypical because the stereotype meshed so neatly with their unfolding world-historical analysis. The extrapolation of the struggles of the 1840s into proletarian revolution was an act of faith, the predicted transition from 'class in itself' to 'class for itself' resting on no more than a loose analogy with the rise of the bourgeoisie. Certainly it is not unreasonable to maintain that faith became increasingly blind when, despite the collapse of the upsurge of 1848, the grave-digging inevitability of victory was so confidently reiterated.[16] Like Bahro, Gorz quite rightly argues that this conviction has involved a mythologised proletarian ideal; and that the failure of the empirical working class to conform to the prescribed model has encouraged all manner of substitutionist tendencies and projects.

Yet Marxism also contains a divergent conception, in which workers' common class identity and political insurgency are not a mechanical outcome of material necessity. The long *practical* involvement of Marx and Engels in the international working-class movement reflected a *contingent* theory of revolution: a task to be actively accomplished, not passively awaited. Marx does not 'guarantee the success of the revolution in advance or take it for granted. He only indicates its possibilities historically.'[17] Significantly Lukács, after starting with the 'essentialist' position of Marx in *The Holy Family,* concludes that 'the objective theory of class consciousness is the theory of its objective possibility'; and that the scientific analysis of the conditions for the development of this potential is thus a priority for Marxists.[18]

It is important to disentangle several distinct sources of Marx's identification of the working-class as agent of revolution. First was the search for a 'universal class' to set in place of Hegel's state bureaucracy; and the discovery of the proletariat as a class whose 'radical chains' entailed that its particular emancipation could be achieved only through *general* social emancipation. Second was the anthropological conception of purposeful social labour as the defining characteristic of humanity, its 'species-being'; the proletariat's function was the embodiment of this human creativity. Third was the connection with the 'philosophy of practice': if consciousness and action combined dialectically with material reality to transform social existence, the labour process could be viewed as the elemental form of human praxis and proletarian revolution its crowning manifestation. The fourth reflected the labour theory of value: if labour was the foundation of social productivity, it seemed to follow that the working class was pivotal for social transformation. The final proposition was that of (relative) immiseration: as the principal victims of capitalist 'progress' and capitalist crisis, workers would surely be driven to revolt, and would continue to revolt until they had eliminated the underlying causes of their misery.

These arguments are evidently varied and differ in the degree to which they are 'philosophically' and 'empirically' derived. In sum they cannot be dismissed as cavalierly as Gorz imagines. Yet it is true that Marx's analysis contains an apparent contradiction which he seems nowhere to have appreciated. If capitalist production progressively degrades and disables the proletariat, reducing the worker to a 'crippled monstrosity', how can the worker then take the stage of history as a 'new-fangled man' who overturns capitalist relations of production and domination and ushers in a new social order?

Gorz's answer, as has been seen, is that Marx envisaged the re-appearance of the artisan in the guise of the polytechnic worker in high-technology industry. This is surely a perverse reading of Marx. Perhaps a couple of *aperçus* within the rich and visionary complexity of the *Grundrisse* are open to this interpretation;[19] but throughout the whole body of Marx's writings is a consistent and altogether contrary thesis, and one to which Gorz himself alludes. Though the development of capitalist science and technology provides the material prerequisites for the emancipation of labour, by reducing necessary labour time and immensely increasing productivity, the actual consequences are not liberating but enslaving. The individual worker is no longer identifiably productive; established skills are eroded and displaced; the worker is subordinated to the machine; wages are depressed as women and children are employed in place of adult men; both the intensity and the length of the working day are increased. To quote from *Capital*:[20]

> Factory work exhausts the nervous system to the uttermost; at the same time, it does away with the many-sided play of the muscles, and confiscates every atom of freedom, both in bodily and in intellectual activity. Even the lightening of the labour becomes an instrument of torture, since the machine does not free the worker from the work, but rather deprives the work itself of all content. Every kind of capitalist production, in so far as it is not only a labour process but also capital's process of valorization, has this in common, but it is not the worker who employs the conditions of his work, but rather the reverse, the conditions of work employ the worker. However, it is only with the coming of machinery that this inversion first acquires a technical and palpable reality. Owing to its conversion into an automaton, the instrument of labour confronts the worker during the labour process in the shape of capital, dead labour, which dominates and soaks up living labour-power. The separation of the intellectual faculties of the production process from manual labour, and the transformation of those faculties into powers exercised by capital over labour, is, as we have already shown, finally completed by large-scale industry erected on the foundation of machinery. The special skill of each individual machine-operator, who has now been deprived of all significance, vanishes as an infinitesimal quantity in the face of the science, the gigantic natural forces, and the mass of social labour embodied in the system of machinery, which, together with those three forces, constitutes the power of the 'master'.

Marx assumed that workers were *bound* to rise up against such denial of their humanity. One might suspect that his image of the revolutionary proletarian was coloured by the qualities of those activists with whom he collaborated: Parisian communists, survivors of Chartism, delegates to the First International, German social-democrats. Did he regard these 'organic intellectuals'—no doubt disproportionately drawn from an artisan stratum —as typical, or at least prototypical, of the proletariat in general? This may in part explain his view of the working class. But probably more important was the fundamental principle of Marx's epistemology: the educative power of experience and action. *Struggle* was the yeast in the development of consciousness; revolutionary confidence and commitment would be fostered by a perhaps lengthy learning process based on collective action. And here, indeed, is one possible line of explanation of the failure of revolutionary expectations: that workers learned the *wrong* lessons! Gains *could* be made piecemeal, positions defended, areas of relative autonomy secured; many workers, and particularly those with enduring records of collective struggle, did have more than their chains to lose. In other words: against Gorz's thesis that full proletarianisation made revolutionary consciousness impossible, it could be argued that it was the partial and uneven character of proletarianisation which had this effect. In was Marx's prognosis of complete homogenisation of labour which proved inaccurate; and thus his prediction of the revolutionary outcome of such homogenisation was never put to the test.

Why does Gorz invent this allegedly Marxist concept of the neo-artisan? The cynic might reply: as a foil for his own notion of the neo-proletarian. The thesis that advanced capitalism gave birth to a new category of polytechnic workers was not Marx's, but rather the enthusiasm of a number of left-wing French sociologists in the 1960s.[21] Gorz himself was clearly influenced by this tendency, though more sceptical than some of his contemporaries.[22] But his treatment of the 'non-class of non-workers' is no more satisfactory than the account of the 'new working class' presented by Mallet and others two decades ago. Indeed, Gorz replicates many of the weaknesses which he claims to have discovered in Marx's theory of the traditional proletariat.

The Gorzian analysis is unconvincing at a number of different levels. First, contemporary workers are contrasted with the stereotype of a traditional skilled craftsman: the bearer of class consciousness, anticapitalist assertiveness, and aspirations for workers' control. This model clearly owes a great deal to the specifically French context, in which many features of artisan production were an enduring element in capitalist development and made their mark on the character of the labour movement. Nevertheless, Gorz's socialist (or anarcho-syndicalist) craftsman is a highly romanticised stereotype; while his account of the transition from occupationally conscious artisan to alienated mass worker is absurdly simplistic. The dynamics of capitalist production relations, with their complex patterns of division of labour and hierarchies of control, have always involved elaborate trajectories of skill, de-skilling, and at times *re*-skilling. Ever since the early nineteenth century, socialists and capitalists alike have repeatedly discerned the final abolition of skill and associated job controls. From Marx's notion of 'real subsumption' within the 'modern industry' of the mid-nineteenth century, to Braverman's account of the 'degradation of work' in the twentieth,[23] to Gorz's present work, the story is remarkably the same. Yet the question seems unavoidable:

how is it that any skills or worker autonomy are left to be degraded?

The answer is of course that trends within the capitalist labour process are always contradictory and uneven, and mediated by class struggle. Transformation is rarely as abrupt and decisive as the most highly dramatised accounts suppose. To establish his argument that a new epoch has arisen, Gorz should pay far more heed to the criticisms he himself directs against Marx. What is needed, in short, is less *a priori* assertion and far more detailed evidence.

Even were Gorz's general diagnosis of the trends within the labour force accepted, there is a second problem: the very notion of a 'non-class of non-workers'. In employing this term, he neatly contradicts his own prior arguments: for if work is *defined* as heteronomous and alienated labour, then those in the 'secondary labour market' performing the most degrading tasks in the most uncongenial conditions are surely *quintessential* workers. It would appear that Gorz is here entangled in his own rhetorical devices: not the best posture for analytical illumination.

More substantively, the whole treatment of the 'neo-proletariat' follows French sociological tradition in fusing actuality with aspiration. Who *are* the 'marginalised majority'? What do the situations of the jobless school-leaver, the under-employed graduate, the de-skilled professional, the un-employed industrial worker, or the redundant executive have in common? And what do their *perceptions* of these situations, and their responses to them, have in common either? What evidence is there that, as Gorz insists, such groups typically reject work, and with it authority in general? Like so many French theorists of 'post-industrialism', the grandiose vision overwhelms critical perception. Indeed Gorz blithely contradicts his own thesis with the argument (pp. 39–40) that unskilled and alienated workers, far from rejecting work and management control, commonly embrace passivity, eschew initiative, and seek to extend commodity relations. Nor is it evident that the unemployed customarily turn against work. 'Gis-a-job' is not the cry of those who have abandoned the work ethic; there is by now extensive evidence that many unemployed exper-ience guilt and psychic deprivation; that possession of even an oppressive and damaging job is an essential part of their social identity and self-esteem.

There is little evidence, either, that hierarchy and authority have lost their legitimacy in the eyes of the 'neo-proletariat'. Would that it were so! Today in Britain, the notion of 'de-subordination' seems a little less convincing than a decade ago. Unemployment, economic crisis and in-security have evoked an authoritarian rather than a libertarian response. Thatcher's appeal to the Victorian virtues of hard work and law and order has clearly won substantial backing within the working class—as, of course, did the imperialist pomp and blood-letting in the South Atlantic. Nor did the ranks of the un- and under-employed strike an obviously discordant posture on either occasion. In short, the anarchic neo-proletariat seems a rather less plausible construct than Marx's original notion of the revolutionary working class.

I have devoted some space to Gorz's treatment of the working class in Marx and in contemporary society, since his title indicates this as his central concern. But I suspect that many readers might consider more important the issues indicated in his subtitle: *An Essay on Post-Industrial Socialism.*

The dominant conceptions of socialism for the past century have defined a pivotal function for the state, as owner/controller of the means of production and as provider of collective services. The reform/revolution debate has centred primarily on whether the state's strategic functions should be enhanced by constitutional gradualism, by a radical seizure of its apparatus, or by its destruction and replacement by a new, workers' state. For Fabians and social-democrats, the consolidation of the state as general social representative may be the ultimate goal; for Marxists, merely a transitional stage to the suppression of class antagonisms which permits its own 'withering away'. Uniting these diverse conceptions is an acceptance—whether enthusiastic or apologetic—of a bureaucratic model of socialism.

Implicit in these traditions is an 'objectivist' view of the state: a set of institutions, positions and officials with prescribed functions, their powers underwritten by 'special bodies of armed men, etc.'. This is a perspective increasingly under question, as the traditional equation of socialism with state control is itself challenged. Both doubts were well articulated in a study published after Thatcher's first electoral victory:[24]

> For as long as we can remember, the question of the transition to socialism has been polarised between two positions: on the one hand gradualism, on the other 'the seizure of state power'. But recently there seems to have been an increasing recognition that this debate is sterile. The obvious lack of possibilities for reform, coupled with our eye-opening experiences of 'participation', have disabused us of hopes in gradualism. There is no way that society can be transformed through institutions that have been developed precisely to take away our power.
>
> On the other hand, a politics which pins everything on 'the seizure of state power' leaves many socialists feeling uncomfortable. They are sceptical about the possibility of overnight change, knowing it will be difficult to generate popular support for socialism when the question of just what it is we are fighting for is left so unreal. Neither capital nor the state can be seized, because they are not *things.* They are *relations* which cannot be grasped and held down, they have to be un-made. In a strange way our critique of the 'seizure of state power' line shares much with our doubts about gradualism: 'capturing power' by either means is not the same thing as taking control.

It is today a familiar argument that, within capitalism, the state form replicates the pattern of social relations of production; while under 'actual-ly existing socialism' the similarities are more notable than the differences. Whether this is explained in terms of the dictates of accumulation, the pervasive influence of commodity relations, or the distinctive interests and perspectives and relative autonomy of the state bureaucracy, it is evident that socialist strategy requires a more detached and critical attitude to the state.

The problem of the state is directly reflected in the constituency to which socialism should appeal. For British socialists and labour movement activists, 'public enterprise' and the 'welfare state' are typically regarded with pride and without question as signals of socialist advance. Arguments to the contrary have normally been associated with attacks by right-wing social-democrats on the nationalisation commitment in the Labour Party constitution. The whole tenor of the debate indicates however that the mainstream of labour movement thought it out of touch with popular opinion. Almost certainly, for most members of the working class the welfare state is not *their* welfare state. The services provided are typically inadequate, hemmed in by bureaucratic regulation, subject to inexplicable delay. The manner of delivery is often grudging, patronising, humiliating. Nationalisation is rarely seen as advantageous either to employees or to consumers. State officialdom is widely regarded as arrogant, incompetent, unaccountable. The whole apparatus of state activity is generally perceived as an ever-increasing burden on the incomes of ordinary workers.

Of course some of these arguments and attitudes represent popular mythology, fanned by political misinformation and media hostility. But the stereotypes have proved so powerful because they resonate with people's real experiences. There can be no prospect of mobilising popular support for an extension of state activity, or even to defend what already exists, if the state is popularly viewed as impoverishing and oppressive rather than liberating and enriching. This point, too, has been well made before:[25]

> Our daily contact with the state is a crucial arena of class struggle. In the past, however, if as socialists we have concerned ourselves with struggles with the welfare state at all, we have tended to concentrate on questions of resource provision: more and better housing, more hospitals, better teacher-pupil ratios and higher pensions. Increasingly, however, we are coming to realise that it is not enough to fight to keep hospitals open if we do not also challenge the oppress-ive social relations they embody; that it is insufficient to press for better student-teacher ratios in schools if we do not also challenge what is taught or how it is taught. Socialists involved in struggles over resources are realising that many people choose precisely *not* to give their support to 'fighting the cuts', defending or extending the state apparatus, because they quite reasonably have mixed feelings about the social relations which state institutions embody.

The question of quantity, one might say, is subsidiary to that of the quality of state activity.

Hence it is not surprising that Labour manifestoes and Alternative Economic Strategies based essentially on a policy of more—more nationalisation, more state services, more controls over private economic activity—have failed to win enthusiastic backing. On the contrary: Tory deployment of the rhetoric of individual choice and personal freedom suggests a far more sensitive understanding of working-class aspirations.

Against this background, Gorz's discussion of the interrelationship between state, socialism and individualism is of urgent import. Some of his arguments on the themes of self-determination in personal life and in grassroots collective relations have become familiar through the women's movement and libertarian socialist currents. His distinctive contribution is to link these concerns to a more abstract analysis of the spheres of individual autonomy and collective control, and to a critical assessment of the nature and limits of state activity under socialism.

The propositions which Gorz develops stand or fall independently of his prior analysis of the 'neo-proletariat'. In my view, his emphasis on the inevitable space between individual and social being is wholly persuasive. The necessity of macro-social determination of many aspects of collective life does not entail that individuals will experience true freedom in submission to such control. Nor should socialism imply the socialisation of all aspects of everyday life: diversity and creativity require the preservation of private social space. Also persuasive is Gorz's insistence that state power *is* necessary within any form of socialism, but that equally essential are autonomous collectivities to sustain the maximum possible self-determination and also to curb any tendencies to state aggrandisement.

Gorz's argument on this score is clear and convincing, and particularly relevant in Britain today. The traditional programme of state socialism repels more than it attracts, and for reasons which socialists should consider legitimate. The model of 'actually existing socialism' is rejected by most workers themselves as drab, monolithic and oppressive. It is not enough to insist that socialism here would be different; it is a question of demonstrating how and why this should be so. To do this, we on the Left must agree ourselves where we are going; must redefine for our own day a social vision which recaptures from the right the appeal to individual freedom while sustaining the traditional principles of conscious collective determination of social existence.

Marxists, as Bahro has commented, 'have a defensive attitude towards utopias. It was so laborious to escape from them in the past. But today utopian thought has a new necessity'.[26] How many of us have found it easy to dismiss those questions which occur to anyone but passionate believers in socialism as an abstract ideal: how would the major practical problems of social and economic organisation be resolved under socialism?

Of course we can't offer detailed blueprints; of course it is absurd to speak of releasing collective creativity and then lay down the lines which must be followed. But is it unreasonable to expect some sort of answer to such questions as: what will happen to the motor industry? Will the private car survive? What about motorways? How will a national road network be determined, and who will build it? With this, as with a myriad other areas of possible enquiry, the ritual response that the workers will decide for themselves when the time comes sounds suspiciously like a lack of vision or of honesty. The case for socialism carries little conviction unless at least some plausible *options* can be spelled out.

Bahro, it will be recalled, outlined what he termed 'the economics of the cultural revolution' according to five central principles: 'the goal of production as rich individuality'; 'a new determination of the need for material goods and the availability of living labour from the standpoint of the optimization of conditions of development for fully socialized individuals'; 'a more harmonious form of reproduction'; 'accounting for a new economy of time'; and 'individual initiative and genuine communality'.[27] Gorz develops his utopia along parallel lines, popularising many of the themes from Bahro's weightier tome, and adding a distinctively 'green' complexion to the argument: a reflection of his previous insistence that 'the ecological movement is. . . a stage in the larger struggle'.[28]

As has been seen, Gorz seeks to eschew *both* those forms of economic strategy which merely aim to 'socialise' (and manage more 'efficiently') the large-scale high-technology apparatus of contemporary capitalism; *and* the diametrically opposed conception of a return to 'primitive communism', with material life restricted to production with rudimentary equipment in small communities. His notion of a 'dual society' is more than a simple compromise; it is an imaginative synthesis which demands close critical consideration by socialists.

There are four problems in his analysis which I would wish to emphasise. The first is a highly diffuse perspective of the obstacles and enemies confronting a struggle for the type of society proposed. 'In modern societies, power does not have a subject' (p. 63): Gorz's thesis is scarcely novel.[29] But does this mean that socialists have merely to dismantle an impersonal 'system'? And in the short term, does it make *no* difference who occupies positions of 'functional power'? Capitalism indeed sets oppressive limits to the options available within its framework; but precisely because its operation is internally contradictory, those who exert political and economic management and direction can and must choose among alternatives. And if the discretion of *individual* rulers is limited (though given the supermarketed ersatz charisma of contemporary political leaders, and the extensive patronage at their disposal, surely far from insignificant), the power of the *ruling class* may be far more momentous.[30] Gorz's abstract and elusive references to 'domination' hint at this, but he nowhere confronts the problems inherent in a socialist challenge to the mechanisms and vested interests of class rule.

This issue connects with a second: Gorz oscillates between a highly determinist model of the 'juggernaut of capital', and (no doubt reflecting his existentialist background) a tendency to voluntarism and idealism. The sway of capital is at times attributed, not to material relations but to the 'rationality of productivism'; its abolition thus demands a transformation in social philosophies, 'the rejection of the accumulation ethic'. Correspondingly, freedom is to be achieved 'by a constitutive act which, aware of its free subjectivity, asserts itself as an absolute end in itself within each individual' (p. 74). This is sheer mysticism. It is right to insist that the abolition of capitalism must be a cultural as much as a material revolution; but Gorz here seemingly proposes that socialism will be established through spiritual conversion alone.

The third problem is also related: like Bahro, Gorz is very imprecise in locating the *agency* of socialist advance. Given his stress on the individualism, the non-class identity of the 'neo-proletariat', what is it that can give their gratuitous subjective acts a common direction and purpose? He speaks of 'the movement formed by all those who refuse to be nothing but workers' (p. 11), and insists portentously that 'only the movement itself, through its own practice, can create and extend the sphere of autonomy' (p. 116); but this is the sum total of Gorz's guide to strategy. Implicit in such remarks is an assumption of spontaneous collectivism, akin to that which Gorz derides in Marx's treatment of the working class, but far less grounded in evidence and analysis. A century of debate on socialist political strategy—the party, parliamentarism, reform/revolution— is not engaged or contested; it is simply ignored.

The fourth problem is of a different order. In discussing the integration of different systems of production, and the relationship between state and civil society, Gorz appears to assume a specifically national context. Despite the attention in many of his previous writings to issues of internationalism, this dimension is absent here. How would the movement towards socialist production relations and a 'dual society' confront the problems of the world market, the sway of multinational capital, the policies of domination of the superpowers? Is *world* revolution a necessary condition of transformation in individual societies—and if so, does this not multiply the problems of strategy and organisation among socialists? And on a global scale, is the conquest of the sphere of necessity as close to our grasp as Gorz's discussion assumes?

On issues such as these, *Farewell to the Working Class* provokes far more questions than it resolves. In what is not designed as a fully-fashioned manifesto, this is not necessarily a weakness. 'There is no wealth but life': Ruskin's maxim, the inspiration of so many early British social-

ists, was expunged from the consciousness of later generations of bureaucratic and technocratic social-democrats. Even radical currents within the
labour movement are typically marked by the philistine priorities of
capitalist production. Campaigns for the right to work, demands for
workers' control, implicitly accept the segmentation of life into a
(dominant) sphere of full-time wage labour and a (subordinate, devalued)
sphere of activity outside the bounds of commodity production.

There have of course been challenges to this dominant 'workerism',
not least under the impact of feminism. On the Left, declining faith in
Leninist orthodoxies has been associated with renewed discussion of
strategies for humanistic/libertarian socialism; but attention has been
mainly concentrated in narrow intellectual coteries; in particular it is hard
to detect more than a token influence within the organised labour movement.[31] Symptomatic is the fate of *A Life to Live,* written by Clemitson
and Rodgers in response to mass unemployment and the 1979 election
defeat, an eloquent plea for a right to a fuller life as an alternative to both
unemployment *and* employment.[32] Specifically addressed to the unions
and the Labour Party, their case for a worthier demand than the 'right to
work' has seemingly passed unnoticed.

Institutionalised within the sclerotic structures of the labour movement, British socialism has become modest and banal in its long-term
vision even when superficially radical in its short-term programme. Utopian
imagination—the tradition of William Morris—is more often an embarrass-
ment than an inspiration. As 1983 has brutally demonstrated, official
socialism, with its 'combination of narrow trade unionism and failed state
intervention',[33] no longer has a popular constituency. No more do the
industrial and political organisations of labour possess a language with
which to relate to those they supposedly represent. Will the current crisis
stimulate an effort to rediscover the essence of socialism, in a form appropriate to the closing years of the twentieth century, and in terms which
can inspire more than a dedicated minority? Gorz's utopia provides a
valuable contribution to such a quest.

NOTES

1. André Gorz, *Farewell to the Working Class: an Essay on Post-Industrial Socialism* (Pluto Press, 1982). Quotations in this review are followed by a page reference in the text.
2. For example M. Abrams and R. Rose, *Must Labour Lose?* (Penguin, 1960). The
   notion that 'affluence' and 'embourgeoisement' had destroyed workers' readiness to support Labour was confronted in a massive research study, the results
   of which appeared only after Wilson's two election victories had already given a
   practical refutation; see J.H. Goldthorpe et al., *The Affluent Worker: Political
   Attitudes and Behaviour* (Cambridge University Press, 1968).
3. Such revisionism (in some respects the linear antecedent of the SDP breakaway
   from Labour) was most elegantly proposed in the writings of C.A.R. Crosland;

in particular *The Future of Socialism* and *The Conservative Enemy* (Cape, 1956 and 1962)

4. For instance E.J. Hobsbawm's 1978 lecture and the subsequent debate, published in *The Forward March of Labour Halted?* (Verso, 1981); and Tony Lane, 'The Unions: Caught on the Ebb Tide', *Marxism Today*, September 1982 (and the ensuing controversy).

5. For the first fifteen years of *Les Temps Modernes*, Sartre had been sole editor.

6. Examples are *Strategy for Labour: a Radical Proposal* (Beacon Press, 1964); *Socialism and Revolution* (Anchor Press, 1973); *The Division of Labour: the Labour Process and Class-Struggle in Modern Capitalism* (Harvester Press, 1978); *Ecology as Politics* (South End Press, 1980).

7. Ivan Illich, *Tools for Conviviality* (Calder and Boyars, 1973).

8. *Marx-Engels Collected Works,* Vol. 4, (Lawrence and Wishart, 1975), p. 37.

9. Gorz makes no explicit reference here to the more bucolic utopian vision outlined in *The German Ideology,* but it surely lies behind this passage.

10. *Capital,* Vol. 3 (Lawrence and Wishart, 1959), p. 820.

11. The parallel with Durkheim's discussion of 'mechanical solidarity' is presumably not accidental.

12. Presumably this is a deliberate allusion to *The German Ideology,* in which Marx and Engels refer to 'Saint Max' Stirner.

13. One of the first popular assertions of this theme was in R.C. Tucker, *Philosophy and Myth in Karl Marx* (Cambridge University Press, 1961).

14. Rudolf Bahro, *The Alternative in Eastern Europe* (NLB, 1978), p. 195.

15. Hal Draper, *Karl Marx's Theory of Revolution*, Vol. 1 (Monthly Review, 1977), pp. 136-7.

16. Notably in Marx's peroration to the penultimate chapter of volume 1 of *Capital,* reproducing two decades later the revolutionary scenario of the *Communist Manifesto.*

17. Shlomo Avineri, *The Social and Political Thought of Karl Marx* (Cambridge University Press, 1968), p. 144.

18. Georg Lukács, *History and Class Consciousness* (Merlin Press, 1971), p. 79.

19. Gorz gives several references to the *Grundrisse;* the only other text specifically mentioned is the *Critique of the Gotha Programme.* In neither work, as far as I can see, does Marx posit the emergence of a polytechnic worker *within capitalism.* What he does argue in the *Grundrisse* (Penguin, 1973), p. 701, is that the productivity resulting from advanced technology 'will redound to the benefit of emancipated labour, and is the condition of its emancipation'; that is, *after* the abolition of capitalist production relations. For a similar argument see *Capital,* Vol. 1 (Penguin, 1976), p. 618.

20. *Capital,* Vol. 1, pp. 548-9. For additional examples of the same argument see *Grundrisse,* pp. 692-4, 700-9; *Capital,* Vol. 1, pp. 483, 526-7, 544-5, 559, 619, 667; *Inaugural Address* and *Critique of the Gotha Programme* in *The First International and After* (Penguin, 1974), pp. 77-8, 352.

21. Notably Serge Mallet, with his notion of the 'new working class' of technically qualified workers. For critical discussions of this approach see Michael Mann, *Consciousness and Action Among the Western Working Class* (Macmillan, 1973); Michael Rose, *Servants of Post-Industrial Power?* (Macmillan, 1979); Richard Hyman and Robert Price, *The New Working Class?* (Macmillan, 1983).

22. See for example his essay 'Technology, Technicians and Class Struggle' in *The Division of Labour.*

23. Harry Braverman, *Labour and Monopoly Capital: the Degradation of Work in the Twentieth Century* (Monthly Review, 1974).

24. London Edinburgh Weekend Return Group, *In and Against the State* (Pluto

Press, 1980), p. 130.
25. Ibid., pp. 76–7.
26. *The Alternative*, p. 253.
27. Ibid., pp. 405–7.
28. *Ecology as Politics*, p. 3.
29. 'Capital is, therefore, not a personal, it is a social power', (*Manifesto of the Communist Party* in *Marx-Engels Collected Works*, Vol. 6, 1976, p. 499). 'competition subordinates every individual capitalist to the immanent laws of capitalist production, as external and coercive laws' (*Capital*, Vol. 1, p. 739).
30. See, for example, Göran Therborn's discussion of 'Finding the Ruling Class' in *What Does the Ruling Class Do When It Rules?* (NLB, 1978).
31. I do not mean to overlook the involvement of many union activists in both the practical and the theoretical aspects of 'workers' alternative plans' or the initiatives of some left-wing Labour councils; here, one suspects, is a source of some of the cadres of the 'movement' to which Gorz refers. At the same time, it is necessary to recognise the extent to which such activities are patronised, ignored or opposed by the official union hierarchies.
32. Ivor Clemitson and George Rodgers, *A Life to Live: Beyond Full Employment* (Junction Books, 1981). The book carries a Foreward by Neil Kinnock; it will be interesting to see what becomes of his endorsement of a 'life ethic' rather than a work ethic.
33. Hilary Wainwright in *The Forward March of Labour Halted?*, p. 132.

MARX, BLANQUI AND MAJORITY RULE

Monty Johnstone

1

Is the support of the majority of the population necessary for the socialist transformation of society? Or should a revolutionary party or organisation be prepared to take power without such support and hold on to it even against the wishes of most of the people? The issue, pivotal to socialist debate on democratic theory and practice, divided revolutionaries a hundred and fifty years ago as it divides them today.

The first Marxist party, the League of Communists, was formed in 1847 from the union of two communist currents, which had differed radically on their attitudes to democracy. One trend, represented by the leaders of the League of the Just, sprang from the conspiratorial Babouvist-Blanquist tradition and has been involved in Blanqui's abortive Paris rising of May 12, 1839, of which Engels had written that he did 'not consider such things creditable to any party.'[1] Like most pre-Marxist socialists they were elitist and paternalistic, striving to change society by capturing power for an enlightened minority, which would act for the good of the people without requiring to obtain and retain the support of a majority among them. The other current was that of Marx, whose early 'ultra-democratic opinions'[2] in favour of 'the self-determination of the people'[3] had been extended and combined with the social and economic democracy which he and Engels were advocating through a revolutionary change in the class basis of society led by the working class.

Marx and Engels only agreed to enter the new League after being assured that the leaders of the old one 'were as much convinced of the general correctness of our mode of outlook as of the necessity of freeing the League from the old conspiratorial traditions and forms'.[4] The first League congress was held in London in June 1847 and a thoroughly democratic constitution was drawn up, which, as Engels later noted, 'barred all hankering after conspiracy, which requires dictatorship'.[5]

Following the congress the League published in London a trial number of a Marxist journal entitled the *Kommunistische Zeitschrift*, appearing in September 1847 with the slogan 'Working men of all countries, unite!' under the title. Its introductory declaration of policy made it very clear with which of the two communist currents the new League identified

itself. 'There certainly are some communists who, with an easy conscience, refuse to countenance personal liberty and would like to shuffle
it out of the world because they consider it is a hindrance to complete
harmony,' they wrote, stressing that they themselves were not among
those communists who are out to destroy personal liberty'. On the
contrary, they were convinced 'that in no social order will personal freedom be so assured as in a society based upon communal ownership'. It
was necessary, they went on, to 'work in order to establish a democratic
state wherein each party would be able by word or in writing to win a
majority over to its ideas'.[6]

At the League's second congress that November Marx and Engels were
commissioned to draw up its 'detailed theoretical and practical programme',[7] which was to appear early the next year as the famous
Manifesto of the Communist Party. It unequivocally rejected the old
Utopian notions of the proletariat as 'a class without any historical initiative *(Selbständigkeit)* or any independent political movement', and made
clear its support for 'the gradual, spontaneous class organisation of the
proletariat'[8] as a 'movement of the immense majority',[9] striving to become the ruling class and 'win the battle of democracy'.[10]

This did not however mean the disappearance of the other current in
communism, which has continued to find reflection in major controversies
right up to the present time. Historically this trend found its clearest and
frankest expression in the ideas of Louis Auguste Blanqui, who argued,
and organised, for power to be taken by a revolutionary minority on
behalf of, and if necessary against the wishes of, the majority of the
people and held in their best interests until such time as they had been
educated without reactionary influences and production had been greatly
increased. It would 'then be possible to speak of self-government'.[11] It is
a measure of the distortions to which Marx's ideas have been subject in
the hundred years since his death that precepts and practices with a
striking affinity to these of Blanqui's should be held to be Marxist both
by most of those who subscribe to them as well as by critics of Marxism.
It is the purpose of this essay to compare the ideas of Blanqui and the
tradition from which they sprang with those of Marx and Engels on the
question of majority and minority rule on the basis of an examination
of their relevant writings.

2

Blanqui was heir to the Jacobin-Blanquist political tradition as trans-
mitted by Buonarroti. That tradition has roots in Rousseau's concept of
popular sovereignty as an expression of a metaphysical 'general will'—
'always constant, unalterable and pure'—which he distinguished from 'the
will of the people', which could be mistaken.[12] (This is a distinction that
is still made in some quarters between the 'true' will of the people and

what the majority of the people actually want at a given time.) Rousseau argued that sovereignty should be attributed solely and exclusively to the people, who must be the authors of every law. However, he asked, 'how would a blind multitude, which knows not what is good for it, execute of itself an enterprise so great, so difficult, as a system of legislation? ' The general will was always right (*droite*) but the judgment directing it was not always enlightened. 'It must be made to see objects as they are, sometimes as they ought to appear', he wrote. The people needed guides to teach them 'to know what they require'.[13] It was moreover important, 'in order to have a clear declaration of the general will, that there should be no partial association in the state'[14]—in other words, no political parties, because he considered them disruptive of the desired social harmony. Whoever refused to obey 'the general will', should be constrained to do so, which he said in a famous phrase 'means nothing else than that he shall be forced to be free'.[15]

In the French Revolution Robespierre and the Jacobins, inspired by Rousseau, were the most intransigent champions of popular sovereignty. Having obtained power in June 1793 as a result of a popular Paris insurrection and removed their Girondin opponents from the National Convention, they introduced the democratic Constitution of 1793 based on universal male suffrage. However the exigencies of war, rebellion and a deteriorating economic situation led them to suspend its operation and enforce a virtual one-party dictatorship from October 1793 to July 1794. The purged National Convention and its Committees of General Security and Public Safety, vested with full executive powers, were to be 'the sole custodians and executors of the "general will" '.[16] Robespierre presented the increasingly centralised rule by the Paris-based 'provisional government of France', resting on the support of a minority of its people, as 'the despotism of liberty against tyranny'. The terror which it applied, was, he said, 'an emanation of virtue' and 'a consequence of the general principle of democracy applied to the most pressing needs of the country'.[17]

After Robespierre had been overthrown on July 27, 1794 (9th Thermidor) and fallen victim to the same guillotine to which he himself had been instrumental in assigning so many other revolutionaries, the new Thermidorian rulers repealed the economic controls of their predecessors and introduced the Constitution of 1795 with a limited franchise favouring the propertied classes. It was against this shift to the right that Babeuf and his friends organised their 'Conspiracy of Equals' in 1795-6. It aimed to carry through an insurrection to overthrow the government and restore the democratic Constitution of 1793 with modifications and supplement it by the establishment of a pre-industrial form of communism (based primarily, though not exclusively, on distribution rather than production) involving common landholding and the establishment of social equality. At the centre of the conspiracy was a small, secret, self-appointed 'Com-

mittee of Public Safety', grouping around itself a wider circle of sympathisers who were only very partially informed of its plans and objectives.
Propaganda was undertaken among the *sans-culotte* masses of Paris, from
whom however the hoped for support was not forthcoming. The conspiracy was betrayed and Babeuf and others paid with their lives.

The essential ideas of Babeuf and his associates (Babouvism) were set
out in 1828 by one of their number, Buonarroti, in his *Conspiration pour
l'Egalité dite de Babeuf*, which was to have a profound effect on Blanqui
and other revolutionaries of this period. Babeuf's secret committee were
convinced, Buonarroti tells us, that it would be 'neither possible nor
without danger to appeal straight away to popular assemblies to elect a
legislature and a government in accordance with the Constitution of
1793', which did not provide the people with sufficient 'guarantees'
against 'the errors into which it might itself be drawn'.[18] A people whose
opinions have been formed under a regime of inequality and despotism,
wrote Buonarroti,

> is hardly suited, at the beginning of a regenerative revolution, to choose by its
> votes the men required to lead and consummate that revolution. This difficult
> task can only be entrusted to wise and courageous citizens, strongly imbued with
> patriotism and a love of humanity. . . whose knowledge is in advance of their
> contemporaries' and who, despising wealth and vulgar honours, seek their
> happiness in rendering themselves immortal by securing the triumph of equality.
> Perhaps it is necessary at the beginning of a political revolution, even out of
> respect for the true sovereignty of the people, to be concerned less with winning
> the votes of the nation than with placing supreme power, in the least arbitrary
> way possible, in wise and strong revolutionary hands.[19]

The secret committee decided that it would exercise such a revolutionary
dictatorship until the people of Paris could be called on to elect a national
assembly endowed with supreme authority. The committee would however keep itself in existence and carry out detailed 'research' to determine
which candidates to propose and then to 'watch over the conduct of the
new assembly'.[20]

Inspired by Babouvist communism, Blanqui sought to organise a
relatively small, centralised, hierarchical elite to prepare and lead an
insurrection, which would replace capitalist state power by its own
temporary revolutionary dictatorship. The *Société des Saisons*, a secret
society led by Blanqui and Barbès, consisting mainly of Paris workers or
artisans, attempted to carry through the best known of such Blanquist
risings in Paris in May 1839. The conspirators seized the *Hôtel de Ville*
and proclaimed themselves the legitimate authority in France. They
expected that this audacious offensive action would galvanise the people
into joining them against their oppressors. There was however no such
popular response and not more than eight hundred people in all were

involved in the action, which was defeated after a few days' fighting.

In 1848, immediately after the French February Revolution, Blanqui adopted different tactics. Instead of a clandestine organisation, he formed the *Société républicaine centrale* as an open body, holding public meetings six evenings a week which attracted hundreds of people, although a little later he reconstituted it on the lines of the old secret societies. Organised around an elite core of Blanqui's fellow-insurrectionists of 1839, its purpose, as Samuel Bernstein notes, 'was to be at once a pressure group and a propaganda machine', which 'endeavoured earnestly to start up a groundswell of popular sentiment that might seriously damage the established institutions to their foundations'.[21] Blanqui opposed the idea of organising a *putsch* as he had attempted to do in 1839. 'If we seize power by a bold *coup de main*', he declared perceptively, 'who can answer for the durability of our power?' What was needed was 'the mass support of the people, the insurgent faubourgs' of Paris rising as they had against the monarchy on August 10, 1792.[22] He called for the granting of 'complete and unlimited press freedom' and other liberties, and for the arming of the workers.[23] At the same time he retained his basic Babouvist belief that the majority of the people were not yet ready to choose their own rulers. This now found expression in his demand for the 'indefinite postponement' of the elections which had been fixed for a constituent national assembly. He claimed that 'the freedom of suffrage would be only apparent, all the hostile influences would inevitably conspire to falsify the will of the people'.[24] In the countryside the influence of the clergy and the aristocracy predominated. 'A cunning tyranny has stifled all spontaneity in the heart of the masses', he wrote. 'The unfortunate peasants, reduced to the status of serfs, would become a stepping stone for the enemies that oppress and exploit them.' If elections were held before there was time for the people to see the light (*'que la lumière se fasse'*) they would result in the victory of reaction and would lead to civil war.[25]

More than two decades later Blanqui developed these ideas further in his essay, 'Communism—The Future of Society', written in 1869–70, in which he called for a revolutionary *'dictature parisienne'*. To the suggestion that it constituted 'an admission of minority and violence' to put off elections 'until the full freeing of consciences', he rejoined: 'No! A majority acquired by terror and gagging is not a majority of citizens but a herd of slaves. It is a blind tribunal which for seventy years has heard only one of the two sides. It owes it to itself to listen for seventy years to the opposite side. Since they have not been able to plead together, they will plead one after the other.' In 1848 the republicans had paid the price for granting total freedom to their adversaries. There must be 'no freedom for the enemy' this time, he insisted, setting aside the 'unlimited press freedom' which he had demanded in 1848.[26] 'The day when the gag is removed from the mouth of Labour it will be to enter the mouth of Capital', he went on. 'One year of Parisian dictatorship in 1848 would have spared France and history the quarter of a century which is nearing its end. If this time ten years are needed, there should be no hesitation.' The government of Paris, he claimed in Robespierrist vein, 'is the government of the country by the country, hence the only legitimate one. . . it is a true national representation.'[27] Such a conception of 'true representation' clearly has nothing to do with anything empirically verifiable, but corresponds rather to an 'ideal' or metaphysical form. It is in this sense that Blanqui conceived of democracy of which, he claimed, the communists of his school 'have not ceased to constitute the most audacious vanguard'.[28]

The major task of Blanqui's revolutionary dictatorship would be educational rather than coercive. 'The army, the judiciary, Christianity, public bodies—merely fences. Ignorance—a formidable bastion. One day for the fence; twenty years for the bastion.'[29] The introduction of communism, would have to proceed 'step by step' and 'always completely voluntarily'[30] after the expulsion from the country of aristocrats and 'the black (clerical) army, male and female'.[31] Ultimately there would remain 'nothing of that execrable thing called government'.[32] Blanqui apparently envisaged arriving at some sort of withering away of the state corresponding to Saint-Simon's aim of replacing the government of men by the administration of things.[33] He distinguished himself from the Utopians, however, by rejecting disputes between socialist schools on the nature of the society which they hoped to establish. They 'argue heatedly on the river bank to decide whether there is a field of maize or of wheat on the other side', he wrote. 'Well, let us cross first. We shall see when we get there.'[34] It did not appear to worry him greatly that many people, seeing that they were not going to be consulted about what would be planted there for them, might be reluctant to cross for fear that they might be confronted with neither maize or wheat but deadly nightshade!

3

Marx and Engels held Blanqui in high esteem as a courageous and incorruptible revolutionary. In *The Class Struggle in France,* describing the period from 1848 to 1850, Marx wrote that 'the *proletariat* increasingly organises itself around *revolutionary socialism,* around *communism,* for which the bourgeoisie has invented the name of *Blanqui*'.[35] In 1861 Marx described him as 'the head and the heart of the proletarian party in France'.[36] At the time of the Paris Commune Marx noted the refusal of Thiers, who headed the Versailles government, to exchange Blanqui whom it held prisoner for Archbishop Darboy, held by the Commune. 'He knew', wrote Marx, 'that with Blanqui he would give the Commune a head.'[37]

In April 1850, when Blanqui was incarcerated in France (he spent more than thirty-three of the seventy-six years of his life in nearly thirty different gaols), Marx and Engels concluded a short-lived agreement with French Blanquist leaders in exile in London. Together with them and the left-wing Chartist leader Harney, they established a Universal Society of Revolutionary Communists. Its aim was defined as 'the downfall of all privileged classes, the submission of those classes to the dictatorship of the proletarians (*la dictature des prolétaires*) by maintaining the revolution in permanence (*la révolution en permanence*) until the achievement of communism, which shall be the final form of the constitution of the human family'.[38]

This agreement was made at a time when Marx and Engels still expected a revival of revolution and were anxious to work with the leaders of the main proletarian trends which they thought would be involved in France and Britain. By the late summer of 1850, however, they had reached the conclusion that European capitalism had entered a period of prosperity which precluded a new revolution in the period ahead. This realistic appraisal brought them into conflict with an important minority in the leadership of the League of Communists, headed by Willich and Schapper. At a meeting of the League's Central Authority on September 15, 1850, Schapper declared: 'The question at issue is whether we ourselves chop off a few heads right at the start or whether it is our own heads that will fall. In France the workers will come to power and thereby *we* in Germany too. Were this not the case I would indeed take to my bed.'[39] Marx argued that Schapper and Willich saw revolution 'not as the product of the realities of the situation but as the result of an effort of *will*'.[40] Marx was here echoing the criticism he had made in 1844 of the belief in 'the *omnipotence* of the will' held by Robespierre,[41] and of the Jacobin methods of coercion and terror, where 'political life seeks to suppress its prerequisite, civil society and the elements composing this society, and to constitute itself as the real species-life of man devoid of contradictions'. This it could achieve, he said, 'only by coming into *violent* contradiction with its own conditions of life'.[42]

Marx's condemnation of such voluntarism applied to the whole Jacobin-Babouvist-Blanquist tradition, with which it had appeared that Schapper had broken when, with other leaders of the old League of the Just, he joined with Marx and Engels to form the League of Communists. It was to this that he was now reverting under the heady impact of the 1848 revolutions.[43] It is not surprising therefore that most of the Blanquists sided with Schapper and Willich when the League split on this issue. On October 9, 1850 Marx, Engels and Harney wrote to the Blanquists to indicate that they had already for some time considered the Universal Society of Revolutionary Communists as *de facto* dissolved.[44]

When Marx and Engels still considered that 'a new revolution is impending', they drew up their famous March (1850) Address on behalf of the Central Authority of the League of Communists,[45] which was to be described as 'Blanquist' by Eduard Bernstein and others who have followed him.[46] In fact, although on immediate tactics it had points of convergence with the Blanquists, which provided the basis for the brief agreement with them at that time, its strategy was quite different from theirs. Instead of envisaging a Communist *coup,* or even revolution, it foresaw a revolutionary drama in two acts, in the first of which a broadly based workers' party should help to bring the petty bourgeois democrats to power and pressurise them to make the maximum inroads into capitalist property.[47] The Address recognised that 'the German workers are not able to attain power and achieve their own class interests without completely going through a lengthy revolutionary development'.[48] When Schapper outlined his immediate perspective of the workers coming to power in Germany, Marx pointed out that this view clashed with that of the March Address and the *Communist Manifesto,* of which he had approved.[49]

The *Manifesto* had spoken of Germany being 'on the eve of a bourgeois revolution' which must establish bourgeois supremacy, whilst predicting that 'the bourgeois revolution will be but the prelude to an immediately following proletarian revolution'.[50] The tactics followed by Marx and Engels in Germany in 1848–9 do not bear out Stanley Moore's use of this quotation to support his thesis that from 1844 to 1850 Marx' and Engels' tactics 'were primarily influenced by the tradition of Babeuf, Buonarroti and Blanqui'.[51] After returning to their homeland little more than two months after writing the *Manifesto,* they joined the Democratic Party, 'the party of the petty bourgeoisie',[52] whose most advanced wing they formed[53] until the spring of 1849, and concentrated on editing the *Neue Rheinische Zeitung* as a radical, broadly based 'Organ of Democracy'.[54] The formulation quoted from the final peroration of the *Manifesto* should be ascribed to a flourish of over-optimistic rhetoric by its young authors rather than to Blanquist tactics. It contrasts sharply with the more sober recognition by Engels in his preliminary draft of the *Manifesto* in October 1847 that a communist revolution would be 'slowest and most difficult to carry out in Germany'[55] and his statement only six or seven months earlier that 'the workers are still far from sufficiently mature to be able to come forward as the ruling class in Germany'.[56]

Around the time that they drew up the March Address, Marx and Engels also wrote a long review article criticising the conspirators of the Paris secret societies as 'the alchemists of revolution', who were 'characterised by exactly the same chaotic thinking and blinkered obsessions as the alchemists of old'.[57] Conspiracies like that organised by Blanqui in 1839 'never of course embraced the broad mass of the Paris proletariat', even though 'the 1839 revolt was decidedly proletarian and communist'. However experience had proved, they insisted, that 'in the modern revolution this section of the proletariat is insufficient and that only the proletariat as a whole can carry a revolution through'.[58]

4

Marx's and Engels' rejection of Blanqui's conception of an educational dictatorship by a revolutionary minority flowed from political and philosophical premises diametrically opposed to the elitist tradition. Marx's first two published articles, written in 1842, are among the most powerful philippics ever penned against press censorship. In them he rebutted the thesis that human beings are 'immature' and need for the sake of their 'education' to be protected from 'the siren song of evil'. In this view, wrote Marx, 'true education consists in keeping a person wrapped up in a cradle throughout his life, for as soon as he learns to walk, he learns also to fall, and only by falling does he learn to walk. But if we all remain in swaddling-clothes, who is to wrap us in them? If we all remain in the cradle, who is to rock us? If we are all prisoners, who is to be prison warder?'[59] Arguing that censorship is 'a law of suspicion against freedom', resting dubiously on the Jesuit maxim that the end justifies the means, he proclaimed: 'Let us allow the sirens to sing!'[60]

A similar aversion to a paternalist tutelage of the masses was forcefully expressed the next year in Marx's *Contribution to the Critique of Hegel's Philosophy of Law*. He found 'truly repulsive' Hegel's insistence on a 'guarantee' that delegates elected to representative assemblies should be individuals who would exercise 'only their objectively recognisable and tested qualities'. Hegel was, he wrote, 'infected through and through with miserable arrogance' which 'grandly looks down on the "self-confidence" of the "people's own subjective opinion" '.[61] The criticism of course applies equally to the 'guarantees' which we saw the Babouvists insisting on against the 'errors' of the electors.

Marx's classical objection to all this kind of elitism is found in his third thesis on Feuerbach, written in 1845:

> The materialist doctrine that men are products of circumstances and upbringing, and that, therefore, changed men are products of other circumstances and changed upbringing, forgets that it is men who change circumstances and that the educator must himself be educated. Hence, this doctrine is bound to divide society into two parts, one of which is superior to society (in Robert Owen, for example).
> The coincidence of the changing of circumstances and of human activity can be conceived and rationally understood only as revolutionising practice.[62]

Like Blanqui Marx and Engels recognised the need for independent organisation to provide resolute and clear-sighted leadership in the struggle against the bourgeoisie.[63] To this end they sought to promote the building of working class parties, the forms of which varied very greatly in different periods and in different countries.[64] Unlike Blanqui, however, they sought to give these parties thoroughly democratic structures[65] and to link them with the 'real movement' of the working class rather than to 'shape and mould' the labour movement according to 'sectarian principles of their own'.[66] Above all, as Engels was to explain, 'for the ultimate triumph of the ideas set forth in the *Manifesto* Marx relied solely and exclusively upon the intellectual development of the working class, as it necessarily had to ensue from united action and discussion'.[66a] 'Substitutism', as it has subsequently been called, was out. 'The emancipation of the working classes must be conquered by the working classes themselves', as Marx had insisted.[67] In view of this, they declared it was impossible for them to cooperate with those people in German Social Democracy 'who openly state that the workers are too uneducated to free themselves and must be freed from above by philanthropic big bourgeois and petty bourgeois', who claimed that they alone possessed 'the "time and opportunity" to acquaint themselves with what is good for the workers'.[68]

Setting down the essential differences between Marxism and Blanquism, Engels wrote in 1874:

> From Blanqui's conception of every revolution as the *coup de main* of a small revolutionary minority follows of itself the necessity of a dictatorship after it succeeds: the dictatorship, of course, not of the whole revolutionary class, the proletariat, but of the small number of those who carried out the *coup* and who are themselves already in advance organised under the dictatorship of one or a few individuals.[69]

Here is expressed the essential difference between the dictatorship of the proletariat conceived by Marx and Engels to be carried out by 'the whole revolutionary class', and Blanqui's revolutionary dictatorship to be exercised on behalf of the working class by an elite. It was Marx who first used the term 'dictatorship of the proletariat', which he saw as constituting 'the transition to the *abolition of all classes* and to a *classless society*'.[70] Contrary to widespread belief, there is no record of Blanqui ever having used the expression, although some of his followers were to do so at certain times, notably in 1850, under the influence of Marx.[71]

5

In *The Civil War in France* Marx highlighted the tendencies of the Paris Commune which he considered most noteworthy for an experience which he called 'the conquest of power by the working classes'[72] and Engels was to characterise as 'the dictatorship of the proletariat'.[73] They stand in striking contrast to Blanqui's ideas on revolutionary dictatorship.

In *The Civil War in France,* and the two first drafts that he wrote of it during the seventy-two days of the Commune, Marx underlined above all the creative initiative that it released among the masses on the 'basis of really democratic institutions'[74] reflecting 'the people acting for itself by itself'.[75] He presented the Commune as 'a thoroughly expansive political form, while all previous forms of government had been emphatically repressive'.[76] In his first draft he quoted an extract from the London *Daily News*, which deplored the fact that the Commune was 'a concourse of equivalent atoms, each one jealous of another and *none endowed with supreme control over the others*'. Marx underlined the last phrase and noted that 'the bourgeois. . . wants political idols and "great men" immensely'.[77]

The Commune, far from being a one-party system, was divided into a Blanquist majority and a mainly Proudhonist minority, with various other political groups like the middle class *Union Républicaine* functioning freely. Universal suffrage was preserved along with freedom for the bourgeois supporters inside Paris of the counter-revolutionary Versailles government to stand in the elections to the Council of the Commune, in which they obtained fifteen out of eighty seats. Not till two weeks after the Versailles troops started attacking the outskirts of Paris and bombarding the city did the Commune begin to suspend hostile papers,[78] an action that Marx considered fully justified as a *wartime* measure.[79]

Before the Commune, Marx and Engels had opposed a Paris rising.[80] After the proclamation of the third republic on September 4 1870, they expressed their agreement with a perspective of 'restraint' and 'using the freedoms which the republic will necessarily grant for the organisation of the party in France'.[81] Ten years later, looking back on the Commune, Marx recognised that it had been 'merely the rising of a city under exceptional conditions' and that 'a compromise with Versailles useful to the whole mass of the people' of France was 'the only thing that could be reached at the time'.[82]

The Commune was not the result of a Blanquist rising. Indeed so little had Blanqui expected such an event that he had left Paris, sick and depressed, shortly before its proclamation. As Kautsky remarked unkindly but aptly, the Blanquists 'just had the bad luck that the insurrections which they regularly prepared failed, and the one which succeeded caught them unprepared'.[83] The Commune resulted from a spontaneous defensive response to Thiers' attempt to seize the artillery of the National Guard on March 18, 1871. Once it had been proclaimed, Marx and Engels gave it their unstinting, though not uncritical, support. The perspective for which they worked was not the Blanquist one of the dictatorship of Paris over France, which Engels had dismissed as 'a strange idea' since it was the thing 'on which the first French revolution had foundered'.[84] Marx envisaged, on the contrary, 'all France organised into self-working and self-governing communes, the standing army replaced by the popular militias' and 'the state-functions reduced to a few functions for general national purposes'.[85] In his first draft of his *Civil War* he devoted a five-page section specifically to the peasantry. In it he sought to show how the Commune represented not only the interests of the working class but also of the middle strata and 'above all the interest of the *French peasantry*'. He proposed measures of assistance to the peasant, whereby 'being immediately benefitted by the Communal Republic, he would soon confide in it'.[86]

In his 1891 Introduction to *The Civil War in France,* Engels showed how the experience of the Commune led the Blanquists to act contrary to Blanqui's doctrine:

> Brought up in the school of conspiracy, and held together by the strict discipline which went with it, they started out from the viewpoint that a relatively small number of resolute, well-organised men would be able, at a given favourable moment, not only to seize the helm of state, but also by a display of great, ruthless energy, to maintain power until they succeeded in sweeping the mass of the people into the revolution and ranging them round the small band of leaders. This involved, above all, the strictest, dictatorial centralisation of all power in the hands of the new revolutionary government. And what did the Commune, with its majority of these same Blanquists, actually do? In all its proclamations to the French in the provinces, it appealed to them to form a free federation of all French Communes with Paris, a national organisation which for the first time was really to be created by the nation itself.[87]

6

Unlike Blanqui, Marx not only envisaged preserving universal suffrage ('nothing could be more foreign to the spirit of the Commune than to supersede universal suffrage by hierarchic investiture'[88]), but also extending it under a workers' government so that 'like the rest of public servants, magistrates and judges were to be elective, responsible and revocable'.[89] Already in the 1840s Marx and Engels had given their enthusiastic support to the Chartists, as they were to do in the 1860s to the Reform League, for whom universal manhood suffrage was the central demand. Marx wrote in 1852, with rather a large dose of wishful thinking,[90] that 'universal suffrage is the equivalent for political power for the working class of England, where the proletariat forms the large majority of the population, where, in a long, though underground civil war, it has gained a clear consciousness of its position as a class, and where even the rural districts know no longer any peasants'. For that reason he considered that its implementation in Britain would be 'a far more socialistic measure than anything which has been honoured with that name on the continent'.[91] This did not however prevent Marx and Engels from supporting it in continental countries as well.

In the 1848 Revolution the right of every German over 21 to vote and be elected features prominently as the second point in the *Demands of the Communist Party in Germany,* drafted by Marx and Engels as the programme of the League of Communists in the revolution and repeatedly published in the press and in leaflet form in 1848 and 1849.[92] It was clearly central to what Engels had in mind when he demanded a German constitution 'based on the sovereignty of the people and the elimination from the regime actually existing in Germany of everything that contradicted the principle of the sovereignty of the people'.[93]

Referring to the convening of the French Constituent National Assembly in May 1848 which had been so bitterly opposed by Blanqui, Marx wrote in *The Class Struggles in France*:

> If universal suffrage was not the miracle-working magic wand for which the republican worthies had taken it, it possessed the incomparably higher merit of unchaining the class struggle, of letting the various middle strata of bourgeois society rapidly get over their illusions and disappointments, of tossing all the sections of the exploiting class at one throw to the apex of the state, and thus tearing from them their deceptive mask.[94]

And later in the same work, dealing with the constitution first drafted by that assembly, he observed:

> The fundamental contradiction of this constitution consists in the following: The classes whose social slavery the constitution is to perpetuate, proletariat, peasantry, petty bourgeoisie, it puts in possession of political power through universal suffrage. And from the class whose old social power it sanctions, the bourgeoisie, it withdraws the political guarantees of this power. It forces the political rule of the bourgeoisie into democratic conditions, which at every moment help the hostile classes to victory and jeopardise the very foundations of bourgeois society.[95]

The potential threat of universal suffrage to bourgeois society in a country where the working class constitutes a relatively small part of the population is here very strongly put. Alarmed by the growth of the left in the elections of March 1850, the bourgeois National Assembly proceeded to 'violate the sovereignty of the people' by 'robbing three million Frenchmen of their franchise'.[96] The bourgeoisie, as Marx put it, was openly confessing: ' *"Our dictatorship has hitherto existed by the will of the people; it must now be consolidated against the will of the people."* '[97]

Commenting on the vote in the National Assembly in May 1850 reintroducing a property qualification, Marx wrote: 'Universal suffrage had fulfilled its mission. The majority of the people had passed through the school of development, which is all that universal suffrage can serve for in a revolutionary period. It had to be set aside by a revolution or by reaction.'[98] The last sentence is descriptive (or predictive) rather than prescriptive. A successful working class revolution in France at that time would necessarily have borne the imprint of Blanqui and his comrades, 'the real leaders of the proletarian party', who, as we have seen, opposed universal suffrage and vainly sought to dissolve the assembly resulting from it and set up a revolutionary government in its place.[99] Marx recognised that the Assembly 'represented the nation' and that the attempt 'forcibly to negate its existence' had 'no other result' than the imprisonment of Blanqui and his associates.[100] The French working class was still at a level of development where it was 'incapable of accomplishing its own revolution'.[101] Marx justified the June 1848 workers' uprising as a defensive rather than an offensive action. 'The Paris proletariat was *forced* into the June insurrection by the bourgeoisie. This sufficed to mark its doom. Its immediate, avowed needs did not drive it to engage in a fight for the forcible overthrow of the bourgeoisie, nor was it equal to this task.'[102]

The idea that Marx stood for the abolition of universal suffrage by revolution is contradicted by his writings already quoted on the 1871 'proletarian revolution', as he designated the Paris Commune.[103] In his first draft of *The Civil War in France* he wrote that 'the general suffrage, till now abused either for the parliamentary sanction of the Holy State Power, or a play in the hands of the ruling classes' was 'adapted to its real purposes, to choose by the communes their own functionaries of administration and initiation'.[104]

Marx was well aware that, particularly in countries with a peasant majority, universal suffrage could be used to hold back the working class and sanction reactionary regimes. He discussed this process very clearly in *The Eighteenth Brumaire of Louis Bonaparte*. However he did not conclude from this, like Blanqui, that the peasant majority should be disenfranchised and dictated to by the revolutionary workers of Paris. On the contrary, he stressed the need to work for unity between the peasantry and the urban workers—'their natural ally and leader'—so that *the proletarian revolution will obtain that chorus without which its solo becomes a swan song in all peasant countries'.*[105] The French workers, he had explained in *The Class Struggles in France*

could not take a step forward, could not touch a hair of the bourgeois order, until the course of the revolution had aroused the mass of the nation, the peasants and petty bourgeois, standing between the proletariat and the bourgeoisie, against this order, against the rule of capital, and had forced them to attach themselves to the proletarians as their protagonists.[106]

Engels was to express the same idea nearly thirty years later after the experience of the Paris Commune. He wrote in 1878 of a basis being created in France for the workers to

ally themselves with the hitherto hostile mass of peasants and thus make future victories not simply as up till now into the short-lived triumphs of Paris over France but into decisive triumphs of all the oppressed classes of France under the leadership of the workers of Paris and the big provincial towns.[107]

We have in these statements the essentials of a theory of working class hegemony, which would be elaborated early this century by Lenin and applied by the Bolsheviks under his leadership with such world-shaking effect in the October Revolution.

For Marx and Engels, proletarian revolution did not presuppose the necessity for the working class to have become *sociologically* the majority of the population, as has sometimes been asserted,[108] but rather, whether this was the case or not, to have won majority *political* support. It was not enough to have obtained the backing of the majority of the working class, if this only constituted a minority of the people as a whole. A proletarian revolution, wrote Engels in 1847, 'in the first place will inaugurate a *democratic constitution* and thereby, directly or indirectly, the political rule of the proletariat. Directly in England, where the proletariat already constitutes the majority of the people. Indirectly in France and in Germany, where the majority of the people consists not only of proletarians but also of small peasants and urban petty bourgeois, who are only now being proletarianised and in all their political interests are becoming more and more dependent on the proletariat and therefore soon will have to conform to the demands of the proletariat.'[109] In 1895 Engels insisted that for French socialists 'no lasting victory is possible unless they first win the great mass of the people, that is, in this case, the peasants'.[110]

Marx rejected talk of universal suffrage revealing some classless 'will of the whole people'. The latter consisted, in class-divided societies, of 'the separate contradictory "wills" of the separate social estates and classes'. Universal suffrage acted 'as the compass needle which, even if it is only after various fluctuations, nevertheless finally points to the class which is called upon to rule'.[111] Marx and Engels did not believe in throwing away, or interfering with the working of the compass when it gave uncongenial readings. Engels wrote to Paul Lafargue in 1892: 'Look what a splendid weapon you have now had in your hands in France for forty years in universal suffrage if only you'd known how to make use of it!'[112] Forty years before, Louis Bonaparte had brought back universal suffrage to obtain a majority for himself. Engels implied that Socialists should have welcomed its restoration and used it to win and register a majority *for themselves.*

In *The Origin of the Family, Private Property and the State* Engels recognised that 'the possessing class rules directly through the medium of universal suffrage', but only for so long as the working class is 'not yet ripe to emancipate itself'. To the extent that the proletariat 'matures for its self-emancipation', it 'constitutes itself as its own party and elects its own representatives, and not those of the capitalists. Thus universal suffrage is the gauge of the maturity of the working class.'[113]

In countries where universal manhood suffrage had in its essentials been won, Marx stressed the possibility and importance of its being 'transformed from an instrument of deception *(duperie)*, which it has been hitherto, into an instrument of emancipation'.[114] It would be difficult to imagine a greater contrast between the confidence in the people's ability to change society for themselves expressed in the potential ascribed to universal suffrage here by Marx, and the paternalistic portrayal of helplessness conveyed by Blanqui's picturesque imagery of universal suffrage as 'the poor slave of the ever-sovereign triad Sword-Moneybags-Cassock, marching to the ballot box with the gendarme and the priest holding him by the scruff of the neck and Capital kicking him up the backside'.[115]

Writing in 1895, in his famous Introduction to Marx's *Class Struggles in France,* Engels quoted Marx's phrase and argued that with the successful use of universal suffrage by German Social Democracy 'an entirely new method of political struggle came into operation', which should be followed in other countries.[116] He recognised that their 1848 expectations of successful proletarian revolutions were over-optimistic due to the potential for capitalist economic development and underdeveloped mass consciousness and organisation. 'History has proved us, and all who thought like us, wrong', he wrote referring to those expectations.[117] He was not implying, as is sometimes suggested,[118] that he and Marx had earlier plumped for a Blanquist scenario of minority revolution, since he went on to emphasise that 'the *Communist Manifesto* had already proclaimed the winning of universal suffrage, of democracy', in contrast to revolutionaries in Latin countries who 'had been wont to regard suffrage as a snare, as an instrument of government trickery'.[119] The *Manifesto,* as we have seen, had stressed the majoritarian character of the proletarian movement in contrast to 'all previous historical movements (which) were movements of minorities, or in the interest of minorities'.[120] Engels, in his 1895 Introduction, was reinforcing this idea on the basis of historical experience and relating it to the new situation where in Western countries universal manhood suffrage, or something approximating to it, had been increasingly introduced. 'The time of surprise attacks, of revolutions carried through by small conscious minorities at the head of unconscious masses, is past', he wrote. 'In order that the masses may understand what is to be done, long, persistent work is required.'[121] His perspective was of German Social Democracy winning, alongside the workers, 'the greater part of the middle strata of society, petty bourgeois and small peasants' and growing into 'the decisive power in the land, before which all other powers will have to bow, whether they like it or not'.[122]

7

In 1872 Marx expressed the opinion that the transition to socialism might be attained by peaceful means in countries like America and Britain.[123]

However at no time in their lives did Marx and Engels come to believe such a possibility to exist in more than a limited number of states with particular 'institutions, customs and traditions'. Marx said in the same speech that 'we must recognise that in most continental countries the lever of revolution will have to be force'.[124]

Engels, writing to Paul Lafargue on April 3, 1895, insisted that he only favoured the peaceful tactics outlined in his 1895 Introduction 'for the *Germany of today* and even then *sous bonne réserve*'. For France, Belgium, Italy and Austria they 'could not be followed in their entirety and for Germany they could become inapplicable tomorrow'.[125] Engels had agreed reluctantly to the deletion from his Introduction of some passages and formulations, which leaders of the German Social Democratic Party were afraid might be used as a pretext for the government bringing back the Anti-Socialist Law, which had been in force from 1878 till 1890. In doing so he insisted that 'the obligation to legality is a juridical, not a moral one. . . and that it completely ceases when those in power break the law. . . Legality as long and as far as it suits us, but no legality at any price, not even lipservice to it!'[126]

Marx rejected the 'kind of logic which keeps within the limits of what is permitted by the police and not permitted by logic' (except where 'circumstances demand caution') under despotic regimes.[127] However, he favoured making use of bourgeois legality in the interests of democracy. He noted in September 1878:

> If in England or the United States the working class wins a majority in Parliament or Congress, it could in a legal way get rid of the laws and institutions blocking its development. . . in so far as social development required this. However the 'peaceful' development could quickly change into a 'violent' one through a rebellion by those with a stake in the old order; if they (as in the American Civil War and the French Revolution) were crushed by force, then it would be as rebels against the 'legal' power.[128]

Even such a strong critic of Marxism as Popper accepts that 'citizens have not only a right but a duty' to offer 'violent resistance to attempts to overthrow democracy' when (as is the case posited by Marx) such resistance is 'unambiguously defensive'.[129]

Communists, as Engels wrote in 1847, considered a revolution by peaceful means to be desirable but believed it at that time to be blocked by their opponents.[130] Hence they could not but work for and welcome a situation where, on the basis of universal suffrage, 'the representative body concentrates all the power in its hands, where it is possible constitutionally to do what one wants as soon as one has the support of the majority of the people' as he wrote in 1891, adding that such a democratic republic would also be 'the specific form for the dictatorship of the proletariat.'[131]

8

For Marx and Engels the democratic nature of a socialist revolution was not determined by whether conditions allowed it to be carried through peacefully or violently, constitutionally or unconstitutionally. It depended on its enjoying the support of the majority of the people. The majoritarian nature of the proletarian movement was emphasised, as we have seen, in the *Communist Manifesto,* which went on to declare that its ends could 'be attained only by the forcible overthrow of all existing social conditions'.[132] Similarly, in an interview with the *Chicago Tribune* given on December 18, 1878, Marx explained that although 'there will be a bloody revolution in Russia, Germany, Austria and possibly in Italy. . . these revolutions will be made by a majority. No revolution can be made by a party, but by a nation'.[133]

The winning of a majority was considered essential by Marx and Engels not only on grounds of expediency, but also because of the democratic nature of the socialist project. If Engels was to write in 1885 that 'if ever Blanquism—the fantastic idea of overturning an entire society by the action of a small conspiracy—had a certain *raison d'être,* that is certainly so now in Petersburg',[134] it was because he saw it as an 'exceptional case', where such action against the 'unexampled despotism' of tsarism could 'release explosive forces' among a people who were 'approaching their 1789'[135]—i.e. a *bourgeois* revolution. Such methods would be quite inappropriate for a socialist revolution aiming to establish 'the self-government of the producers'[136] with 'the haughteous masters of the people' replaced by 'their always removable servants. . . continuously under public supervision'.[137] In such a revolution, wrote Engels, where it is a question of a complete transformation of the social organisation, 'the masses must themselves *already* have grasped what is at stake, what they are going in for with body and soul'.[138] Moreover the prospect of the withering away of the state was based, as Engels made clear, on 'a free and equal association of producers',[139] to the effective development of which minority rule would constitute an insuperable obstacle.

From the beginning Marx had rejected the elitist and doctrinaire approach which proclaimed, 'Here is the truth, kneel down before it!' As against that, he wrote in 1843: 'We develop new principles for the world out of the world's own principles. We do not say to the world: Cease your struggles, they are foolish; we will give you the true slogan of struggle. We merely show the world what it is really fighting for, and consciousness is something that it *has to* acquire, even if it does not want to.'[140] This was the spirit in which Engels wrote to Kautsky forty years later, arguing that a socialist government should give independence to colonial countries and let them find their way 'completely of their own accord'—even though it would involve all sorts of uncertainties and disorders—through whatever 'social and political phases (they) have to pass before they also arrive socialist organisation'. And Engels emphasised: 'One thing alone is certain: the victorious proletariat can force no blessings of any kind on any foreign nation without undermining its own victory by so doing.'[141]

Marx's and Engels' whole political philosophy and practice marks them off unambiguously from the elitist Jacobin-Babouvist-Blanquist political tradition with what Talmon calls its 'totalitarian democratic ideal' and of which he curiously claims Marxism to be 'the most vital among the various versions'.[142]

The incompatibility of Marxist and Blanquist views on the nature of revolution and post-capitalist society, which this essay has sought to demonstrate, does not of course prove that Marx and Engels were right and Blanqui, or those who consciously or unconsciously share his views today, are wrong. This question, which has considerable importance and relevance for current international socialist controversies, has to be evaluated in its own right both analytically and empirically in the light of the very considerable experience of revolution and post-revolutionary states accumulated in this century. That, however, would take us far beyond the scope of the present essay.

NOTES

1. F. Engels, '*The Times* on German Communism', January 1844, Marx/Engels *Collected Works*, Lawrence & Wishart, 1975 onwards, hereafter *CW*, Vol. 3, p. 411.
2. This was the characterisation made by the Prussian censor in March 1843, quoted by A. Cornu, *Karl Marx et Friedrich Engels* (Paris, 1958) Vol. 2, p. 102.
3. K. Marx, *Contribution to the Critique of Hegel's Philosophy of Law*, *CW*: 3, p. 29.
4. F. Engels, 'On the History of the Communist League', Marx/Engels, *Selected Works* (Moscow/London, 1950) hereafter *SW*, Vol. 2, p. 314.
5. Ibid., p. 315.
6. D. Ryazanov, ed., *The Communist Manifesto of Karl Marx and Friedrich Engels* (London, 1930) Appendix E, p. 292. Ryazanov thinks the article was probably written in collaboration by the London members of the League of Communists headed by Karl Schapper. (ibid., pp. 20–21).
7. Marx/Engels, Preface to 1872 German edition of *Manifesto of the Communist Party*, *SW*: 1, p. 21.
8. *CW*: 6, p. 515; Marx/Engels, *Werke* (Berlin, 1956–1968), hereafter *MEW*, Vol. 4, p. 490.
9. *CW*: 6, p. 495.
10. Ibid., p. 504.
11. Auguste Blanqui, *Textes Choisis* (Paris, 1971), hereafter *TC*, p. 189.
12. J.J. Rousseau, *The Social Contract*, trans. by H.Z. Tozer (London, 1909), p. 198 (Book IV, Chapter 1).
13. Ibid., p. 133 (Book II, Chapter 6).
14. Ibid., p. 124 (Book II, Chapter 3).
15. Ibid., p. 113 (Book I, Chapter 7).

16. George Rudé, *Revolutionary Europe—1783-1815* (London, 1964), p. 151.
17. Robespierre, *Discours et Rapports à la Convention* (Paris, 1965), p. 222. (Speech of February 5, 1794.)
18. P. Buonarroti, *Conspiration pour l'Egalité dite de Babeuf* (Paris, 1957), Vol. 1, pp. 109, 102. English translation by B. O'Brien, Augustus M. Kelley (New York 1965).
19. Ibid., p. 111.
20. Ibid., pp. 114-15.
21. Samuel Bernstein, *Auguste Blanqui and the Art of Insurrection* (London, 1971), p. 145.
22. *TC*, pp. 109-10.
23. Ibid., pp. 111-12.
24. Ibid., p. 112.
25. Ibid., p. 114.
26. Ibid., pp. 165-6.
27. Ibid., pp. 166-7. cf. Robespierre (November 5, 1792) arguing that the action of Paris was *'comme fondé de procuration tacite pour la société tout entière.'* Quoted by Alfred Cobban, *Aspects of the French Revolution* (London, 1971), p. 164.
28. *TC*, p. 161.
29. Ibid., p. 151.
30. Ibid., pp. 151-2, 167-8.
31. Ibid., pp. 164-5, 168.
32. Ibid., p. 156.
33. S. Bernstein, op. cit., p. 312.
34. *TC*, p. 46. It is true that Marx and Engels refused to set down 'recipes for the cookshops of the future' (K. Marx, *Capital,* Moscow, 1954, Vol. 1, p. 17) but their indications of the general lines of socialist and communist society have provided two present-day Marx scholars with sufficient material for a book of over five hundred pages on the subject. (See R. Dlubek/R. Merkel, *Marx und Engels über die sozialistische und kommunistische Gesellschaft,* Berlin–GDR, 1981).
35. K. Marx, *The Class Struggles in France* (1850); *CW:* 10, hereafter *CSF,* p. 127. Emphasis in original.
36. Marx to Dr Watteau, November 10, 1861, in R. Garaudy, *Les sources françaises du socialisme scientifique* (Paris, 1948), p. 217. German translation in *MEW:* 30, p. 617.
37. K. Marx, *The Civil War in France* (1871), *SW:* 1, p. 489.
38. D. Ryazanov, 'Zur Frage des Verhältnisses von Marx zu Blanqui', *Unter dem Banner des Marxismus,* II, 1/2 (Frankfurt a/M., 1928), Appendix 1, p. 144. A not entirely satisfactory English translation is given in *CW:* 10, p. 614.
39. *CW:* 10, p. 628. Emphasis in original.
40. Ibid., p. 626. Emphasis in original.
41. K. Marx, 'Critical Marginal Notes on the Article by a Prussian' (1844), *CW:* 3, p. 199. Emphasis in original.
42. K. Marx, 'On the Jewish Question' (1843), ibid., p. 156. Emphasis in original.
43. Schapper appears later to have regretted this. See Marx to Engels, April 16, 1856, Marx/Engels, *Selected Correspondence* (Moscow/London, 1956), hereafter *SC,* p. 111, and E.P. Kandel, ed., *Marx und Engels und die ersten proletarischen Revolutionäre* (Berlin–GDR, 1965), pp. 117-8.
44. *CW:* 10, p. 484.
45. Ibid., pp. 277-87.
46. E. Bernstein, *Die Voraussetzungen des Sozialismus und die Aufgaben der*

Sozialdemokratie (Stuttgart, 1899), p. 29; G. Lichtheim, *Marxism* (London, 1961), pp. 124–5; B.D. Wolfe, *Marxism* (London, 1967), pp. 153–4, 157, 163.

47. *CW:* 10, pp. 280, 284, 286.
48. Ibid., p. 286.
49. Ibid., pp. 626, 629.
50. *CW:* 6, p. 519.
51. S. Moore, *Three Tactics: The Background in Marx* (New York, 1963), pp. 22, 32–33.
52. *CW:* 10, p. 277.
53. Engels to Florence Kelley-Wischnewetzky, January 27, 1887, *SC,* p. 476.
54. This was how every issue of the paper designated itself immediately under the title.
55. F. Engels, *Principles of Communism* (1847), *CW:* p. 352.
56. F. Engels, *The Constitutional Question in Germany* (June 1847), ibid., p. 84.
57. *CW:* 10, p. 318. The article was written in March and April 1850.
58. Ibid., pp. 316, 320-1.
59. 'Debates on Freedom of the Press' (May 1842) *CW:* 1, p. 153.
60. Ibid., p. 161.
61. *CW:* 3, pp. 124, 127. According to J.L. Talmon (*Political messianism,* New York, 1960, p. 205) the young Marx in this work is 'entirely within the totalitarian-democratic tradition'!
62. *CW:* 5, p. 7.
63. *Communist Manifesto, CW:* 6, p. 497.
64. See my essay, 'Marx and Engels and the Concept of the Party', *Socialist Register* 1967, pp. 121–58.
65. See ibid., esp. pp. 123, 143.
66. *Communist Manifesto,* loc. cit.
66a. Preface (1890) to German edition of *Communist Manifesto, SW:* 1, p. 30.
67. General Rules of the IWMA (drawn up by Marx in October 1864), *SW:* 1, p. 350.
68. Marx/Engels, 'Circular Letter', September 17-18, 1879, *SC,* pp. 395, 389–90.
69. F. Engels, 'The Programme of the Blanquist Communard Refugees', *MEW:* 18, p. 529.
70. Marx to J. Weydemeyer, March 5, 1852, *SC,* p. 86. Emphasis in original.
71. See Hal Draper, 'Marx and the Dictatorship of the Proletariat', Etudes de Marxologie (6), *Cahiers de l'Institut de Science Economique Appliquée* (Paris, September 1962) No. 129 (Série S, No. 6), pp. 5–73.
72. Marx's speech at dinner for delegates to London Conference of First International, 1871, in M. Molnar, *Le Déclin de la Première Internationale* (Geneva, 1963), p. 238. German translation in *MEW:* 17, p. 433.
73. F. Engels, Introduction (1891) to Marx's *Civil War in France, SW:* 1, p. 440. For an argument that, although Marx did not apply the term to the Commune, it did constitute what he understood by the dictatorship of the proletariat, see my essay, 'The Paris Commune and Marx's Conception of the Dictatorship of the Proletariat', in John Hicks & Robert Tucker, eds., *Revolution and Reaction —The Paris Commune 1871* (Amherst, Massachusetts, 1973) pp. 80–95.
74. *SW:* 1, p. 473.
75. First draft, K. Marx, *The Civil War in France* (Peking, 1966) p. 141.
76. *SW:* 1, p. 473.
77. First draft, op. cit., p. 157. Emphasis in original.
78. See F. Jellinek, *The Paris Commune of 1871* (London, 1937) pp. 227, 295.
79. *SW:* 1, p. 478.
80. Marx to Engels, September 6, 1870, *MEW:* 33, p. 54.
81. Engels to Marx, September 7, 1870; Marx to Engels, September 10, 1870,

ibid., pp. 59, 60. See also Marx's Second Address of First International on Franco-Prussian War (September, 1870), *SW:* 1, pp. 451-2.

82. Marx to F. Domela-Nieuwenhuis, February 22, 1881, *SC,* p. 410.
83. K. Kautsky, *Terrorismus und Kommunismus* (Berlin, 1919) p. 57.
84. Engels to Marx, July 6, 1869, *MEW:* 32, p. 336.
85. First draft, op. cit., p. 171.
86. Ibid., pp. 173-7. Emphasis in original.
87. *SW:* 1, p. 438.
88. Ibid., p. 472.
89. Ibid., p. 471.
90. It should however be remembered that in Chartist times, at least till 1848, with a more militant working class, universal suffrage would certainly have represented a greater danger to the established order than it was to do later. This is not without some bearing on the fact that it was bitterly resisted by the ruling class in the earlier period but happily extended to the majority of male urban workers by Disraeli in 1867 as a device to 'dish the Whigs'. (See Royden Harrison, *Before the Socialists* (London, 1965) pp. 80-1, 112-33.
91. K. Marx, 'The Chartists' (August 1852), *CW:* 11, pp. 335-6.
92. *CW:* 7, pp. 3, 601.
93. F. Engels, 'The Assembly at Frankfurt' (May 1848) ibid., p. 16.
94. *CSF,* p. 65.
95. Ibid., p. 79.
96. K. Marx, *The Eighteenth Brumaire of Louis Bonaparte* (1851-1852) *CW:* 11, hereafter *EB,* p. 147.
97. *CSF,* p. 131. Emphasis in original.
98. Ibid., p. 137.
99. *EB,* pp. 109-10.
100. Ibid.
101. *CSF,* p. 56.
102. Ibid., p. 69. Emphasis in original.
103. *SW:* 1, p. 463.
104. First Draft, op. cit., p. 169.
105. *EB,* pp. 191, 193. Emphasis in original.
106. *CSF,* p. 57.
107. F. Engels, 'The European Workers in 1877' (1878), *MEW:* 19, p. 133.
108. This view was attributed to Marx particularly by German Social Democratic theorists. See, e.g. H. Cunow, *Die Marxsche Geschichts-, Gesellschafts- und Staatsauffassung* (Berlin, 1920), p. 329: 'In Marx's view the proletariat will only come to rule when it already comprises the majority of the population.' Karl Kautsky wrote in his *Dictatorship of the Proletariat* (Manchester, 1919): 'The dictatorship of the proletariat was for (Marx) a condition which necessarily arose in a real democracy, because of the overwhelming numbers of the proletariat.' However, he modified this on the next page, when he stated that 'as a rule the proletariat will only attain to power when it represents the majority of the population, or, at least, has the latter behind it. . . This was the opinion of Marx and Engels.' (pp. 45-6).
109. *Principles of Communism, CW:* 6, p. 350. Emphasis in original.
110. *SW:* 1, p. 124.
111. K. Marx, 'The Berlin *National-Zeitung* to the Primary Electors' (January, 1849) *CW:* 8, pp. 271-2.
112. Engels to Lafargue, November 12, 1892, Engels/Lafargue, *Correspondance* (Paris, 1959) Vol. 3, p. 229.
113. *SW:* 2, p. 291.

114. *Considérants du Programme du P.O.F.* (1880) K. Marx, *Oeuvres.* Economie I (Paris, 1963) p. 1538.
115. *TC,* p. 172.
116. *SW:* 1, pp. 119-120, 123-4.
117. Ibid., p. 115.
118. See, e.g. S. Moore, op. cit., p. 54.
119. *SW:* 1, p. 119. The *Manifesto* did not actually speak of universal suffrage, but Engels was indicating here that it was implied by the Manifesto's formulation 'to win the battle of democracy' (*CW:* 6, p. 504).
120. Ibid., p. 495.
121. *SW:* 1, p. 123.
122. Ibid., pp. 124-5.
123. Speech on the Hague Congress (September 8, 1872) *The First International after Marx* (London, 1974) p. 324.
124. Ibid.
125. Engels/Lafargue, *Correspondance,* op. cit., p. 404. Emphasis in original.
126. Engels to Richard Fischer, March 8, 1895. *MEW:* 39, pp. 425-6.
127. K. Marx, *Critique of the Gotha Programme* (1875), *SW:* 2, p. 31.
128. Notes on Reichstag Debate, *MEW:* 34, pp. 498-9.
129. K.R. Popper, *The Open Society and its Enemies* (London, 1980) Vol. 2, p. 152.
130. *Principles of Communism, CW:* 6, p. 349.
131. F. Engels, Critique of Draft Social Democratic Programme (1891) *MEW:* 22, pp. 234-5.
132. *CW:* 6, pp. 495, 519.
133. Marx/Engels, *Gesamtausgabe (MEGA),* Probeband (Berlin, 1972), p. 277.
134. Engels to V.I. Zasulich, April 23, 1885, *SC,* pp. 459-60.
135. Ibid., p. 459.
136. *SW:* 1, p. 471.
137. First Draft, op. cit., p. 169 (in Marx's uncorrected English).
138. *SW:* 1, p. 123. My emphasis.
139. *Origin of the Family, SW:* 2, p. 292.
140. Letter (September 1843) from *Deutch-Französische Jahrbücher, CW:* 3, p. 144. Emphasis in original.
141. Engels to K. Kautsky, September 12, 1882, *SC,* p. 423. Translation of first sentence slightly modified after *MEW:* 35, p. 358.
142. J.L. Talmon, *The Origins of Totalitarian Democracy* (London, 1970) p. 249.